MAXIMUM
BANDWIDTH

MAXIMUM BANDWIDTH

Written by Dan Blacharski

Maximum Bandwidth

Library of Congress Catalog No.: 97-67037

ISBN: 0-7897-1294-6

99 98 97   6 5 4 3 2 1

Interpretation of the printing code: the rightmost double-digit number is the year of the book's printing; the rightmost single-digit number, the number of the book's printing. For example, a printing code of 97-1 shows that the first printing of the book occurred in 1997.

Screen reproductions in this book were created using Collage Plus from Inner Media, Inc., Hollis, NH.

Contents at a Glance

Maximum Bandwidth

Appendixes

Table of Contents

6   IsoEthernet   137

9   HiPPI   211

Appendixes

Credits

PRESIDENT
Roland Elgey

SENIOR VICE PRESIDENT/PUBLISHING
Don Fowley

PUBLISHER
Joseph B. Wikert

PUBLISHING DIRECTOR
Brad R. Koch

GENERAL MANAGER
Joe Muldoon

EDITORIAL SERVICES DIRECTOR
Elizabeth Keaffaber

MANAGING EDITOR
Thomas F. Hayes

DIRECTOR OF MARKETING
Lynn E. Zingraf

ACQUISITIONS EDITOR
Tracy M. Williams

SENIOR PRODUCT DIRECTOR
Lisa D. Wagner

PRODUCT DIRECTOR
Becky Campbell

PRODUCTION EDITOR
Julie A. McNamee

EDITORS
Lisa M. Gebken
Brian Sweany
Tom Lamoureux
San Dee Phillips

STRATEGIC MARKETING MANAGER
Barry Pruett

WEB MASTER
Thomas H. Bennett

PRODUCT MARKETING MANAGER
Kristine R. Ankney

ASSISTANT PRODUCT MARKETING MANAGER/DESIGN
Christy M. Miller

ASSISTANT PRODUCT MARKETING MANAGER/SALES
Karen Hagen

TECHNICAL EDITOR
Brad Lindaas

MEDIA DEVELOPMENT SPECIALIST
David Garratt

TECHNICAL SUPPORT SPECIALIST
Nadeem Muhammed

ACQUISITIONS COORDINATOR
Tracy M. Williams

SOFTWARE RELATIONS COORDINATOR
Susan D. Gallagher

EDITORIAL ASSISTANT
Virginia Stoller

BOOK DESIGNER
Ruth Harvey

COVER DESIGNER
Glenn Larsen

PRODUCTION TEAM
Kay Hoskin
Heather Howell
Tim Neville
Sossity Smith
Lisa Stumpf

INDEXER
Chris Barrick

Composed in *Century Old Style* and *ITC Franklin Gothic* by Que Corporation.

To my wife Lotus and son Shanti; and to Joe, Kevin, Jeff, and all the rest of my old cronies who I haven't seen in so many years.

About the Author

Dan W. Blacharski is a technology and business writer, novelist, and satirist with several years experience. He has written several articles and books, and currently works out of his home in Santa Cruz, California.

Acknowledgments

I would like to acknowledge and thank Tracy Williams of Que, for her continual support and encouragement throughout the entire production of this book. I would also like to acknowledge the fine work of development editor Becky Campbell, who was a great help. I must also tip my hat to many other individuals involved, from the artists to the typesetters, and from the technical editors to the salespeople.

Thanks and appreciation are also due to the many vendors, manufacturers, and developers who were kind enough to provide me with information, photographs, and product data.

And lastly, a nod of thanks goes to my son Shanti, for taking me away from my computer every now and then and reminding me what a spring day looks like.

We'd Like to Hear from You!

QUE Corporation has a long-standing reputation for high-quality books and products. To ensure your continued satisfaction, we also understand the importance of customer service and support.

Tech Support

If you need assistance with the information in this book or with a CD/disk accompanying the book, please access Macmillan Computer Publishing's online Knowledge Base at:

http://www.superlibrary.com/general/support

Our most Frequently Asked Questions are answered there. If you do not find the answer to your questions on our Web site, you may contact Macmillan Technical Support by phone at **317/581-3833** or via e-mail at **support@mcp.com**.

Also, be sure to visit QUE's Desktop Applications and Operating Systems team Web resource center for all the latest information, enhancements, errata, downloads, and more:

http://www.quecorp.com/desktop_os/

Orders, Catalogs, and Customer Service

To order other QUE or Macmillan Computer Publishing books, catalogs, or products, please contact our Customer Service Department:

Phone: 800/428-5331
Fax: 800/835-3202
International Fax: 317/228-4400

Or, visit our online bookstore:
http://www.mcp.com/

Comments and Suggestions

We want you to let us know what you like or dislike most about this book or other QUE products. Your comments will help us to continue publishing the best books available on computer topics in today's market.

Lisa Wagner
Senior Product Director
QUE Corporation
201 West 103rd Street, 4B
Indianapolis, Indiana 46290 USA
Fax: 317/581-4663
E-mail: **lwagner@que.mcp.com**

Please be sure to include the book's title and author, as well as your name and phone or fax number.

We will carefully review your comments and share them with the author. Please note that due to the high volume of mail we receive, we may not be able to reply to every message.

Thank you for choosing QUE!

Introduction

In the earliest days of networking, dumb terminals were used to send data to a mainframe. This concept was decidedly one-sided, and if someone wanted a bit of information, it was necessary to approach the high priests in the glass house, perhaps bring an offering of some sort, and wait two or three weeks. Then, the report you got would invariably not be what you had originally requested.

Then, we got PC networks, run by file-sharing network operating systems such as NetWare. We still couldn't get at that data behind the glass wall, but we could share printers and text files with one another. However, these LANs were limited in terms of bandwidth. For example, although Ethernet runs at 10Mbps, users typically enjoy a maximum of only about 4Mbps, which is then further divided by the number of users on the network. For example, if there are 10 users on the network, each user gets only 400Kbps of bandwidth.

Hardly enough for multimedia! Although at one time this was more than adequate, the increasing demand for bigger and more critical applications on the LAN has created more traffic jams and congestion, which, in turn, drives the need for high-speed networking.

Eventually, end users decided they wanted to get at those massive stores of corporate data, and wanted to transmit multimedia files as well. However, sending a multi-megabyte file full of images overburdened those early PC networks, which were, after all, designed to handle data only, and not very much of it, at that.

Larger files, multimedia, and greater demand for easy access to corporate data all contributed to the need for high-speed networking technology, such as Fast Ethernet and ATM. Another major factor in the drive to high-speed networks is the move to intranets, a technique that uses Internet protocols to send and receive data both internally and externally.

The open nature of TCP/IP, the dominant Internet/intranet protocol, has created unparalleled levels of data access. Users, regardless of location or platform, can connect to the internal network from any dial-up Internet account, through almost any ordinary Web browser. Making data access this easy comes with a price: More people will want more data. Because it's so easy to get, those users will probably access it more frequently. For years, networking was a frustrating experience for the end user, who faced delays, crashes, and dependence on a centralized information system. Thus, as end users wised up, took advantage of new technology, and then asked for more, the need for high-speed networking arose.

High-speed networking technologies, such as Fast Ethernet, Frame Relay, FDDI, and ATM, are just now beginning to bring massive changes to networking. The desktop PC revolution made PCs inexpensive and widely accessible; advances in high-speed networking will similarly bring access to large databases, graphics, and multimedia to the masses. The endless delays, bottlenecks, and the often-heard comment "my, the computer's slow today" may be a thing of the past. These new high-speed technologies are increasingly affordable, and many are likely to become commodity items within a few years.

In the following chapters, we will take a closer look at these high-speed technologies, their histories, usage, and implementation. We will see how 10Mbps Ethernet has evolved into 100Mbps, and then 1,000Mbps Ethernet; and how ultra-high channel technologies are being used to connect high-speed devices. ■

What's In Store for the Future?

In the future, the "Information Superhighway" will bring high-speed Internet access, video-on-demand, and networked appliances to every home. However, this future cannot be accomplished with traditional networking technology. An all-optical network would remove the bottlenecks common to traditional networks, and thereby potentially increase the amount of data carried by each fiber a hundred-fold.

The first step towards such a network has been taken by the National Transparent Optical Network Consortium (NTONC), a group of researchers, manufacturers, and telecommunications providers led by Lawrence Livermore National Laboratory. Members of the consortium include Pacific Bell, Sprint, Northern Telecom, United Technologies Research, Hughes Aircraft, Rockwell International, and Columbia University. NTONC has proposed a $40 million project that would create a prototype optical network in California. Eventually, NTONC hopes to develop technology that could be used to carry up to 100 Terabits per second (Tbps) of data—a capacity far beyond anything currently available or underway. At this phenomenal rate, data would be streaking across the network at ten million times the rate of standard 10Mbps Ethernet.

The NTONC project hopes to create a testbed network to demonstrate wavelength division multiplexing (WDM) device technologies and control strategies required to develop a terabit-per-second optical network. These speeds will be achieved by using WDM as a means of expanding fiber system bandwidth by allowing multiple colors of light to be sent over a fiber that currently accommodates only one color. The group will deploy a four-node, bi-directional ring network carrying both OC-48 Synchronous Optical Network (SONet) and ATM traffic.

Initially, the project, which will be funded in part by the Defense Advanced Research Projects Agency (DARPA), would establish a network around the San Francisco Bay Area, using Pacific Bell and Sprint's existing fiber optic cables. Later, the network would expand to Southern California.

As is the case with new technologies, it is necessary for us to face a slew of acronyms and new terms. Even to the most technically proficient among us, these can be confusing. A glossary has been added to the end of this book to serve as a quick reference to these new terms.

Representations Used in this Book

There are several graphical representations in this book to make it easier to read and understand. The following items point you to specific information:

ON THE WEB

This icon and format signal URL addresses for the Internet and World Wide Web of places that have related products or information, such as the Que home page at:

http:\\wwwm.quecorp.com

N O T E Notes give advice or general information related to the specific topic. ▉

CAUTION

This paragraph format warns of hazardous procedures that may cause irreparable damage.

What About Sidebars?

Sidebars are supplementary material that expands on the specific topic being discussed. While this information is not vital to the discussion, it may provide valuable insight or further explanation.

The Evolution of High-Speed Networking

At one time, 10Mbps of bandwidth was all anyone ever needed. Those days, however, have gone out with 10M hard drives and black-and-white screens. Trends in both management and technology have driven the need for faster networks. Companies are "leaner and meaner," middle management has been eliminated, and end users are being given more responsibility. Fortunately, the technology has evolved at the same time, allowing these end users to gain faster and greater access to corporate data of all types. ■

Faster LANs

The old 80/20 rule, which states that 80 percent of network traffic exists locally, or within the LAN segment, and 20 percent in the backbone, is no longer valid. This design model held that an internetwork, which was generally created by connecting LANs with routers, ran most traffic over each individual LAN. Routers were optimized to handle this traffic pattern. Later, however, companies started to centralize servers on the corporate backbone, creating a new pattern of traffic and destroying the old 80/20 rule. Furthermore, increased segmentation in a traditional routed network has led to a much higher percentage of backbone traffic, resulting in more congestion. Multiple segments on a shared backbone result in tremendous congestion, as more and more traffic competes for a piece of that 10Mbps of bandwidth (see Figure 1.1). In this shared scenario, each segment gets only a proportional share of the 10Mbps; that is, if there are six nodes attached to the shared hub, each one only gets one-sixth of the 10Mbps.

FIG. 1.1

A shared backbone can result in network congestion.

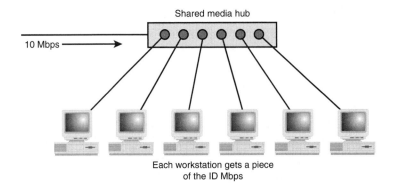

Shared media hub

10 Mbps

Each workstation gets a piece
of the ID Mbps

There are dozens of ways to correct this bottleneck problem, including deployment of a switched network. Figure 1.2 shows the same network, divided into segments, with each segment receiving its own 10Mbps of bandwidth.

The switching paradigm can be made even more efficient by adding Asynchronous Transfer Mode (ATM) technology, which adds a high-speed connection between switches and other devices, Quality of Service (QoS) guarantees, and connectivity with legacy LANs.

Token Ring networks have also suffered from the same bottleneck problems as Ethernet. The advent of Ethernet switching has effectively eliminated the technical advantages of Token Ring. That is, Token Ring's deterministic nature had been advantageous because it eliminated the possibility of packet collisions. However, this advantage is minimized when compared with an Ethernet switching environment, where collisions are far less common than in a routed Ethernet environment.

FIG. 1.2
A segmented network
eliminates bottle-
necks.

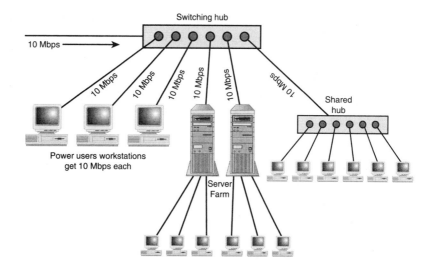

Although Token Ring may not have a technical advantage over Ethernet any longer, many
IBM shops have large Token Ring investments that they may wish to preserve. Short of a
wholesale migration to ATM, there are some solutions. Although moving to Fiber Distributed Data Interface (FDDI) can solve Token Ring bottleneck problems on a short-term
basis, the problems that result from shared bandwidth still exist. Segmentation of the LAN
offers a performance boost, although Token Ring switching is still a fairly new, and fairly
expensive technology. The switching approach merely breaks up the ring into multiple
smaller rings, which are then linked together with switches. Because there are several
smaller rings, each user will not have to wait as long for a token to come around.

Before a Token Ring switching environment is deployed, a serious cost/benefit analysis
should be undertaken. Management will often find that in the long run, a switched Token
Ring network will be less advantageous from a cost perspective than moving to a switched
Ethernet or ATM environment.

Analyzing the Need for a High-Speed
Networking Architecture

Of course, not everyone needs a high-speed networking architecture. A ten-person company running basic word processing and spreadsheet applications would be wasting
money to deploy such a system. In fact, in many cases, deploying ATM is simply overkill—sort of like using an Indy racecar to drive to the corner supermarket. If you do need
a high-speed network, it may not be necessary to deploy it throughout the enterprise.

Some workgroups dealing with high-bandwidth applications may require the speed, whereas others may not; or it may make sense to deploy a high-speed backbone only.

If you think you may need a high-speed network, the first thing to do is take a look at the existing network infrastructure, see where the bottlenecks are, and determine what your current and future needs will be. The best way to approach this is with a formal "Needs Analysis." This process should be implemented by a committee, which includes not only the Information Services (IS) organization, but management, and representatives from each department in the company. At least some of the departmental representatives should be end users; ideally, each department would have two delegates (one management and one end user). This analysis should examine at least the following issues in detail:

- What type of data is currently being sent across the network, and what type of data is expected to be sent over the next three years?

- What forces are behind the need for a high-speed network? (Bigger files, broader access, multimedia, corporate intranet?)

- Does every department have a need for high-speed networking, or is it limited to certain areas? If so, pinpoint those areas.

- What problems exist in the current network infrastructure? What are the alternatives for addressing these problems?

Another critical component of the initial analysis is a complete inventory and diagram of the existing network, including servers, segments, remote sites, and peripheral devices. All bottlenecks, suspected bottlenecks, and potential bottlenecks should be pinpointed on this diagram. From this existing diagram, and armed with information about bottlenecks, you can begin mapping out your future network.

Make sure to include any new, or potentially new sites that you plan to add, new applications, and new or upgraded equipment. When possible, hubs should be replaced with switches to maximize bandwidth to each individual end user. Generally, Token Ring workgroups should be replaced with switched Ethernet environments, if the investment is not too large. And in general, even if you are not planning to deploy a high-speed technology such as ATM immediately, this changeover should be kept open as a possibility, and any new equipment acquired should be purchased with high-speed expansion in mind. Cabling, for example, is an especially critical consideration when planning for the future. Although CAT-3 UTP wiring may be more than adequate for the present, deploying CAT-5 UTP will leave the door open to an ATM deployment in the future.

Addressing Bottleneck Issues Without High-Speed Networking

Ch
1

After the initial needs analysis, it should become clear whether or not a high-speed infrastructure is needed, or whether any existing bottlenecks could be resolved without such a drastic measure. Although for a larger network, migration to a high-speed technology is probably the way to go, a smaller network may benefit from interim techniques, such as segmentation or performance optimization. Ultimately however, if significant growth is foreseen for the future, a migration to high-speed networking is desirable, even if it is more than what is needed for the present.

Performance tuning and optimization can take several different forms. Managers may wish to apply one or all of them, although network changes should always be executed one at a time in order to get an accurate evaluation of the results of each change. Adding network changes in this cautious manner will also greatly assist in troubleshooting when the inevitable installation glitch occurs. Following are some simple areas to start optimizing your network.

1. The first place to start is to simply discover whether or not you have the latest device drivers, bug fixes, and patches in place.
2. Network performance can often be enhanced with an upgrade of resources, including cabling, PCs, and other networking devices such as routers and switches. Upgrading the network hosts and the links that connect them is certainly a valid approach, although often the most costly one.
3. Tuning, load balancing, and prioritization. In a distributed environment, load balancing helps to "even out" the processing, so that one processor is not overburdened while another is not being fully utilized. Prioritization is becoming an increasingly common feature of networks; this simply assigns different values to different end users or processes. Under a prioritized scheme, a given network service would be given to a high-priority user before the low-priority user. When applied to threads in a multithreaded environment, such as Windows NT, a thread assigned high priority status will get a larger share of processor time when the processor is busy.
4. Re-visit network design. As the network's topology evolves, it may be beneficial to rearrange the bridges and routers, or apply segmentation and switching to the network.

Even if you do not send huge files back and forth, you may still be having performance problems. If this is the case, some performance optimization may be in order; in fact, this may increase the performance of the network to such a degree that deploying a new high-speed infrastructure is unnecessary.

Even if it becomes apparent that performance optimization can solve the current problems, the future must be taken into account. Although performance optimization is always a positive thing, you may still want to deploy some sort of new high-speed architecture to make room for future needs. However, there are companies, probably lots of them, that will never ship a multimedia file over their networks, will never create a data warehouse, and will never need to connect multiple sites. For these companies, performance optimization may be just the ticket.

There are several commercial software tools, tips, and tricks available for this purpose. Some of these include:

- Windows NT 4.0's Administrative Tool includes a *Performance Monitor,* which generates performance metrics and issues alarms if preset thresholds are exceeded. Other operating systems include similar tools, either as a part of the operating system itself or through an add-on utility. Although these monitors do not repair the performance problem themselves, they are valuable in alerting the administrator to its existence.

- *Inadequate memory* is a frequent cause of problems and the first area to consider when performance seems sluggish.

- A *cache bottleneck* can occur if there is not enough memory to create a truly useful cache. This problem usually occurs at the server, although it can occur at the workstation level when very complex programs, such as CAD/CAM or scientific visualization, are being run. Examining the amount of cache hits and cache misses, or the amount of data the system actually uses from the cache, will yield some important information about the cache's effectiveness. Increasing the size of the cache may yield more performance. Some operating systems, including Windows NT 4.0, have a self-tuning cache.

- The *I/O bus* may be a source of problems if it is inadequate or of an older design. Furthermore, multiple physical disks may lose their effectiveness if they are all placed on a single bus; placing some of the disks on a separate I/O bus may yield a performance boost.

Deciding on a High-Speed Networking Architecture

Just a few years ago, there was no such thing as high-speed networking. Now, there are numerous options from which to choose, although the major options are Fast Ethernet

(100Base-T), Asynchronous Transfer Mode (ATM), and FDDI. The following chapters will give an overview of each option, and the relative advantages of each one.

ATM is particularly well-suited to multimedia because of its incredibly high throughput and scalability, as well as its Quality of Service (QoS) guarantees. FDDI was one of the first high-speed architectures, and has matured significantly over the past five years. This option, however, can be quite costly. Fast Ethernet, on the other hand, can be deployed on existing Category 5 Unshielded Twisted Pair (UTP) cabling, and many Fast Ethernet cards run at dual speeds of both conventional (10 Mbps) and Fast (100 Mbps) Ethernet speeds.

Cost Analysis

For most of us, even in the biggest companies, cost weighs heavily on our decision-making processes. In order for a high-speed networking architecture to be deployed successfully, it must be given high priority not only by IS, but also by management. Gaining the support of management is critical here, simply because of the resources that must be devoted to a network upgrade.

Many IS departments are under the budget knife, and get only a minimal budget increase or a budget cut. As high-speed networking technology matures, price cuts can be expected to provide some relief.

Costs of an ATM rollout can be higher than expected; however, if careful planning has not been done. In addition to the cost of the ATM adapters and wiring, there may be significant hardware upgrade costs as well. Consider that if a shop is upgrading from Ethernet to ATM, you are enabling each client to transmit at data rates of as much as 15 times that of standard Ethernet. Although this speed increase has its benefits, and may indeed be a general goal of the company, the existing workstations and servers may be incapable of handling the load. The older servers, which may have handled the load adequately under a 10Mbps network, simply may be unable to keep up with this tremendously higher data rate. More RAM and additional disk space may have to be added; in some cases, it may make sense to simply replace the entire server.

Furthermore, if ATM is being deployed to the desktop level, each individual desktop machine will have to be examined for its ability to handle the level of output of which ATM is capable. All those 486s may need to be relegated to lower-priority areas; newer Pentium-level processor machines may need to be deployed to take full advantage of the high-speed architecture. For example, if a high-speed architecture, such as ATM, is connected to a legacy 10Mbps Ethernet network, the 486s may still be used in the legacy system. These hardware upgrades must be factored into the initial cost estimate.

Integration with Existing Infrastructure

In some cases, it may be best to deploy the high-speed architecture gradually, or apply it only to certain areas within the company's WAN structure. In this case, the new architecture must be able to integrate with the existing one. In many cases, this is a simple matter. In the case of Fast Ethernet, integration is remarkably straightforward and can occur gradually. Many modern Ethernet NICs offer a dual 10/100Mbps mode to provide for easy migration without having to replace the adapter. Through a software technique known as LAN emulation—effectively a "bridge" from ATM to LAN technology—an ATM network can easily communicate with legacy Ethernet and Token Ring networks.

Summary

The 80/20 rule, which stated that 80 percent of network traffic exists locally and 20 percent over the WAN, has nearly been reversed as corporate networks grow and more end users clamor for access to corporate data. As a result, the need for high-speed networks has grown. While traditional, shared low-speed network hubs may be able to accommodate small networks, switching has become a more dominant paradigm for busier environments.

Before deploying a high-speed network, one must analyze the need for it. While impressively fast, the architectures discussed in this book are not for everyone; in many cases, a switched 10Mbps Ethernet network will be more than adequate. In some cases, congestion can be addressed without deploying a new network architecture, using techniques such as performance optimization, keeping up to date with the latest drivers and bug fixes, and upgrading network hosts. ●

CHAPTER 2

Asynchronous Transfer Mode (ATM)

Of all the computer technologies that generate confusing acronyms, Asynchronous Transfer Mode (ATM) is the biggest offender. If you can get past deciphering LANE (LAN Emulation), VLAN (Virtual LAN), LUNI (LAN Emulation User Network Interface), FUNI (Frame User Network Interface), MPOA (Multiprotocol over ATM), and the dozens of other acronyms this technology has created, ATM can actually be quite useful, and may even eventually replace classical LAN technologies such as Ethernet and Token Ring. However, it will be a long time before such an event takes place; so in the meantime, the focus is on making high-speed and classical networks interoperate. ■

Overview of ATM

ATM can be deployed throughout the enterprise, down to the desktop level, and has the potential for use as a complete, end-to-end system. Few technologies have this level of scalability. ATM holds tremendous potential, although widespread acceptance has been slow due to the costs involved in replacing legacy networks, and the comparative lack of expertise.

ATM has a big advantage over other high-speed networking technologies such as Fast Ethernet, especially as a backbone technology. Unlike Fast Ethernet, most of the available ATM bandwidth is utilized, and ATM is readily expandable. The emerging Gigabit Ethernet model may not make a viable alternative to ATM because, like standard Ethernet and Fast Ethernet, Gigabit Ethernet will still suffer from the same lack of bandwidth management and low utilization rate—which means that its full potential can never be achieved. It's perhaps more efficient (although certainly more expensive) to implement ATM across the board, down to the desktop level, than it is to implement Fast and Gigabit Ethernets throughout the enterprise.

Speed and efficiency are not the only advantages ATM has to offer over other technologies. In this chapter, we will look at several of the other pluses of ATM, which include superior manageability, adaptability, and efficiency of performance.

ATM Background

ATM has its roots in asynchronous time division multiplexing (ATDM). ATDM differs from synchronous time division multiplexing (STDM), a technique commonly employed by the public switched telephone network in which time slots are based on hardware rather than software.

Multiplexing techniques create a high-speed channel by combining several lower-speed channels. In the synchronous model, the clock is used as the basis for allocating bandwidth time; with each tick of the clock used as the basis for assigning subchannels. Although it is simple, it is also inflexible. Each subchannel has a fixed bandwidth allocation, whether it is used or not. Consequently, if a particular subchannel is not used, its fraction of the aggregate link is wasted.

Modern cell-switching technologies, such as ATM, are based more closely on ATDM, where the hardware clock is replaced with a virtual channel identifier that can be controlled by software. Although this software approach is more complex, it is also much more flexible. Earlier ATM switches, however, lacked dynamic routing capabilities that could direct connections between multiple switches. Consequently, these early networks could not support end-to-end connections.

Applications for ATM

An ATM network can be used for almost any type of traffic, including data, voice, or video. The claim that there are no applications that require ATM's superior bandwidth is largely a myth. Besides graphics, audio, and video, intranet applications and groupware are ideal candidates for ATM. Through LAN Emulation (LANE) techniques, existing applications running on NetWare, Windows, DECnet, TCP/IP, MacTCP, or AppleTalk can run over the ATM network without modification.

ATM's highly efficient architecture can handle almost any type of traffic. It uses a small, fixed packet size of 53 bytes (48 bytes of data with a 5 byte header); sending the packets directly over the network through a switching mechanism. It's this small, fixed packet size that makes ATM an ideal technology for time-sensitive applications such as video. An Ethernet frame, on the other hand, can range from 64 to 1,516 bytes. Some applications will merely use the maximum frame size available to it; and when these large frames move over the network, they can cause slow-downs, which is especially problematic for any time-sensitive traffic that may be moving over the network at the same time.

Because there is no prioritization mechanism in classical Ethernet, a frame containing time-sensitive data could conceivably get stuck behind a larger frame of low-priority data—sort of like when you're driving your sports car down the coastal highway and get stuck behind a gravel truck.

Fast Ethernet may be a less desirable desktop solution than ATM if videoconferencing is being run over the network, because Fast Ethernet technology does not offer the same Quality of Service (QoS) guarantees as ATM. (See "Quality of Service (QoS)" later in this chapter.) QoS guarantees are essential to avoid jittery video. ATM is designed to support traffic with various cell flow requirements, and can therefore be used to run voice, video, data, and more, all on the same link.

Quality of Service (QoS)   An ATM connection, or virtual circuit, is established when one ATM end station requests a connection to another ATM end station. The connection request results in a negotiation that takes place between the caller and the ATM network. This negotiation takes place transparently to the end user, but under the hood, the network itself is negotiating parameters, such as QoS class, bandwidth, and burst length. This end-to-end negotiation will result in a contract of sorts that exists between the network and the end station; whereby the network guarantees a certain QoS level, and the end station guarantees that it will send only the amount of traffic that was negotiated.

One of the biggest advantages of ATM is its QoS guarantees. There are four service classes, each with different QoS levels. QoS is essential for applications such as video or audio, where all packets must arrive in a timely fashion in order for the presentation to be coherent. Without these QoS priorities established ahead of time, the network could get bogged down with low-priority transmissions; effectively disrupting and delaying what should be high-priority traffic. The classes of service are as follows:

- *Class A.* Constant Bit Rate (CBR), a "reserved bandwidth" service, generates a continuous, steady stream of bits, and is best applied to traffic requiring minimal bandwidth. Under Class A, the end station provides the network with parameters for the specific connection; the network will then allocate resources to accommodate those parameters. CBR also accommodates traffic that may be time-sensitive or intolerant to loss of cells, such as voice or video.

- *Class B. Variable Bit Rate-Real Time (VBR-RT).* VBR is also a "reserved bandwidth" service, and like Class A, the network will allocate the necessary resources to establish a connection with an end station to match the parameters requested by that end station. However, VBR establishes a peak rate, sustainable rate, and maximum burst size. This quality level is appropriate for voice or video applications.

- *Class C. Variable Bit Rate-Non Real Time (VBR-NRT).* Class C quality level is useful in applications where a slight delay may be more acceptable, such as in video playback, or transaction processing.

- *Class D. This class consists of unspecified bit rate (UBR) and available bit rate (ABR).* UBR is nonreserved, and as such, the network does not allocate resources for a requested connection. Both UBR and ABR are for bursty traffic that can tolerate delays or cell loss. UBR is a "best effort" type of service, and has no QoS guarantee. ABR, also a "best effort" service, adds management to Class D and will yield a lower cell loss rate. ABR sustains less cell loss than UBR by allowing the network to be periodically polled, and adjusting the transmission rate based on the results. Typical applications using UBR service are less demanding programs, such as data entry, data transfer, or remote terminal applications.

The various service classes and the types of applications appropriate to each one are detailed in Table 2.1.

Table 2.1   ATM Quality of Service—Application Chart

Application Area	CBR	rt-VBR	nrt-VBR	ABR	UBR
Critical Data	**	*	***	*	n/s
LAN Interconnect	*	*	**	***	**

Application Area	CBR	rt-VBR	nrt-VBR	ABR	UBR
LAN Emulation Data transport/ Interworking (IP-FR-SMDS)	*	*	**	***	**
Circuit emulation -PABX	***	**	n/s	n/s	n/s
POTS/ISDN - Video Conference	***	n/a	n/a	n/s	n/s
Compressed audio	*	***	**	**	*
Video distribution	***	**	*	n/s	n/s
Interactive multimedia	***	***	**	**	*

Advantages of each QoS relative to each application area are ranked as follows:
***Optimum; ** Good; * Fair; n/a No Advantage; n/s Not Suitable.
SOURCE: ATM FORUM

The above classes are hardware-based and usually configurable. Some vendors go beyond these four basic classes to offer more specific options; or may even allow users to define their own QoS parameters.

Video and Telephony Applications   Video over ATM would promote applications such as distance learning or videoconferencing. The ATM Forum is already drafting standards to meet the requirements of video over ATM. Both MPEG-2 and International Telecommunications Union (ITU) H.320 standards apply to video compression, and video over ATM. MPEG-2 specifically addresses ATM because it allows for variable bit rate (VBR) video streams. The ATM Forum has a specification for direct MPEG-2 over ATM, although it is limited to unidirectional video on demand applications and does not apply to videoconferencing.

ATM Telephones

ATM-based telephony may become more commonplace through a new technique known as *euphony*. Many telephones and other consumer appliances contain embedded processors, but very few of them have the inherent ability to be networked. Euphony, developed at AT&T Bell Labs, establishes a low-cost network processor that can be embedded in ATM end points or consumer appliances. Because euphony performs both signal processing and networking at the same time, it is ideal for use as an ATM-based telephone. Although this technology is still developing, euphony may form the framework for the networked, computerized home of the future.

ATM Speed

ATM's speed far exceeds that of many other network technologies. In its current state of development, it runs at 155Mbps, although theoretically, there is no limit. In fact, plans have been made to increase the top implemented speed specification from 622 to 2.488 Gbps, making three different physical layer specifications: OC-3 (155Mbps), OC-12 (622 Mbps), and OC-48 (2.488Gbps). For the most part, OC-48 is still experimental, although it can be achieved merely by combining 16 OC-3 switches. Also unlike other high-speed technologies, ATM is designed to operate over large distances, making it an ideal technology for a wide-area network (WAN).

SONET and the OC-N Structure

The prefix "OC" stands for Optical Carrier, and is part of the Synchronous Optical Network (SONET) structure. SONET is an ultra-high speed fiber optic system, with transmission rates from 51.84Mbps (OC-1) to 2.488Gbps (OC-48). It is used primarily by public carriers and organizations with very large WANs.

25Mbps ATM   For companies who do not see a need for 155Mbps ATM, an alternative can be found in the new 25Mbps offering, which is a less expensive alternative. A handful of ATM vendors have products that support ATM25, which may offer an easy way to start migrating to high-speed networking. ATM25 is not only less expensive than 155Mbps ATM, it is also less expensive than Fast Ethernet. In fact, ATM25 may be more advantageous than Fast Ethernet in ways other than expense. 100Mbps Ethernet, or even Gigabit Ethernet, suffers from the same limitations as standard 10Mbps Ethernet: a poor utilization rate, no congestion control mechanism, and lack of scalability.

Although it makes an excellent backbone technology, there are numerous advantages to deploying ATM across the board to every desktop in the enterprise. The advent of multimedia, voice and video, and greater demand for corporate data in general, all point to the need for a more powerful desktop. ATM25 may be just the ticket to handle the needs of most power users.

ATM25, unlike full ATM and Fast Ethernet, can be deployed on CAT-3 UTP cabling, and may present many companies with all the bandwidth they need, as well as an efficient way to bring ATM to the desktop. Only one pair of CAT-3 UTP is required; the same as 10Base-T Ethernet. However, before deploying an ATM25 network, you may want to consider switched Fast Ethernet as an alternative and weigh the relative advantages. ATM25 does offer the advantage of bandwidth management and QoS guarantees, but in the short-term, Fast Ethernet may be simpler to deploy.

IBM is one of the few vendors currently offering an ATM25 solution, with the IBM 8285 Nways ATM Workgroup Switch, as shown in Figure 2.1.

FIG. 2.1
IBM 8285 Nways ATM
Workgroup Switch.

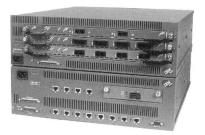

The IBM Nways unit can connect up to 12 users, and can be easily managed by HP OpenView or IBM NetView.

The efforts of the Desktop ATM25 Alliance, founded in 1994 to promote ATM25, have been handed over to the ATM Forum, which has ratified ATM25 as an official standard. This means that more vendors are likely to start offering ATM25 switches in the near future.

Low-Speed ATM   There are many smaller businesses that need ATM's data transfer capabilities, but do not need a high-speed service, making low-speed ATM an ideal solution and a possible alternative to ISDN or Frame Relay for those small businesses who wish to employ a public carrier instead of running their own internal ATM network. Pacific Bell's low-speed service starts at 128Kbps. Customers can configure their systems in 64 kilobit increments up to 1.5Mbps. Once the business grows, Pacific Bell can easily upgrade the service to full-speed ATM (155Mbps).

ATM Bandwidth Utilization

ATM's traffic shaping and traffic policing features allow the ATM network to accommodate traffic with varying requirements, and also to fully use available bandwidth. These features are discussed in more detail in the "Managing Traffic over ATM" section in this chapter.

ATM's Quality of Service levels also lay the groundwork for efficient traffic management. The purpose of the QoS levels is to determine which cells gets to travel over the network in which order. The best way to leverage this capability to its fullest extent is to have a rigorous priority scheme. A priority scheme would transmit cells in order, sending any CBR traffic first, VBR-Real Time traffic next, and then VBR-Non-Real-Time traffic after that. It is essential that CBR traffic gets highest priority, because it is not bursty. If VBR traffic were to get highest priority, for example, other service categories may not get a chance to transmit if several VBR circuits transmit at their peak rates.

Another way to provide for efficient use of bandwidth is to again grant high priority to CBR traffic, and to use a weighted type of allocation scheme for other service categories.

The queuing algorithm is also a major determining factor in efficient bandwidth utilization. A FIFO (First In First Out) queuing algorithm places all virtual circuits (VCs) in one service class in the same queue. Under this algorithm, all VCs within the service class are affected equally by congestion. By adding Per-VC accounting to FIFO, all VCs in one service class are still placed in the same queue, but congestion is detected individually for each VC. The last method allocates each VC its own queue, so if congestion occurs on one VC, it will not affect other VCs.

Integrating ATM Into Existing Networks

Congestion is one of the biggest problems in networks, and one of the biggest reasons we upgrade to new network architectures. As we saw in the previous section, ATM offers several different ways to manage traffic and make the most efficient use of available bandwidth. Although subdividing a large network into smaller subnetworks and joining them with bridges may solve some problems, it can cause other problems, increase complexity, and can even add more bottlenecks than it relieves. Switched Ethernet or Token Ring at the workgroup level, connected by an ATM backbone, may be a much more effective solution for relieving congestion.

Switching, while more efficient than routing, still has its limitations. In a switching system, every frame moving over the wires has a different destination, and the switch acts as a traffic cop, making decisions for every frame. Therefore, whether or not 100 Mbps Fast Ethernet is being deployed, the real speed in a switching system is dependent on the processor contained in the switch itself. For a further discussion of Fast Ethernet, see Chapter 3, "Frame Relay." In ATM the connection is negotiated ahead of time and the cells can be transferred more quickly than in a switched environment.

Deploying ATM over a single office LAN, however, may be overkill. A congested LAN may best be addressed by techniques such as better management, performance optimization, or deployment of Fast Ethernet; or better yet, a combination of all three.

ATM Cost Savings

The cost of deploying ATM is rapidly dropping. Although at first glance, ATM may seem costly compared to a standard 10Base-T Ethernet configuration, it may prove to be a cost-effective solution when compared to the alternative of constantly adding more segments, routers, hubs, and switches.

Because of its QoS guarantee, ATM presents an efficient way to send voice over the network. Because voice packets arrive in a timely fashion over an ATM network, the resulting speech is clear, and does not suffer from lost packets that cause garbled audio.

An ATM-based WAN could carry both voice and data, and consequently, save a company a tremendous amount of toll fees. Still, although ATM transmission quality is good, it's not good enough to equal that of standard telephone service; and therefore may be limited to internal use—at least for the present. Ultimately, it could be possible to bypass long-distance fees entirely by running voice calls over ATM to the point nearest to each call's destination. At that point, the call would be handed off to the local telephone network.

ATM Security

Security-conscious administrators will also enjoy the advantages of ATM. Because it is connection-oriented, it is inherently more secure than a connectionless LAN, such as IP or Ethernet. In a classical LAN, an intelligent hub must be deployed to check the MAC addresses against a master list of users; and typically, some sort of MAC address filtering is applied to every frame. In the event of unauthorized access, the intelligent hub will shut down the appropriate port. Besides being inefficient, this approach can degrade performance. ATM offers a more straightforward approach to access control. Under ATM, each call is processed before the connection is established. If access is denied, the workstation attempting access will be barred from that connection; but the port is not shut down.

Standards Development (ATM Forum)

The ATM Forum is the standards body responsible for developing the many ATM standards necessary to deploy this technology and for promoting usage of ATM throughout the industry. Established in 1991, the ATM Forum now consists of over 750 member companies. Members include both hardware and software companies, including FORE Systems, 3Com, Intel, and Bay Electronics; telecommunications companies such as British Telecom and Cable Vision Systems; large integrators such as Electronic Data Systems; and software vendors such as Net2Net.

Continued development will lead to more widespread use of ATM, not only for data and multimedia, but for voice as well. Currently, voice can be carried over ATM at the Constant Bit Rate (CBR) QoS level. However, using CBR for voice may be inefficient, because it forces the user to reserve bandwidth for voice, even if no voice is being transmitted. Variable Bit Rate (VBR) would be more efficient, because bandwidth could be allocated as needed. Although the ATM Forum has not yet officially approved VBR for voice traffic, some vendors, including IBM, are already implementing this strategy.

The ATM Forum has made significant progress towards standardizing and promoting ATM technology. Some of its major accomplishments include:

Ch
2

- *LAN Emulation (LANE).* LANE is a software function that permits existing LANs to communicate both with similar LANS and with ATM-attached stations over ATM. The ATM Forum has completed the LAN Emulation over ATM V.1.0 and LAN Emulation Direct Management Specifications. LANE allows a LAN client to access the ATM network through a LANE server running special software that mitigates the differences in addressing schemes, and converts LAN packets into ATM cells and vice versa.

- *Multiprotocol over ATM (MPOA).* MPOA permits Layer 3 protocols (IP, IPX, and Connectionless Network Protocol (CLNP)) to operate directly over ATM, either between two ATM hosts, or with hosts attached to other networks. The ATM Forum has already established MPOA requirements and the architectural framework, although definitions and specifications are still in progress. For a further discussion of MPOA, see the MPOA section later in this chapter.

- *Traffic Management.* ATM's traffic management techniques provide for traffic control, which minimizes congestion and makes optimal use of available bandwidth. The Traffic Management V 4.0 specification is nearly complete.

- *Service Aspects and Applications (SAA).* SAA includes application programming interfaces (APIs), interworking with Frame Relay, SMDS, and Circuit Emulation Services. The Frame UNI specification is complete; the Circuit Emulation Switching (CES) Interoperability Specification is still underway.

- *Private Network-to-Network Interface (PNNI).* PNNI establishes a methodology for ATM switches to communicate within a private ATM network. PNNI will allow for the creation of a multiprotocol switched private network. Already established is the Interim Interswitch Signal Protocol (IISP). The full PNNI V 1.0 specification is nearly complete.

- *Physical Layer.* The physical layer defines the physical characteristics of interfaces and signals, and shows how ATM cells are placed into transmission frame structures of a physical-layer data stream. Accomplishments include the ATM Physical Medium Dependent Interface Specification for 155Mbps over Twisted Pair Cable, DS1 Physical Layer Specification, UTOPIA, Mid-Range Physical Layer Specification for Category 3 Unshielded Twisted Pair, and 6.312Mbps UNI Specification. Still underway are the E1 Public UNI, E3 Public UNI, 622.05Mbps, and 155.52Mbps Physical Layer Specification for Category 3 UTP.

- *Signaling.* ATM signaling establishes a procedure for setting up each call (or connection), and for negotiating the QoS for each connection. The signaling specification allows for the creation of switched virtual circuits (SVCs), an inherently more flexible model than the permanent virtual circuit (PVC) model used in frame relay networks. Completed specifications include the ATM User-Network

Interface (UNI) Specifications V.2.0, V.3.0, V.3.1, and Interim Local Management Interface (ILMI) Management Information Base (MIB) for UNI V.3.0 and 3.1.

■ *Broadband ISDN Inter-Carrier Interface (B-ICI).* B-ICI is used to establish inter-switch communications in public networks. Completed specifications include B-ICI V.1.0 and B-ICI V.1.1. B-ICI V.2.0 is nearing completion.

■ *Network Management.* The ATM network management specifications establish a protocol MIB for each interface in the ATM network. Network management specifications include Customer Network Management (CNM) for ATM Public Network Services, M4 Interface Requirements and Logical MIB, and Common Management Information Protocol (CMIP) Specification for the M4 Interface.

■ *Testing.* The ATM testing specifications establish a suite of tests for evaluating conformance, interoperability, and performance of implementations of the ATM specifications. The suite includes the Protocol Implementation Conformance Statement (PICS) Proformas for the DS3 Physical Layer Interface, SONET STS-3c Physical Layer Interface, 100Mbps Multimode Fiber Physical Layer Interface, and DS1 Physical Layer. Additional tests still in progress include the PICS Proforma for the UNI ATM Layer, Conformance Abstract Test Suite (ATS) for the ATM Layer for Intermediate Systems, Interoperability Test Suite for the ATM Layer, and Interoperability Abstract Test Suite for the Physical Layer.

■ *Frame User Network Interface (FUNI).* The FUNI specification establishes a frame-based (as opposed to the more common cell-based) interface for ATM services.

■ *Residential Broadband (RBB).* RBB, which is still being defined, will establish an end-to-end, residential ATM system that will ultimately connect common household devices and appliances, including set-top boxes and PCs.

■ *Security.* The ATM Forum is still developing security specifications.

N O T E   Because there are so many different ATM standards still under development, it may be beneficial to deploy your ATM network with equipment and software from a single vendor to guarantee interoperability. ■

ATM Implementation and Infrastructure

ATM can be deployed either as a backbone technology, or, if a gradual deployment is desired, over just a single workgroup. Later, the ATM network can expand to include additional workgroups or switched LAN segments, at which point the ATM backbone would be implemented.

Ch
2

After the ATM backbone has been established, it is possible to directly attach any server or router that is common to multiple workgroups directly to the backbone. A gradual migration can take place by running the ATM backbone in parallel with the existing backbone. A gradual approach to ATM migration may consist of the following steps:

Step 1. During the first step, ATM is initially introduced into the network. Although it can be initially introduced as a backbone technology, another more gradual approach introduces it to a single workgroup. If deployed in a single workgroup, an ATM-compliant router or switch can accommodate traffic between the new ATM workgroup and the existing Ethernet or FDDI backbone (see Figure 2.2).

FIG. 2.2

A phased implementation of ATM can start with introducing an ATM workgroup into an Ethernet corporate network.

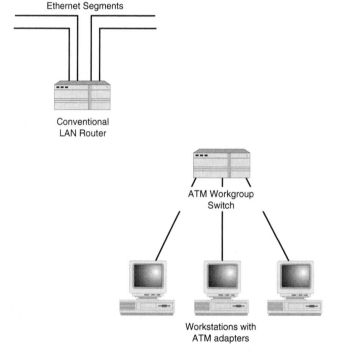

Ethernet Segments

Conventional
LAN Router

ATM Workgroup
Switch

Workstations with
ATM adapters

Introducing ATM to accommodate a particular workgroup with high-speed bandwidth needs is fairly common, and an excellent way to introduce the technology into the enterprise. However, some may wish to start by implementing an ATM backbone (see Figure 2.3).

A backbone allows individual LANs to connect to the central data center and with one another. Using an ATM switch, as opposed to an FDDI backbone, for example, minimizes the possibility of congestion at the data center by providing a dedicated, high-speed link to each backbone router and common server. ATM's bandwidth and congestion management techniques can be applied to optimize available bandwidth even further.

FIG. 2.3
A corporate network with an ATM backbone optimizes the use of ATM's congestion management and bandwidth features.

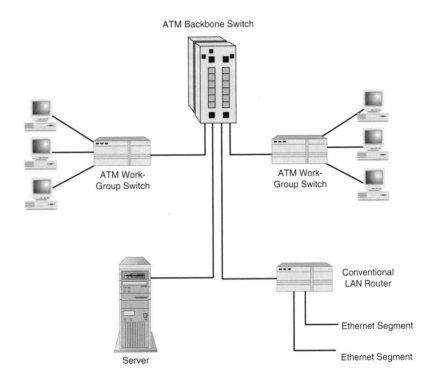

ATM Backbone Switch

ATM Work-Group Switch

ATM Work-Group Switch

Conventional LAN Router

Ethernet Segment

Ethernet Segment

Server

Step 2. After ATM has been established either in a workgroup or as the corporate backbone, all subsequent workgroup installations should be ATM-based. During phase two of the ATM installation, the ATM network grows to encompass both an ATM-based backbone and ATM-based workgroups. The several ATM-based workgroups are then interconnected, thereby forming a backbone (see Figure 2.4), or building on the existing ATM backbone created earlier. Any common server or central router is attached to the backbone. ATM can then run in parallel with an existing FDDI backbone or, if none exists, the backbone is created simply by interconnecting the ATM workgroups.

Once multiple workgroups have been established, it may be advantageous to consider Virtual LAN technology (VLANs) to allow logical associations of users to work on the same workgroup, without having to physically reconnect them. The VLAN can encompass devices attached to ATM workgroups as well as legacy devices, thereby allowing for a more gradual migration.

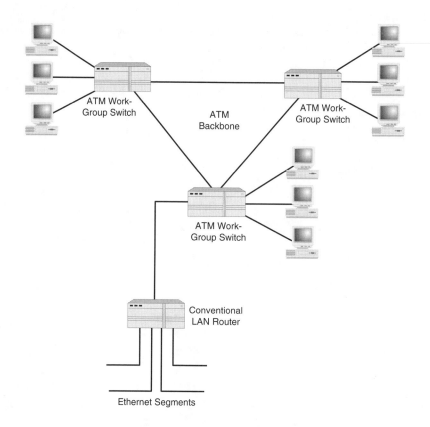

FIG. 2.4
Build an ATM backbone by connecting ATM workgroups.

Managing ATM

Once you have your ATM network in place, how do you keep track of it? Managing an ATM network, although it may take an initial learning curve and require some education, may ultimately be simpler than managing a standard shared-media LAN such as Ethernet.

A standard LAN environment may consist of multiple LANs joined to a backbone by bridges or routers. These bridges and routers require a great deal of administration; in particular, one of the most difficult aspects of managing a network is dealing with moves, additions, and changes. Every time someone moves to a new desk, the administrator may need to go to the wiring closet and physically change the wiring. ATM's VLANs eliminate this requirement, and let administrators make moves, additions, and changes from a management workstation via software.

Standard reactive network analysis products and protocol analyzers cannot handle high-speed technologies like ATM. A standard protocol analyzer is designed to analyze a single network segment. Packet capture is difficult when data is moving at high speeds, but analysis and management must be addressed before an ATM network can be completely successful. Because of the difficulties involved in capturing packets, it is important to focus on a more proactive management model.

Analysis and Management Tools   A new breed of products such as Net2Net's (Hudson, Massachusetts) Cell Blaster target ATM networks with a set of analysis and management tools for managing switches and connections (see Figure 2.5). Because Cell Blaster includes an SNMP agent, administrators can manage ATM from any SNMP-based management platform. Net2Net's combination hardware and software device is one of few products capable of capturing ATM cells for analysis. After capture, Cell Blaster sends the information to Windows-based analysis and reporting applications. Cell Blaster differs from standard packet capture devices in that it does not sample traffic. Sampling would interfere with the integrity of ATM's fixed-size cells. Instead, Cell Blaster filters and captures the traffic at its full rate of 155Mbps.

ON THE WEB

Check out Net2Net at the following address:

http://www.net2net.com

FIG. 2.5
Net2Net's Cell Blaster is used to analyze and manage ATM networks.

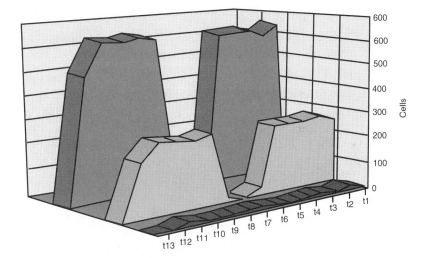

Performance Monitoring   Further development of tools like Cell Blaster will be critical to the acceptance of ATM as a standard transport mechanism. Another solution to the management problem has been proposed by FORE Systems. FORE, along with several other vendors, has proposed extending Remote Monitoring (RMON) to ATM networks. The availability of RMON would add performance monitoring services to the ATM network.

ON THE WEB

Check out Fore Systems at:
http://www.fore.com

An RMON agent monitors the network and generates an SNMP alert if a predefined threshold has been exceeded. Under this proposed model, RMON software would be embedded in the ATM switch, and would greatly assist network managers in monitoring and analyzing traffic, increasing availability and troubleshooting.

The ATM Forum's ATM RMON specification defines a management information base (MIB), built on existing RMON MIB technology, for gathering and analyzing information on ATM cells. This new specification will facilitate the development of new applications for monitoring ATM networks.

ATM Media and Topology   Although early implementations of ATM networks were limited to fiber optic cable, the variety of media on which ATM is capable of running has expanded. The most common type of cabling scheme for ATM running at speeds of up to 155Mbps has become Category 5 unshielded twisted pair (UTP) and Type 1 shielded twisted pair (STP). Category 3 UTP cannot be used for full speed ATM (155Mbps or higher) but can be used for ATM25 (25Mbps). Connectors used include:

- *RJ-45 connectors.* A shielded RJ-45 is commonly used on a network using UTP cabling, and will work with any type of UTP cabling, including CAT-5.
- *DB-9 connectors.* Used on Type 1 STP cabling in conjunction with four-position data connectors, usually in a Token Ring LAN.
- *Four-position data connectors.* Also frequently used on Type 1 STP cables, these are usually implemented at the wall jack.

CAUTION

It's critically important that CAT-5 UTP installations conform rigorously to the EIA/TIA 568A Commercial Building Wiring Specification. Cabling and all components, including connectors and wall jacks, must conform to this rating. It is easy, and quite common actually, to forget about upgrading short pieces of CAT-3 cabling in the wiring closet when upgrading to CAT-5; nonetheless, every single piece of CAT-3 cable must be upgraded.

ATM networks deploy a star topology, with an ATM switch located centrally, and each desktop wired to the switch.

Distance limitations of the physical medium get progressively smaller as Ethernet increases in speed; that is, Fast Ethernet suffers from a shorter hop length than does 10Mbps Ethernet; Gigabit Ethernet has a shorter hop still. When run over CAT-5 UTP

copper wire, ATM also suffers from a distance limitation of 100 meters and two interconnects. Multimode fiber, on the other hand, provides a maximum of 2,000 meters per segment and up to 15 kilometers for single-mode fiber.

COMSAT Corp. (Bethesda, MD) bypasses the issue of cabling and distance limitations
entirely with a new commercial ATM satellite service. The technology is expected to allow
telecommunications carriers and multinational companies to extend their ATM networks
around the globe. COMSAT offers the first commercially available ATM satellite service
that meets ITU standards, which gives users the ability to deploy an ATM network to
anywhere in the world at DS-3 (45Mbps) speeds. Just released in March 1997, the
COMSAT system represents a major breakthrough in terms of bringing more companies
the ability to communicate over great distances.

ON THE WEB

Visit the Web site for Comsat at:
http://www.comsat.com

The COMSAT service offers standard ATM traffic management facilities, including priority scheduling, congestion control, and resource management notification. The service is
compatible with all major ATM network components, and can support an ATM link at
rates from fractional T1 to DS-3. COMSAT customers can access the ATM satellite service through their ALA-2000 (ATM Link Accelerator) and ALE-2000 products (see Figure
2.6), which are satellite interfaces that are located at the customer's premises.

FIG. 2.6
COMSAT ALA-2000
and ALE-2000
satellite ATM
interfaces make it
possible to deploy an
ATM network anywhere
in the world.

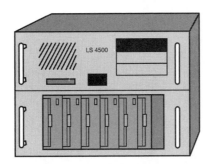

Managing Traffic over ATM   An ATM network uses traffic shaping, policing, and
congestion control to manage traffic.

- *Traffic shaping.* This function is executed at the user-to-network interface (UNI)
  level, and guarantees that the traffic matches the negotiated connection that has
  been established between the user and network. Traffic shaping is accomplished
  through the Generic Cell Rate Algorithm (GCRA), which has been defined as part

of the UNI 3.0 standard by the ATM Forum. Traffic shaping can be implemented by the ATM network adapter, hub, bridge, or router.

■ *Traffic policing.* Traffic policing is done by the network itself. It guarantees that the traffic running over each connection is within the parameters that have been established for each individual connection. Policing is done through a "leaky bucket" technique (see Figure 2.7) at the switch level. This is a buffering technique that flows traffic into a buffer (or "bucket"), then allows it to "leak" out at a constant rate, regardless of how fast it flows into the bucket. If the in-flow exceeds the negotiated rate for a long enough period of time, the buffer will overflow. At that point, the switch will then examine each ATM cell's Cell Loss Priority (CLP) bit.

FIG. 2.7
"Leaky Bucket" traffic policing.

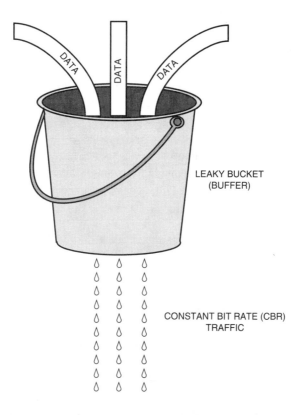

LEAKY BUCKET
(BUFFER)

CONSTANT BIT RATE (CBR)
TRAFFIC

The CLP bit is used by the switch to identify whether or not each cell conforms to the terms of the negotiated rate for the individual connection. A non-conforming cell will then be sent through the network only if there is enough capacity. If there is not enough capacity, the cell is discarded and must be re-sent by the originating device. CBR traffic relies on one leaky bucket because it uses a sustained rate; VBR traffic uses dual leaky buckets because it must monitor both a sustained rate over a discrete period of time, and the maximum bandwidth used for the connection.

In the case of discarded cells, the ATM Adaptation Layer determines whether or not all cells were received; if not, the recipient may request that the sender retransmit the entire packet, but not the individual cell.

■ *Congestion Control.* Although congestion is infrequent in CBR and VBR traffic, it may occur in ABR traffic, depending on the network load. The ABR-negotiated applications are, again, those that can tolerate delays, so the congestion will affect these connections to a lesser degree. However, congestion control is applied to ABR traffic to mitigate this effect.

There are two types of congestion control: link-by-link and end-to-end, both of which are still under consideration by the ATM Forum. It is most likely that the final specification will combine some elements of both schemes. End-to-end flow control is the most common, and has the advantage of being more readily available and less expensive than link-by-link. However, it requires a considerable amount of buffer space. The end-to-end type of scheme controls transmission rates at the network edge, where the LAN is connected to the ATM device. The link-by-link method, on the other hand, uses less buffer space. As of yet, no vendors have offered equipment that supports link-by-link flow control. This method would provide control over each virtual connection individually. The link-by-link method affords greater and more precise control.

Routing ATM   Before ATM can be widely deployed, different vendors' switches must be interoperable. The Private Network-to-Network Interface (PNNI) specification, established by the ATM Forum, is a dynamic routing protocol that facilitates inter-operation by creating a switched virtual circuit (SVC) routing system. PNNI lets multiple switches work together as if they were a single switch. PNNI will disseminate network topology information to all switches on the network, allowing them to calculate the best path for any given packet. PNNI will also provide alternate routes in case of a linkage failure.

The Private Network-to-Network Interface dynamic routing protocol is used to let companies establish a multi-vendor ATM switching network, where all of the various components are interoperable, regardless of vendor. Ultimately, under PNNI, a SVC routing environment could be established for thousands of switches.

PNNI has two functions: it disseminates topology information to all switches in the network, thereby allowing paths to be calculated between network endpoints. Further, PNNI extends the User-to-Network Interface (UNI), adding features that include alternate routing in the event of link failures.

PNNI is similar to the Open Shortest Path First (OSPF) protocol used in classical LANs. Without it, every ATM switching system would have to maintain a picture of the total topology, and information on every node in the network. Each time a connection request is made by a client, the PNNI is used to compute the best path, based on the topology information and QoS requirements.

ATM-based routing can take on a centralized model or distributed model. A centralized ATM implementation uses a route server that stores topology and resource information in a central server. The central route server must be constantly connected to the network; and a central route server approach establishes an unfortunate single point of failure.

Several vendors, including FORE Systems and Cascade Communications, offer a distributed routing model. Although more complex, a distributed routing model is more scalable, and avoids the single point of failure found in the centralized model. This distributed routing model is based on the ATM Forum's PNNI standard, or some variation of the common Open Shortest Path First (OSPF) algorithm. A link-state routing model uses a distributed map database model, with each switch describing its own local environment and propagating it throughout the network. As topology changes, any update is again propagated throughout the network.

ON THE WEB

Find out more about the distributed routing model at Cascade's Web site: **http://www.casc.com**

LAN Emulation (LANE)

LANE addresses the many differences between classical LANs and ATM. Whereas a classical LAN is connectionless, ATM is connection-oriented; also, a classical LAN uses Medium Access Control (MAC) addressing, while ATM uses its own addressing mechanism. With so many differences, how do you get classical and ATM networks to talk to one another? A difficult proposition, but necessary, if companies with huge investments in Ethernet and Token Ring are to even consider ATM technology.

LANE Services   LANE accomplishes this network interconnection by hiding the underlying ATM network at the Data Link (MAC) layer, effectively allowing ATM to peacefully co-exist with Ethernet and Token Ring LANs and all the applications that run on them. LANE is an ATM Forum standard that consists of three separate services, and unfortunately, three more acronyms:

- *LAN Emulation Configuration Server (LECS)*. LECS is used to configure LANE clients.

- *LAN Emulation Server (LES).* The LES provides an existing classical LAN with access to the ATM network, by resolving Ethernet and Token Ring MAC addresses into ATM addresses. Every device has a unique Network Service Access Point (NSAP) address along with a MAC layer address. The NSAP address is a 20-byte address, whereas the MAC address is 48 bits. The ATM switch automatically discovers the NSAP address through an auto-registration process.

  The NSAP address is used by one ATM device to request a connection to another ATM device. A LANE client must know the NSAP address of the target device before requesting a connection, however. The LANE client will first discover the device's MAC address, and armed with the MAC address, the client can then send a message to the LES to discover the NSAP address. Only then, once the client is equipped with the NSAP address, can it communicate with the remote device.

- *Broadcast and Unknown Server (BUS).* Because ATM is connection-oriented, there is no inherent mechanism for connectionless broadcast traffic. However, under LANE, a BUS server can accommodate broadcast, multicast, or unknown unicast packets from any LANE client, simply by sending data to all members of the VLAN in a one-to-many connection. The BUS's broadcast capability offers an efficient way to broadcast video. With a traditional 802.x broadcast, the video is distributed to all members of the shared media LAN. With ATM's BUS mechanism, the broadcast is received only by those end users who need to receive it, or those members who have been specified by the managers as members of a particular VLAN. This in itself can reduce the possibility of a broadcast storm and ensure that network resources are not being wasted.

LES, LECS, and BUS services can be implemented in different physical locations, either in a workstation or in a switch device; or they can all be implemented in a single workstation.

LANE Addressing   Each LANE client has two addresses, a standard 48-bit MAC address, and a 20-byte ATM Address. It is here, within the LANE software, that the addresses are negotiated. Each client has a translation table of destination MAC addresses. If a destination address is contained in the table, the message can be sent with the existing virtual connection. If there is no destination address in the MAC translation table, however, the client must undertake an address resolution process by sending a request to the LES, which then uses LANE's Address Resolution Protocol (ARP) to discover the valid destination and send it back to the client.

CAUTION

Confusing Acronyms Alert! Most vendors refer to the LAN Emulation Server, described above, as LES. However, some also refer to the entire mechanism of LECS, LES, and BUS collectively as "LAN Emulation Services," and also refer to LAN Emulation Services as LES. Throughout this book, LES will be used to refer only to the LAN Emulation Server element of LANE.

LANE allows the ATM end station to establish a traditional MAC-layer connection through the presence of a LANE driver that resides in each end station or access device. This MAC-layer connection then allows traditional LAN protocols, including TCP/IP, to run over an ATM network. This model allows for the creation of virtual LANs (VLANs). This logical association removes the necessity of specifying the physical connection between the host and the client; therefore, an end user can move from place to place and still remain part of the same VLAN.

One ATM network can support multiple VLANs. All LANE clients are provided with a list of all VLANs they are allowed to join. The list of VLANs is provided to the client by the LECS automatically. By establishing this list, the administrator can retain control over access to each VLAN in the network. This methodology is capable of delivering ATM down to the desktop level, and will go a long way towards making ATM technology widely accepted.

LANE Connectivity   There are two possible types of connectivity that can be achieved with LANE:

- *LAN-to-ATM.* This configuration allows an end node on a Token Ring or Ethernet network to access a server on the ATM network. The Ethernet or Token Ring end station does not need to have any type of ATM adapter or LANE software; instead, the node holds only a standard network interface card. The ATM adapter on the server end masquerades as a standard NIC for the benefit of the end node, allowing the connection to take place. The individual Token Ring or Ethernet LAN is connected to the ATM network using a switch or bridge.

- *LAN-to-LAN.* This configuration uses ATM as a backbone for connecting multiple Ethernet or Token Ring LANs.

LANE allows ATM to support and communicate with existing 802.x networks; that is, an end station on an Ethernet or Token Ring network under LANE would see the ATM adapter is merely another Ethernet or Token Ring card.

Although stations on the emulated LAN can communicate with the core ATM network, they are still, in fact, Ethernet or Token Ring, and are unable to take advantage of the ATM-specific features such as Quality of Service (QoS).

Although LANE services are typically implemented on one workstation, it is also possible, and perhaps advantageous, to distribute the LANE function. By distributing emulation, you avoid a single point of failure, and minimize the amount of clients connected to one server.

Virtual LANs (VLANs)

Administrators who spend half their time in the wiring closet will appreciate ATM's Virtual LAN (VLAN) model. A VLAN, sometimes referred to as an Emulated LAN (ELAN), is a logical association of users that share a single broadcast domain.

Ch
2

In a classical shared-media LAN environment, each workstation is connected to a port on a routing device. Every time the user moves or a workgroup is rearranged or disbanded, the administrator has to change and reconfigure each corresponding physical port. The ability to manage moves, additions, and changes via software is a tremendous advantage to the network administrator. Not only does this give the administrator time for a few more coffee breaks, it can result in a tremendous cost savings for the company—and minimize the risk of error or breakage in the physical wiring.

VLAN Administration   Every end user can belong to multiple VLANs, regardless of physical location. The administrator handles VLAN membership through the LANE software, specifically, in the LANE Configuration Server (LECS) module.

The VLAN allows the administrator to implement a policy-based management scheme, enforce rules and constraints, and ensure service quality for specific applications. VLANs are a natural security mechanism, in that members of one VLAN can communicate only with other members of the VLAN. Of course, an individual can belong to multiple VLANs. This makes it easy to isolate workgroups for security purposes. The VLAN allows the administrator to manage the network from a business-oriented focus, rather than a strictly technological focus.

These VLAN management capabilities could, for example, impose restrictions on who can access which VLAN, what time of day a user can get access, and what applications can be accessed; they could also be used to establish allowed bandwidth for each user and application. Several vendors offer, or are developing, policy-based management utilities.

VLAN Interoperability   It's critically important to be able to establish interoperability between multiple vendors' VLAN equipment in a larger enterprise. When the first VLANs were implemented, there were no interoperability standards, and companies had to deploy only one vendor's VLAN strategy. Cisco Systems, along with several other networking vendors, have developed a way to establish interoperability between VLANs through the existing IEEE 802.10 Standard for Interoperable LAN/MAN Security (SILS). Cisco's idea is to encourage vendors to support the existing 802.10 standard as a way to establish interoperability between multi-vendor VLANs.

The IEEE 802.10 specification, which was ratified in 1992, needs no modification to apply to VLANs. The standard was originally created by the IEEE to address security within a shared LAN or MAN (metropolitan area network). However, a particular 4-byte field within the 802.10 frame can be used to carry VLAN identification information instead of the security data for which it was originally intended. Cisco proposes using this 4-byte field in the physical router and switch, as a way to route network traffic out to each appropriate VLAN. The field would be used to tag individual frames and route them to the VLAN to which they belong.

VLAN Traffic Routing   The VLAN concept has evolved rapidly, first appearing around 1994 in the form of broadcast control. Under this model, broadcasts between switching ports and user stations were controlled, effectively improving performance by reducing the amount of broadcasts moving through the switch. This was done with filtering tables, which were used by the switch to determine which ports or MAC addresses had been grouped together as a VLAN. The use of filtering tables is adequate for smaller networks, but because the switch must examine each packet, some performance degradation would result. This simple filtering technique would be inadequate for a campus-wide environment.

Later, a technique known as packet tagging was introduced and subsequently accepted by the IEEE 802.1Q committee to allow broadcast domains to span the entire campus. This also introduced more bandwidth management functions, including load distribution, and allows VLANs to be established across a high-speed uplink.

Many networks have multiple backbone types, such as FDDI, Fast Ethernet, and ATM. The purpose of the VLAN is, ultimately, to allow end users to communicate across these different backbones, while still avoiding the necessity of establishing separate physical links for each connection. Packet tagging works well across different backbone types; furthermore, a mapping protocol developed by Cisco Systems can be applied to automatically configure the VLAN across the campus network, regardless of backbone type. Cisco's VLAN Trunk Protocol (VTP), part of Cisco's Internetworking Operating System (IOS) software, is used for switch-to-switch and switch-to-router communications. The protocol is used to propagate all VLAN configuration data throughout the network.

Integrating Legacy LANs with ATM

An existing, connectionless LAN uses broadcast techniques to send messages to every segment and end station on the network. ATM, on the other hand, is a connection-oriented technology. With the exception of the Broadcast and Unknown Service (see the

"LANE Services" section earlier in this chapter) mechanism, data is sent directly between the originating and target device. These data paths take the form of either permanent virtual circuits or switched virtual circuits. A PVC is configured manually, although the SVC is dynamically created via software at the ATM switch.

Frame Relay   ATM traffic can be mixed with frame relay over the same high-speed network, thanks to a new standard promoted by the ATM Forum and the Frame Relay Forum. The Frame Relay to ATM PVC Service Interworking Implementation Agreement (FRF.8 standard) establishes the framework for moving a frame relay site to a higher-bandwidth ATM site, without having to make an immediate choice between the two technologies. The service is offered by some long-distance carriers, including AT&T, LDDS, MCI, and Sprint. The service seamlessly connects each carrier's frame-relay WAN service to any ATM service, including corporate ATM backbones.

The service offered by long-distance carriers renders protocol conversion software unnecessary when running both ATM and frame relay, and allows a company to deploy a mixed model using ATM for high-volume sites and frame relay for branch offices. Frame relay to ATM interworking can be used to transparently link frame relay sites to ATM sites (see Figure 2.8). Under this type of hybrid network, protocol translation is carried out by the carrier, allowing an ATM switch to communicate with a frame relay switch. The service requires no special software on either end. The translation takes place seamlessly within the frame relay cloud. In short, Service Interworking simply converts frame relay frames into ATM cells for delivery to the ATM customer premises equipment (CPE), and vice versa.

FIG. 2.8
Service Interworking
between frame relay
and ATM Services.

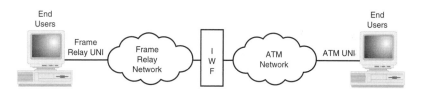

The interworking agreement furnishes a mechanism for traffic management and congestion control by offering a method for converting frame relay traffic conformance parameters to ATM traffic conformance parameters.

The specification offers two modes of encapsulation for each PVC:

- *Transparent mode*—forwards encapsulations unaltered.
- *Translation mode*—supports internetworking of routed or bridged protocols.

One of these two modes are selected at configuration time.

Furthermore, two methods of multiplexing are supported by this frame relay to ATM proposition: one-to-one, where a single frame relay logical connection is mapped to a single ATM virtual circuit; or many-to-one, where multiple frame relay logical connections are mapped to a single ATM virtual circuit.

The technique, known as "service interworking," describes the process whereby a frame relay user interworks with an ATM service user. During this interface, the ATM service user does not perform any frame relay-specific functions, and the frame relay service user does not perform any ATM-specific functions. The interworking is actually performed by the interworking function (IWF), since the ATM terminal itself cannot support the frame relay core services. The IWF itself can be contained in a single device or distributed across multiple devices.

Service interworking differs from the older network interworking model, where frame relay frames are actually transported over ATM and processed by the ATM terminal. Network interworking is essentially a mechanism for connecting two frame relay end-points over an ATM backbone. Under Network Interworking, the ATM terminal must be configured to interoperate with the frame relay network; under Service Interworking, the ATM terminal is unaware that the remote device to which it is attached is in a frame relay network.

The network interworking mechanism is seldom used and is extremely difficult to implement, requiring considerable software changes to the equipment on the ATM network. Service interworking, on the other hand, requires no software or equipment changes to take place.

Frame User Network Interface (FUNI)   A similar option to the frame relay to ATM interworking is the Frame User Network Interface (FUNI) specification, which sends frames over ATM. FUNI is implemented on the user's premises, and although it is very similar to frame relay, it is actually incompatible. FUNI is not frame relay, but actually a frame-based ATM solution that unlike the frame relay to ATM service interworking specification, permits signaling and flow control features to be extended to the customer premises. Advocates of FUNI claim that Service Interworking generates too much overhead.

FUNI is geared to sites with connection speeds of 1.5Mbps and below, and can support fractional T1 rates.

It is important to note that ATM is usually thought of as a cell-based mechanism, although the ATM specification does not mandate a cell-based interface. FUNI has the same frame header and trailer formats, with the service data unit (SDU) in between, as does the frame relay frame format. However, the frame relay UNI differs from the FUNI in its interpretation of the header information.

FUNI offers all the advantages of ATM, including traffic parameters and signaling, although it applies only to variable bit rate (VBR) data. Through the Frame Relay Forum's FR-to-ATM Service Interworking Function (S-IWF), FUNI is compatible with frame relay services over permanent virtual circuits. Consequently, a FUNI user can communicate with a frame relay user over an ATM network. For data-only needs, FUNI offers several advantages, especially a higher payload due to the frame model.

To implement FUNI, the corporate user deploys special software in the on-site equipment, and a complementary frame-based interface and software application resides in the ATM switch. At the ATM switch, the frames are converted to ATM cells and sent into the network. Cells coming from the network are reassembled into frames and sent to the user. Unlike the carrier-based technique described previously, FUNI was not designed to provide full interoperability between ATM users and frame relay users; it was designed to provide a frame-based transport over ATM. FUNI does have a frame structure similar to frame relay, and operates on the same type of equipment as frame relay, although it has nothing else in common. Unfortunately, not all ATM services are available over FUNI, including some of the QoS service classes.

FUNI can carry all variable bit rate (VBR) traffic, although it does not handle Constant Bit Rate (CBR). FUNI is compatible with frame relay, and any user running FUNI can communicate with a frame relay user through the ATM network.

SNA/APPN   ATM can also be linked to a System Network Architecture/Advanced Peer-to-Peer Networking (SNA/APPN) installation, through IBM's High Performance Routing (HPR) feature. The HPR feature establishes native access to a wide-area ATM network, connecting SNA and APPN directly to ATM through LAN emulation or frame relay emulation. As a result, users on the SNA installation will be able to run their applications over an ATM network without modification. Without the HPR feature, SNA does not lend itself to high-speed networking; but this ATM link will bring SNA into the era of high-speed networking.

The APPN/ATM Internetworking specification maps ATM's QoS guarantees to APPN's HPR class of service routing specifications. The IBM specification is implemented in routers, hubs and other devices; and allows the SNA network to migrate to ATM services merely by installing an ATM adapter on the router. HPR has some similarities to ATM's QoS guarantees, including congestion control and class-of-service levels.

802.x   The Ethernet-to-ATM issue is still being addressed by the ATM Forum and various ATM vendors. The biggest issue in Ethernet-to-ATM is address modification. Ethernet uses a 48-bit hardware address, while ATM uses a header address consisting of two 16-bit components.

Ch
2

Although ATM's 20-byte NSAP addressing scheme differs from the traditional 48-bit MAC address used in standard Ethernet and Token Ring LANs, it is still possible for the two to communicate. LANE software has a mechanism that transparently maps the MAC addresses to the Network Service Access Point (NSAP) ATM addresses, and converts ATM cells to 802.x packets and packets to cells. This software-based resolution mechanism is what allows the ATM network and the 802.x network to interoperate.

LAN Emulation (LANE), of course, is the most obvious way to integrate a legacy LAN into an ATM environment. LANE provides a way for Ethernet and Token Ring LANs and the applications running on them to operate over an ATM network without modification. This is necessary, at least for the present time, because LAN-based operating systems such as Windows NT and NetWare do not run natively on ATM.

Hewlett-Packard and FORE Systems offer a solution for an integrated Ethernet and ATM switch solution with an ATM module for HP's AdvanceStack Switch 2000. The module will let users integrate an existing 10Base-T, 100Base-T, 100VG-ANYlan, or FDDI workgroup with an ATM backbone. With the ATM module, the HP device will appear as an edge device to the ATM network, while functioning as a switch to the LAN.

Integrating IP with ATM

The tremendous rise of the Internet has pushed TCP/IP into the forefront as companies rush to deploy Web sites and corporate intranets. An intranet, however, can be very traffic-intensive, especially if the IS department is trying to provide access to a large back-end database, graphics, and multimedia to hundreds of users.

It's possible to leverage the advantages of both IP and ATM to create an efficient, high-speed intranet capable of carrying heavy traffic and big files. Straight IP networks use a series of algorithms to calculate each packet's optimal path. When ATM and IP are integrated, a process known as *cut-through* is implemented. The cut-through process takes advantage of the fact that IP packets tend to travel in clumps. The idea is that the first packet in a long stream is approached with the same set of standard IP algorithms in order to derive the best path. However, subsequent packets can be switched directly at higher speed by ATM switches. This IP switching technique can give the IP traffic a big boost. This fact has not been lost on the major ATM vendors, many of which are now offering IP switching capabilities in their ATM switch products.

The latest version of IP, IPv6, makes integration with ATM networks even easier, because header information has been placed in fixed locations within the packet. This fact makes it possible to execute routing via hardware. The previous version of IP suffered from a variable length header, which meant that routing had to be software-based. For more details about IP switching and high-speed intranets, see the "Intranets" section of Chapter 12, "High-Speed Telephony and Internet Access."

The ATM Forum's Private NNI Working Group has developed an Integrated Private Network-to-Network Interface (IPNNI), which may furnish another way to send IP traffic over an ATM network. IPNNI is an alternative to more traditional routing protocols, such as the Routing Information Protocol (RIP) and Open Shortest Path First (OSPF), and takes into account ATM parameters such as QoS and delay constraints.

Although LANE by itself does map MAC addresses to ATM, LAN emulation results in some problems, including additional protocol overhead. Also, applications running over an emulated LAN cannot utilize ATM's QoS attributes. Lastly, a performance issue comes from the fact that LANE imposes a maximum frame size on all devices in the emulated LAN. The maximum transmission unit (MTU) is limited to 1,500 bytes, even though an ATM-attached device could handle a larger frame size.

The Internet Engineering Task Force (IETF) has issued a specification for native IP support over ATM. Running IP natively over ATM eliminates the need for LANE software, and gives the IP network a performance advantage over an emulated LAN. IETF RFC 1577 defines how the IP network is mapped to the ATM fabric. This RFC defines an IP address resolution protocol (ARP). Under this model, an ARP server is deployed. Using an ARP server is similar to a LANE server, but instead of issuing MAC addresses in response to queries from the emulated LAN, it issues network-layer addresses.

Direct IP-to-ATM mapping is more powerful and advantageous than LANE in several ways. It reduces the overhead that otherwise results from the address translation mechanism. An ARP request is sent to the ARP server directly, the server then issues an ATM address, thereby giving the station making the request all the information it needs to make the ATM connection. LANE, on the other hand, is comprised of several additional steps, which result in more broadcast traffic. Furthermore, direct mapping allows the connection to handle larger MTUs. IP-to-ATM still requires a router to connect the sub-networks, which makes it a more costly solution.

MPOA (Multiprotocol over ATM)

Similar to IP switching is Multiprotocol over ATM (MPOA). MPOA, however, is not a routing protocol by itself, instead, it is merely an architecture that allows an ATM client to query a router to discover the best path through an ATM network. Whereas IP switching has not been standardized, MPOA is expected to be ratified as an official ATM Forum standard. Although it has not yet been ratified, several vendors are already rolling out prestandard implementations of MPOA.

The MPOA standard routes multiple, existing protocols over an ATM backbone, and unlike native IP-to-ATM schemes, provides the advantages of ATM's QoS guarantees. MPOA uses a central switch along with edge devices. The routing function is distributed to the edge router, which stores routes in its cache. An edge router or edge device exists at the edge of the ATM network, and facilitates connectivity between an ATM network and an existing LAN.

MPOA defines a high-performance way to route not only IP, but other protocols over the ATM fabric. It also lets the network administrator create a virtual subnet that spans routed boundaries to create a VLAN. Lastly, MPOA allows applications outside of the ATM network to make use of ATM's QoS guarantees.

MPOA extends the LANE concept, and maps network layer addresses to ATM. MPOA allows other routing protocols, such as IP, to make use of ATM's QoS features. Ultimately, MPOA allows a standard LAN to run over ATM, without having to migrate that LAN to native ATM. Under MPOA, an SVC is created for each data relationship, establishing an efficient one-hop transfer. This software-based router mechanism is used to create virtual subnetworks that are independent of physical location. The MPOA architecture consists of three main components:

- *Edge devices.* An intelligent switch that exists on the edge of the ATM network, that forwards packets between the legacy LAN segments and the ATM infrastructure. The edge device resolves the network-layer address with the ATM address by looking up the ATM address in either the route server, or in its memory cache.

- *ATM-attached hosts.* An adapter card implements MPOA, allowing the ATM hosts to communicate with the legacy LANs that are connected through the edge device.

- *Route server.* The route server is a virtual device, a new concept introduced by MPOA. It is actually a set of functions that allow network-layer subnetworks to be mapped to the ATM fabric. The route server is usually implemented as software added to an existing router or switch. The route server keeps track of network-layer, MAC-layer, and ATM address data, and uses this information to establish a direct link between any two end points.

MPOA's virtual routing model is far more efficient than a physical router. With virtual routing, the edge devices do not have to contain as much intelligence as a full-featured router. Additional routing capabilities can be included through software; furthermore, the virtual router, which consists of switches and route servers, can all be managed via software as if it were a single router. Like LANE, MPOA allows for the creation of virtual subnets with devices that are physically located anywhere in the enterprise.

MPOA also addresses the overhead and performance degradation experienced under LANE and IP-to-ATM, because the network-layer protocols are mapped directly to ATM. Unlike LANE, MPOA can support variable-sized MPUs, and can take advantage of ATM's QoS features. Furthermore, MPOA works with existing routing protocols, making it possible to implement MPOA alongside an existing routed network.

Product Overview

Dozens of traditional networking vendors, along with several start-ups that specifically target ATM, are offering ATM hardware and software. A more lengthy listing can be found on the ATM Forum's Web site (**http://www.atmforum.com**), where they offer a "Product and Services Guide." Here is a brief overview of some of them.

Fore Systems

174 Thorn Hill Rd.
Warrendale, PA 15086
Voice: 412-772-6600
Fax: 412-772-6500
E-mail: **info@fore.com**
Web: **http://www.fore.com**

Fore Systems has been very active in the ATM Forum and the development of the LANE standard. The company's ForeThought LANE software goes beyond the specifications of the ATM Forum's LANE standard by including the following:

- *VLAN manager.* This graphical interface gives managers an easy way to manage and set up VLANs, add and delete hosts and end stations, and manage the LES and BUS processes.

- *Intelligent BUS.* ForeThought's BUS service minimizes broadcast traffic by allowing the BUS to search the LES cache for specific MAC addresses before executing a broadcast.

- *VLAN roaming.* This ForeThought technique uses an automatic address registration technique to allow an end user to physically relocate, without having to have the administrator reconfigure the VLAN.

- *Redundant LANE services.* Running a single LECS in an ATM network can be dangerous, in that it establishes a single point of failure. FORE allows for this process to be distributed or replicated to avoid this possibility.

Ch
2

Fore also has a complete network management software package called ForeView for managing its ATM hardware. ForeView supports most popular network management platforms, including OpenView and NetView. FORE also offers a complete line of ATM adapter cards and switches.

FORE's approach to ATM establishes a layered architecture (see Figure 2.9). The four layers comply with industry standards, and add additional value through FORE's proprietary software, such as Per-VC Queuing, VLAN roaming, and session records for Call Detail Records.

FIG. 2.9
Fore's Forethought Internetwork design presents a four-layered architecture.

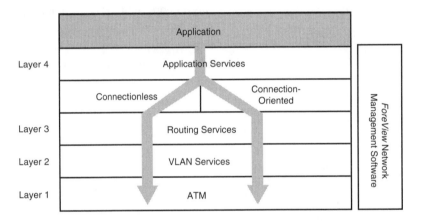

Layer 1: ATM Transport Services. This is the heart of FORE's LANE implementation, and where non-ATM traffic is converted to ATM cells at the network's edge.

Layer 2: VLAN Services. This layer allows users to share a broadcast domain based on logical association, rather than physical location. The VLAN allows end users to form a subnet based on a logical relationship, such as a common project, rather than having to base it on physical connections.

Layer 3: Distributed Routing Services. Under this layer, the old router model is abandoned in favor of a distributed, virtual router. Routing is necessary when deploying a larger internetwork, converting between different MAC types, communicating between devices on different VLANs, or internetworking with an existing network.

Layer 4: Application Services. These services include: security, connection auditing, Quality of Service guarantees and bandwidth reservation, and optimization of resources.

Crosscom

450 Donald Lynch Blvd.
Marlborough, MA 01752
Voice: 508-481-4060 or 800-388-1200
Fax: 508-229-5535
Web: **http://www.crosscomm.com**

CrossComm takes a highly modular approach to ATM internetworking. Its ClearPath family of software and hardware includes a full range of switches and edge routers, and an ATM backplane that establishes a high-speed connection between modules. All CrossComm components are managed by a single network management software, called Integrated Management System (IMS). IMS is built on HP OpenView, and can manage all CrossComm hardware as well as other SNMP devices from other vendors. IMS works with Network General's Sniffer through its built-in RMON probe.

CrossComm's XL80 and XL20 multi-slot platforms afford a great range of scalability. The XL80 is a 16-slot chassis; the XL20 can hold four modules. The XL10 is designed for workgroups, and can hold the same modules used in the XL80 and XL20 units. The CrossPoint Matrix (CPM) backplane is a full duplex, high speed interconnect scheme that builds an internal ATM backbone network within the chassis. Parallel transmission paths in the CPM operate up to 622Mbps (SONET STS-12c rates). Because the matrix design is not a shared media, total throughput on the CPM can be as much as 9.6Gigabits/second.

In addition, CrossComm's CrossLAN Exchange (see Figure 2.10), a turnkey system built on the XL80 chassis, facilitates a complete intranet solution.

FIG. 2.10
CrossComm's Infrastructure for ATM-based Corporate Intranets integrates with existing legacy networks.

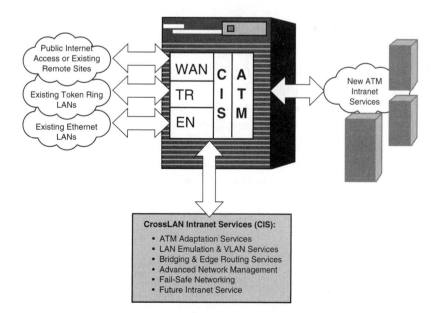

CrossLAN Exchange allows new networks to be built, or existing networks to be upgraded so that they are capable of supporting intranets. The CrossLAN device (see Figure 2.11) incorporates ATM and edge routing technologies onto a single chassis, capable of integrating with an existing Token Ring or Ethernet LAN. The XL80 chassis holds a collapsed ATM backplane that can become the backbone of an ATM-based intranet.

FIG. 2.11
CrossComm CrossLAN Exchange.

Cisco Systems

170 W. Tasman Drive
San Jose, CA 95134
Voice: 408-526-4000 or 800-553-NETS (6387)
Fax: 408-526-4100
Web: **http://www.cisco.com**

Cisco Systems' LANE solution provides for redundancy and fault tolerance, through the company's LANE Simple Server Redundancy Protocol (SSRP), a Cisco Internetwork Operating System (Cisco IOS) for ATM software protocol. This protocol establishes redundancy for all three server components (LECS, LES, and BUS). With SSRP, neither the LECS, LES, or BUS can become a single point of failure in an ATM network.

Cisco offers a full line of ATM products, including switches, adapters, management software and, since its acquisition of StrataCom, the StrataCom Integrated Gigabit switch (IGX) (see Figure 2.12). The latter device is an innovative and highly scalable ATM switch that comes in 8-, 16-, and 32-slot configurations. It supports all QoS service classes, and will permit any amount of bandwidth to be assigned to any slot. Voice transmissions are one of the most bandwidth-intensive aspects of networking; Cisco addresses this with its voice activity detection (VAD) technique. VAD uses a digital signal processor to distinguish between silence and speech on a voice connection. VAD will then generate cells onto the network only during speech, thereby saving bandwidth. Along with voice compression, the VAD technique is used to furnish voice connectivity to a digital PABX through a standard interface.

FIG. 2.12
Cisco Systems'
StrataCom Integrated
Gigabit switch (IGX)
supports all QoS
classes.

Cascade Communications Corporation

5 Carlisle Road
Westford, MA 01886
Voice: 508-692-2600 or 800-647-6926
Fax: 508-692-5052
E-mail: **mktg@casc.com**
Web: **http://www.casc.com**

Cascade's Virtual Network Navigator (VNN), a dynamic routing technology, was
originally developed for use in frame relay networks but has been expanded to

incorporate ATM's QoS parameters and other ATM-specific technology. VNN offers three components:

- Topology database, holding the physical topology and QoS capability of the ATM links.
- OSPF-based topology database distribution algorithm.
- Best-route calculation algorithm.

These three components work with Cascade's Virtual Circuit Manager services, which reside in all switches, regardless of whether they are frame relay, SMDS, or ATM. This is especially useful in a multiservice ATM-integrated network. Cascade products support frame relay to ATM Interworking (for more information on this technology, see the "Integrating Legacy LANs with ATM" section shown previously).

Cascade's B-STDX 9000 and B-STDX 8000 (see Figure 2.13) offer a multiservice WAN platform for interworking between ATM, frame relay and SMDS. This functionality allows the user to establish a migration path to ATM, while still taking advantage of frame relay and SMDS services.

FIG. 2.13

Cascade Communications B-STDX 8000 Multiservice WAN Platform can be used to interwork ATM, Frame Relay and SMDS.

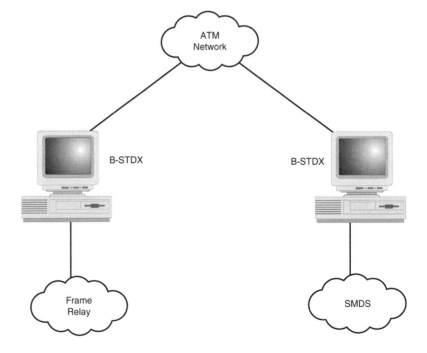

End2End Network Solutions

353 Gold Star Highway
Groton, CT 06340
Voice: 860-446-3030
Fax: 860-446-3039
Web: **http://www.end2end.com**

End2End is a developer of real-time, embedded-system networking solutions, specifically focusing on network interface requirements for high-bandwidth applications. The company promotes a high level of enterprise connectivity, with an innovative technique that integrates web-based, multi-tiered, distributed component software architecture using an ATM switch infrastructure. End2End's new ATM-FastLane family of real-time device drivers targets the real-time embedded systems market, and permits developers to integrate ATM technology into data and telecommunications products.

Ch
2

Summary

ATM uses a small, fixed packet of 53 bytes, making it ideal for transmitting delay-insensitive information such as video or voice. ATM delivers the advantage of Quality of Service, allowing the network manager to specify four different service classes that may correspond to different types of data. ATM's speed exceeds that of many other network technologies. It is capable of running at 155Mbps (OC-3), 622Mbps (OC-12), and 2.488Gbps (OC-48). For those who want ATM but don't need the extremely high speeds, 25Mbps ATM can be an inexpensive alternative.

Because ATM is connection-oriented, it is inherently more secure than any of the Ethernet implementations. LAN Emulation (LANE) is used to allow the ATM network to communicate with legacy networks, including Ethernet and Token Ring. After deploying the ATM network, it will be necessary to acquire new network management and monitoring tools. Fortunately, there are several vendors providing this capability. ATM networks are capable of interworking with frame relay, SNA, IP, and other network infrastructures. ●

CHAPTER 3

Frame Relay

Frame relay, a wide-area networking system that relies on permanent circuits between end points, offers a high throughput and allocates transmission resources only when active communications are taking place. Typically used for data transmissions only, frame relay is well-suited 2for bursty transmissions and for connected multiple-branch office sites. However, recent innovations have made it possible to send voice traffic over the frame relay network as well—presenting an opportunity for tremendous savings on long-distance bills. ■

Overview of Frame Relay

In the past, leased lines were often used to connect corporate sites, divisions, and branches. Greater demand for connectivity led to the need for a more efficient and less costly solution. To meet this demand, frame relay was developed to provide a better way to connect multiple LANs, data networks, and their peripherals.

Over the past few years, there has been a noticeable trend of moving away from the lower-speed leased line connections and Systems Network Architecture (SNA), in favor of frame relay. Recent innovations allow frame relay to be used to carry voice and fax transmission over the same network, resulting in an even greater level of savings. Placing voice over frame relay can provide additional savings of between 30 to 50 percent, depending on the corporate network characteristics.

SNA Architecture

IBM's Systems Network Architecture (SNA) was first released in 1974 to impose strict control over communications between various devices. Originally, it was meant as a network architecture with a central host; later it was adapted to accommodate multiple hosts. Each device that provides physical services in the SNA network gets a Physical Unit (PU) definition, which defines its position in the hierarchy between terminal and host. A PU 2 device controls workstations; a PU 4 device is a communications controller or front-end processor, and a PU 5 device is a mainframe processor. Logical Units (LU), on the other hand, define the type of data that flows between the PUs. SNA supports both local and remote links, and several extensions and gateways have been created that allow PC-based networks to communicate with an IBM mainframe or minicomputer network.

Frame relay is especially useful for WAN connections, and many corporations with multiple branches employ the technology. Cost savings become greater when a company brings more sites into the frame relay network. The frame relay network can be managed internally or through a provider. Ultimately, frame relay is simple and flexible. If a skilled in-house team is in place, it may be more effective to run the network internally.

Frame Relay Background

StrataCom president Dick Moley is often considered the "father of frame relay." In the late 1980s, Moley, along with others, saw the paradigm of taking frames and dividing them into cells for fast transport as a tremendous opportunity. Moley's StrataCom, along with Digital Equipment, Cisco Systems, and Northern Telecom, founded the Frame Relay Forum. In 1991, the first frame relay network was deployed by WorldCom, which joined the Forum later on.

Another major advantage to frame relay is access speed. Frame relay typically offers a 56Kbps connection, significantly higher than the 9.6Kbps found in leased lines.

Under the leased line model, a customer had to request a 64Kbps access line (DS0) for branch offices, and a 1.55Mbps (DS1) line for headquarters. When the inevitable congestion occurred, another DS1 had to be acquired from the service provider, and additional Customer Premises Equipment (CPE) had to be deployed—translating into a significant expenditure for additional bandwidth. Now, higher-speed frame relay gives customers more bandwidth without additional CPE. For those users who do not want to initiate a wholesale migration to ATM, high-speed frame relay is a workable and inexpensive alternative that can extend the life of frame relay equipment.

The type of traffic being carried by frame relay has changed; where it was used originally for data only, it is now being used for voice, video, and other types of traffic. However, newer applications and an increase in demand for data has led to the need for more bandwidth and higher-speed networks. The Frame Relay Forum addressed these needs by amending its User-to-Network Interface (UNI) and Network-to-Network Interface (NNI) Implementation Agreements (IAs) to accommodate DS3 speeds of up to 45Mbps.

Ch
3

Applications for Frame Relay

One of the biggest segments of the frame relay market is IBM networking. While traditionally IBM networking environments utilized wide area leased line networks, frame relay can furnish a viable alternative. Originally, X.25 was meant to provide the open environment necessary for IBM computing, however, IBM never widely supported X.25. Frame relay, on the other hand, equips IBM with a smooth and efficient way to integrate LANs into the SNA environment. A big advantage is that customers can use existing hardware to support frame relay.

IBM's Network Control Protocol (NCP 7.1), released in 1994, allowed SNA networks to use frame relay for the first time. Usage of frame relay gives SNA shops the advantage of link consolidation, that is, each access link can support multiple virtual circuits. Since that time, frame relay has quickly become the preferred technology for networks running at T1/E1 speeds (2Mbps) and above.

The technology has been growing in popularity, because of its easy management, cost advantage, and multiprotocol support. Multiprotocol networking has been one of the biggest drivers in frame relay's growth. Integrating LANs into SNA environments in particular has caused a number of corporations to consider frame relay.

Types of Frame Relay Networks

A frame relay solution can take the form of private network services, public network services, or a hybrid of the two.

A private frame relay network (see Figure 3.1) can operate over several different interfaces, including V series interfaces, fractional E1, and both BRI and PRI ISDN. The private option gives the corporate user greater control over the network, better trunk utilization and can take advantage of some existing equipment.

FIG. 3.1

A private Frame Relay network takes advantage of existing equipment.

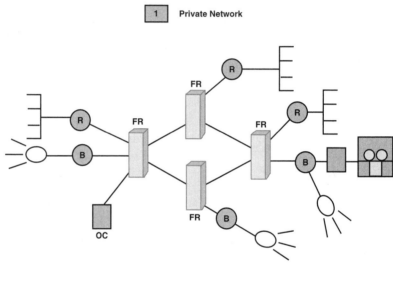

1   Private Network

▼ Leverages Existing Network
  Equipment, Protects Investment
▼ Improves Trunk Utilization
▼ Control over Core Network is Maintained

A public frame relay network, on the other hand, can significantly reduce costs of ownership, and may be advantageous in situations where there has not been a big investment in existing customer-premises equipment (see Figure 3.2).

The hybrid option is used by some large sites, especially where different branches may have different needs (see Figure 3.3). In this case, the needs of each site can be determined, and the most appropriate configuration installed.

Deploying frame relay is surprisingly simple. A new location can be added simply by adding an access port and configuring the permanent virtual circuits (PVCs). Compared to a leased-line solution, frame relay is much more cost-effective, and can often bring significant performance improvements.

FIG. 3.2
A public Frame Relay network delegates management to the service provider.

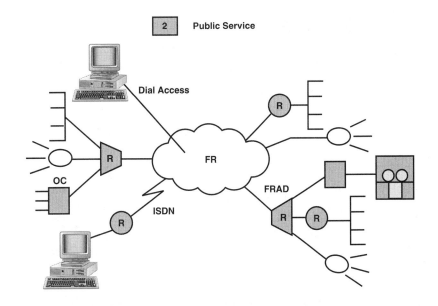

▼ Service Provider Manages Backbone, Ownership Costs are Reduced
▼ Single Network Access Supports Multiple Remote Connections and Protocols
▼ Connection-oriented Environment Maintains Privacy and Security

FIG. 3.3
A hybrid Frame Relay network can be used when costs and needs differ between sites.

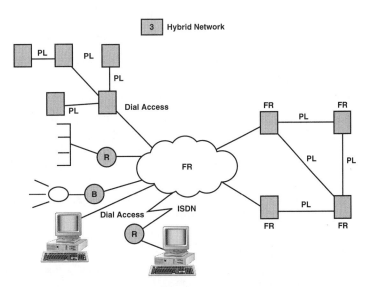

▼ Provides Control over Critical Network Links
▼ Allows Cost/Benefit Analysis on Site-by-Site Basis
▼ Optimizes Network Price-to-Performance Ratio

Ch
3

Frame Relay Speed

Since the Frame Relay Forum modified them to accommodate high-speed frame relay, the User-to-Network Interface (UNI) (FRF 1.1) and Network-to-Network Interface (NNI) (FRF 2.1) Implementation Agreements (IAs), now support three high-speed physical layer interfaces:

- HSSI (High-Speed Serial Interface) (52Mbps)
- DS3 (Digital Service 3) (45Mbps)
- E3 (35Mbps)

Originally, UNI and NNI specified speeds only up to T1/E1 levels (2Mbps). The UNI's basic function is to specify signaling and management functions between CPE and a frame relay network device. The purpose of the NNI, on the other hand, is to establish bidirectional signaling and management between two frame relay networks.

Standards Development (Frame Relay Forum)

The Frame Relay Forum was founded in 1991 to promote national and international frame relay standards. The group has grown quickly, and now has chapters in North America, Europe, Australia/New Zealand, and Japan.

The Forum's standards, known as Implementation Agreements, are as follows:

- *FRF.1.1.* User-to-Network Interface (UNI) Implementation Agreement
- *FRF.2.1.* Frame Relay Network-to-Network Interface (NNI) Implementation Agreement Version 2.1
- *FRF.3.1.* Multiprotocol Encapsulation Implementation (MEI) Agreement
- *FRF.4.* Switched Virtual Circuit (SVC) Implementation Agreement
- *FRF.5.* Frame Relay/ATM Network Interworking Implementation Agreement
- *FRF.6.* Frame Relay Service Customer Network Management Implementation Agreement (MIB)
- *FRF.7.* Frame Relay PVC Multicast Service and Protocol Description
- *FRF.8.* Frame Relay/ATM PVC Service Interworking Implementation Agreement
- *FRF.9.* Data Compression Over Frame Relay Implementation Agreement

Over the next year, the Frame Relay Forum's Technical Committee and working groups will be focusing on these additional IAs:

- *FRF.10.* Switched Virtual Circuits (SVCs) at the Network-to-Network Interface (NNI)

- *FRF.11.* Voice over Frame Relay (VoFR). This IA will specify a mechanism for transporting packetized low-bit-rate voice over frame relay networks. The first phase will support preconfigured connections, and will promote multivendor interoperability.

Newer initiatives that may lead to more IAs in the future include:

- *Frame Relay Fragmentation.* This will enable fragmentation and reassembly of frames at the FR UNI.
- *Multi-Link Frame Relay at the User-to-Network Interface (UNI).* This will enable frame relay devices to use multiple physical links (a type of frame relay inverse MUXing, or multiplexing). In other words, inverse MUXing is able to take multiple, smaller noncontiguous circuits, run data over them in a synchronous fashion, and achieve the equivalent of a higher-speed link.
- *Frame Relay-to-ATM (FR/ATM) Switched Virtual Circuit (SVC) Service Interworking.* This effort will define FR/ATM service interworking supporting SVCs.
- *Frame Relay Network Service Level Definitions.* This will establish frame relay network performance definitions. These definitions will give service providers the ability to deliver uniform service levels over diverse networks, and will also give users a metric that can be used to determine whether service levels have been rendered.

Implementation and Infrastructure

A traditional LAN internetwork uses hub routers with a star topology. Frame relay has come to address the needs of the LAN internetwork, changing the role of the hub somewhat. The routers take a less centralized role, instead moving to the edge of the frame relay cloud and functioning as a LAN-to-WAN gateway.

Frame relay itself performs the packet switching that would have otherwise been accomplished by the hub router. Because frame relay facilitates the use of fewer hub routers, there is an obvious cost advantage. Also, because there are fewer hub routers, the hop count is reduced, an additional side benefit for larger networks.

A frame relay network, because it is connection-oriented, enters a series of paths in each switch. A logical entity known as a virtual circuit is created, that allows all data that moves between a given source and destination to travel over the same path over a period of time. The virtual circuit model simplifies network design, because each virtual circuit precisely matches the requirements of each feeder router. The configuration of these virtual circuits is largely automatic and extremely fast.

The physical connection of the frame relay network is a synchronous connection at either 56 Kbps or 64Kbps, and occurs through a Channel Service Unit/Data Service Unit (CSU/DSU). In addition, a series of Permanent Virtual Circuits (PVCs) are established to provide the most logical connection between locations. The PVCs operation is controlled by two parameters; the Committed Information Rate (CIR) and Burst Excess (Be).

Frame relay is a router-based technology. Routers usually use a store-and-forward mechanism to send data over the network; in this model, the entire frame must be received by the router before any processing begins. Although the store-and-forward methodology does offer some benefits, such as the ability to check a packet for errors before directing it to the appropriate network, it also introduces delays and a slower response time, which increases as the number of hops increase.

Frame relay technology lends itself to peer networking, where each site is directly connected to one another in a mesh, or cloud topology. Some routers can also operate in a partial mesh environment.

N O T E There are vendor implementations of frame relay that differ from the "standard" frame relay discussed later in this section. ▨

Frame relay simplifies the routing operation. Packets move from the LAN to a single frame relay port with multiple virtual connections to each destination network. The frames are switched very quickly, and each virtual connection has a set priority ranking. This rate can be exceeded under some circumstances, such as a burst of traffic, if the bandwidth is available. For more information about packet priorities in frame relay, see the "Voice and Fax Over Frame Relay" section later in this chapter.

Routing Frame Relay

LAN internetworking can be enormously complicated; frame relay can simplify internetworking by minimizing the number of routers required.

The physical configuration of the router is as follows: the router is attached to the frame relay network and the LAN. This LAN interface corresponds to the type of LAN at each location. The physical port is dependent on the individual network infrastructure, and even the country in which it is deployed. Most services use V.35 or X.21 ports, and some routers support multiple interfaces. The frame relay router must rigorously conform to the frame relay protocol. In addition, the router gets its information about the virtual connections by signaling the user-to-network interface (UNI).

Routers used in leased line networks have one physical port for each leased line. Vendors embrace a rule known as the *split horizon*, which states that an incoming packet cannot be placed on the same network interface from which it originated. The purpose of the split horizon rule is to prevent data from bouncing back and forth indefinitely in a routing loop if a link fails. Although this is critically important in a private line, it does not apply to frame relay, where one physical interface may support multiple remote connections.

Because different PVCs originate from the same physical interface, a frame must be able to be sent back out on the same physical port from which it originated in order to send it back out on a different PVC. Under frame relay, a routing loop is avoided through a different technique that recognizes each PVC independently. A frame relay router will send a frame back over the same physical port, but will not permit it to be sent back over the same PVC.

Frame Relay Media and Topology

Frame relay networks are typically implemented in a star topology, much like the older leased line networks they are meant to replace. Under a star topology, one location works as the central point of traffic for multiple locations. Because more traffic passes through the central point, this location requires greater bandwidth allocation than the others. Classical frame relay networks are configured with a series of permanent virtual circuits (PVCs) between every end station.

Some frame relay products, including those from ACT Networks, can function not only over cable, but also over wireless media. ACT has implemented a satellite-based frame relay network service called SkyFrame, in which each earth-bound station transmits one carrier, which is modulated by the aggregated channels that originated from that station. The data is packetized and multiplexed, and each carrier is assigned a frequency and bandwidth. The receiving earth stations will then accept packets based on their addresses.

This satellite technology represents an innovative way to integrate terrestrial frame relay networks into a single, integrated network. Like ACT's other frame relay products, SkyFrame supports frame packetizing, voice compression, and network management. A big advantage of the SkyFrame technology is that a satellite hub is unnecessary, thereby eliminating a very large initial expense that can easily reach a half-million dollars. Furthermore, intelligent processing is distributed between all connected sites, creating a virtual switching system and minimizing complexity to yet another level.

In each earth station, the SkyFrame unit, frame relay switch, or other frame relay assembler/disassembler (FRAD) accesses the satellite through the use of modulator and demodulator cards and RF terminals. This specialized system of separate modular and demodulator cards (as opposed to a single modem card) is unique to SkyFrame. The modulator card includes the frame relay switch, and the demodulator card includes the

Ch
3

packet filtering processor. The satellite system is most effective for small to medium-sized integrated voice/fax/data networks. Connectivity to a larger number of sites would be cost-prohibitive, because of the number of demodulators that would be required.

Vendor-Specific Frame Relay Implementations

Some vendors offer proprietary products or implementations for some facets of frame relay technology that are not yet formal standards. While some of these products can provide capabilities that a company is in dire need of using, always be wary about implementing proprietary technology if you need to interface your network with products from other vendors or service providers. Asking a lot of questions of the vendors involved (both the vendors selling and the vendors whose equipment you will need to interoperate with) will help ensure your network remains interoperable.

Definitions

The CIR is a throughput rate to which a customer subscribes, and is the maximum amount of bandwidth the provider agrees to send through each PVC. The PVC cannot exceed the maximum speed the customer equipment is capable of providing, however. In reality, the CIR is usually not set to this maximum speed, but is set to a rate equivalent to an average calculated usage.

The Bc, or committed burst rate, is a parameter that measures the maximum number of data bits on a PVC that a network will transfer under normal conditions and over a given period of time.

The Be, or excess burst rate, is a parameter that measures the maximum number of uncommitted bits on a PVC that a network will attempt to deliver over a given period of time.

The Bc sets out a guaranteed level of bits that the network will transmit over the PVC, and the Be sets out an additional amount that the network will transmit if the bandwidth is available. The frame relay switch will mark any frame that exceeds the Bc but not the Be as Discard Eligible (DE). Frames that are so marked will be dropped first under congested conditions. The frame is then retransmitted by the originating device.

The Tc is a sliding value, which is the time period over which the PVC is monitored. It is dependent on the other parameters.

Switched Frame Transfer Mode (SFTM)   Some companies offer—or will be offering in the future—switching technology that gives frame relay users permanent virtual circuits (PVCs) that include some of the same benefits offered by switched virtual circuits (SVCs). Switched Frame Transfer Mode (SFTM) technology lets users switch voice and data over a public or private frame relay network. SFTM overcomes the traditional methodology of using PVCs, which calls for a point-to-point connection between each location for each application.

Unlike PVCs, SFTM technology lets administrators combine traffic onto a single direct connection, so each destination only requires a single switch. The technology lets a user hang on to the existing permanent virtual circuit backbone, while being able to switch traffic for applications such as voice.

Cell Technology and Dynamic Routing A different approach to frame relay technology is taken by another company whose products slice frames into small cells, similar to ATM cells. Processing begins immediately, instead of waiting for the entire frame to be received (store-and-forward). Under this model, the first cells of a subdivided frame may reach the final destination while the end of the frame is still in the process of being fragmented. The disadvantage of the store-and-forward mechanism is that the store-and-forward router must encapsulate some protocols in IP frames in order to transmit them, which results in additional decreases in response time.

The technique of dividing the frame into cells avoids the necessity for encapsulation. In a standard encapsulation method, every node must interpret the frame header before taking any action. The alternative methodology relies on dynamic routing tables, and allows each node to act like a switch that automatically relays each cell in the proper direction without any additional processing. In the event one route fails, the connection is dynamically restructured.

The system also offers prioritization of data at the cell level instead of frame relay's standard of prioritizing at the frame level. Every data type can be assigned a priority level, and then data will enter the circuit according to its priority. Again, this is a proprietary scheme and not part of the actual frame relay specification; nonetheless, it adds significant value to the frame relay network. Prioritization at the frame level is probably better than none at all, but it still carries one big drawback: it is still possible for a prioritized frame to experience a delay if it gets stuck behind a series of longer frames.

Think of frame prioritization this way: the priority frame is you, when you go to the grocery store to buy a single item. There's only one checkout lane open, and the lady in front of you has two baskets full of groceries, wants to write a check on an out-of-state bank account, and forgot to show the clerk her fistful of coupons until the last minute. Priority or not, you still have to wait. By cellularizing the frames, no cell will experience much of a delay, because they are all the same size. (Grocery stores apply the same logic to the "nine items or less" checkout lane.)

Ch
3

Frame Relay and ATM

Frame relay and ATM complement each other well, and the interworking of the two technologies enjoys broad industry support, including work between the ATM Forum and the Frame Relay Forum. Use of frame relay in an ATM environment can significantly extend the reach of ATM. Because of ATM's Quality of Service guarantees, ATM is especially good for bursty applications. Frame relay adds value when used in combination with ATM, by presenting a valuable standard for wide area networks.

Although voice over ATM is currently more popular than voice over frame relay, it is certainly possible to send voice over frame relay, and many customers save big money by doing so. However, ATM has the more mature technology for sending voice over the network.

Large companies often deploy a mix of ATM and frame relay, perhaps using ATM at headquarters, and frame relay at the branch level. Although frame relay and ATM networks may coexist as separate networks, eventually, frame relay will be used to send traffic into the ATM network. Many new ATM networks support frame relay access; eventually, most LAN interconnects will center on frame relay going into an ATM network.

In the past, it has been a common misconception that the frame relay and ATM technologies are mutually exclusive. Nothing could be further from the truth. The two technologies are remarkably similar, and actually evolved from the same technology, that is, Integrated Services Digital Network (ISDN) standards. The only real difference between the two is in the size of the packet, or cell. While frame relay uses a variable packet size, ATM uses the fixed 53-byte packet size, making it more applicable to multimedia, video, and other delay-sensitive traffic.

Frame Relay Interworking

A seamless connection between ATM and frame relay can be established, thanks to the Frame Relay to ATM Service PVC Interworking Implementation Agreement (FRF.8), a new standard jointly promoted by the Frame Relay Forum and ATM Forum. The standard allows network managers to use both technologies in a single network, instead of having to make a difficult decision between the two. The FRF.8 standard will let users connect frame relay sites with data-intensive, high-speed ATM sites. Interworking is an ideal technology for those who wish to plan for an ATM migration, but want to take the long view. Under the Service Interworking plan, a customer could upgrade the central site to ATM, while retaining frame relay equipment in branch offices.

FRF.8 details the interworking of the frame-based frame relay and cell-based ATM protocols. Before a frame relay packet can enter into an ATM backbone, the frame must be broken into cells, including an identifier cell and data cells. In reverse, ATM cells are consolidated, and converted into a frame.

Interworking can work in transparent mode or translation mode. In transparent mode, the customer premises equipment (CPE) performs the reverse translation. The CPE is typically an ATM router. In translation mode, the frame relay network performs the translation. The biggest difference between the two modes is that in translation mode, multiple protocols can run over one permanent virtual circuit (PVC). In transparent mode, a separate PVC is required for each protocol. In a larger network running multiple protocols, translation mode can be a big benefit.

Fortunately for the end user, service interworking is largely transparent. The older specification, known as Network Interworking, called for the ATM equipment at the customer site to convert ATM traffic into frame-relay packets before communicating with a frame relay device.

The four biggest service carriers, AT&T, LDDS WorldCom, MCI Communications, and Sprint all offer interworking services to seamlessly interface frame relay WAN services to any ATM service. Interworking allows for the central office to migrate to ATM, while allowing branch offices to stay with frame relay. One major appeal of interworking is that protocol conversion is not a concern. The protocol conversion is transparent within carrier networks, and does not require any special software in the end devices.

In a combined ATM and Frame Relay network, frame relay is often deployed at remote locations or branches, with ATM used at headquarters. Service interworking is utilized to convert between the two technologies (see Figure 3.4).

Interworking technology is also optimal for those frame relay users who use frame relay for data, and do not need the higher bandwidth offered by ATM at all sites. Interworking is offered by most long-distance carriers. Sprint was one of the first to offer this hybrid service in the spring of 1996, and other carriers provide the protocol translations required to let the ATM switch communicate with the frame relay switch.

FIG. 3.4

Service Interworking connects a frame relay network to an ATM network.

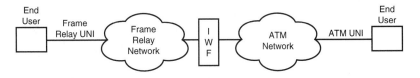

Frame User Network Interface (FUNI)

Those in the ATM camp offer a technology known as FUNI, which is a type of frame-based ATM networking, as an alternative to frame relay. Although ATM is primarily thought of as a cell-based transport technology, the FUNI specification does not actually require it; and so FUNI was born to send frames, instead of fixed-length cells, over an ATM network. For more discussion on FUNI, see Chapter 2, "Asynchronous Transfer Mode (ATM)."

FUNI lets customers use low-cost, frame-based equipment, and uses the ATM switch to segment frames back into ATM cells. FUNI software can run on the same hardware devices that support frame relay, and there are a number of similarities between frame relay and the FUNI specification.

The FUNI places software in the user equipment, and a frame-based interface and FUNI software in the ATM switch. The frames are segmented into cells at the ATM switch interface, sent into the network, and reassembled into frames and sent on to the recipient. FUNI was not intended to provide interoperability between frame relay and ATM, although the two do have similar structures and can run on the same type of hardware.

It isn't possible, however, to simply connect frame relay equipment into the ATM network's FUNI and expect it to function. Furthermore, FUNI does not support all ATM services. Specifically, services that require use of ATM adaptation layers (AALs) other than 3, 4, and 5 are not available over FUNI, and the Available Bit Rate (ABR) class of service is not available as well.

Voice and Fax over Frame Relay

Voice calls are usually sent over dedicated leased lines, although the leased line is by far the most costly way to handle long-distance voice calls. It does, however, yield the highest quality audio fidelity. Although it is usually thought of as a data-only technology, frame relay can be an effective and inexpensive way to transmit voice over the network.

Voice over frame relay can cost about a tenth of the cost of using a virtual private network. The price differential is due to the method of pricing; frame relay is priced either by the frame, or at a flat monthly rate. Standard long-distance voice, on the other hand, is charged by the minute. Using frame relay for voice can pay for itself very quickly, just by eliminating some of the long-distance fees. Several vendors are starting to deploy voice over frame relay, including ACT Networks (see Figure 3.5).

A great deal of attention has been devoted to sending voice over frame relay networks, despite its limitations and relatively low level of quality. When voice is digitized over a plain ordinary telephone service (POTS) line, it is done with the Pulse Code Modulation

(PCM) standard for digital voice which runs at 64 Kbps. This PCM standard represents what we recognize as toll-quality voice, or the voice we normally hear on a standard long-distance call. But in order to send voice over a low-speed data line, some sort of compression must be applied to the digital voice.

FIG. 3.5
ACT Networks Frame Relay Voice/Data topology connects remote sites to headquarters, bypassing the long-distance telephone companies.

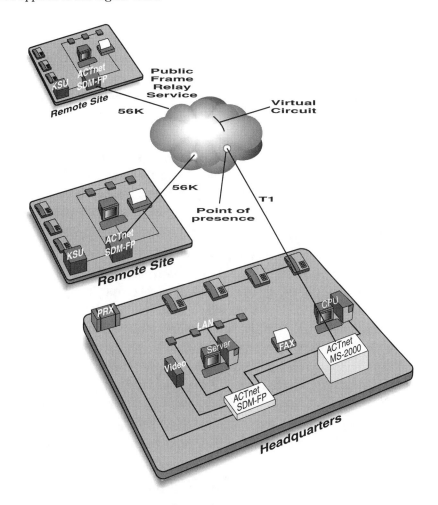

Besides compression, two other issues may also have an impact on voice quality; these are delay and dropped packets. Delay, sometimes known as *jitter*, is the variation in the delay experienced by consecutive packets.

Compression   Unlike most data transmissions, voice cannot tolerate delay. Until very recently, packetized voice transmission was impossible. However, consider how most people speak. Unless you've had a few too many cups of coffee, you have a great many pauses in your speech; probably a lot more than you realize. This dead space may be necessary for comprehension, but to the network, it's only dead space, and doesn't need to be transmitted.

Currently, packetized voice transmission is achieved not by digitizing the entire voice transmission, complete with pauses and redundancies, but by evaluating and picking out only what is essential to comprehension. This is accomplished through eliminating repetitive sounds, and eliminating pauses (silence suppression). Only about a fifth of what is contained in speech is necessary for accurate transmission; the balance consists of pauses, repetition and background noise. Human speech, by nature, includes a great deal of repetition, just because of the vibrations that take place in the vocal chords. If you listen carefully, you can pick out repetitive or drawn-out sounds, such as the "s" sound in the word "ice," or "snake."

After eliminating repetitive sounds and pauses, the voice can be more efficiently compressed. The information that remains can then be digitized and placed into packets, which can be sent over a frame relay network. Voice packets are typically smaller than data packets, because a smaller packet will experience less transmission delay over the network.

Delay Jitter can occur in a public network for reasons that cannot be controlled by a buffer. For example, if a packet from frame relay customer "A" arrives at an intermediate switch, but that switch is occupied with a packet from frame relay customer "B," some jitter may occur. In this case, customer A's packet would be placed into a buffer by the intermediate switch, and it processed only after customer B's packet has been passed on. Buffering can present some significant delays, especially if customer B has an exceptionally long packet.

Frame relay, remember, allows variable length packets—so here we are again, with our one item in the supermarket, behind the lady with two carts and a fistful of coupons. There is a limit to buffering, however, and if the jitter introduced in the intermediate switch is more than the receiving device can handle, the quality of the voice transmission degrades.

A fast public frame relay backbone will virtually eliminate the problem of jitter. A frame relay service running on an ATM backbone will eliminate it further, because ATM is based on fixed-length cells, and the problem of a small packet getting stuck behind a larger one is eliminated.

Asynchronous Time Division Multiplexing Ironically, older technology, which used Time Division Multiplexing (TDM), did not suffer from compression or jitter problems. TDM divided the bandwidth into as many equal time periods as there were input channels. Every data channel got an opportunity to transmit, whenever its corresponding time period, or packet, was sent. Because the time interval was predictable, there was no jitter, and since TDM worked over a point-to-point link, there were very few dropped packets.

The only problem with TDM technology, however, was that every time packet had to be dedicated to voice. Now, a person's normal speech pattern is full of pauses. Some of those packets that existed under the TDM system contained these pauses, which was an inefficient use of bandwidth.

The obvious way to make better use of the bandwidth was to use statistical multiplexers (also known as Asynchronous Time Division Multiplexers (ATDM). With ATDM, a data channel can make use of any time packet. That is, if a channel is experiencing a period of silence, it does not have to transmit that silence anymore; instead, the packet that would otherwise be dedicated to carrying nothing could be given to another channel. Although ATDM made better use of bandwidth, it introduced the concept of jitter. Some of this jitter can be mitigated with a buffering technique that buffers arriving packets, and reassembles them in order before converting them to analog form.

Frame relay uses a type of statistical multiplexing. However, further differences are evident in a public frame relay network versus a private frame relay network.

Packet Prioritization   There are some additional considerations when considering adding voice to a frame relay network. For example, the audio quality of voice over frame relay will not be as good as standard toll traffic. For this reason, most users opt to limit voice over frame relay to inter-company communications, and not use it for external calling.

Prioritization is perhaps the most important part of voice transmission. Without it, the individual packets containing the voice data would not arrive in the correct order, and the result would be garbled speech. Use of switched virtual circuits (SVCs) lends itself to these types of advanced features, including QoS guarantees and bandwidth reservation similar to ATM networks.

Although the frame relay standard does not provide for these types of ATM services explicitly, some vendors have incorporated them into their products.

Packet Drop   Packet drop in the public frame relay network poses another problem. The service provider may deploy congestion control methods that consist of discarding packets that exceed the particular customer's Committed Information Rate (CIR). Therefore, all packets that exceed a customer's CIR will be marked with a Discard Eligible (DE) bit. If a congested state arises, these marked packets can be dropped, which can again cause the quality of the voice transmission to degrade. Frame relay itself has no provision for notifying the transmitter to resend the packet, but since frame relay works with other transport protocols (such as SNA or IP), that task can be picked up by the other protocols.

Ch
3

Frame Relay Assembler/Disassembler (FRAD) Voice over frame relay is a recent innovation, and mostly produces voice transmissions of marginal quality, which limits it to internal use. Obviously, a caller doesn't want to sound garbled when talking to a big client. But the technology holds a great deal of potential, and some frame relay devices are starting to apply proprietary technology to achieve better quality. Basically, a voice-over-frame relay device is similar to a standard frame relay assembler/disassembler (FRAD), except that it encapsulates voice traffic into a frame relay frame for transmission. Some voice-enabled FRADs, however, offer value-added features, such as the ability to connect with a PBX.

The most critical element to consider when selecting a FRAD for voice transmission is the delay. Voice traffic, obviously has to be delivered in real time, or as close to it as possible. If it is not, your top salesman's silver-tongued voice may come out sounding like he has a mouthful of marbles. In a delay-insensitive network that sends data only, frames can be re-sent, and received out of order, but since they eventually get put back together on the receiving end, this makes little difference.

In the public telephone network, every voice channel enjoys a dedicated bandwidth of 64Kbps. In order to send voice and data over the same pipe and achieve the cost savings that voice over frame relay promises, voice traffic needs to be compressed. Products use a compression algorithm to achieve this, although different algorithms may yield different levels of audio fidelity on the receiving end. Many voice-enabled FRADs can compress data into 8Kbps channels, thereby placing eight calls over that 64Kbps pipe that would otherwise carry only one. Some FRADs will even compress voice into 4.8Kbps channels. Although this high level of compression can squeeze more calls into a single pipe (and achieve a corresponding cost savings), the lower levels of compression will yield better quality audio conversations. FRADs range in their ability to compress voice channels from a ratio of 2:1 to 16:1.

Integrated Frame Relay Assembler/Disassembler (IFRAD) A standard, garden-variety FRAD will handle data only. However, recent innovations have brought about the Integrated FRAD (IFRAD), a device that can accommodate voice, data, and fax over a public or private frame relay network. These devices will negotiate delay and jitter that would otherwise occur in voice traffic through a series of bandwidth management techniques. ACT Networks was one of the first to provide voice over frame relay, and now offers a line of IFRADs that use a standards-based interface to translate any data protocol into a frame relay packet. Unlike other FRADs, ACT's IFRADs can packetize voice and fax communications, thereby eliminating toll charges for inter-site calls.

Deployment of Voice and Data Technology on a Frame Relay Network Some vendors and analysts claim that voice traffic should be limited to ATM networks, although if an ATM network is not already in place, this can be a costly solution, at least for the initial setup. The frame relay solution is surprisingly simple; the PBX is just hooked up to the data network, and long-distance charges disappear.

Voice transmission over frame relay is limited, there is a four-hop limit to voice travel. If voice travels more than four nodes before it reaches its destination, there will be delays and the quality of voice traffic will degrade.

Private network managers can control routing over the network; some public carriers also offer virtual circuit-to-virtual circuit engineering support. Carriers are under pressure by smaller users who do not have large private networks, and do not want to bear the expense of an ATM migration, to offer voice over frame relay services.

Ideally, voice over frame relay is suited for a corporate environment with several branches, where all the branches must communicate with headquarters. Because of the hop limitation, the most efficient way to execute voice transmission in the private network is to let branches transmit directly to headquarters, and then allow the headquarters to re-send the voice traffic through a switch and PBX to the destination.

A MAN or WAN configuration, however, requires traffic flow to be monitored carefully to avoid congestion at headquarters. An integrated frame relay assembler/disassembler (IFRAD) that can handle both voice and data is essential here, and each branch must have one. An IFRAD can cost up to $10,000 each. The headquarters must either have an equivalent number of FRADs as there are branches, or use a concentration FRAD, which is a single device that can communicate with all peripheral FRADs.

NOTE There is currently no fixed standard for VoFR technology, although the Frame Relay Forum is actively working on developing these standards. Consequently, several vendors are now offering successful, although proprietary, methods for integrating voice onto frame relay.

Voice over frame relay may be exceptionally useful for intra-company communications. Frame relay users often have excess bandwidth available. Even if additional bandwidth must be added, the incremental cost of doing so is minimal compared to paying for standard long-distance services. By adding voice to the frame relay network, users can make more efficient use of bandwidth, while also providing an inexpensive option for voice traffic between company sites.

SNA and Frame Relay

Network managers enjoy many benefits from integrating SNA with frame relay. For example, under a traditional SNA network (see Figure 3.6), a multipoint circuit will tend to be slow, and modifying configuration is complicated. Under a frame relay/SNA network

Ch
3

(see Figure 3.7), each location has a direct network connection, and will therefore enjoy a faster response time. Additionally, the multipoint configuration is logically maintained, making reconfiguration simpler.

FIG. 3.6

In a traditional SNA network, a single outage can affect multiple sites and degrade performance. SOURCE: Frame Relay Forum

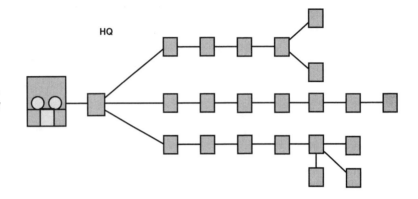

▼ **Multipoint Circuits are Slow, Affecting Response Times**
▼ **Modifying Configurations as Traffic Loading Changes is Difficult, Time Consuming, and Expensive**
▼ **Single Circuit Outage Affects Multiple Sites**

FIG. 3.7

In a frame relay/SNA configuration, each location has a direct network connection, and reconfiguration is logical and fast. SOURCE: Frame Relay Forum

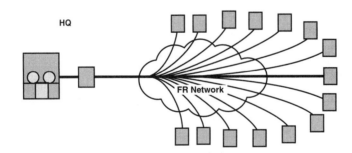

▼ **Each Location has Direct Network connection**
▼ **Multipoint Configuration Maintained Logically; Reconfiguration is Fast and Easy**
▼ **Network Performance and Survivability Increases**

More network managers are turning to frame relay to support mission-critical SNA applications. This technology can be used to eliminate reliance on SNA/SDLC multidrop leased lines, while still maintaining NetView network management. In addition, multiple protocols can be run over a single PVC. As an alternative to a leased line, frame relay can save a great deal, with estimates ranging from 30 to 50 percent.

SNA installations can utilize frame relay, while still making use of their existing equipment and network management practices.

Because multiple protocols, including SNA, can be encapsulated in a frame relay network, SNA and LAN traffic can be combined on a single frame relay link. FRADs, routers, and other devices can therefore handle both SNA and LAN traffic simultaneously.

An SNA network using a point-to-point non-switched line can be migrated from SDLC to frame relay with no changes to applications or hardware. All that is required is to upgrade the communications software located in the controllers; those controllers that cannot be upgraded can be connected to a FRAD to establish connectivity. Because frame relay uses the same hardware framing as Synchronous Data Link Control (SDLC), all SDLC equipment can be used within the context of the frame relay network.

SNA multipoint hardware configurations will have to be changed to point-to-point configuration before deploying frame relay, however. This is because frame relay supports one-to-many and many-to-many connections over a single line, where SDLC requires a multidrop line for a one-to-many configuration. An SNA controller, router, or FRAD encapsulates SNA as multiprotocol data.

For a larger Advanced Peer-to-Peer Network (APPN), a FRAD or SNA controller is a better option than a router, because FRAD and SNA controllers are optimized to carry SNA over frame relay. Networks using an IP backbone may do better with a router, because a router will support IP routing protocols and technologies. Distributed peer-to-peer networks should use an SNA controller running SNA/APPN.

Because SNA applications are usually mission-critical, prioritization and bandwidth allocation must be applied to mitigate the effects of other traffic bursts. There are two approaches to bandwidth management:

- Assign a higher priority to sending SNA data over LAN IP/IPX data if both are multiplexed over the same virtual connection.
- Send the data streams over two separate virtual connections and apply frame relay's Committed Information Rate (CIR) mechanism to allocate bandwidth dynamically to each virtual connection.

Some FRADs and routers support the latter type of bandwidth allocation, and so a separate PVC may not be required.

One option for moving SNA over a frame relay network is to encapsulate SNA in TCP/IP. There are several advantages to this option. First of all, TCP/IP encapsulation will establish a nondisruptive rerouting mechanism in the event of link failure. Although frame relay carriers typically offer rerouting services from within the frame relay cloud, users are still not protected against line failures in the local exchange carrier or permanent virtual circuit.

Local acknowledgment, on the other hand, will keep a session up while the routers dial the backup line. Once the primary link has been re-established, the router will then transparently move traffic back to the primary link, and hang up the backup link. One disadvantage of TCP/IP encapsulation for frame relay is the additional overhead, and loss of SNA functionality and the usage of SNA's class of service guarantees.

Pricing Structures

Frame relay rates can vary a great deal, and can be somewhat confusing. Tariffs are regulated by the FCC, but several of the smaller vendors, especially, are petitioning for rate reductions.

Sending voice over frame relay saves money, again thanks to the unique pricing structures involved. MCI Communications, for example, charges about four cents a minute for a 64Kbps committed information rate (CIR). With compression, as many as eight voice calls can go over that one connection. Other service providers, such as AT&T, charge a fixed monthly fee, although this, too, presents an opportunity for savings.

Neither a monthly-fixed or per-minute rate scheme is inherently superior; the best savings will depend on the individual company's usage patterns. Although additional bandwidth will probably be needed, adding bandwidth is incrementally cheaper.

Besides access fees, the access loop and port charges must also be considered, as well as the cost of the physical equipment. However, once you do the math, it becomes obvious that the equipment will pay for itself fairly quickly; particularly when sending voice traffic, frame relay presents numerous advantages. Depending on several factors, most notably the amount of savings realized from long-distance bills, the frame relay network could pay for itself inside a year. If you can get over the fact that sound quality will simply not be equal to that of a standard, ordinary telephone service (POTS) connection, you can save a bundle.

The phone company sends voice over a dedicated 64Kbps link; frame relay sends voice over its links only after it is compressed into 8Kbps channels. This means that eight calls can be placed over that link that would otherwise carry only one call.

Most companies structure their charges around the CIR. The purpose of the CIR is to set an amount of bandwidth that the customer expects to stay within. If a burst is sent that exceeds the CIR, any packet above the CIR will be marked for possible discard. If congestion occurs, the marked packets may be lost. The originating node can resend packets; and if the material being sent is data only, the loss has negligible results. However, if the originating node has sent a voice transmission, sending the voice packet again is useless, because voice must arrive in the correct order in order to be clear. It is therefore important for the customer to balance the need for clarity against the need to save money, if there are plans to send voice over the frame relay network.

Product Overview

Frame relay hardware and software, including FRADs and other customer-premises equipment, is plentiful and available to accommodate every possible need.

MCI Communications Corporation

http://www.mci.com

MCI's HyperStream Frame Relay service gives administrators the ability to incrementally increase the speed of their service. As a result, users can inverse multiplex up to eight T-1 connections, which would result in a bandwidth rate of 12.288Mbps. Frame relay usually runs at a maximum of 1.544Mbps. To achieve multiplexing, users must invest in a multiplexer device, but the costs are minimal compared to migrating to another technology, such as ATM. There are no standards for frame relay inverse multiplexing however, and users are limited to Digital Link's 3800 multiplexer.

The standards-based packet data service is highly adaptable to new networking requirements, and is offered from 500 domestic access points. It can be accessed from speeds ranging from 28.8Kbps to 12.288Mbps. With this service, multiple applications and users can share the same network access line and CPE. The company's usage-based pricing is economical, since users pay only for the bandwidth used.

MCI's Priority PVC service, an enhancement to HyperStream, adds another innovation: the ability to assign three priority levels to frame relay permanent virtual circuits. Priority schemes, such as those offered by ATM's Quality of Service levels, allow delay-sensitive traffic to travel over the network first to ensure prompt delivery of mission-critical or other types of traffic, such as packetized voice or video. The service is the first frame relay offering that gives customers the ability to establish a priority scheme for individual PVCs. The service works by polling PVCs marked as high priority four times as often as it does PVCs marked for low priority. Because the low priority PVCs are still polled, low priority traffic still is able to get through under a heavy load. Without a priority service, the only approach to sending delay-sensitive traffic is to increase the committed information rate (CIR) of the frame relay port—a more costly solution than the nominally-priced Priority PVC service.

Ch

3

ACT Networks, Incorporated

http://www.acti.com
188 Camino Ruiz
Camarillo, CA 93012
Voice: 805-388-2474
Fax: 805-388-3504

ACT Networks is a leader in the voice over frame relay market, and is the first to release a product specifically designed for central office applications. ACT's FX-1000 product is the first release of the company's ACT FrameXchange product family. This product family is targeted at the carrier market and leverages ACT's leadership in voice over frame relay to provide central-office-based solutions to frame relay service providers. Most currently available frame relay products are designed to be installed at CPE, the FX-1000 is the first designed for central office-based applications. According to Martin Shum, CEO of ACT, "Carriers can offer Native Voice over Frame Relay utilizing their existing frame relay fast packet infrastructure and significantly lower the cost of transporting voice when compared to the existing circuit switched network."

Shum believes that service providers will be able to offer voice services at a fraction of the cost of existing public switched telephone networks. Potential services may include virtual private networks, directory assistance, and help desk applications.

The FX-1000 is designed to be installed at the frame relay service providers' Point of Presence (POP) and can convert 24 channelized T-1 voice circuits into a frame relay composite using a Committed Information Rate of 256Kbps or less.

ACT's family of NetPerformer frame relay products make use of ACT's proprietary NetPerformer cell-based prioritization and switched virtual circuit technology, along with voice and data compression algorithms, to deliver quality voice traffic over the frame relay network. Because NetPerformer uses a cell-based technology that subdivides frames into ATM-like cells, it is capable of carrying SNA and other legacy protocols over the frame relay network. The company's ACTNet products further offer standards-based networking for voice, fax, data, and LAN traffic over point-to-point, public frame relay and private frame relay networks.

All of ACT's products can be managed with the company's ACTview 2000, an SNMP-based network management system based on HP OpenView.

Netrix

http://www.netrix.com
13595 Dulles Technology Drive
Herndon, VA 20171
Voice: 703-793-2088
Fax: 703-742-4048

Netrix is strong in the voice-over-frame relay market, and offers a family of products designed to unify the transmission of data and voice applications.

Cisco Systems

http://www.cisco.com
170 West Tasman Drive
San Jose, CA 95134
Voice: 408-526-4000 or 800-553-NETS (6387)
Fax: 408-526-4100

StrataCom, a major vendor of frame relay equipment, was acquired by Cisco in April, 1996. The acquisition will give Cisco the ability to furnish an end-to-end solution across public, private, and hybrid networks.

Now a major vendor of customer premises equipment (CPE) for frame relay networks, Cisco has developed a technology known as the Frame Relay Broadcast Queue to mitigate problems commonly found on larger frame relay nets, and improve performance and stability.

Cisco's proprietary Frame Relay Broadcast Queue feature identifies all broadcast traffic, including routing and SAP (Service Advertisement Protocol) updates, and places it in a queue. This queue is managed independently of the standard interface queue, has its own buffers, and its own configurable service rate. The broadcast queue will get priority when it transmits at a rate that is below the configured maximum.

This mechanism offers three major benefits:

- The bandwidth utilized by the broadcast queue is limited, and normal data traffic is given a percentage of the bandwidth. This is especially important for SNA traffic that may be sensitive to delays.
- The amount of buffering allocated to broadcasts can be increased without affecting the performance of user data protocols such as LAT.
- The possibility of losing routing updates is minimized, because a large special queue can be configured to store replicated routing updates.

Ch
3

Summary

Although frame relay was originally created to connect far-flung LANs, it has evolved significantly over the past few years, and is often used as a replacement for a traditional leased line. Its ability to interwork with ATM, SNA, and other technologies make SNA an excellent WAN technology; in addition, new standards designed to send voice over a frame relay network will make it even more versatile.

There are dozens of uses and potential uses for frame relay besides traditional data, including voice and fax transmissions. Voice support can be especially useful for companies with international branches. ●

CHAPTER 4

Fast Ethernet

Standard 10Base-T Ethernet is still the most common type of network architecture in use today. It is used to connect PCs and peripherals on unshielded twisted-pair (UTP) wiring, usually in a star topology with a central hub. Fast Ethernet, or 100Base-T, increases the amount of available bandwidth tenfold, while still maintaining a high degree of compatibility with the 10Base-T network. ▨

Overview of Fast Ethernet

Fast Ethernet is especially useful for workgroups using high-bandwidth applications, such as CAD, multimedia, or graphic design. Even the laptop can run Fast Ethernet with the addition of an interface card, although external Fast Ethernet devices such as PCMCIA cards do not offer the same performance as that of an internal Fast Ethernet card. This is largely because most laptops still use only a 16-bit PC Card bus, which inherently limits performance. The new CardBus extension, however, is capable of 32-bit operation, and lends itself to a throughput that is similar to that of a standard desktop computer. A few laptop vendors, including Toshiba, IBM, NEC, and Hewlett-Packard, already offer laptops with CardBus extensions, and a handful of vendors, most notably Xircom, are already offering CardBus-based Fast Ethernet cards.

Fast Ethernet is the most logical migration path to take from standard Ethernet. With the widespread availability of hybrid 10/100 network interface cards (NICs), migration is simple, and a company's existing investment in 10Mbps Ethernet devices and cabling can be preserved.

Fast Ethernet is often used in workgroups, and can provide fast access to a backbone network. Relatively inexpensive, Fast Ethernet is frequently bridged to a Fiber Distributed Data Interface (FDDI) backbone that can add a greater measure of reliability and availability. Fast Ethernet can also be integrated into an ATM network through the LAN Emulation (LANE) specification. (See Chapter 2, "Asynchronous Transfer Mode.")

Evolution of Fast Ethernet

10Mbps Ethernet has been the standard for nearly 20 years; until the 1990s, there was little need to develop a higher-speed technology. However, in recognition of the need for a higher-speed Ethernet, Grand Junction Networks (now part of Cisco Systems) began work on Fast Ethernet in 1992 to address bandwidth problems that were starting to occur as a result of greater demands for data and bigger applications. Along with Grand Junction, other principal sponsors of the Fast Ethernet specification were DAVID Systems, Digital Equipment Corporation, LAN Media, Standard Microsystems, Intel Corporation, National Semiconductor, SUN Microsystems, SynOptics Communications, and 3Com Corporation.

There are now actually three 100Mbps standards. Between these three standards, end users have a wealth of products and strategies from which to choose:

- 100Base-T (Fast Ethernet), 802.3u
- 100VG-AnyLAN (Hewlett-Packard's proprietary 100Mbps product), 802.12
- FDDI (initially standardized in ANSI X3T12, FDDI is now ISO standard 9314)

A strategic alliance between CNet USA Technology, Davicom Semiconductor, Inc., and United Microelectronics Corp. to develop next-generation Fast Ethernet products, based on a single-chip design, may result in significantly lower prices. CNet plans to incorporate its line of Fast Ethernet products with Davicom's integrated Fast Ethernet technology, which consists of single-chip solutions manufactured by United Microelectronics. The result will be lower-cost and higher-speed NICs. The agreement draws on designs from all three companies, and will result in CNet delivering highly affordable Fast Ethernet NICs that can be deployed in PCs, workstations, and servers. The solution is based on Davicom's DM9101, which combines the functionality of multiple chips into a single chip. The DM9101 integrates the physical layer and the transceiver function into a single component, which not only makes Fast Ethernet more efficient, but also lowers the overall cost.

Standards Development (IEEE)

The 100Base-T standard has been established by the IEEE (Institute of Electrical and Electronics Engineers) 802.3 committee. The basic premise behind the design of Fast Ethernet is the reduction of the duration that each bit is sent by a factor of 10, which effectively increases the packet speed to 10 times that of standard Ethernet. Packet format and length, error control, and management information is still the same as 10Base-T.

Fast Ethernet replaces 10Base-T Ethernet's Attachment Unit Interface (AUI) with a Media-Independent Interface (MII) layer, which establishes a single interface for the three 100Base-T media specifications. These three physical layers are:

- *100Base-TX*. A two-pair system for Category 5 UTP and STP cabling.
- *100Base-T4*. A four-pair system for Category 3, 4, or 5 UTP cabling.
- *100Base-FX*. A multi-mode, two-strand fiber system.

All three layers can be interconnected through a hub.

The IEEE 802.3 committee's draft standard for Fast Ethernet includes several sections that will be added to the IEEE 802.3 specification:

- Clause 21: Introduction to 100Mbps Baseband Networks
- Clause 22: Reconciliation Sublayer and MII
- Clause 23: Physical - 100Base-T4
- Clause 24: Physical - 100Base-X
- Clause 25: PHY for 100Base-TX
- Clause 26: PHY for 100Base-FX

Ch
4

- Clause 27: Repeater for 100Mbps/s
- Clause 28: Autonegotiation
- Clause 29: System Considerations for Multisegment 100Base-T Networks
- Clause 30: Management

In addition to the IEEE, the Fast Ethernet Alliance assembled 80-some companies to promote the usage of Fast Ethernet. The alliance has since disbanded, claiming that it had achieved its goals.

Several vendors currently support 100Base-T. One of the biggest advantages of Fast Ethernet is that it is based on a mature technology, and in many cases, represents the most logical "next step" in building a high-speed network.

Implementation and Infrastructure

In order to achieve its increase in speed, 100Base-T divides the bit-timing used in 10Base-T by 10. *Bit-timing* is the length of time a bit requires for transmission. Consequently, the network can wait one-tenth of the amount of time for responses. An end result of this is that the distance that a data packet travels must be minimized in order for 100Base-T to work.

10Base-T permits three repeater hops between any two workstations; 100Base-T only allows two, and the repeaters can only be 5 meters apart. The 100Base-T cable length is a maximum of 100 meters between the repeater and each workstation, which makes a total of 205 meters for the network diameter. 10BaseT, on the other hand, affords a generous 2,500 meters.

Network Diameter

The term "network diameter" can be somewhat misleading, and may lead one to believe that the entire Fast Ethernet network cannot exceed 205 meters. In fact, "network diameter" only refers to the cable distance between any two end-stations on the same LAN segment or collision domain.

The 802.3 specification does not explicitly provide for full-duplex transmission, although there are initiatives to include full-duplex transmission in the specification. Nonetheless, there are a few vendors who already support full-duplex operation in their products. Full-duplex doubles the available bandwidth of a link between a network card and a switch, by disabling collision detection and thereby allowing the card and switch to send and receive at the same time. Full-duplex segments can use the same type of cabling used by standard half-duplex connections.

CSMA/CD

Ethernet—whether it is standard, Fast, or Gigabit—is based on the transmission protocol *Carrier Sense Multiple Access/Collision Detection (CSMA/CD)*. Consequently, data can be moved between 10Base-T and 100Base-T stations without any type of protocol translation. Because no translation is needed between the two speeds, no routers are required; a simple bridge will suffice in most cases.

To put it in political terms, CSMA/CD represents a sort of enlightened Marxian concept where all stations have an equal opportunity to transmit over the network. No one station is given priority over the other; the lowliest frame of word processing data is accorded the same rights and privileges as the big, bad cigar-chomping frame of multimedia. If a station detects that there is currently no signal on the channel, it can transmit freely, regardless of content—and while it is doing so, all others must wait.

However, it does happen that two stations both detect the opportunity at the same time, and both start transmitting at precisely the same moment. In such a case, the two signals collide, the transmission stops, and both stations wait a random period of time before attempting to retransmit.

The term *collision* is somewhat misleading. When applied to automobiles, a collision can certainly be disastrous, but it is a natural part of the Ethernet specification. It is merely the mechanism used to resolve situations where two or more nodes attempt to access a shared channel at the same time. Collisions occur frequently and on a regular basis, and are not necessarily anything to worry about, unless the percentage of packets that collide exceeds around 30 percent. A collision event only occupies a very small period of time— only a very small fraction of the amount of time it takes for a successful packet to be transmitted.

Ch
4

Topology

Fast Ethernet is typically built on a star topology, as was the case with 10Mbps Ethernet. However, only two repeaters can be used, and each workgroup makes up a separate LAN segment or collision domain.

Cabling

Because many sites already have Category 5 or fiber optic cabling installed, the same cabling already in use for the 10Base-T network can often be used for 100Base-T, allowing many companies to maximize their existing investments in their installed network system. Migration from standard to Fast Ethernet is remarkably straightforward and cost-effective. Users of Fast Ethernet can enjoy 10 times the power of standard Ethernet, while not having to pay 10 times the price for access (see Figure 4.1).

The costs of 10/100 and 100Mbps products are rapidly decreasing, with Fast Ethernet adapters costing not much more than a standard card. Fast Ethernet may also be a good alternative to ATM, FDDI, or other fast networking technologies for cost-conscious companies; a Fast Ethernet card is hundreds of dollars cheaper than an ATM card and it is far simpler to deploy.

The diameter of the network can be extended by applying a two-port switch, which will permit another 200-meter hop to be added to a collision domain.

FIG. 4.1

Fast Ethernet Cable Topology.

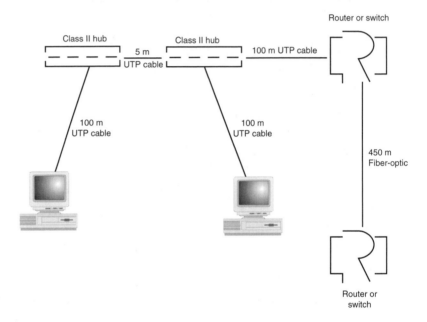

Fiber optic cable affords greater distances to Fast Ethernet than Category 5 cable, as follows:

- Distance between a 100Base-T hub and a fiber bridge, router, or switch is 225 meters.
- Distance between two fiber bridges, routers, or switches in a half-duplex network is 450 meters.
- Distance between two fiber bridges, routers, or switches in a full-duplex network is 2 KM.

These limitations are more stringent than those of standard Ethernet. 10Mbps Ethernet imposes a *3-4-5 rule* of three populated segments, four repeater hops, and five total segments. However, this rule cannot be applied to Fast Ethernet, which greatly decreases the total possible diameter of a Fast Ethernet network.

The Layers of Fast Ethernet

In Fast Ethernet, the *Media Access Control (MAC)* is separated from the *Physical Layer Device (PHY)* by the *Media Independent Interface (MII)*. The MII is used to allow different PHYs to support different media. The MII is typically transparent to end users, and is implemented as a chip-level interface. The *Media Dependent Interface (MDI)*, on the other hand, is the physical connection system for attaching to a medium. This takes the form of the same RJ-45 type connector used in 10Base-T networks.

There are five component specifications in the 100Base-T standard, including MAC, MII, and the three options for physical layers of 100Base-TX, 100BaseT4, and 100Base-FX. These specifications, which have been adopted by the IEEE and ISO/IEC standards bodies, are discussed in subsequent sections.

Physical Layer   The physical layer standard supports the following transmission schemes:

- 100BASE-TX two pairs of Category 5 balanced cable, or two pairs 150 Ohm shielded balanced cable as defined by the International Organization for Standardization/ International Electrotechnical Commission (ISO/IEC) specification 11801.
- 100BASE-FX two strand multi-mode fiber as defined by ISO 9314.
- 100BASE-T4 four pairs of Category 3, 4, or 5 balanced cable as defined by ISO/IEC specification 11801.

In 100Base-TX and 100Base-T4, the twisted-pair segment can be up to 100 meters long, just as was the case for a 10Base-T segment. However, 25-pair cable bundles cannot be used, and there is no support for coaxial cable or bus wiring methods.

100Base-TX is a half-duplex connection similar to 10Base-T. One pair of wires is used to transmit, and the other is used to receive. It requires CAT-5 UTP cable and uses a 4B/5B block code transmission scheme.

4B/5B Block Code Transmission Scheme

Fast Ethernet borrows the 4B/5B data encoding scheme from FDDI technology. Under 4B/5B, each *group*, or block of four bits, is represented as a five-bit symbol, which is in turn associated with a bit pattern. The bit pattern is then encoded, using a method called non-return to zero inverted (NRZI), making further electrical encoding more efficient. 4B/5B encoding is significantly more efficient than Manchester signal encoding, which is used in 10Base-T Ethernet networks.

The 100Base-TX physical layer uses two pairs of CAT 5 UTP or Type 1 STP cable, with one pair used for transmitting and the other for receiving. This is exactly the same

Ch
4

configuration as used in 10Base-T Ethernet. Furthermore, the UTP connector is an RJ-45, also the same as with 10Base-T, although the punch-down blocks used for the wiring closet must be CAT-5 certified. 100Base-TX is full-duplex capable. The specification's auto-negotiation scheme allows each node to define its modes of operation, including whether or not it is operating at full duplex. Full-duplex operation has not been formally standardized yet, but a handful of vendors have already released network interface cards and switches capable of implementing full duplex operation.

100Base-T4 works with CAT-3 cabling, which is more limited in terms of performance. Because CAT-3 cable does not meet FCC standards, four pairs are required. The transmission is divided between the wires, and uses an 8B6T block code transmission scheme. In 100Base-T4, three pairs of wire are used for transmitting and receiving, and the fourth listens for collisions.

The 100BASE-T4 Physical Layer uses four pairs of CAT 3, 4, or 5 UTP cabling; three are used to send and receive, and the last one is used to detect collisions.

100Base-FX physical layer specifies two strands of fiber cable: one for transmitting and one for receiving.

Media Access Control (MAC) Layer   100Base-T, like 10Base-T, runs on the same MAC protocol layer of the Data Link (Layer 2) section of the OSI model, making 100Base-T easy to integrate into a 10Base-T network. A simple diagram of the main components of the standard is shown in Figure 4.2. The MAC is separated from the PHY by a MII layer, which allows different PHYs to support different media. For the most part, the MII is transparent and implemented as a chip-level interface.

FIG. 4.2
Fast Ethernet and the
OSI Model.

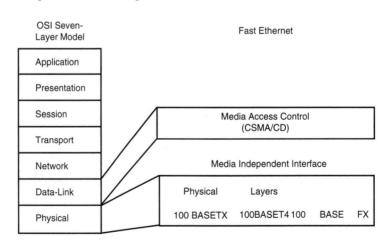

The MAC layer uses the same protocol, CSMA/CD, as 10Mbps Ethernet, with the only difference being speed. A major advantage here is that users can leverage prior experience with standard Ethernet and apply it to a Fast Ethernet implementation. In addition, all of the same network management and monitoring tools used in 10Base-T can still be used in a 100Base-T network.

The IEEE is considering an alternative to the existing backoff algorithm, known as the *Binary Logarithmic Access Method (BLAM),* which addresses the issue of channel capture.

A condition known as *channel capture* exists when the Ethernet MAC layer is temporarily biased toward one station on a loaded network. This situation results in one station being the contention winner more frequently for the channel. This peculiar situation is a result of probabilities inherent in the CSMA/CD method.

For example, if two stations send a packet at the same time, the packets will collide and be discarded, and both stations will transmit again after calculating a random period of time in which to wait. The contention winner sends the packet, but the contention loser still has one to send. The winner now wants to send a subsequent packet, while the loser still wants to send the first. The winner's collision counter is reset since the first packet has been successfully transmitted, and as a result, the winner selects a random number from a smaller range of numbers than does the loser. The initial winner has a higher probability of winning the contention again.

The Media Independent Interface (MII) Layer   The MII is a new specification, embraced by the IEEE and ISO/IEC, which defines an interface between the MAC layer and the three physical layers. It can support rates of both 10Mbps and 100Mbps, and is implemented in a network device either internally or externally. When implemented internally or directly in the network device, the MII connects the MAC layer directly to the Physical Layer. It can also be implemented externally in a network device with a 40-pin connector.

Hub Types

A *repeater*—a physical layer device sometimes known as a hub or concentrator—regenerates data moving between network components. Fast Ethernet supports both Class I and Class II repeater hubs.

The terms hub and repeater are sometimes used interchangeably, although they are not technically the same thing. A *hub* functions as a common point of termination for multiple nodes, usually of a single architecture. An intelligent hub typically includes management features, and can monitor network activity. A *repeater* connects two network segments in the same network. Once the repeater receives the signals from one segment, it amplifies it, and then relays it to the next segment. A repeater may be incorporated into a hub.

Class I and Class II Repeaters

In 10Base-T, repeaters are largely all the same, but under Fast Ethernet, there are two types: Class I and Class II. *Class I repeaters* transmit line signals between ports by translating them to digital signals, then retranslating them to line signals. This is necessary when connecting different physical media in the same segment. A *Class II repeater* does not perform any type of translation, but instead merely repeats the incoming line signal immediately. This type of repeater is used when connecting the same media type to the segment. Both types of repeaters have multiple shared ports; nodes attached to the ports must function either all at 10Mbps or 100Mbps.

Hubs   Fast Ethernet networks using a Class I hub will not permit more than a single hub to exist between two end nodes (see Figure 4.3). If more than one Class I hub is used, a bridge, router, or switch must be placed between each hub (see Figure 4.4).

FIG. 4.3
Class I hub
configuration.

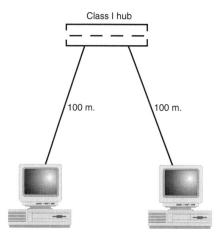

Class I hub

100 m.   100 m.

A Class I hub has a bigger timing delay, and works by translating line signals from the incoming port into a digital signal, and then translating the digital signal back to a line signal when it is sent out on the other port. This mechanism lets different techniques (100Base-TX, 100Base-FX, 100Base-T4) be integrated through the same hub.

A Fast Ethernet network using a Class II hub, on the other hand, will permit two hubs to be interconnected without a bridge, router, or switch. However, a bridge, router, or switch still must be placed between every two sets of hubs.

The Class II hub has a smaller timing delay and does not use a translation process. Consequently, the Class II hub can accommodate only segments that are using the same signaling mechanism.

FIG. 4.4

Class I hub configuration with two hubs.

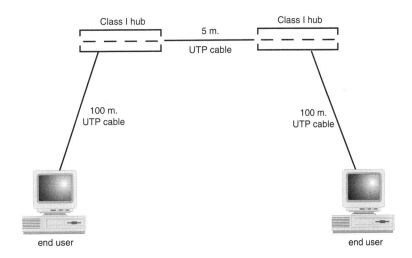

Both options, however, seem limiting when compared with the multi-level cascading options allowed in standard 10Mbps Ethernet. A non-standardized Class III hub has been designed by Garrett Communications (see Figure 4.5). Although using stackable Fast Ethernet hubs can expand the port count, this vendor's product still requires the wiring for each node to go to the central wiring closet, and may mean a significant amount of rewiring. Garrett's devices provide three levels of cascading, which are unavailable in any other vendors' Fast Ethernet products. The IEEE has not defined a Class III hub repeater, however.

The distance between the hub port and end node (assuming UTP cabling) is 100 meters. Using a Class II hub, end stations can be 205 meters apart, with each segment being 100 meters and 5 meters being used to connect the two hubs. There is no provision in the Fast Ethernet standard for coaxial cable or bus wiring.

There are different types of 100Base-TX hubs. A pure 100Base-TX repeater functions like a 10Base-T repeater, where a signal is received on one port and then broadcast to all the remaining ports. This type of hub, however, does not support a gradual migration from 10Base-T.

A switching hub, on the other hand, can combine 10Base-T and 100Base-TX. With a switching hub, the signals are not broadcast to all ports; instead, the hub looks at the data packet's header to see the destination address, and then sends it only to the appropriate port. This approach means less traffic over the network, because unnecessary traffic is not being sent.

Ch
4

FIG. 4.5
Class III hub configu-
ration (non-standard).

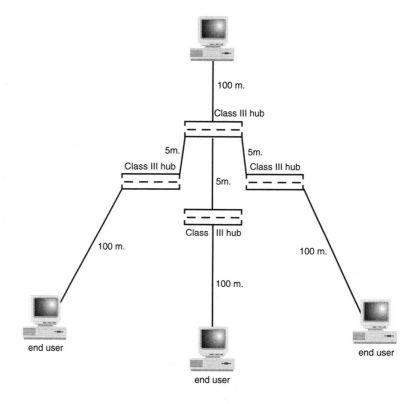

Fast Ethernet also has the advantage of being able to work with a switching hub or a shared hub, again in order to maintain the existing 10Base-T connections while still taking advantage of newer technology. In a shared hub configuration, all devices connected to the hub share 100Mbps of bandwidth. In a switched hub configuration, however, each device connected to a hub port gets its own 100Mbps of bandwidth.

A stackable hub can be deployed to add more users. The stack, regardless of how many units are included, is still considered a single repeater for the purposes of measuring hop count and cable length.

Repeaters   A Class I repeater is used to connect different physical media in the same collision domain. For example, it could be used to connect a 1000Base-TX link with a 100Base-T4 link. A Class I repeater functions by translating the incoming signal to digital signals, and then retranslating them to line signals. Only one Class I repeater can exist in a single collision domain.

A Class II repeater, on the other hand, connects identical media in the same collision domain. That is, it can only be used to connect 100Base-TX with 100Base-TX, 100Base-T4 with 100Base-T4, or 100Base-FX with 100Base-FX. Because no translation is required, the repeater transmits the incoming line signal immediately to the other port. Two Class II repeaters can exist in a single collision domain.

Network diameter rules are shown in Tables 4.1 and 4.2.

Table 4.1   Diameter for One Repeater Configurations

Configuration	Diameter
100Base-TX, Class I	200 meters (100 meters for each segment)
100Base-TX, Class II	200 meters (100 meters for each segment)
100Base-T4, Class I	200 meters (100 meters for each segment)
100Base-T4, Class II	200 meters (100 meters for each segment)
100Base-FX, Class I	272 meters
100Base-FX, Class II	320 meters
Mixed 100Base-T4 and 100Base-FX, Class I	231 meters (100 meters for T4 and 131 for FX)
Mixed 100Base-T4 and 100Base-FX, Class II	304 meters (100 meters for T4 and 204 for FX)
Mixed 100Base-TX and 100Base-FX, Class I	260.8 meters (100 meters for TX and 160.8 for FX)
Mixed 100Base-TX and 100Base-FX, Class II	308.8 meters (100 meters for TX and 208.8 meters for FX)

Table 4.2   Diameters for Two Repeater Configurations (Must Use a Class II Repeater)

Configuration	Diameter
Mixed 100Base-TX and 100Base-T4	205 meters (100 meters for each segment and 5 meters to connect the repeaters)
100Base-FX	228 meters
Mixed 100Base-T4 and 100Base-FX	236.3 meters (100 meters for T4, 5 meters to connect the repeaters, and 131.3 meters for FX)
Mixed 100Base-TX and 100Base-FX	216.2 meters (100 meters for TX, 5 meters to connect the repeaters, and 111.2 meters for FX)

Ch
4

Bridging and Routing

Bridging and routing are the two primary methods used to connect 10Mbps Ethernet with 100Mbps Ethernet. The bridging solution is the easiest of the two; routing requires purchase of additional routing equipment in addition to the 100Base-T hub. One hub should be installed for each collision domain.

To go beyond the 205-meter limitation of 100Base-T, a bridge or router can be added. Bridges are often the simpler solution; compared with a router-based system, bridging is inexpensive and very simple to deploy, while also allowing the network to go beyond the stated topology limits of 100Base-T.

Migration to Fast Ethernet

A gradual migration to Fast Ethernet can be accomplished easily, allowing the addition of extra bandwidth as it becomes necessary. The first place to start is to examine existing cabling; this will determine which physical layer of Fast Ethernet can be deployed.

Many existing Ethernet installations are based on CAT-5 UTP; if this is the case, the more common 100Base-TX adapters can be deployed on existing cable. Although CAT-3 cabling can be used to run Fast Ethernet using a 100Base-T4 adapter, this is the more complex option of the two, and does not leave much room for further upgrades to other technologies, such as ATM. Therefore, it is recommended to use CAT-5 cabling if at all possible.

Another disadvantage to using a CAT-3 configuration is that all four pairs, or eight wires, must be used to achieve the 100Mbps speed. However, sites with four pairs of CAT-3 wiring commonly use one set for telephone connections—therefore, not enough pairs are left to deploy 100Base-T4.

Furthermore, 100Base-T hubs should be deployed as new devices are added to the network.

All existing applications and protocols will run over the new Fast Ethernet network; no software upgrades will be required to enjoy the greater bandwidth afforded by Fast Ethernet.

Hybrid Network Interface Cards   One of the best migration strategies is to start out deploying the hybrid 10/100 NICs where greater bandwidth is needed. Give the "power users" the first upgrades, replacing their older 10Base-T adapters with 10/100s, as well as those users in the workgroups that need additional bandwidth, such as those dealing with multimedia or large databases.

A good strategy is to deploy a 10/100 adapter on each new PC that is installed, regardless of where it is located. The hybrids are not much more costly than a standard NIC, so it makes economic sense to deploy the hybrid whenever a new NIC must be deployed.

Integrating Fast Ethernet in a standard Ethernet network is amazingly straightforward. As mentioned earlier, most vendors' 100Base-T NICs are actually hybrid devices that support speeds of both 10Mbps and 100Mbps. Many are *auto-sensing*, which means that they will automatically detect whether it is connected to a standard or Fast Ethernet hub. Auto-sensing NICs lets a manager undertaking a gradual migration install of 10/100 NICs and connect them to a 10Base-T hub, then later upgrade to a 100Base-T hub without having to change or even reconfigure the NICs.

Fast Ethernet Backbones   As a backbone technology, 100Base-FX—the fiber version of Fast Ethernet—is a viable alternative to FDDI. There are several compelling reasons to deploy Fast Ethernet as a backbone technology, not the least of which is its simplicity and the fact that it is a well-understood and widely supported technology. Under an FDDI backbone running an Ethernet network, there is an inherent frame translational latency; this is not experienced with a Fast Ethernet fiber backbone. A full implementation of Fast Ethernet may deploy a fiber optic backbone using 100Base-FX, while running a 100Base-TX connection to servers and power users.

CAUTION

100Base-TX supports only CAT-5 twisted-pair cable (although CAT-5+ is certainly acceptable). CAT-5+, if available, is rated at 350 MHz instead of the standard 100 MHz. It is essential that the cabling comply with EIA/TIA-568-A standards. Although a network may have been wired with CAT-5 cabling, after testing, they may perform as if they were wired with CAT-3. This may be caused by the residual use of CAT-3 in the hub closet; therefore, be sure to replace this cabling as well.

Fast Ethernet Servers   At the server level, Fast Ethernet can address the congestion that typically occurs in that area. A server farm connected with standard Ethernet may be overwhelmed, especially with the installation of higher-powered servers running bandwidth-intensive applications. By giving each server a Fast Ethernet port, much of this congestion can be relieved.

Fast Ethernet Desktops   At the desktop level, most users may still need only 10Mbps Ethernet, with the exception of some power users running applications such as CAD or graphics programs. If there are few power users in the company, one option may be to retain the 10Mbps links to the desktop in most cases, at least initially, and give the few power users that need it a dedicated 10Mbps link with a LAN switch.

Running Fast Ethernet to all desktops may result in some congestion because the desktop Fast Ethernet streams cannot be multiplexed if both desktop and server connections are running at the same speed. Therefore, how widely Fast Ethernet is deployed is dependent on the nature of the network backbone and its ability to handle the 100Mbps streams. However, most adapter cards run at both 10Mbps and 100Mbps speeds; when a new card must be purchased, these hybrids are the best option. These cards usually permit the client to automatically switch between 10Mbps and 100Mbps with no modification. However, hybrid hubs and switches must also be purchased to be able to accommodate both speeds.

With each desktop having the capability to run at 100Mbps, even if it is not deployed immediately, the network has built into it the ability to migrate even further when the need arises. 100Mbps desktops can be multiplexed onto a *Gigabit Ethernet backbone*, a newer technology that companies may want to consider as a future path. For additional information on gigabit Ethernet, see Chapter 5, "Gigabit Ethernet."

Network Management

In much the same way as a widened freeway seems to attract more cars, a faster network will quickly attract more data and applications. In addition to the adapters, hubs, and switches, monitoring and management must also be considered. The network manager must have analyzers that can handle the increased speed; more sophisticated monitoring and management tools may also be required.

Remote Monitoring (RMON) probes are ideal for more complex, high-speed networks. These can help track data flow and spot problems early on. These same tools can be used for capacity planning. Older network analyzers, however, are for the most part not scalable to higher-speed networking technologies. Part of the expense of migrating to Fast Ethernet, or any high-speed network technology for that matter, is the purchase of new management software and hardware.

There are two ways a LAN analyzer can monitor a standard half-duplex link in a switched Fast Ethernet network. One is through a mirror port on a switch; the other is by connecting to a hub port that is connected to the switch (see analyzer A2 in Figure 4.6).

Port mirroring allows a switch to copy data from the switch port to a mirror port (also called the *monitor port*). The network analyzer is then attached to the mirror port, and the administrator can specify which ports should be mirrored. Consequently, a single analyzer can be used to monitor all segments.

However, not all switches support port mirroring. In this case, the analyzer can still monitor a single switch segment by connecting the analyzer to the hub port on the segment that needs to be monitored. Unfortunately, the analyzer must be physically reconnected for each segment that needs to be monitored.

FIG. 4.6
Port mirroring in a switched Fast Ethernet network.

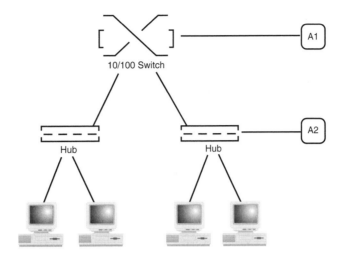

It is not as easy to monitor a full-duplex link as it is to monitor a half-duplex link. Because a full-duplex connection is made up of two devices, the LAN analyzer cannot be used without first changing the connection to half-duplex.

Again, Shomiti has been innovative in this regard with a new device that is capable of monitoring a full-duplex segment. The company's Century Tap family offers a fairly unique way to view traffic on as many as 12 Fast Ethernet segments with a single device. The device is actually a set of wiring taps used to insert a Shomiti Century LAN Analyzer into a full-duplex link. The Century Tap will monitor both sides of the full-duplex link, and mirror the data streams to the Century LAN Analyzer. Because the taps are not repeaters, they do not add a hop count to the segment; they are essentially simple Y-cables for Ethernet links.

Another innovation is available from 3Com: the new *Transcend dRMON Edge Monitor System*. The Edge Monitor System offers continuous RMON coverage in a switched or Fast Ethernet environment. By working with 3Com's DynamicAccess software on the company's family of NICs, the Edge Monitor System gives network administrators the tools needed to manage the entire network with remote monitoring.

The RMON product offering uses 3Com's *SmartAgent intelligent technology*, which resides on the NIC and allows end nodes to become part of the monitoring and analysis system. The Edge Monitor runs on a Windows NT Workstation and manages RMON data collection for an entire multicast domain. It aggregates RMON data from the SmartAgent software on each end node, and is able to compile that information into a complete and integrated picture of network traffic. A Java-enabled browser, connected to the World Wide Web, can be used to remotely monitor the Edge Monitor data from any PC with access to the Internet.

Ch
4

Virtual LANs

Virtual LANs (VLANs) may also help to alleviate some of the complexity that will inevitably result from a move to a Fast Ethernet network. Because higher speed capabilities mean more data will be sent throughout the network, every end node on the network will suffer from an increased rate of broadcast traffic. Segmenting the network will help to avoid experiencing the congestion that Fast Ethernet was meant to avoid in the first place.

One way to achieve segmentation is through a VLAN, which exists on top of the existing network topology and establishes multiple, logical topologies. This approach avoids a scenario where all broadcasts travel across the entire network; the administrator can establish these virtual subnets to determine where specific traffic will flow. Several vendors offer support for VLANs in their equipment and software.

Essentially a series of virtual broadcast domains, the Fast Ethernet VLAN offers an alternative to physically segmenting the network with bridges, switches, or routers. For a further discussion of the VLAN concept in general, see the "VLAN" section in Chapter 2, "Asynchronous Transfer Mode."

Although there are some disadvantages to VLANs, such as slower speed and added overhead, there are plenty of benefits. Some advantages of VLANs, whether applied to a Fast Ethernet or ATM network, are as follows:

- Moves, adds, and changes are simpler because they can be configured via software from a central console as opposed to having to physically execute the move in the wiring closet.

- The VLAN presents a way to apply security to the network, by allowing the administrator to configure which VLANs can be accessed by which clients. A VLAN is a closed group, and users in one defined group cannot access another VLAN to which they have no access.

- Broadcast activity is minimized because traffic does not have to traverse the entire network, thereby increasing network performance.

- Workgroups can be organized logically, as opposed to workgroups being based on physical location or media. This flexibility affords the administrator the ability to regroup LAN segments almost instantly, without having to take a server down or change the physical infrastructure of the network.

Although Fast Ethernet VLANs have not yet been standardized by the IEEE, a method of tagging switched packets on a VLAN has been approved. This packet tagging mechanism identifies each packet, specifying which VLAN the packet belongs to. This packet tagging mechanism, proposed originally by Cisco Systems, uses the existing IEEE 802.10 security protocol. Packet tagging makes use of an existing security field added to packets, as per the 802.10 specification; but instead uses the same field to add a VLAN identification number.

Ethernet Switching

A switch differs from a repeater in that it affords each port full bandwidth. A device connected directly to a switch has a LAN segment all to itself. If a repeater is connected directly to a switch, the devices connected to the repeater share the bandwidth of that port. Simple Fast Ethernet may be more advantageous than switched Ethernet, but the two technologies can both have a place in the network.

Under switched Ethernet, the full 10 or 100Mbps of bandwidth is available to each port. However, switched Ethernet requires the addition of a switching hub, but existing Ethernet adapters can remain in place. Fast Ethernet requires new hubs and new adapters. Switched Ethernet, then, is the less costly method of upgrading because no new adapters or cabling must be installed. One reason to move to switched Ethernet instead of Fast Ethernet may be if a company has a large installed base of older PCs which are not optimized for Fast Ethernet's throughput. Fast Ethernet will do little good on an older machine that cannot handle the speed. For situations where new PCs are being installed, however, Fast Ethernet is often the best option.

Ethernet switching can go a long way toward alleviating network congestion and minimizing delays. Switching affords an increase in available bandwidth, and an easy upgrade path to ATM should the need for even greater bandwidth arise. Switched Fast Ethernet makes a very cost-effective backbone solution and an ideal platform for multimedia.

A switched network is similar to a bridged network in some respects—that is, the server broadcasts can still have an impact on the network's performance. This broadcast traffic can be addressed with a VLAN, which segments the switched network and attempts to impose controls over the broadcast traffic. In addition, the VLAN simplifies management and adds a level of security to the network. Layer 3 switching can be used to shunt traffic between VLANs. This solution avoids having to purchase additional routers by handling routing within the switch hardware.

Shared Ethernet and switched Ethernet represent two different approaches; shared Ethernet will be less expensive per port, although the network diameter will be severely limited. For smaller shops, this may not be an issue, and a shared topology may be the best option. Switched Fast Ethernet is more costly per port, but the diameter restrictions are eliminated. Another advantage of switched Fast Ethernet is that it can run in full-duplex mode, thereby establishing 200Mbps of bandwidth for the backbone connection.

Ch
4

Coexistence with Other Network Technologies

Fast Ethernet can be deployed along with other high-speed technologies, including FDDI and ATM. With a network using an FDDI backbone, Fast Ethernet can be sent to the desktop easily and inexpensively. The major differences between FDDI and 100Base-FX are that FDDI's transmission scheme and topology is similar to Token Ring, while 100Base-FX uses Ethernet packets and a star topology.

Fast Ethernet can be sent to the desktop from an FDDI backbone easily and inexpensively. FDDI can bridge to Fast Ethernet in the same way as it does to 10Mbps Ethernet. For example, the FDDI ring is downlinked to a 10Mbps workgroup via an FDDI-Ethernet router; a FDDI-Fast Ethernet router facilitates a connection with 100Mbps servers or workgroups. The router can be hardware-based or software-based; in the latter case, the software virtual router exists in the Fast Ethernet NIC.

Fast Ethernet can also co-exist with ATM, although the two technologies approach bandwidth problems from a different perspective. While ATM is a top-down technology that starts with the WAN, Fast Ethernet is a bottom-up solution that focuses on high bandwidth to the desktop and server.

Fast Ethernet Basics

To summarize, the basic rules in Fast Ethernet are:

- A twisted pair segment can be 100 Meters.
- The diameter of a collision domain can be 205 meters using two Class II repeaters, or 200 meters using one Class I repeater.
- There may be three segments and two Class II repeaters; or two segments and one Class I repeater between any two end stations on the network:

Physical Layer	Segment Length	Number of Repeaters
100Base-TX	100 meters	2
100Base-T4	100 meters	2
100Base-FX	412 meters	2

- The 100Base-T specification includes an auto-negotiation scheme, which permits each station to select an operating mode based on the station to which it is connected.
- Both data and the hub ports themselves can be designated as either high or normal priority. For data to get the high-priority label, an upper-level software application is used, which sends the data packet, along with the corresponding high-priority label, down to the MAC layer where it is transmitted. A hub can be configured so that any

given port's traffic is always given high priority. Normal priority data can still get through; however, any normal priority packet that has not been serviced within a given time period, usually 300 microseconds, will be automatically upgraded to high priority.

100VG-AnyLAN

This little-used—proprietary—alternative to Fast Ethernet created by Hewlett-Packard supports the same 100Mbps traffic as Fast Ethernet, but takes a slightly different approach. Whereas Fast Ethernet is based on Ethernet's CSMA/CD access method, 100VG uses a technique called *Demand Priority*. Hewlett-Packard promotes 100VG as a solution that takes the best aspects of both Token Ring and Ethernet. Like Fast Ethernet, existing adapter cards must be replaced in order to use the new technology. However, there are no hybrid 10Mbps/100VG cards, while the market is rich with hybrid 10/100Mbps Ethernet cards that permit an easy migration.

100VG can run on CAT-3 four-pair UTP cable, although Fast Ethernet, in its 100Base-T4 implementation, also has that capability. Fast Ethernet is less expensive, easier to use, and supported by many vendors, making it by far the technology of choice in most shops.

Many VG cards come equipped with two RJ-45 connectors: one that connects to the VG hub, and one that can connect to a 10Base-T hub. However, both cannot be used simultaneously, making a hybrid network impossible. The purpose of the dual connectors is to allow for a simplified migration; when the VG card is plugged into the 10Base-T hub, the VG card works like a standard 10Base-T Ethernet card. A VG hub cannot accommodate a 10Base-T card, however. In addition, in order to migrate to a 100BaseVG network, not only would all the NICs have to be replaced, but all of the hubs and management tools would have to be replaced as well.

100VG was designed to accommodate both Ethernet and Token-Ring frame types. Based on the IEEE 802.12 standard, it is capable of transmitting both 802.3 Ethernet and 802.5 Token-Ring frames at 100Mbps. However, both frame types cannot be accommodated simultaneously. The VG network will be configured to use either the Ethernet or Token-Ring frame format.

The standard was ratified by the IEEE in June 1995. Like Fast Ethernet, 100VG is based on a star and hub topology.

Fast Ethernet's dependence on CSMA/CD makes it contentious—that is, the constant collisions and re-sending of packets degrades actual performance. In reality, there is nowhere near a full 100Mbps of bandwidth being used. 100VG, on the other hand, shuts off CSMA/CD, delivering a much greater efficiency to the network and a higher *de facto* speed.

Ch
4

The Demand Priority mechanism used in 100VG eliminates packet collisions and establishes some basic prioritization for delivery of time-sensitive traffic. 100Base-T is, by its very nature, not suitable for delay-sensitive applications such as videoconferencing. 100VG, on the other hand, is deterministic, so all stations on the network are guaranteed access at regular intervals.

100VG's Demand Priority scheme permits a station to send its high-priority traffic first. The 100VG architecture uses the hub to decide on network access. Each hub will poll all active ports, and if a station requests permission to send data, the hub will permit it to generate a single frame. The hub will then move on to the next port and repeat the process. However, if a hub receives a high priority request, it will immediately give access to the high-priority station. The other stations will not time out, however, because the hub keeps track of requests for access. If the time lag gets out of hand, the hub will assign high priority status to normal priority stations.

A VG node, like most other types of nodes, can receive a packet at any time, but transmission is governed by a set of media access rules. In Fast Ethernet, the media access rules are implemented within the nodes themselves, so there is no centralized control. The media access rules for VG, on the other hand, are implemented at the hub.

Unlike the Marxian concept of CSMA/CD where everyone has equal rights, VG's Demand Priority is a sort of benevolent dictatorship. The node will petition the hub for the right to transmit; the hub will then decide when to allow the transmission. VG, Token Ring, and FDDI have similar access characteristics. The theoretical advantage to this mechanism is that those nodes which do not need to transmit are left alone; in Token Ring and CSMA/CD, all nodes must continually occupy themselves by either passing tokens or being polled.

Another advantage is that 100VG can accommodate Ethernet and Token-Ring frames in their native sizes; this is not available in Fast Ethernet. This may be an advantage in a situation where two Token-Ring segments are separated by a 100VG backbone. Because Token-Ring frames are larger than Ethernet frames, segmentation of the frames would be required to connect the Token Rings across a Fast Ethernet backbone. No such segmentation would be required to connect them over a 100VG backbone.

Hewlett-Packard originally supported only 100VG-AnyLAN exclusively, but later came to embrace 100Base-T as well in its product line, giving its customers a choice between the two technologies—and perhaps acknowledging to itself that 100VG, despite any real or alleged technical superiorities, will never overtake Fast Ethernet in the marketplace. This move had the effect of making the technology more viable, because customers would not be locked into one or the other. In fact, it is now possible to run a mixed network with both 100VG and 100Base-T workgroups.

A handful of vendors have followed suit by supporting both technologies. These include AT&T Microelectronics (Allentown, PA), Cabletron Systems (Rochester, NH), and Texas Instruments (Dallas, TX).

100VG-AnyLAN was originally meant to be the replacement for Ethernet, but because it does not meet the IEEE requirements to be called Ethernet, it was given its own separate specification (803.12). Because it cannot truly be called "Ethernet," this separate specification has actually had the result that 100VG-AnyLAN has not been widely accepted. The *VG* in 100VG-AnyLAN stands for *voice grade*, and the *AnyLAN* term is derived from the standard's support of both Ethernet and Token Ring.

A 100VG network uses a scalable star topology, allowing it to support 10BaseT Ethernet and IEEE 802.5 Token-Ring networks. Given that hubs are of the same frame type, it is possible to upgrade an existing 10BaseT or Token Ring LAN to 100VG without changing topology. A 100VG hub can support either Token Ring or Ethernet, but not both simultaneously. A router can be used to move traffic between 100VG networks using Ethernet and one using Token Ring.

The major difference in 100VG and 100BaseT is the fact that 100VG does not use CSMA/CD for its network transmission access method. It is this difference that separates 100VG from Fast Ethernet. Instead, 100VG uses a Demand Priority scheme, a collision-free methodology that can be used to give packets priority in the queue. Under the Demand Priority scheme, only one node can access the segment at a time, effectively bypassing the whole issue of collisions.

Although 100BaseT is the IEEE's official 802.3 Fast Ethernet standard, the standards body has declared 100VG-AnyLAN to be a new, 802.12 standard. However, this concession means little; 802.3 is still the predominant standard for UTP wiring.

Both technologies run on the major network operating systems.

Ch
4

Troubleshooting Fast Ethernet Components

An Ethernet frame used to contain a Type field, which contains a number that describes the protocol being carried by the frame. This information may be especially useful in troubleshooting, because it will tell you which protocols are involved in the particular problem. The Fast Ethernet specification replaces the Type field with a set of frame specifiers, although several implementations still use the Type field.

The 48-bit Ethernet address, or the *Organizationally Unique Identifier (OUI)*, is also useful in troubleshooting. This address is divided into two 24-bit sections; the first denotes a manufacturer, and the second is used by the manufacturer to denote a unique address for each Ethernet interface.

Knowing the manufacturer's number used in the OUI may assist in identifying which computer may be causing a problem in the network. However, some manufacturers may subcontract the manufacturing of subcomponents to other companies, making it impossible to use this number to derive any useful information. Nonetheless, this represents a valuable place to start when trying to pinpoint the source of a problem.

Appendix C, "OUI Listing," lists each manufacturer and its unique identifier.

Product Overview

Besides low cost and easy migration, 100Base-T enjoys wide industry support. Ethernet experts are abundant, and there are literally hundreds of companies offering Fast Ethernet products and services. This high level of competition inevitably results in reasonable prices for the technology.

Although Fast Ethernet adapters are rapidly becoming commodity items, different vendors struggle to differentiate their products from one another by offering unique technologies and added value. However, although these unique technologies may be innovative, they are usually non-standard and incompatible with other vendors' equipment.

The cost of hybrid 10/100Mbps Ethernet NICs is rapidly dropping, and is in fact, rapidly approaching the price of a standard 10Mbps card. As more vendors compete for a piece of this market, the cost of moving to Fast Ethernet will become almost negligible. The cost of Fast Ethernet hubs and routers is also dropping, although not quite as fast as the price for the NICs themselves. Although some companies may want to preserve their investments in the older 10Mbps cards, when it comes time to deploy a new machine, a 10/100 dual-speed NIC is definitely the way to go.

Farallon Computer

http://www.farallon.com
2470 Mariner Square Loop
Alameda, CA 94501
Voice: 510-814-5000
Fax: 510-814-5023
E-mail: **farallon@farallon.com**

Farallon's Plug-and-Play 10/100 Ethernet NICs offer all the recommended features, including auto-sensing and multi-protocol support. Cards are available for both Macintosh and PCI-based PCs. Because they are compliant with the IEEE 802.3u standards for 100Base-TX, the cards are compatible with other vendors' compliant 100Base-T products.

The company offers the only Macintosh adapters based on 3Com's Parallel Tasking 10/100 Ethernet technology; the cards support all popular Macintosh protocols, including MacTCP, MacIPX, MacSNMP, and AppleShare.

Cogent Data Technologies

http://www.cogentdata.com
691 South Milpitas Boulevard
Milpitas, CA 95035
Voice: 408-945-8600
Fax: 408-262-2533

Cogent (now part of Adaptec) is one of a handful of Fast Ethernet vendors that offer products complying with the 100Base-T4 specification, which can run on CAT-3 cabling. Although the bulk of the Fast Ethernet market is for Category 5 installations, those environments with large Category 3 installations may want to examine this type of technology as an option.

Asanté

http://www.asanté.com
821 Fox Lane
San Jose, CA 95131
Voice: 408-435-8388, 800-662-9686
Fax: 408-432-7511

Asanté differentiates itself from the pack of Ethernet vendors with its *Goldcard Connector technology*. This little device eliminates the noise and delay of cables, and simplifies installation. With it, up to 15 Asante Fast Ethernet hubs can be stacked, and two stacks can be placed within a single collision domain. Furthermore, Asante's Fast Ethernet hubs offer Class II operation, and can be daisy-chained to other Fast Ethernet hubs while still retaining a single collision domain.

3Com

http://www.3com.com
5400 Bayfront Plaza
Santa Clara, CA 95052
Voice: 408-764-5000 or 1-800-NET-3COM
Fax: 408-764-5001

Ch
4

For the most part, older ISA-bus PCs cannot take advantage of the speeds offered by Fast Ethernet; typically, the legacy PCs retain their 10Mbps Ethernet connection while newer PCI-bus PCs are hooked into the Fast Ethernet LAN. 3Com, however, offers a way to get those legacy machines with the program. 3Com Corporation offers the first Fast Ethernet NIC for *Industry Standard Architecture (ISA) bus systems*, with its Fast EtherLink ISA 10/100BASE-TX Parallel Tasking NIC. The adapter lets users leverage their existing PCs, while still enjoying the benefits of Fast Ethernet.

Cisco Systems

http://www.cisco.com
170 West Tasman Drive
San Jose, CA 95134
Voice: 408-526-4000 or (800) 553-NETS (6387)
Fax: 408-526-4100

Cisco's Catalyst 5000 and Catalyst 2900 Fast Ethernet switches offer built-in traffic management facilities. Cisco is the only vendor to support embedded RMON across all of its Fast Ethernet switching platforms. RMON is integrated with the CiscoView device management application, giving network managers access to a wide range of statistics, history, and other data through either SNMP or Cisco's TrafficDirector management application.

Cisco was also the first to offer embedded VLAN capabilities in its family of Fast Ethernet switches. Both the Catalyst 5000 and 2900 are capable of handling as many as 1,024 switched VLANs.

Both RMON and VLAN features are managed by CiscoWorks for *Switched Internetworks*, a management software utility that furnishes the administrator with an integrated view of the Fast Ethernet networks.

Cnet

2199 Zanker Road
San Jose, CA 95131
408-954-8000 or 800-486-2638
E-mail: **info@cnet.com**

Cnet offers a wide variety of Fast Ethernet products with sophisticated features. Among these products are a six-port 100Mbps switching hub, hybrid 100/100 switching hubs, 12-port repeaters, and full-duplex capable NICs. Many of these products include SNMP (Simple Network Management Protocol) agents to provide for network management, as well as an auto-negotiation feature.

Summary

Fast Ethernet increases the bandwidth of standard 10Mbps Ethernet tenfold, while still maintaining compatibilty with the older standard. The cost of hybrid 10/100 network interface cards is rapidly decreasing, to the point where they are nearly the same price as a 10Mbps card. The physical layer specification of Fast Ethernet allows for use of Category 3, 4, or 5 cabling, as well as fiber for greater network diameters. 100VG-AnyLAN is a little-used alternative to Fast Ethernet.

100VG was created by Hewlett-Packard, and differs from Fast Ethernet in that it does not use the CSMA/CD method of collision control. Instead, it uses a Demand Priority mechanism which avoids packet collisions. ●

Ch
4

Gigabit Ethernet

With the release of the 100Mbps Fast Ethernet standard in 1995, Ethernet was established as a scalable technology. Now, fast networks can take advantage of the mature and reliable technology of the Ethernet. This presents a major advantage because of the high reliability of an Ethernet network, widespread availability of hardware and software, and substantial and readily available experienced personnel. Gigabit Ethernet raises the bar once again on this technology.

Because it preserves the Ethernet frame structure, Gigabit Ethernet software and management remains compatible across 10Mbps, 100Mbps, and 1,000Mbps. Possibly one of the earliest uses of Gigabit Ethernet will be the aggregation of 100Mbps Ethernet and 100Mbps Fiber Distributed Data Interface (FDDI) with a 1,000Mbps hub.

Fast Ethernet, in the few short years in which it has existed, has rapidly come down in price to the point where it is only slightly more costly than 10Mbps Ethernet. Although there are currently only very few pre-standard Gigabit Ethernet products available, Gigabit Ethernet is likely to follow the same pattern as Fast Ethernet, representing an easy and cost-effective backbone technology. ■

Local area networks (LANs) are taking on greater significance in the workplace, and have come to accommodate more complex and mission-critical applications. Furthermore, LANs are being called on to carry more data and an increased traffic load. The old 10Mbps Ethernet LAN may become inadequate in these growing networks. Fast Ethernet (100Mbps Ethernet) offered us some relief, but as Fast Ethernet becomes a desktop technology, we need an even higher bandwidth for the backbone. Gigabit Ethernet is the most obvious upgrade path for those who want to preserve their Ethernet investment when more bandwidth is required.

Ethernet has gone through some significant changes since it was first developed in the mid-1970s. Initially, it ran at less than 3Mbps. At 10Mbps, it became a widely used LAN technology; later, it increased to 100Mbps, and now, 1,000Mbps. Ethernet is used throughout the world; in fact, the majority of network installations are based on the Ethernet. The widespread acceptance of the Ethernet means that companies that choose to deploy Gigabit Ethernet will enjoy access to the plentiful resources that are available, which include products, information, and skilled technicians.

Gigabit Ethernet marks the fourth ultra-high performance option, with the first three being Asynchronous Transfer Mode (ATM), Fibre Channel, and High Performance Parallel Interface (HiPPI). ATM, despite being an immensely useful backbone technology, may have limited applications for the LAN. Fibre Channel has advantages as well, but has yet to be thoroughly tested and lacks widespread vendor support. HiPPI is a mature and robust technology, but applies only to internetworking—that is, in connecting multiple LANs.

Gigabit Ethernet, on the other hand, offers a versatile solution for communications in a large Ethernet-installed base. Like HiPPI, Gigabit Ethernet can be applied to internetworking; and like ATM, it can be used as a backbone technology. Yet at the same time, Gigabit Ethernet can be used on the LAN level, potentially even down to the desktop for applications such as scientific visualization or CAD/CAM (computer-aided design/computer-aided manufacturing).

The rapid deployment and acceptance of Fast Ethernet virtually requires the existence of Gigabit Ethernet, simply because the backbone must have more capacity and performance than its endpoints. We must wonder, therefore, what will come next, when down the road Gigabit Ethernet eventually finds its way to the even more powerful desktop of the future. A Terabit Ethernet specification may not be physically possible, but it is certainly an intriguing idea to consider. There have, however, been a few rumblings (although nothing official has yet to be proposed) about a 10Gbps Ethernet specification.

But let us not get ahead of ourselves. Gigabit Ethernet is still in the development stages at this point, although some pre-standard hardware is already available. However, the

Institute of Electrical and Electronics Engineers (IEEE) expects to have a formal standard by March 1998, and you can be sure that hundreds of vendors will be in line to offer compliant products shortly after that date.

Overview of Gigabit Ethernet

Remember when a 10M hard drive was enormous? Then 20M and 40M hard drives came out, and you couldn't imagine how you could ever fill it. Now, anything less than a 1G hard drive is inadequate. Gigabit Ethernet technology is in that same space right now. Very few people can imagine any practical purpose for 1,000Mbps transmissions; in fact, the vast majority of network transmissions are still well under the 10Mbps specified by standard Ethernet. Just wait—within a few years, high-speed networking will be the norm, and a 10Mbps connection will be as obsolete as a 10M hard drive.

Although the vast majority of desktops are still running at 10Mbps connections, more companies are starting to experiment with running Fast Ethernet, or 100Mbps connections, to the desktop level—at least to the desktops of their power users with the "heavy artillery" type of applications. As this trend continues, it will be necessary to implement an even higher bandwidth technology for use as a backbone. Obviously, it is not possible to multiplex 100Mbps desktops to a 100Mbps backbone. Here's where Gigabit Ethernet comes in. Although we can't currently imagine running 1,000Mbps to the desktop, there are many instances where the combination of 100Mbps to the desktop and a 1,000Mbps backbone make sense.

Like Fast Ethernet (which runs at 100Mbps), Gigabit Ethernet will manifest itself first in the form of dual-speed network interface cards (NICs), which can run at both 100 and 1,000Mbps speeds, an innovation that makes migration much simpler. Like Fast Ethernet, Gigabit Ethernet represents an easy upgrade path, because it uses much of the same technology as standard 10Mbps Ethernet. There is no significant learning curve involved, but the new technology can accommodate newer, graphics- and data-intensive applications that require higher transmission rates, including scientific modeling, data warehousing, and videoconferencing.

Despite limitations in terms of prioritization and collision detection, Gigabit Ethernet is extremely fast. However, although it can theoretically accommodate a transmission speed of up to 1G/sec, Gigabit Ethernet is still based on the same technology as 10Mbps and Fast Ethernet, and is subject to the same limitations. There are often unpredictable delays inherent in Ethernet, there are no Quality of Service (QoS) guarantees, and Ethernet networks of any type use as little as 40 percent of the available bandwidth because of its contentious nature. Of course, depending on the network configuration, usage patterns,

Ch
5

and dozens of other factors, the actual utilization rate may be higher (in other words, your mileage may vary). Still, 40 percent of 1,000Mbps is still 400Mbps, a fairly substantial rate of bandwidth by any measure.

Between Gigabit Ethernet and ATM, Gigabit Ethernet is by far the easier and cheaper of the two to deploy, especially if an Ethernet network is already in place. One of the biggest advantages of Gigabit Ethernet is that it is compatible with the installed base of 10Mbps and 100Mbps Ethernet. By preserving the basic 802.3 MAC frame, backwards compatibility is maintained, while packet transmission of 1,000Mbps is possible using fiber optics and, most likely, four-pair CAT-5 copper cable as well.

Gigabit Ethernet's goal is to take advantage of existing technologies. It makes use of Fibre Channel's physical layer, although the difference between the two technologies is that Gigabit Ethernet is more generic, and is useful primarily as a LAN technology. Fibre Channel, on the other hand, is used for more specialized applications, such as clustering and high-speed input/output storage.

NOTE   It is important to note that the PCI bus design will be able to accommodate Gigabit Ethernet. The current 32-bit PCI implementation already can accommodate several hundred megahertz; a 64-bit PCI bus would easily handle Gigabit Ethernet. ▮

Service Guarantees

There is some work being done to apply service guarantees to Gigabit Ethernet. Basically, this involves the IEEE 802.1Q specification, which makes use of the virtual LAN (VLAN) packet header to identify traffic priority. Although for networks with a large percentage of time-sensitive traffic, ATM may be an optimal choice, these new QoS mechanisms may be applied to allow Ethernet to accommodate both data and video.

In addition to the increased bandwidth being afforded through Fast Ethernet and Gigabit Ethernet, new protocols, such as *RSVP* (the IETF's Resource Reservation Protocol), will allow for bandwidth reservation over an Ethernet network to accommodate time-sensitive traffic. In addition, new standards such as 802.1Q and 802.1p will allow the existence of a VLAN on the Ethernet network. Furthermore, usage of advanced video compression mechanisms, such as MPEG-2, will facilitate easier transport of video (over other network architectures as well as Gigabit Ethernet).

Virtual LANs

The 802.1Q specification addresses the issue of VLANs, and promotes a standardized method for frame tagging which is used to denote membership in a VLAN. The existence of frame tagging makes it possible for a VLAN to be implemented with equipment from multiple vendors, and makes it possible for these vendors to incorporate the feature directly in their switching products.

N O T E When your network has several VLANs, how does a packet know which one is its destination? How can information on what VLAN a packet belongs to be communicated across multivendor devices? Frame tagging represents a major breakthrough in allowing VLANs to be established using equipment from multiple vendors. ▨

The move toward LAN switching as a replacement for departmental routing has paved the way for VLANs. The VLAN makes an attractive alternative to routers, because VLANs permit switches to contain broadcast traffic in the same way a router does. Implementing switches and VLANs makes it possible for network segments to be smaller, while still allowing large broadcast domains. VLANs also have the wonderful side benefit of allowing moves, adds, and changes to occur without having to manually reconfigure and reconnect each station. (See Chapter 4, "Fast Ethernet," for more information on VLANs.)

The 802.10 VLAN standard, originally proposed to the IEEE by Cisco Systems, makes use of the 802.10 frame header format's ability to hold security information. The standard takes the portion of the header that was originally meant to hold security information, and instead uses it for VLAN frame tagging. The specific 802.1Q standard is a major enabling milestone in VLANs, and will ultimately permit a VLAN to be created with multi-vendor equipment.

N O T E 802.10 is the IEEE Standard for Interoperable LAN/MAN Security (SILS) and currently contains IEEE Std 802.10b, Secure Data Exchange (SDE). You can find out information about all IEEE Computer Society standards on its Web site at **http://www.computer.org**. ▨

Ch
5

There are numerous benefits to employing VLAN technology, not the least of which is simplified management of a dynamic network. Traditionally, if a user moves to a different subnetwork—which occurs all too frequently in a rapidly changing corporate environment—the IP addresses must be manually updated. Under a VLAN, members retain their IP addresses and membership in a given subnet, regardless of physical location. This dynamic management capability lends itself to the establishment of a *virtual workgroup*, where workgroups can be easily created, changed, and disassembled as needed without regard to physical location of the membership.

Many networks have come to embrace switching, resorting to routing only when absolutely necessary, because of the inherent performance advantages of switching over routing.

A switch, however, cannot filter LAN broadcast traffic, which may require the network to be partitioned with routers. LAN switches that support VLANs can, however, control broadcast traffic more effectively, and minimize the need for routers even more. A server or end station disseminating broadcast traffic will send that traffic only to the other members of the VLAN. A switch port that contains no end stations belonging to a particular VLAN would not promulgate the broadcast.

Standards Development

The IEEE 802.3z Task Group, responsible for the development of a Gigabit Ethernet standard, is expected to announce a formal standard by March 1998. Few products are available at this time, although once the standard has been ratified, you can be sure that vendors will be rushing to provide them.

Although the final standard is not expected to be released until 1998, work on Gigabit Ethernet actually started as early as 1995, when the IEEE 802.3 standards committee created a High-Speed Study Group. The group's dual goals were to establish a half-duplex shared bandwidth technology, and a full-duplex switched technology for more bandwidth.

The IEEE subcommittee has made significant progress in establishing a specification for a 100-meter CAT-5 UTP physical interface for Gigabit Ethernet. The proposed 1000Base-T specification would allow Gigabit Ethernet to run over four-pair CAT-5 cabling for distances of up to 100 meters. CAT-5 cabling is already in use in many network installations. In addition, a short-haul copper link standard has been proposed for use in the switching closet or computer room. This specification would allow a distance of up to 25 m.

Furthermore, the Gigabit Ethernet standard will conform with the 802.2 LLC (Logical Link Control) interface and the 802 Functional Requirements Document, with the exception of Hamming distance.

N O T E   *Hamming* is an error correction and detection code. *Hamming distance* is the number of bit positions in which two code words differ. If two code words are a hamming distance *d* apart, then *d* single-bit errors to convert one into the other will be required.

Network management for Gigabit Ethernet will remain more or less constant, and the proposed standard will actually be a supplement to the existing 802.3 standard.

The Gigabit Ethernet Alliance (**http://www.gigabit-ethernet.org**) is an open forum that promotes the further development of Gigabit Ethernet. The alliance's goals include:

- Support Gigabit Ethernet standards activities currently being conducted in the IEEE 802.3z working group

- Contribute technical resources with the goal of achieving consensus on technical specifications
- Provide resources to establish product interoperability
- Promote communications between suppliers and consumers of Gigabit Ethernet products

Gigabit Ethernet Goals

Theoretically, there is no limitation to how big a Gigabit Ethernet network can be. The IEEE has established three objectives for distances:

- A multi-mode fiber-optic link with a maximum length of 500 m.
- A single-mode fiber-optic link with a maximum length of 2 km.
- A copper link with a maximum length of 25 m.

Also under investigation is the possibility of establishing the CAT-5 UTP link with a maximum length of 100 m.

Resource Reservation Protocol (RSVP)

The IETF's *Resource Reservation Protocol (RSVP)* represents a technology for creating integrated services networks. As an internetworking end-to-end protocol, RSVP reserves resources for different classes of service, based on whatever techniques are available for classes of service on the underlying network type. For example, RSVP will reserve resources using FDDI techniques on an FDDI network, ATM techniques on an ATM network, and so forth. RSVP may certainly be applied to Gigabit Ethernet.

RSVP is a handy little protocol that makes it possible to set up QoS levels for IP networks, giving an Internet Protocol (IP) network some of the same service guarantee capabilities as an ATM network. Most of the big software vendors have plans to support this new protocol. RSVP works by starting out at the client level, sending information about bandwidth requirements from router to router, and then to the destination client. The client application signals the network, requesting the class of service it needs, and then communicates this information from router to router.

For full-duplex support, Gigabit Ethernet MAC uses the IEEE 802.3x Full-Duplex specification and the IEEE 802.3x frame-based flow-control mechanism. In half-duplex, the MAC supports Carrier Sense Multiple Access with Collision Detection (CSMA/CD).

Above the MAC layer, Gigabit Ethernet is the same as the original IEEE 802.3 standard.

Ch
5

Fibre Channel Standards

Gigabit Ethernet actually uses a combination of technologies, including those from the IEEE 802.3 Ethernet specification and the ANSI X3T11 Fibre Channel specification (see Figure 5.1).

FIG. 5.1

The Gigabit Ethernet protocol stack draws some of its specifications from Fibre Channel.

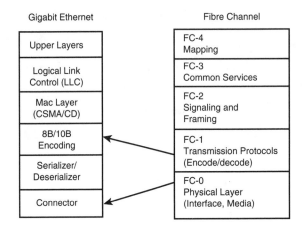

The fiber version of the Gigabit Ethernet protocol stack uses the Fibre Channel specification's FC-0 layer at the bottom. FC-0 defines the physical interface and media, including cables, connectors, and drivers.

Gigabit Ethernet also adopts 8B/10B encoding from the FC-1 Fibre Channel specification. This type of encoding specifies byte synchronization and the encode/decode scheme.

▶ **See** Chapter 10, "Fibre Channel," **p. 227**

In March 1997, the Gigabit Ethernet alliance met a major milestone when the feature set of the Gigabit Ethernet standard was finalized by the IEEE 802 Plenary meeting. As of this milestone, no new features will be added. Furthermore, the Project Authorization Request for the 1000Base-T long-haul copper media was approved at the meeting. Although the committee still does not have a formal specification for running Gigabit Ethernet on copper wire, this milestone indicates that it is on its way.

Different physical layers that have been incorporated into the standard include:

- *1000Base-CX.* For interconnection of equipment clusters.
- *1000Base-SX.* For horizontal building cabling.
- *1000Base-LX.* For backbone building cabling and campus interconnections.

The IEEE specification for Gigabit Ethernet as it stands now deploys fiber only, although the work already done by task force members indicate that running it over copper will be a reality by the time Gigabit Ethernet becomes a formal standard.

PMC-Sierra, a Task Force member, is first in line with a proposal for a new standard for an Unshielded Twisted Pair (UTP) CAT-5 physical layer on Gigabit Ethernet. The PMC-Sierra proposal establishes a simple, low-cost Complementary Metal-Oxide Semiconductor (CMOS) physical layer interface that will facilitate the rapid development of full-duplex Gigabit Ethernet links over CAT-5 UTP copper wiring. The physical layer interface proposed by PMC-Sierra uses currently available semiconductor technology.

The IEEE 802.3z Gigabit Task Force issued the first draft of the Gigabit Ethernet specification in January 1997, and the last feature was added in March 1997. After this point, no new features will be added to the specification. The final specification is expected to be approved as a standard in March 1998. The task force's objectives in taking on Gigabit Ethernet are as follows:

- Speed of 1,000Mbps at the Media Access Control/Physical Layer Signaling (MAC/PLS) service interface.
- Use 802.3 Ethernet frame format.
- Meet 802 Functional Requirements (FR), with the possible exception of hamming distance.
- Simple forwarding between 1,000Mbps, 100Mbps, 10Mbps.
- Preserve minimum and maximum frame size of current 802.3 Std.
- Full and half duplex operation.
- Support star-wired topologies.
- Use CSMA/CD access method with support for at least one repeater/collision domain.
- Support fiber media and, if possible, copper media.
- Use ANSI Fibre Channel FC-1 and FC-0 as basis for work.
- Provide a family of Physical Layer specifications which support a link distance of:

    At least 25 m on copper (100 m preferred)

    At least 500 m on multimode fiber

    At least 3 km on single-mode fiber

- Support maximum collision domain diameter of 200 m.
- Support media selected from ISO/IEC 11801.
- Adopt flow control based on 802.3x.
- Include a specification for an optional Media Independent Interface (MII).

Implementation and Infrastructure

One of the advantages of Gigabit Ethernet is that it makes Fast Ethernet (100Mbps) useful on the desktop level. 100Mbps desktops can be multiplexed onto a Gigabit Ethernet backbone, effectively giving each desktop a tremendous resource for running high-powered applications.

There have been some questions about whether Gigabit Ethernet can run as both a shared and switched media technology; until the IEEE releases a ratified standard, there are several unanswered questions. Some users may worry, and with some justification, that existing workstations and servers may not be able to accommodate the throughput offered by Gigabit Ethernet, and some existing internetworking equipment may not be able to be upgraded to the new technology. The focus for the IEEE is likely to be on creating a switched Gigabit Ethernet environment; there is some question as to whether shared Gigabit Ethernet should even be part of the formal specification.

A shared Gigabit Ethernet technology would use the same CSMA/CD access mechanism as other Ethernets; switched Ethernet suspends CSMA/CD on full-duplex connections so traffic can travel in both directions at once. The elimination of CSMA/CD causes a problem, at least in the eyes of the IEEE. When the 100VG-AnyLAN (for a discussion of 100VG, see the "100VG-AnyLAN" section in Chapter 4, "Fast Ethernet") group proposed making their standard the official Fast Ethernet standard, they lost out to 100Base-T; because the standards body decided that without CSMA/CD, it could not still be called Ethernet. 100VG does not use the CSMA/CD access mechanism; it uses a Demand Priority scheme instead. Demand Priority is a contentionless method used to allow stations to transmit high-priority packets first. Instead of collision detection, Demand Priority determines network access in the hub. The hub polls all ports consecutively. When a station requests permission to end data, the hub permits it to generate one frame, then moves on to the next port. If the hub receives a high-priority request to send, however, it will complete its current transmission, allow the high-priority packet to be sent, and then resume its normal polling operation.

▶ **See** "100VG-AnyLAN," **p. 97**

Performance Issues

The Gigabit Ethernet Alliance presented two schemes to the 802.3z Task Force to address performance in a shared Gigabit Ethernet network: one that uses carrier extensions, another that uses a buffered repeater.

Carrier Extension   There are a number of proposals for modifying the CSMA/CD protocol to accommodate the high speeds offered by Gigabit Ethernet, while still allowing a 200-m collision domain. The most basic proposal involves a simple carrier extension technique that is added onto CSMA/CD.

The *carrier extension proposal* presents a scheme whereby if a device on the network transmits, the signal will stay active for a longer time before another device will attempt to send. This lets an Ethernet frame travel a longer distance, and thereby increases the potential network diameter.

Buffered Repeater   The second alternative proposed by the Gigabit Ethernet Alliance for improving performance is a buffered repeater. The buffered repeater scheme is somewhat unconventional. Traditionally, shared Ethernet is a half-duplex technology. However, if collision detection is placed on the repeater, end stations do not have to retransmit; therefore, they can transmit over a full-duplex link. This reduces the possibility of collision, and again allows for a larger network diameter.

In full-duplex operations, a switching hub can be used. A full-duplex link offers high efficiency, and with switching, the bandwidth of the hub is a multiple of the link speed. A Gigabuffer Repeater is halfway between a standard repeater and switching hub. This buffered repeater still uses full-duplex links, but shares the 1Gbps between the links through flow-control arbitration.

Collision Domain   When dealing with the CSMA/CD protocol, you must consider something called the *collision domain*. The collision domain is equal to the maximum separation between any two stations in the network, which is in turn limited by the minimum length transmission time. As the speed at which data travels over the medium increases, the amount of time necessary for sending a minimum length frame decreases. As a result, the collision domain diameter also decreases.

In order to preserve a 200-m collision domain diameter, the minimum frame size needs to be increased. Carrier extension is used to achieve a 200-m collision domain diameter in Gigabit Ethernet, while still retaining Ethernet's standard minimum frame size. This technique appends a short frame with non-data symbols to make up a desired minimum transmit time. However, increasing the minimum transmit time by appending non-data symbols will result in decreased network efficiency.

A hub can be deployed to mitigate some of the decreased efficiencies. Three types of hubs can be applied with a Gigabit environment:

- A traditional repeater running at half-duplex
- A switching hub at full-duplex
- A Gigabuffer Repeater

The last device is a buffered repeater that uses full-duplex links, but uses flow control to share the bandwidth between the links.

Ch
5

The objectives of the IEEE in terms of the Gigabit Ethernet physical layer is to support link lengths used in building wiring standards. These lengths include a horizontal length of 100 m, backbone length of 500 m, and campus length of 3 km. Because there is a 200-m maximum collision domain, links cannot exceed 100 m unless used in full duplex mode. All of the physical layer specifications, however, are limited to star topologies.

Virtual Collisions and Packet Bursting: Enhancements to CSMA/CD   A proposal to the IEEE 802.3z committee has been made by NBase Communications to enhance the CSMA/CD algorithm with facilities for virtual collisions and packet bursting. Although CSMA/CD is scalable to higher speeds, as we learned from moving to 100Mbps Ethernet from 10Mbps Ethernet, some issues arise as a result of that scaling. The twin concepts of adding facilities for virtual collisions and packet bursting are an attempt to mitigate the problems that arise from scaling CSMA/CD to 1,000Mbps speeds.

Specifically, packet bursting looks at scaling issues, while virtual collisions add an extra measure of support for time-sensitive applications. Packet bursting may be used only with CSMA/CD carrier extension; both packet bursting and carrier extension have been included in the IEEE draft documents.

Virtual collisions, despite the fact that only minor modifications would be required to CSMA/CD, were not adopted because of scheduling issues and because most members believe that most Gigabit Ethernet installations will be full-duplex. Nonetheless, the concept of virtual collisions merits a closer examination, not only because of its innovative nature, but simply because the entire standard is still in the standards process. The final specification is still being hashed out.

Because Ethernet is inherently a contention-oriented, connectionless technology, it does not lend itself to support of delay-sensitive traffic because it has no prioritization mechanism. However, end users have come to demand that their networks support multimedia and other types of traffic for which delay cannot be accepted. Indeed, multimedia support is coming to be a part of everyday business.

Virtual Collisions   A virtual collision-based Gigabit network can accommodate nearly 200 simultaneous MPEG-1 sessions, or 30 MPEG-2 sessions. A Gigabit network capable of running multimedia may best be deployed as a mixed switched and shared environment.

There are some significant differences between standard data traffic and multimedia traffic. Whereas data is bursty, multimedia is more constant in its flow, but it is critically important that multimedia packets arrive on time in order to avoid jitter, garbled voice, and dropped frames. CSMA/CD, by its very nature, sends packets out of order. To ensure a smooth multimedia reception, the network needs to guarantee a predetermined level of bandwidth, and alleviate such phenomena as *channel capture*, where one transmitting node gains an advantage by repeatedly being the contention winner.

However, a deterministic calculation is required to designate certain types of traffic as high priority. Ethernet, however, is probabilistic, not deterministic.

The virtual collision technique calls for a star topology with a single hub in the center. This technique makes a small adjustment to CSMA/CD to establish a more deterministic network with a priority mechanism. The concept is remarkably simple—to make use of the collision time to deliver one good frame, in order to guarantee that one of the stations involved in a collision has a successful transmission (as opposed to both stations' frames being discarded). Although one station involved in the collision does have a successful transmission, the others still must retransmit. The one good frame is the first to arrive at the hub.

Channel capture in a virtual collision scheme is avoided by ensuring that the gap between the successful transmission and the subsequent transmission is larger than the network's round-trip delay. As a result, the other stations involved in the collision are given priority over the station that delivered the good frame, thereby avoiding a situation where the first contention winner takes control of the channel and prevents any other stations from transmitting.

To comply with the virtual collision model, each station must monitor the network for an idle period of no less than 76 byte times, which is equivalent to round-trip delay plus a 12-byte *inter frame gap (IFG)*. Transmission can then occur, but the 76-byte idle time must once again be observed before undertaking another transmission.

A typical collision scenario without virtual collision takes the following sequence of events:

1. Station 1 sends a frame, and the repeater distributes it to all ports.
2. Station 2 has not yet detected station 1's transmission, so it starts one of its own.
3. When the repeater receives the second transmission, it acknowledges that a collision has occurred, and will then jam all ports.
4. Station 1 receives the jam and stops transmitting. Both stations wait a random period of time before retransmitting.

With virtual collisions enabled, the scenario is a little different:

1. Station 1 transmits a frame; the repeater receives it and proceeds to distribute it to all ports.
2. Again, Station 2 has not yet received the first transmission, and believes the channel is free and so it starts a transmission of its own.
3. The repeater receives Station 2's transmission. However, instead of jamming all the ports, the repeater merely ignores the frame, and Station 2 stops transmitting.

Ch
5

4. Station 1 is allowed to complete its transmission, and Station 2 is required to retransmit after Station 1 has completed its successful transmission.

One very desirable benefit of virtual collisions is that it doubles the network diameter, which has been significantly reduced under Fast and Gigabit Ethernet compared with 10Mbps Ethernet. Typically, the round-trip delay of the network must be less than the collision window. However, under Virtual Collisions, the end-to-end delay (half of the round-trip delay) of the network must be less than the collision window. Consequently, virtual collisions give us an easy way to double the potential diameter.

Packet Bursting   The packet bursting model has been adopted by the committee and incorporated in the first draft of the Gigabit Ethernet standard.

Carrier extension by itself results in a higher probability of collisions and low network utilization for frames under 512 bytes. *Packet bursting* is a simple method that improves bandwidth utilization in a heavily loaded network for short frames, and decreases the likelihood of a collision.

As an addition to carrier extension, packet bursting recoups some of the performance lost when carrier extension is applied, by sending a burst of frames whenever the first frame has passed a collision window of 512 bytes, and applies carrier extension only to the first frame in the burst. A carrier extension signal is inserted between all frames in the burst, to prevent other stations from starting to transmit while the burst is occurring.

The benefit of this model is that the overhead of the carrier extension symbols are averaged over several frames instead of just one frame, thereby improving utilization when short frames are sent.

Cabling

Gigabit Ethernet is intended to function mostly as a backbone technology, and can run over coaxial cables to 25 m. However, there are plans to develop a specification for CAT-5 UTP, the standard cabling used with 10Mbps and 100Mbps Ethernet.

As you saw with Fast Ethernet, as the bit rate increases, the maximum network diameter decreases. Fast Ethernet shrank the maximum diameter to 200 m (100 m from hub to desktop); Gigabit Ethernet will reduce the diameter further, to about a tenth of that, unless the 802.3z task force can come up with a way to preserve the 200 m maximum set forth in Fast Ethernet. It does appear, however, that this goal will be met.

Figure 5.2 shows the relative cable lengths available for the different Ethernet specifications.

FIG. 5.2

Ethernet cable lengths.

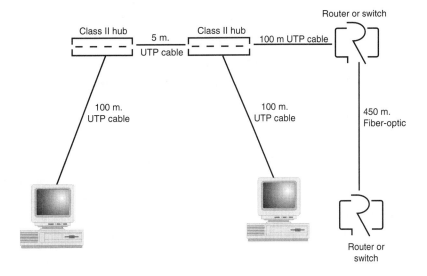

Furthermore, the task force hopes to address distance issues by specifying a multi-mode fiber-optic link that has a maximum length of 500 m, a single-mode fiber-optic link with a maximum length of 2 km, and a copper link with a maximum length of 25 m.

Single-Mode and Multi-Mode Fiber

Fiber-optic cable consists of five components: the core, cladding, buffer, strength members and jacket. The core is made up of one or more fibers, through which light moves. The cladding is a protective layer with a lower refractive index than the core. Consequently, if light hits the core walls, it is redirected back to its path. The buffer is a plastic layer that surrounds the cladding, and is used to strengthen the cable. Strength members are strands of steel or other material that offer additional reinforcement to the cable, and the fiber-optic jacket is an outer casing.

Single-mode fiber cable has a narrow core that allows the light to take only a single path. It allows for higher transmission speeds, but is more difficult to install. Another advantage of single-mode fiber is that it suffers from the least signal attenuation (distortion). Multi-mode fiber cable, on the other hand, has a larger core. Multiple beams of light can pass through the multi-mode fiber, but the signal will suffer from greater distortion at the receiving end.

These newer cable restrictions may impose a need for upgrading cable in some scenarios. A link that may have functioned well at 2 km under standard Ethernet may have to be scaled back, or else the cable will need to be upgraded to single-mode. At least initially, it will probably be impossible to run a 2 km network on multi-mode fiber; an upgrade to single-mode may be necessary.

Any Ethernet, whether it is 10Mbps or 1,000Mbps, suffers from limitations in terms of how long each segment can be. As the speed of Ethernet increases, the segment length decreases. The following chart illustrates this trend:

Ch

5

	10Mbps	100Mbps	1000Mbps
CAT-5 UTP	100 m	100 m	100 m
STP/Coax	500 m	100 m	25 m
Multi-mode fiber	2 km	412 m (half-duplex) 2 km (full-duplex)	500 m
Single-mode Fiber	25 km	20 km	3 km

All-CMOS Gigabit Ethernet link lengths up to 50 m will use a single bundle of four-pair copper UTP-5 wiring. Dual-bundle eight-pair copper UTP-5 implementations can provide an upgrade path to 100 m. The 50-meter UTP-5 physical interfaces will be used primarily for equipment room switch and server internetworking; the 100 meter UTP-5 physical interfaces will be used for traditional workgroup connections and backbone configurations.

Ultimately, for it to be widely accepted, Gigabit Ethernet must be available on the lower-cost UTP-5 interface. If it were to be presented as a fiber-only technology, the upgrade costs would be too high for too many users who prefer to retain their existing investments.

Upgrading to Gigabit Ethernet

Gigabit Ethernet is not likely to be deployed to the desktop level, at least initially. According to the Gigabit Ethernet Alliance, there are five areas where upgrading to Gigabit Ethernet would be advantageous:

- *Switch-to-server links*. This simple upgrade replaces a Fast Ethernet switch with a Gigabit Ethernet switch, thereby establishing a 1,000Mbps connection to a server farm.

- *Switch-to-switch connections*. This involves upgrading 100Mbps links between Fast Ethernet switches or repeaters to 1,000Mbps links between hybrid 100/1,000Mbps switches. As a result, the new switches could support more Ethernet segments.

- *Switched Gigabit Ethernet backbone.* This involves aggregating Fast Ethernet switches with a Gigabit Ethernet switch or repeater. A Fast Ethernet backbone switch that may be aggregating multiple 10/100 switches can be upgraded to a single Gigabit Ethernet switch that aggregates multiple 100/1,000 switches. Once the backbone has been upgraded to Gigabit Ethernet, the server farms can be connected directly to the backbone with a Gigabit Ethernet NIC, thereby increasing throughput to the servers. In addition, the network itself can support more segments, more bandwidth for each segment, and more nodes in each segment.

- *Shared FDDI backbone.* This upgrade is achieved by connecting FDDI hubs or Ethernet-to-FDDI routers with Gigabit Ethernet switches. The FDDI hub would be replaced with a Gigabit Ethernet switch or repeater.

- *Upgrade high-performance desktops.* Eventually, a Gigabit Ethernet NIC will be available to connect high-end desktops to Gigabit Ethernet switches or repeaters.

Regardless of the upgrade path, applications and network operating systems will require no changes whatsoever.

The 802.3z Gigabit Ethernet Task force has set out the following goals:

- Facilitate half- and full-duplex operations at 1,000Mbps.
- Employ the standard 802.3 Ethernet frame format.
- Use CSMA/CD with support for one repeater for each collision domain.
- Facilitate backward compatibility with 10Base-T and 100Base-T technologies.

In the future, it is most likely that Gigabit Ethernet and ATM will dominate the high-speed market, with Gigabit Ethernet servicing the LAN and ATM servicing the WAN. Gigabit Ethernet can provide a viable backbone technology, however, and is significantly less expensive than ATM. Both Gigabit and ATM are likely to take some of the spotlight away from FDDI as a backbone technology, the latter of which is costly and offers less bandwidth.

Ch
5

At least for its first few years of existence, Gigabit Ethernet at the desktop level is not likely to occur outside of a few highly specialized areas. The most likely upgrade paths for gigabit Ethernet are:

■ Switch-to-server connections for high-speed access to applications and file servers. This is the simplest type of upgrade (see Figure 5.3).

FIG. 5.3
Upgrading a Switch-to-Server Connection to Gigabit Ethernet.

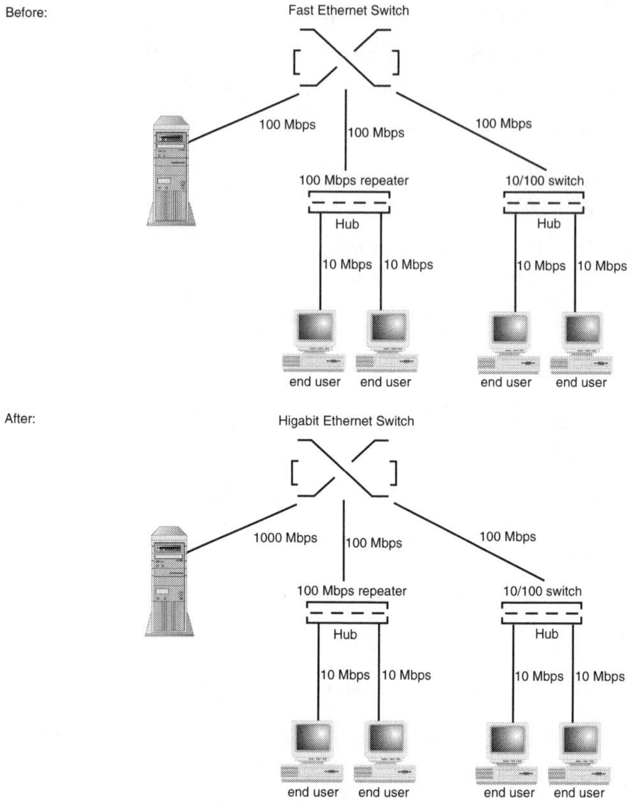

Before:

Fast Ethernet Switch

100 Mbps   100 Mbps   100 Mbps

100 Mbps repeater   10/100 switch

Hub   Hub

10 Mbps 10 Mbps   10 Mbps 10 Mbps

end user end user   end user end user

After:

Higabit Ethernet Switch

1000 Mbps   100 Mbps   100 Mbps

100 Mbps repeater   10/100 switch

Hub   Hub

10 Mbps 10 Mbps   10 Mbps 10 Mbps

end user end user   end user end user

■ Switch-to-switch connections, for replacing 100Mbps links between Fast Ethernet switches with 1,000Mbps links between hybrid 100/1,000 switches (see Figure 5.4).

FIG. 5.4
Upgrading a Switch-to-Switch Connection to Gigabit Ethernet.

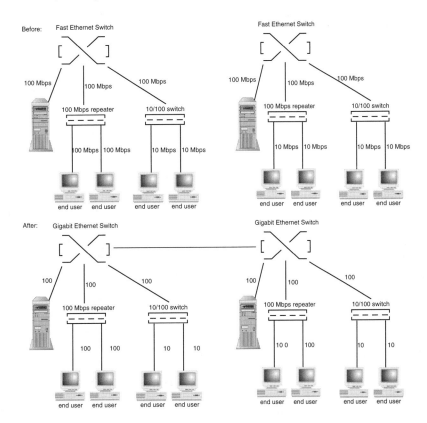

■ Upgrading a switched Fast Ethernet backbone by aggregating Fast Ethernet switches with a Gigabit Ethernet switch or repeater. The older 100Mbps backbone, used to aggregate multiple 10/100 switches, is upgraded to a Gigabit Ethernet switch aggregating multiple 100/1,000 switches. Server farms can then be connected directly to the backbone using a Gigabit Ethernet NIC (see Figure 5.5).

FIG. 5.5

Upgrading a Switched Fast Ethernet Backbone to Gigabit Ethernet.

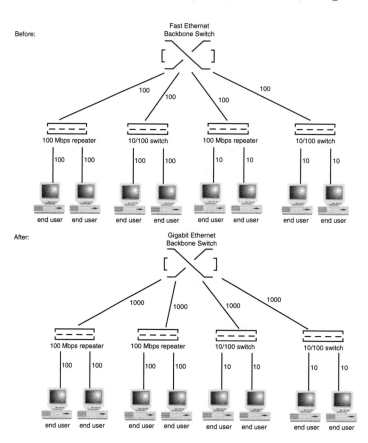

■ Upgrading a shared FDDI backbone. To upgrade the FDDI backbone, the FDDI concentrator is simply replaced with a Gigabit Ethernet switch or repeater. New Gigabit Ethernet interfaces will be required for routers, switches, and repeaters. Fiber-optic cabling is still retained (see Figure 5.6).

FIG. 5.6

Upgrading a Shared FDDI backbone to Gigabit Ethernet.

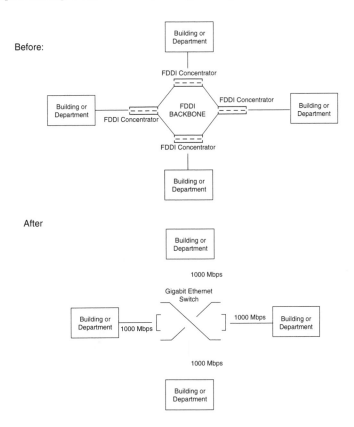

Ch
5

■ Upgrading high-end desktops with gigabit Ethernet NICs. This type of upgrade would be reserved to specialized applications, such as CAD/CAM or scientific visualization (see Figure 5.7).

FIG. 5.7
Upgrading High-End desktops to Gigabit Ethernet.

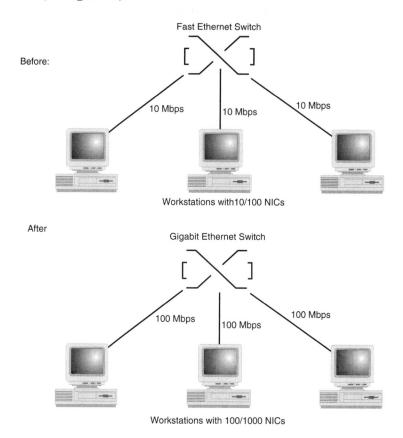

Before:

Fast Ethernet Switch

10 Mbps   10 Mbps   10 Mbps

Workstations with10/100 NICs

After

Gigabit Ethernet Switch

100 Mbps   100 Mbps   100 Mbps

Workstations with 100/1000 NICs

No changes to the network operating system or applications are required with Gigabit Ethernet, making it possible to preserve more of the existing investment than with other types of network architectures.

The best path to Gigabit migration is a gradual one which is transparent to the end user. Because it is based on the same technology as other Ethernets, deployment of Gigabit Ethernet will be quite non-disruptive to the user community.

Uses and Benefits of Gigabit Ethernet   In its early stages, Gigabit Ethernet's primary uses will be in linking Ethernet and Fast Ethernet switches, and for connecting high-performance servers and workstations. Campus backbones are more likely to deploy Gigabit Ethernet in full-duplex mode, which affords the greatest bandwidth and better distance limitations. Half-duplex, however, can still be used for collapsing a backbone in a wiring closet—that is, in scenarios when multiple hubs are aggregated onto a single high-speed repeater. Half-duplex Gigabit Ethernet can also be applied in aggregating servers in the data center.

The ever-increasing speed of CPUs demands the development of higher-bandwidth LANs to carry the traffic that newer machines are capable of producing. According to the IEEE, the development of gigabit technologies will offer the following benefits:

- Backbone, server, and gateway connectivity
- Higher bandwidth for applications such as multimedia, CAD/CAM, and imaging
- The ability to aggregate 100Mbps (Fast Ethernet) switches
- An upgrade path for an installed base of 10/100 Ethernet

It has only been a few years since the introduction of 100Mbps Fast Ethernet, but from that introduction we have learned that it is possible to scale CSMA/CD to higher speeds. Gigabit Ethernet will take one more step in this evolution. A high level of commitment to Gigabit Ethernet throughout the industry has been demonstrated, with more than 80 participants in the standardization process. The Gigabit Ethernet standard will demonstrate compatibility with the existing IEEE 802.3 standard. It will conform to the CSMA/CD MAC with some extensions specific to 1,000Mbps operation.

As was the case with 100Mbps Ethernet, 1,000Mbps Ethernet will require the physical layers to be replaced with new physical layers specific to 1,000Mbps operation. One physical layer will be specified for each type of media (single-mode fiber, multi-mode fiber, coaxial cable, and balanced pair cable). It has been demonstrated that physical layer signaling at 1,000Mbps is feasible on both fiber-optic and copper media.

Ch
5

A big advantage of Gigabit Ethernet is its low cost when compared with other high-speed backbone technologies, and the widespread availability of products and skilled technicians. Fast Ethernet cards have come down in price to nearly the level of 10Mbps cards; Gigabit Ethernet is likely to offer the same competitive price structures as it gains popularity. In addition, it affords an opportunity to preserve existing investments in Ethernet. Once the standard has been implemented, Gigabit Ethernet connections are likely to be offered at between two and three times the cost of a 100Mbps Ethernet interface. At 10 times the bandwidth for three times the cost, it's an obvious bargain. Furthermore, a switched Gigabit Ethernet link is likely to be less costly than a 622Mbps ATM interface.

While in its early stages, Ethernet was restricted to data only, it is now possible to run multimedia and other complex data types over an Ethernet network. This is made possible not only due to the increased bandwidth afforded by Gigabit Ethernet, but because of bandwidth reservation protocols such as RSVP, VLAN specifications, and the ability to mark a packet for high priority.

Gigabit Ethernet supports full-duplex modes for switch-to-switch and switch-to-workstation connections, and half-duplex modes for shared connections. Although its initial deployment will be over optical fiber, Gigabit Ethernet will eventually be able to run over CAT-5 UTP cabling and coaxial cabling as well.

Data warehousing and decision support are just two of many examples of bandwidth-hungry applications that require a new technology to accommodate the tremendous amounts of traffic they generate. These application systems are meant to make enterprise data available throughout the company for the purpose of consolidated analysis and reporting. A data warehouse often consists of multiple gigabytes, or even terabytes in some instances, of information. Just backing up this much information regularly is a major project; it would be very time-consuming and quite impractical without Gigabit Ethernet or one of the other ultra-high speed technologies.

But would desktop computers be able to take advantage of the tremendous speed offered by gigabit Ethernet? Probably not. But remember how quickly the technology advances; by the time Gigabit Ethernet is established, we will have faster desktop machines that just may do the trick.

However, even if the desktops and servers cannot take full advantage of the entire 1,000Mbps of throughput, getting even a few hundred megabytes per second will be easier than aggregating multiple 100Mbps links.

Most existing routers and switches, too, are not built to handle these types of high-speed links; most router and switch vendors will have to release a whole new line of products to accommodate the technology. Network administrators will then have to replace their existing routers and switches in order to use Gigabit Ethernet.

Gigabit Medium Independent Interface

The rapid proliferation of 100Mbps Ethernet (Fast Ethernet) demands a higher-speed technology for use on the backbone. Gigabit Ethernet is an answer to that call. Gigabit Ethernet is architecturally almost identical to 100Mbps Ethernet, with the one exception being that Fast Ethernet's Medium Independent Interface (MII), which connects the Media Access Control (MAC) layer with the physical layers, has been replaced with the *Gigabit Medium Independent Interface (GMII)*.

The goals of the developers of Gigabit Ethernet are to facilitate both full-duplex and half-duplex operations at 1,000Mbps, use the standard IEEE 802.3 Ethernet frame format, use the standard CSMA/CD protocol, and support one repeater for each collision domain. All versions of Ethernet use the same frame lengths and formats, making it possible to transmit frames between Gigabit Ethernet and other Ethernets.

The biggest difference in Gigabit Ethernet as compared with Fast Ethernet is that Fast Ethernet's MII has been replaced with a GMII. The three goals of the GMII are as follows:

- Compatibility with ANSI Fibre Channel specification
- Compatibility with MII
- Manufacturable using existing technology

By making the GMII compatible with the MII, it becomes possible to use existing technology for Gigabit Ethernet, and also provides backward compatibility with 10/100Mbps Ethernet.

FDDI and Gigabit Ethernet

Gigabit Ethernet can be used as an uplink to both FDDI and Fast (100Mbps) Ethernet. Gigabit products, including XLNT's early pre-standard Velocity product, will facilitate this sort of uplink. The Velocity will include four I/O slots for FDDI, 10/100Base-T, 100Base-TX, and Gigabit Ethernet LANs. The switch is capable of three types of frame translations:

- FDDI to Ethernet
- Ethernet-to-Gigabit Ethernet
- Gigabit Ethernet-to-Ethernet

The switch offers 24 100Mbps links to Fast Ethernet, or six switched FDDI rings.

FDDI was introduced in about 1990, and has enjoyed its few years of fame as the leading fiber-optic-based LAN technology. FDDI is often used as a backbone because of its long-distance capabilities. In addition, it is easy to manage and is very resilient. FDDI divides a LAN into dedicated, switched segments in order to relieve the network from some congestion.

Gigabit Ethernet affords an easy migration path from either Fast Ethernet or FDDI. Many existing FDDI backbones can coexist with Ethernet. The FDDI backbone can be upgraded by replacing the FDDI hub with a Gigabit Ethernet switch or repeater. The only upgrade necessary is the deployment of new Gigabit Ethernet interfaces in the routers, switches, and repeaters; and newer versions of analysis and management tools designed to accommodate Gigabit Ethernet. Existing fiber-optic cabling used in the original FDDI backbone is retained, yet the bandwidth available to each segment is significantly greater.

Compared with FDDI, Gigabit Ethernet may make a more optimal backbone technology. Although both FDDI and Gigabit Ethernet offer IP compatibility, FDDI will not transport Ethernet packets.

Ch

5

ATM and Gigabit Ethernet

There has been some debate between analysts over whether to deploy ATM or Gigabit Ethernet as a backbone, although it need not be a choice between one or the other. Those who are firmly planted in the ATM camp insist that ATM should be deployed from end-to-end, including the desktop. This argument is not without merit and, given the budget, would certainly make a powerful network. If starting from scratch, it may even be the more desirable option. However, a full-scale switch-over, or *forklift upgrade* as they call it, in which all Ethernet installations are replaced with ATM, would be a very costly solution indeed.

Perhaps the most measured approach is to view the two technologies as complementary, with ATM used on the WAN backbone and Gigabit Ethernet at the center of the LAN, going down to 10/100Mbps Ethernet on the desktop. In this scenario, Gigabit Ethernet is used as an efficient, high-speed way to access an ATM backbone. ATM presents advantages in some circumstances, while Gigabit Ethernet may be more desirable in others. For example, because of ATM's quality of service guarantees, this may be the best technology for time-sensitive traffic. There are efforts underway, however, to add some prioritization to Gigabit Ethernet to make it more useful for time-sensitive applications, although it is not likely to offer as much in the way of prioritization and quality of service guarantees as ATM.

Even without prioritization schemes, as a high-speed technology for use at the edge of the network, Gigabit Ethernet can present an ideal solution for extending available bandwidth to those servers for which real-time data is not an issue. For those situations where real-time data is a concern, however, ATM's quality of service is essential. Without some sort of quality of service guarantee or prioritization scheme, video comes out jerky and full of lost frames, and audio comes out garbled.

Also, ATM is inherently scalable, ranging from a low of 25Mbps up to more than 10Gbps (OC-192) when configured with multiple connections. It is possible to run both Gigabit Ethernet and ATM and take advantage of both technologies' relative advantages. Because of the inherent flexibility of ATM, it can easily encompass Gigabit Ethernet and other technologies within the ATM WAN through technologies such as *LAN Emulation (LANE)*. However, although LANE affords connectivity between Ethernet and ATM, the emulated LAN will lose the Quality of Service advantages of ATM.

Compared with ATM, Gigabit Ethernet will handle IP traffic natively; ATM requires LANE or Multiple Protocols over ATM (MPOA) to handle IP traffic.

Fibre Channel and Gigabit Ethernet

The Gigabit Ethernet physical layer borrows significantly from Fibre Channel technology quite successfully, despite the fact that Gigabit Ethernet is not a channel-based scheme. Gigabit Ethernet specifies two classes of optical transceivers, in addition to copper media:

- Short wavelength (SWL)
- Long wavelength (LWL)

Fibre Channel more commonly uses SWL optics, which can be used on 50 and 62.5 micron multi-mode fiber (MMF). However, it would be difficult to achieve a long backbone length with SWL devices. LWL will be specified for both multi-mode and single-mode fiber. Maximum link lengths are as follows:

SWL 62.5 MMF	200 m
SWL 50 MMF	450 m
LWL 50 MMF	550–850 m
LWL 62.5 MMF	550–850 m
LWL SMF	3,000 m

Gigabit Ethernet borrows from the first two layers of the Fibre Channel standard, FC-1 and FC-0.

FC-0 defines the physical layer, including the fiber, connectors, and optical and electrical parameters. Both coaxial and twisted-pair versions are defined.

FC-1 defines the Transmission Protocol Layer, including serial encoding and decoding, and error control. This layer defines serial physical transport, timing recovery, and serial line balance. It uses the 8B/10B transmission coding scheme (licensed from IBM and commonly used in SNA environments). Under this mechanism, 8 bits are transmitted as a 10-bit group, with the other 2 bits used for error detection and correction. This mechanism is known as *disparity control*.

At the top of the PHY is the *serializer/deserializer*, which is a layer that supports multiple encoding schemes.

Gigabit Ethernet uses the same CSMA/CD access method as the other Ethernets, although the physical signaling scheme is closer to the ANSI Fibre Channel specification than standard Ethernet.

The 802.3z standard makes significant use of Fibre Channel technology. The first Gigabit Ethernet implementations will use Fibre Channel's high-speed optical components for signaling over optical fiber, as well as Fibre Channel's encoding and decoding

Ch
5

mechanisms for serialization and deserialization. A logical interface between the MAC and PHY layers will be specified to de-couple Fibre Channel encoding, thereby permitting other encoding mechanisms to be used that can support UTP cabling.

Product Overview

Products implementing Gigabit Ethernet, once they become widely available, are likely to be less costly than 622Mbps ATM, making Gigabit Ethernet an attractive option for many network users. Some pre-standard products are already available from a handful of vendors. However, because they are pre-standard, once the standards have been established, these pre-standard devices may require upgrading to comply. Reputable companies generally offer upgrades to the final standard at low or no cost. Always check with the vendor on their upgrade policies before you purchase.

There are about 20 companies already working in the Gigabit Ethernet area, although any products they release are pre-standard. The final standard is not expected from the IEEE until 1998.

Cisco Systems

http://www.cisco.com
170 West Tasman Drive
San Jose, CA 95134
Voice: 408-526-4000 or (800) 553-NETS (6387)
Fax: 408-526-4100

Cisco bought its way into the Gigabit Ethernet market with its acquisition of privately-held Granite Systems, Inc. (Palo Alto, California). Granite is an innovative company focused on multilayer Gigabit Ethernet switching. Granite, which was founded in 1995 to develop high-performance multilayer switching solutions, plans to deliver standards-based, multilayer switching and Gigabit Ethernet through a series of ASIC switching engines. The ASIC technology will be able to be used with Cisco's IOS software and the CiscoFusion architecture.

Packet Engines, Inc.

http://www.packetengines.com
Box 14497
Spokane, WA 99214
Voice: 509-922-9190
Fax: 509-922-9185

Another startup, Packet Engines plans to offer a Gigabit Ethernet MAC layer in its platform, which it will be licensing to other vendors. As a result, those licensees will be able to offer Gigabit Ethernet products much earlier. The company's Gigabit Ethernet MAC is currently shipping.

GigaLabs

http://www.gigalabs.com
290 Santa Ana Court
Sunnyvale, CA 94086
Voice: 800-LAN-8120 or 408-481-3030
FAX: 408-481-3045
E-mail: **info@gigalabs.com**

GigaLabs is one of the first out of the gate with solid Gigabit Ethernet products. The company offers a GigaStar 3000 switch, designed for use as an enterprise network backbone and server connectivity device. Its non-blocking crossbar architecture sports an 18Gbps backplane. It can switch LAN MAC-layer protocols, including Gigabit Ethernet, Fast Ethernet, and FDDI; it can also switch bus protocols, including Sbus and PCI, without converting the bus messages to LAN protocols. GigaLabs sets itself apart through its GigaPipe interface to the GigaStar backplane. GigaPipe allows any I/O subsystem to directly link to the crossbar switch, effectively allowing a switched PCI message to be carried over the same matrix that carries the LAN data packets.

The GigaStar supports up to eight full-duplex Gigabit Ethernet ports with the 18Gbps switching fabric. The company also offers a Gigabit Ethernet NIC for servers and workstations. The GigaStar is based on the company's supercomputer switching technology, and uses a non-blocking crossbar switching fabric to offer low latency and high bandwidth. The GigaStar supports GigaLabs' own I/O switching technology, which allows the server's native I/O subsystem, whether it is PCI or Sbus, without having to convert it to a network protocol. The GigaStar can be managed from any SNMP-compatible management platform, or from GigaLabs' own GigaView network management application.

Ch
5

Alteon Networks, Inc.

http://www.alteon.com
6351 San Ignacio Avenue
San Jose, CA 95119
Voice: 408-360-5500
Fax: 408-360-5501

Alteon is one of a handful of startups focusing on Gigabit Ethernet technology. The company has plans to deliver pre-standard adapters, drivers, and a switch. Alteon has taken the unusual step of establishing a special data frame that is switched between servers. These frames are not limited to the standard 1,518-byte size of Ethernet frames; these special "jumbo" frames can be defined for up to 9K.

Alteon's AceSwitch 110 switch platform has one or two Gigabit Ethernet ports, and eight 10/100 Ethernet ports. Alteon's AceNIC Gigabit Ethernet card supports full-duplex Gigabit Ethernet. The AceSwitch server switching system is fully redundant. Servers equipped with AceNIC adapters can be dual-homed to multiple AceSwitches, so if a failure occurs, no active sessions will be lost. Failover to the standby AceNIC is automatic and transparent, giving servers a high level of reliability.

NBase Communications

http://www.nbase.com
8943 Fullbright Ave.
Chatsworth, CA 91311
Voice: 818-773-0900
Fax: 818-773-0906

NBase Communications has a deterministic method for overcoming distance and time-delay limitations of Gigabit Ethernet. NBase's modification of the standard CSMA/CD algorithm improves bandwidth utilization and doubles the span of the network. This technology simulates the collision of two frames prior to its occurrence. The simulation enables one of the frames to be saved. The repeater will then broadcast the saved frame to its destination, and discard the frame with which it collided. This approach can significantly improve throughput.

NBase's GigaPort Module for the MegaSwitch II represents the company's first Gigabit Ethernet product. The GigaPort can be used to create a Gigabit Ethernet backbone of at least 2 km, with a ratio of 10 10/100 ports to one Gigabit port.

NBase's implementation is based on the existing 100Base-T standard, and uses the Fibre Channel Physical layer. NBase plans to update the products to comply with the IEEE standards once they become finalized.

XLNT

http://www.xlnt.com
15050 Avenue of Science
San Diego, CA 92128

Voice: 619-487-9320
Fax: 619-487-5790
E-mail: **info@xlnt.com**

XLNT is one of the handful of companies with a solid Gigabit Ethernet strategy for bringing Gigabit Ethernet products to the market in 1997. The company, a leader in FDDI technology, is planning a high-end switching product with both FDDI and Fast Ethernet uplinks to Gigabit Ethernet.

XLNT Designs' earliest Gigabit products will facilitate the seamless aggregation of 100Mbps Ethernet and 100Mbps FDDI links. Currently, many companies still deploy desktop systems with 10Mbps Ethernet, although the trend is to move away from shared environments to switched Ethernet for better efficiency. These 10Mbps clients are connected to switches in the wiring closet. Fast Ethernet or FDDI is then used to connect the switches to central servers. XLNT plans to enhance this topology with a Gigabit Ethernet switch, which will be able to consolidate 24 100Mbps links or six switched FDDI rings onto a Gigabit Ethernet link.

Summary

Gigabit Ethernet is compatible with 10Mbps and 100Mbps Ethernet, and may be used as an effective backbone technology. Gigabit Ethernet switches may present an efficient way to get Fast Ethernet (100Mbps) to the desktop.

Gigabit Ethernet is still an emerging standard; the IEEE will not ratify it officially until 1998. However, vendors are building on their previous Ethernet experience, and have already released some pre-standard products.

In its final form, Gigabit Ethernet may have some type of performance guarantee, a first for Ethernet networks. This would be achieved through Virtual LANs (VLANs); the VLAN packet header would be used to identify priority.

Ethernet network diameter decreases as speed increases. Fortunately, there are several ways being investigated to mitigate some of these limitations. The IEEE's goals for Gigabit Ethernet network diameters include 500 meters for multi-mode fiber-optic, 2 kilometers for single-mode fiber-optic, and 25 meters for copper. The IEEE is also investigating the possibility of establishing a CAT-5 UTP link with a length of 100 meters.

Several proposals are under investigation for modifying the CSMA/CD protocol to preserve longer distances. These include using carrier extensions or deploying a buffered repeater. ●

Ch
5

IsoEthernet

The vast majority of network installations are still 10Base-T Ethernet. This architecture has served well for many years, and is still more than adequate for most day-to-day data networking needs.

However, recent trends in productivity applications have created a rapidly growing demand for networked multimedia. End users are clamoring for high-end videoconferencing capabilities, videomail, and other sophisticated applications; but IS managers are reluctant to deliver because of the perceived costs involved. Managers are right to be concerned; offering this type of high-speed-required functionality may involve forklift upgrades. These upgrades can involve ripping out and replacing cables, replacing hubs and other devices, and reconfiguring the entire network with an ultra-high speed architecture such as ATM.

Fork-lift upgrades are often necessary because of the connectionless and contentious nature of Ethernet. Indeed, the very nature of 10Base-T Ethernet produces a high latency and offers no service guarantees; this standard was certainly not created with multimedia in mind.

IsoEthernet lets PC users access interactive network services and applications on demand, including voice, video, and other multimedia. The technology integrates two existing standards: Ethernet and ISDN, and adds an additional 6.144Mbps of bandwidth onto Ethernet's 10Mbps. This extra bandwidth is subdivided into 96 ISDN B-channels, which are used for video and audio traffic. ■

Overview of IsoEthernet

LANs are inherently connectionless and packet-based, and for the most part, used for transporting data only. The dominant LAN technology is still 10Base-T Ethernet, which provides a data connection of up to 10Mbps. The drawback of 10Mbps Ethernet, however, is its contentious nature and high latency, which makes it impractical for multimedia. WANs, on the other hand, are more often used to transport voice through the public telephone network. WAN technologies, such as ATM and SONET, provide a high degree of guaranteed bandwidth, offer lower latency, are connection-oriented, and are better-suited to multimedia. However, an ATM or SONET upgrade may be costly and impractical for many users.

IsoEthernet allows a single network to integrate both LAN and WAN services, and facilitate real-time collaboration, and video or voice traffic. Under standard Ethernet, because of the bursting and packet-oriented nature of LAN traffic, the network has been limited mostly to data transmission. It has not been possible to send time-sensitive over an Ethernet network, because there are no priority guarantees. IsoEthernet, originally created by National Semiconductor, establishes point-to-point connectivity on an N×56K/64Kbps digital switched network through 10Base-T Ethernet cabling, allowing managers to create a virtual workgroup. IsoEthernet multiplexes up to 96 64Kbps B-ISDN channels, and borrows an encoding scheme from FDDI technology to squeeze an extra 6Mbps out of the existing pipe. This additional 6Mbps serves as a dedicated multimedia link. The first 10Mbps is used as the packet channel for standard Ethernet data; the rest provides guaranteed bandwidth for video and voice traffic.

Real-Time Data over 10Mbps Ethernet

Service guarantees, which form an integral part of ATM networks, ensure that multimedia frames arrive in a timely fashion. In a traditional 10Base-T Ethernet network, packets are sent out in consecutive order, but they encounter collisions along the way and must be retransmitted. The result is that on the receiving end of the circuit, the packets are received in non-consecutive order. For plain data, this works out just fine. But when multimedia is sent in this manner, you get inaudible, garbled voices and jittery video.

IsoEthernet is an attempt to facilitate real-time multimedia transport over a standard 10Base-T Ethernet connection.

IsoEthernet lets users of both Macintosh and PCs access interactive network services and applications directly, and on-demand.

No Major Upgrade Required

Over the past few years, we have seen the Ethernet standard evolving to accommodate 100Mbps, and most recently, 1,000Mbps. In its most recent iteration, Gigabit Ethernet, some beginning attempts are even being made to apply service guarantees. The IEEE's 802.9a isochronous Ethernet standard is one more way to beef up existing 10Base-T infrastructures, enabling them to send voice, video, and data over the network.

Integrating IsoEthernet into an existing 10Base-T network can be done seamlessly and with very little trouble and expense. An IsoEthernet hub must be added to the wiring closet, and all multimedia workstations are equipped with IsoEthernet adapter cards. These workstations are then connected to the IsoEthernet hub. The IsoEthernet and Ethernet hubs are connected with an attachment unit interface (AUI).

IsoEthernet easily adds on to an existing network with no major upgrade requirements outside of the cards and hubs. Existing cable and equipment investments are preserved, and there are no changes to applications or other software required. Through these small additions to the network, end users can gain access to public switched telephone network (PSTN) and ISDN services, directly from the desktop and over the existing 10Base-T Ethernet wiring.

Standards Development

The 802.9a standard is actually an evolutionary upgrade from ISO/IEC 8802-3 (or IEEE 802.3) 10Base-T networks. It furnishes both the functionality of packet-based 10Base-T and four Primary Rate ISDN lines over a single interface.

A separate D channel is also provided, and designated as the signaling channel. A 96Kbps Maintenance channel (M channel) is used to transport physical layer control and status data to the remote end of the link. IsoEthernet runs over two pairs of CAT-3 or better UTP wiring up to 100 meters, and uses a star-based network topology.

The 802.9a specification defines the IsoEthernet physical layer, which exists at the bottom of the OSI model. The physical layer is divided into the Physical Medium Dependent (PMD), Physical Signaling (PS), and Hybrid Multiplexing (HMUX) sublayers.

Ch
6

Isochronous Network Communication Alliance

A handful of manufacturers, developers, telecommunications providers, and semiconductor firms have formed a trade group, called the incAlliance (isochronous network communication alliance). The incAlliance's Web site can be found at **http://www.national.com/appinfo/isoethernet/incalliance.html**.

The trade group has given the following goals:

- To promote real-time, interactive multimedia (RIM); computer telephony integration (CTI) products; and services as key tools for businesses

- To educate the industry on the differences between voice, video, and data communications, and how these different services can be integrated and synchronized

- To promote industry growth through joint development initiatives and interoperability testing

- To disseminate information about new isochronous technologies and how they can foster interactive communications solutions

- To provide a roadmap for upgrading networks without a major forklift upgrade

The group hopes to bring isochronous services to the enterprise over existing cable infrastructures. The group supports existing isochronous WAN services (including ISDN and ATM) as well as the new IEEE 802.9a standard—IsoEthernet.

The incAlliance was actually not created to propose a new industry standard, but instead to integrate existing open industry standards into a comprehensive solution. The alliance makes use of existing technical work done by the IEEE, ITU, Electronic Computer Telephony Forum (ECTF), International Multimedia Teleconferencing Consortium (IMTC), ATM Forum, and the Multimedia Communications Forum (MMCF). Companies participating in the alliance are: Apple Computer, Ascom Nexion, AT&T, Databeam, Dialogic, Ericsson Business Networks, IBM, IIT, Incite, Luxcom, MCI, National Semiconductor, PRI Inc., Pacific Bell, Siemens, VCON, and Zydacron.

The alliance also focuses on solutions that adhere to standard interfaces, including TAPI, H.320, T.120, MPEG, Multivendor Integration Protocol (MVIP), and Signal Computing System Architecture (SCSA), which simplifies integration even more.

IEEE Standard

In late 1995, the IEEE finalized the 802.9a specification for Integrated Services Local Area Networks, making IsoEthernet an open standard. The official specification includes the following:

- Mandatory incorporation of the "Auto-negotiation" feature originally proposed by National Semiconductor. This feature has already been incorporated into the IEEE 802.3 specifications for 100Base-T (Fast Ethernet).

- ISDN isochronous Management Information Base (MIB). This is the first time that an IEEE 802 LAN MIB has been combined with an ISDN MIB.

- Incorporation of the ITU's Q.931/Q.932 ISDN signaling procedures

- A parallel draft recommendation of 802.9a by the ITU study Group 15 (audio/video experts group) to be the Guaranteed Quality of Service LAN for H.320 audio/video applications.

The formal name, "Integrated Services Local Area Network 16T (ISLAN16T)," reflects the potentially large market of integrated voice, video and data running simultaneously over a 10Base-T Ethernet network running standard CAT-3, CAT-4, or CAT-5 cabling; while offering a high Quality of Service (QoS) level.

Implementation and Infrastructure

The term "IsoEthernet," now an IEEE standard, is derived from "iso," meaning equal, and "chronous," for time.

IsoEthernet relies on time-division multiplexing (TDM) to isolate the 6Mbps of multimedia from the 10Mbps packet flow. An IsoEthernet hub can be deployed to offload multimedia file-transfers from the packet-based LAN. Separating these time-sensitive applications from the rest of the traffic takes a load off of the standard LAN, minimizing the pauses and delays that would otherwise occur in a video or video stream.

IsoEthernet boosts the performance of a 10Base-T Ethernet network, and adds support for computer-telephone integration (CTI) by adding 96 ISDN-B channels to standard Ethernet. Through use of a physical layer encoding scheme, IsoEthernet reaps an additional 6Mbps of bandwidth on top of the existing 10Mbps. The extra 6Mbps is then available for isochronous communications, and connection-oriented ISDN.

Although the half-duplex, 10Mbps Ethernet bandwidth is inadequate for video and audio, IsoEthernet overcomes this limitation by taking advantage of the full-duplex capabilities of the ISDN telephone network. The connection of Ethernet and ISDN data is made at the desktop and at the hub. Because it connects your LAN with the public network, a point-to-point, videoconferencing connection could be made with any client anywhere in the world.

An extra 6Mbps is certainly not glamorous, when compared with the ultra-high powered throughput of ATM, Gigabit Ethernet, HiPPI, or Fibre Channel. But when applied in this

Ch

6

manner, it provides an excellent platform for running high-quality videoconferencing, MPEG playback, and other sophisticated multimedia applications over the links used for packet-based LAN traffic.

IsoEthernet is one more in a series of upgrades for IEEE 802.3 10Base-T networks. It is used to provide a single, packet-based 10Base-T channel and four Primary Rate ISDN lines over the same interface. In addition to the 10Mbps Ethernet service, it offers 96 isochronous, digital circuit switched 64Kbps Bearer channels (B channels) on a full duplex interface. The aggregated B channels are called a single C channel. A 64Kbps D channel is also provided for use as a signaling channel, and a 96Kbps M channel is included for maintenance; that is, to transport physical layer control and status data to the remote end of the link. Two pairs of CAT-3, -4, or -5 UTP wiring up to the usual 100 meters is employed. It's the same configuration that is used for the standard 10Base-T Ethernet. This wiring configuration is already widely used in many companies.

Combining Ethernet with ISDN

IsoEthernet actually combines two physical layers: Ethernet and ISDN. Currently, 10Base-T relies on a half-duplex packet-switched mechanism, which is not adequate for video and other real-time transmissions. IsoEthernet overcomes this limitation by making use of the ISDN phone network's full duplex, synchronized capabilities. Through use of FDDI's encoding scheme, the 10Mbps of bandwidth is expanded into 16.144Mbps over the same wire. This bandwidth is the equivalent of the standard 10Mbps Ethernet data pipe, plus four ISDN PRI connections of 1.5Mbps each (or 96 64Kbps B channels).

The total of all connections equals 16.144Mbps to every desktop in the network; enough to conduct 15 videoconferencing sessions with up to 30 frames-per-second quality, synchronized voice, and simultaneous data collaboration applications.

The voice or video traffic is sent over the additional 6.144Mbps of isochronous bandwidth. The aggregate of these B channels is designated as a C channel. The remaining 10Mbps is used for Ethernet data packets, just as it always was (see Figure 6.1). The integration of Ethernet and ISDN data is accomplished directly at the desktop PC and hub, through standard UTP cabling. One of the biggest advantages of IsoEthernet is that it can run over existing CAT-3 cabling, while offering the same voice quality that users get with an ISDN phone line.

Existing 10Mbps Ethernet uses a half-duplex, packet switching protocol, which is inadequate for video or real-time communications. IsoEthernet overcomes this limitation by using ISDN's full-duplex, synchronized capabilities. The connection is made at the desktop PC and hub with standard UTP cabling. In all, the total bandwidth equals:

- 10Mbps for standard Ethernet data traffic
- 6.144Mbps of B-ISDN traffic
- A 64Kbps D channel used for signaling
- A 96Kbps M channel used for maintenance

FIG. 6.1
IsoEthernet uses encoding to transform a 10Mbps connection into multiple channels for standard Ethernet and ISDN multimedia traffic.

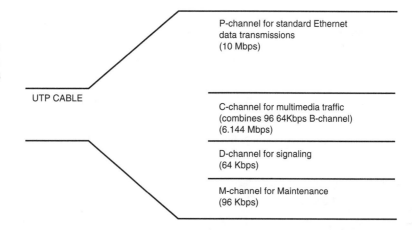

UTP CABLE

P-channel for standard Ethernet data transmissions (10 Mbps)

C-channel for multimedia traffic (combines 96 64Kbps B-channel) (6.144 Mbps)

D-channel for signaling (64 Kbps)

M-channel for Maintenance (96 Kbps)

Physical Layer   IsoEthernet's physical layer, which corresponds to the lowest level of the seven-layer OSI Networking model, is divided into three sublayers:

- Physical Medium Dependent (PMD) sublayer
- Physical Signaling (PS) sublayer
- Hybrid Multiplexing (HMUX) sublayer

The PMD sublayer executes the NRZI (Non-Return to Zero Inverted) encoding scheme, and establishes the interface to the UTP wiring. NRZI is an encoding scheme that inverts a "one" signal, which indicates a change in voltage. But NRZI leaves the "zero" signal, which indicates the absence of a voltage change; in other words, the voltage is un-changed.

The PS sublayer is a transitional layer, which receives data from the HMUX sublayer, adds the Time Division Multiplexing (TDM) information encoded in the 4B/5B encoding scheme, and sends it to the PMD layer. The 4B/5B encoding scheme, commonly used in FDDI, forms the basis of IsoEthernet, and gives it the extra bandwidth it needs. This scheme takes a group of four bits, and represents it as a five-bit symbol, thereby making the encoding 80 percent more efficient.

Standard Ethernet uses the Manchester signal encoding method, a biphase encoding mechanism that is less efficient than 4B/5B.

Ch
6

Communications Channels   The HMUX sublayer establishes an interface with the P channel, the C channel, and the D channel. Again, the P channel is the 10Mbps Ethernet channel; the C channel is the combination of the 64Kbps B channels; and the D channel is the 64Kbps signaling channel.

The P channel is a half-duplex or full-duplex 10Mbps channel, used to carry the packetized Ethernet information using CSMA/CD. This channel is the standard Ethernet channel.

The C channel is a full-duplex, isochronous, circuit-switched channel carrying multiples of 64Kbps.

The M channel is also a full-duplex channel carrying 96Kbps, and is used for carrying low-level control and status information. This channel is where automatic detection, network clock synchronization, error detection, and other maintenance information is carried.

In addition, an extra Start-of-Frame Delimiter channel is included. This 64Kbps channel carries the start of the TDM frame synchronization pattern.

IsoEthernet's C channel functions similar to ISDN, and can be configured in any multiple of 64Kbps. The procedures used to do so are specified in the ITU Q.93x protocol suite commonly used in ISDN and less commonly in ATM links. Consequently, ISDN, ATM, and IsoEthernet networks are easily interoperable.

Specifically, the Q.93I protocol (IEEE 802.9a UNI Signaling) is used for point-to-point connection control and other Supplementary services. The connection control provides the basic services used on the B-channels, including establishment, maintenance, and clearing of the channels. Supplementary services include the following:

- Call transfer, where any C channel call can be transferred to another ISDN or IsoEthernet end station.
- Call hold, where a C channel call can be placed on "hold" and retrieved at a later time, thereby allowing more than one application to use the same connection.
- Conference, where multiple users connected to the ISDN or IsoEthernet network can participate in a joint session. This is the feature that makes both voice-conferencing and videoconferencing possible.
- Point-to-Multipoint and Multipoint-to-Multipoint links. This feature enables applications such as videomail or broadcasts.

Modes of Operation

IsoEthernet can function in three separate modes:

- *Multi-service mode*. All channels are accommodated. The 10Mbps P channel, 6.144Mbps C channel, 64Kbps D channel, 96Kbps M channel, and the 64Kbps Start-of-Frame Delimiter channel are all provided for in multi-service mode.

- *All-isochronous mode*. In all-isochronous mode, the full bandwidth is made available for circuit-switched isochronous data transfer. This provides a total of 248 B channels (15.872Mbps), in addition to the standard D, M, and Start-of-Frame Delimiter channels. The 10Mbps Ethernet P channel is not included in all-isochronous mode.

- *10Base-T mode*. In 10Base-T mode, the IsoEthernet layer functions as a 10Base-T transceiver, and there are no provisions for the C, D, M, or Start-of-Frame Delimiter channels. This mode is the functional equivalent of a standard 10Base-T network.

The mode is automatically configured with the Auto-Negotiation link pulse signaling mechanism, and allows different service channel combinations to become available to each end-user application. Consequently, IsoEthernet and 10Base-T devices can exist on the same LAN. In fact, a 10Base-T network can exist transparently within an IsoEthernet LAN.

The Auto-Negotiation mechanism is common to both 802.3 Ethernet networks and 802.9a IsoEthernet networks. This scheme gives network devices the ability to advertise their modes of operation during power-up, and provides a framework that allows the network devices to automatically configure themselves according to their capabilities. This scheme uses a simple algorithm to allow both ends of a link to discover what common modes of operation are available between them, and to select the most appropriate mode. This Auto-Negotiation mechanism allows an IsoEthernet network to dynamically move between Multi-Service, All-isochronous, and 10Base-T modes.

Multimedia Over IsoEthernet

Integration of data with voice and video at the desktop level will produce unparalleled levels of productivity . Users could easily initiate voice or video conferences directly from their desks, or even create a virtual workgroup. However, multimedia has not been possible over a traditional 10Mbps Ethernet LAN, due to its contentious nature. IsoEthernet adds this level of support through a simple and easy-to-implement mechanism.

IsoEthernet's handy multimedia dial tone supports both the public switched telephone network (PSTN) and ISDN, allowing both types of users to make and receive calls to each other, with the quality of service determined by each end station's capabilities.

Ch
6

IsoEthernet is not an attempt to create a new multimedia network, instead, it becomes a part of the existing WAN.

Basic voice service can be established on the IsoEthernet network, by applying one of the 64Kbps B channels for this purpose. An IsoEthernet segment operating in 10Base-T mode is connected to existing 10Base-T end-stations, establishing Ethernet backwards compatibility. IsoEthernet segments running all-isochronous mode are connected to high-speed video servers, for applications where larger network bandwidth is required.

Furthermore, ATM cells can also be carried over the isochronous network. Signaling requirements for IsoEthernet, ATM and ISDN are all very similar. Because IsoEthernet has the unique ability to provide circuit-mode, cell-mode, and packet-mode services simultaneously, the technology is uniquely positioned to interface with a wide variety of networks with little overhead.

IsoEthernet technology makes it possible for desktop users to enjoy a vast amount of access to applications that were previously inaccessible. In addition to videoconferencing, IsoEthernet has the potential to allow applications such as: Digital fax, broadcast television integration, universal inbox, computer telephones, direct Internet access, and MPEG video playback.

Multimedia gives users the ability to combine voice, video, and data, but requires an efficient and low-latency underlying network structure capable of transporting this delay-sensitive data. Some potential applications are:

- *Multimedia desktop collaboration.* This application lets users hold a real-time multimedia visual conference, while using screen sharing applications and enjoying real-time document collaboration.
- *Multimedia mail.* This is a type of application for distributing multimedia files and messages, and may eventually become an extension to existing communications services.
- *Multimedia information services.* These applications let end users access multimedia information from different sources, and use it in the desktop environment.

Isochronous communications, including IsoEthernet, are ideal for delivering video and data conferencing, multimedia PC network and PBX telephone system integration, automatic call distribution, and other telephony services to the desktop. This remarkably rich set of possibilities has a great deal of potential for telecommuters wishing to integrate with their home base at all levels.

Isochronous Ethernet was created to offer multimedia networking, including voice and video to the desktop level. To accomplish this feat, a technology must be able to:

- Deliver Quality of Service (QoS) guarantees
- Seamlessly integrate with the existing network infrastructure
- Be installed gradually and at low cost
- Offer compatibility with ATM and other technologies

Minor delays in a voice conversation can be a big source of annoyance. But it is more than annoying; delays, echoes, and distortion can be quite disruptive and detrimental to business. An isochronous protocol, such as ISDN, is necessary to ensure the same quality we enjoy over standard telephone connections. Isochronous networks operate in real-time. IsoEthernet adds isochronous capability to standard Ethernet.

ISDN technology has grown in popularity very quickly over the past few years, and most carriers offer an affordable ISDN service. However, there has not been any practical way to deliver ISDN services over the LAN until the availability of IsoEthernet.

Video over IsoEthernet   IsoEthernet delivers full-screen video at 30 frames per second, along with perfect audio synchronization. End users have long clamored for this capability, but MIS has traditionally been reluctant because of the perceived need for major forklift upgrades and new cabling. IsoEthernet can meet these demands for fast frames with existing technology.

Apple Computer's QuickTime Conferencing system has demonstrated that it can make H.320 calls over IsoEthernet. Through IsoEthernet, Macintosh and PowerMacintosh users can tie in with the digital Public Switched Telephone Network services, which can be accessed by IsoEthernet in increments of 56Kbps or 64Kbps B channels while also supporting full-bandwidth 10Mbps Ethernet. With IsoEthernet, multimedia traffic receives high priority, but the Ethernet network itself has no impact on voice and video, even if operating at full capacity.

QuickTime Conferencing users will be able to communicate with others not only on Macintoshes, but also on PCs, and with H.320 videoconferencing systems from companies such as PictureTel. Calls can be made from anywhere over a digital PSTN. In addition, because IsoEthernet facilitates on-demand, real-time interactive communications, videoconferences will no longer need to be scheduled in advance.

IsoEthernet lets Macintosh and PC users gain access to interactive network services and applications on-demand. High-quality videoconferencing, shared whiteboards and other applications, and other services can be achieved through this innovative new technology. Through IsoEthernet, participants in a conference can share an application while simultaneously taking part in a videoconference. However, these high-powered applications will not affect the data network or PC performance.

Ch
6

Video runs at an impressive 30 frames per second, bandwidth is guaranteed and trouble-free. Because IsoEthernet can run over existing CAT-3 or CAT-5 cabling, no expensive wiring upgrades are required.

Real-time multimedia conferencing is a reality through IsoEthernet technology, which can now bring videoconferencing to the desktop level. The videoconference traffic is independent of all other Ethernet traffic, and can connect over a wide area ISDN network.

IsoEthernet and ATM

ATM and IsoEthernet work well together, and both use the same Q.93x-based signaling protocol for establishing point-to-point connections. IsoEthernet, when configured in either the all-isochronous or multi-service mode of operation, can be used as a low-cost desktop ATM solution. It is easy to carry ATM cells over the C channel, which can be configured to meet ATM's load demands.

Work is being done to incorporate support for desktop ATM over IsoEthernet, and also to develop a standard for hub-to-hub connectivity. ATM support means that IsoEthernet can be used as a migration path to a future ATM network, and may give companies a solution for gradual deployment of ATM.

IsoEthernet can be incrementally upgraded. Because it is actually a type of Ethernet, it uses the same Ethernet encoding when communicating to non-IsoEthernet users.

In addition, Asynchronous Transfer Mode (ATM) cells can be sent over the IsoEthernet network. There are a number of similarities between ATM and IsoEthernet; both use the same Q.93x signaling protocol. An ATM cell can be sent over the C channel; and the C channel traffic can be easily converted into cells by the Isochronous Switching/Multiplexing unit for transport over the ATM network.

Quality of Service Guarantees

In order to transmit multimedia over the network, a few basic problems have to be worked out. When sending pure data over Ethernet, packets do not necessarily arrive in order, and in the end, the order is irrelevant because they are eventually reassembled at the receiving end. When receiving a video broadcast, however, it is critically important that the packets arrive in precisely the right order so the integrity of the broadcast is maintained. If the packets arrive slightly out of order, the video will arrive jittery and the audio will be garbled.

Because of the collision-oriented nature of Ethernet, packets naturally arrive out of order. So how is it possible to send multimedia over Ethernet? We start with a Quality of Service approach. Offering a level of service is essential to providing end users with the audio and video quality to which they are accustomed.

Quality of Service (QoS) guarantees, which are offered in other technologies such as ATM but not on Ethernet, offer different levels of safeguards for different types of data. Through these QoS levels, multimedia data can get the type of transport it needs in order to arrive in a timely fashion with a minimum of jitter on the receiving end. Multimedia Desktop Collaboration (MMDC) has the strictest QoS requirements. The Multimedia Communications Forum's Multimedia Communications Quality of Service document, based on ITU guidelines, lays out two sets of requirements for MMDC; the MMDC Teleservices Quality of Service Level, and the MMDC Bearer Services QoS Level. Both levels specify three QoS classes:

- Class 1   basic multimedia
- Class 2   enhanced multimedia
- Class 3   premium multimedia

Unfortunately, many multimedia collaboration solutions deliver substandard quality, out-of-sync audio and video, and jittery reception. However, in order for it to be used for standard business uses, the performance must be superior. This is where the Class 3 (Premium) service in the MMCF specification comes in.

Class 3 service applies to very demanding situations, offering a worst-case delay performance of under 10 ms, and a guaranteed worst-case bandwidth of 1,000Kbps to each user. The performance offered at this level is even enough to support conventional telephone conversations and HDTV transmission.

The Teleservices specification encompasses the LAN, WAN, and Terminal Equipment; the Bearer services specification addresses the network only.

The MMDC Teleservices QoS specifications are explained in Table 6.1 and 6.2.

Table 6.1   MMDC Teleservices QoS Specifications

	Class 1	Class 2	Class 3
Audio transfer delay with echo control	<400 ms	<400 ms	<150 ms
Audio frequency range	>0.3 to 3.4 kHz	>0.3 to 3.4 kHz	>0.05 to 6.8 kHz
Audio level	20dBm	20dBm	20dBm
Audio error free interval	>5 min	> 15 min	> 30 min
Video transfer delay	Still image < 10s	< 600 ms	<250 ms

Ch
6

continues

Table 6.1   Continued

	Class 1	Class 2	Class 3
Video/audio differential delay	N/A	>-400 and <200 ms	>-150 and <100 ms
Video frame rate	N/A	$\geq$5 frames/s	$\geq$25 frames/s
Video resolution	N/A	$\geq$176 x 144	$\geq$352 x 288
Video error free interval	N/A	>15 min	>30 min
DSD/audio differential delay	<1 s	<200 ms	<100 ms
DSD error free interval	>5 min	>15 min	>30 min
Data rate	$\geq$5Kbps	$\geq$50Kbps	$\geq$500Kbps

Table 6.2   MMDC Bearer Services (Private Network) QoS Specifications

	Class 1	Class 2	Class 3
Equivalent transfer delay with echo control	<20 ms	<20 ms	<10 ms
User information transfer rate	$\geq$10Kbps	$\geq$100Kbps	$\geq$1,000Kbps
Error free seconds ratio	>99.5%	>99.75%	>99.9%
Severely impaired seconds ratio	<0.03%	<0.01%	<0.005%

Video/audio differential delay describes the user's perceived difference in delay between the video and audio media. This parameter is defined as the video delay minus the audio delay. A negative value indicates that the video delay is less than the audio delay.

In general, these specifications call for a low latency, guaranteed bandwidth and low jitter rates.

Class 3 (Premium) QoS is meant for professional office staff who need one solution to address several multimedia needs. Class 2 (Enhanced) is more oriented towards small office/home office (SOHO) workers with more modest requirements. Class 1 (Basic) service has the broadest application, and is meant more for users with only occasional needs for multimedia and for whom cost is a major factor.

Some potential applications for each class of service are illustrated in the following table:

Class 1

Video	Still camera color images
Audio	PSTN
Text	Delay < 2 sec
	Jerky delivery
Graphics/Image	Single image
	Delay < 10 sec
	VGA color
Animation	None

Class 2

Video	Talking heads
	Jerky
	> 5 frames/sec
Audio	PSTN
	Apparent synchronization with video
Text	No perceptible delay
	Steady delivery
Graphics/Image	Near real-time delivery of graphics
	GUI support
Animation	Slide show presentations with motion

Class 3

Video	VCR quality
	Multiple video windows
Audio	Capable of two or more channels
	Better than PSTN
Text	No perceptible delay
	Steady delivery
Graphics/Image	No perceptible delay
	High resolution
Animation	Cartoon-like animation

Ch
6

Topology

IsoEthernet can be deployed in a standard star configuration similar to 10Base-T. Each end station is connected to a central hub. A multimedia workstation connected to the IsoEthernet network can run multimedia applications, and can establish a connection with other workstations running the same application. Voice services can also be provided for by using one of the 64Kbps B channels.

In addition, separate IsoEthernet segments can be configured to operate in 10Base-T mode to connect with existing 10Base-T workstations, thereby establishing backward-compatibility with existing standard Ethernet workstations. A third IsoEthernet segment can be configured in All-isochronous mode for linking up to video servers needing a high degree of bandwidth.

Advantages of IsoEthernet

A major selling point for IsoEthernet is its full compatibility with existing ISDN, Ethernet, and ATM infrastructures. Its ease-of-use and compatibility means that the existing infrastructure can be preserved, network subsystems need not be replaced, and IsoEthernet can be introduced gradually. Its WAN compatibility means that there are no hardware gateways required.

Some of IsoEthernet's advantages include:

- Compatibility with existing ISDN and POTS networks
- Transparency with existing Ethernet LAN end users, applications, network operating systems, and protocols
- Guaranteed Quality of Service and bandwidth-on-demand
- Interoperability with H.320, T.120 and MPEG standards
- Capability of running on CAT-3 UTP wiring with no changes
- Multivendor interoperability

IsoEthernet is fully compatible with both Ethernet and ISDN, making it a good solution for gradually introducing multimedia into an existing network. IsoEthernet will seamlessly integrate with both local and long distance ISDN services with no additional gateway required. It is also compatible with the existing H.320 conferencing standard, JPEG code systems, and standard telephony.

Product Overview

Several vendors have products supporting IsoEthernet, including Microsoft's Telephony Applications Programming Interface (TAPI). Numerous hardware products are also available, including network cards and IsoEthernet hubs.

A major element in isochronous solutions are the networking hubs available from companies such as Ascom Nexion, Ericsson Business Networks AB, Luxcom Inc., and Incite. They all offer products with the LAN connections, such as IsoEthernet and Ethernet. They also all offer WAN connections such as E1, T1, BRI, and PRI, which allow networked users to easily communicate remotely while using the same applications and services as the remote station. Furthermore, the 802.9a IsoEthernet-compliant products permit isochronous circuits to be distributed to network users, while still preserving existing LAN wiring systems.

Because IsoEthernet is based on two long-standing technologies, 10Base-T Ethernet and ISDN, no major upgrade is required. Any existing 10Base-T network can be upgraded simply by adding an adjunct hub to the wiring closet, and adding IsoEthernet adapter cards to each PC. Several companies, most notably those participating in the incAlliance, already offer these products at reasonable prices.

Ascom Nexion

http://www.nexen.com
289 Great Road
Acton, MA 01720
Voice: 508-266-4500
Fax: 508-266-2300

The NEXEN 2000 product family is compatible with standard Ethernet 10Base-T UTP cabling, so no new wiring is needed to take advantage of this technology. The existing network infrastructure—including applications, routers, bridges, and switches—can still be used. The NEXEN 2200 uses Isochronous Ethernet technology to integrate the circuit and frame services required by voice, video, and data traffic over existing CAT-3 cabling. With NEXEN 2200, network administrators can deploy multimedia and CTI (Computer Telephony Integration) applications across an existing LAN.

Ch
6

National Semiconductor

2900 Semiconductor Drive
P.O. Box 58090
Santa Clara, CA 95052
Voice: 408-721-5000

National's IsoEthernet ISA Adapter is the only PC adapter that allows integrated multimedia and computer telephony applications to run over a single integrated LAN connection with a quality and feature set equal to that of POTS. National's IsoEthernet Workgroup solution includes the adapter and a workgroup hub/switch. The solution is all that is required to implement an Isochronous Ethernet-compliant LAN. With this solution, the PC has a single link to data systems and terminals, telephone network services, and videoconferencing centers. The adapter can run existing Ethernet data applications, as well as N*64 ISDN compatible voice, video, and data applications on the PC. All traffic, including Ethernet and isochronous, is routed through the standards-based adapter. The software driver modules necessary to facilitate the network connection and installation are included with the adapter. The adapter uses a standard RJ-45 network connector, and supports CAT-3, CAT-4, or CAT-5 wiring with a maximum hub-to-node length of 100 meters.

National Semiconductor's IsoEthernet PC-ISA and NuBus adapter cards were released shortly after ratification of the IsoEthernet standard by the IEEE. National's adapter cards are bundled with hubs from other members of the incAlliance, and they are marketed as complete solutions.

Incite

http://www.incite.com
5057 Keller Springs Rd.
Dallas, TX 75248
Voice: 972-447-8200 or 800-946-2483
Fax: 972-447-8205
E-mail: info@incite.com

Incite offers a specialized hub and accompanying software, to allow video, voice, and data to be integrated over existing cabling. Their Conversational Media line includes a 12-port local hub, four-port WAN hub, Multimedia Manager software for Windows NT servers, and client software. Products such as Incite's allow users to add multimedia to the LAN without a costly forklift upgrade to a new technology, such as ATM. Incite's configuration places a local multimedia hub to connect IsoEthernet clients, existing Ethernet data

LANs, the Windows NT-based multimedia server, and the WAN hub. The software supports SNMP-based network management, and the WAN hub can connect the PBX to the LAN. The Conversational Media line supports H.320 full-motion video and MPEG traffic.

Luxcom

http://www.Luxcom.com
3249 Laurelview Court
Fremont, CA 94538
Voice: 800-322-5000 or 510-770-3300
Fax: 510-770-3399
E-mail: **info@luxcom.com**

Luxcom's isoMAX Isochronous Multimedia Access Switch offers LAN/WAN access and switching services for IsoEthernet desktops, making it easy to gradually integrate multimedia into the workplace. The solution is completely transparent to end users, applications, and network operating systems; WAN access is accomplished through ISDN. Any user attached to the isoMAX switch can place a multimedia call, or a standard telephony call anywhere in the world.

Luxcom's isoMAX solution (see Figure 6.2) includes two components, the isoMAX Hub and isoMAX Server, which are used together to connect, switch, and disconnect multimedia calls. The hub is used to offer an individual interface for each multimedia workstation, and does the actual circuit switching. The hub is designed for the wiring closet. The Server component controls the call setup and release, and is used to establish links with remote stations through the ISDN/PRI interface. Also included in the Server component are SNMP management functions.

The isoMAX offers a departmental solution; and individual isoMAX subsystems can be connected through the Luxcom Series 2000 Multiplexing Hub to create a larger system. The Multiplexing Hub establishes a 100Mbps fiber-optic backbone to support isoEThernet, Ethernet, and token ring LANs, T1/E1 connectivity, and legacy terminal communications.

Ch
6

The isoMAX solution offers the following benefits:

- A ready-to-run multimedia network.
- ISDN and Ethernet on the same desktop connection.
- Support for multimedia conferencing, information retrieval and computer-telephony integration applications.
- Full LAN/WAN compatibility with guaranteed quality of service.
- Integrated BONDING for bandwidth-on-demand.

  ■ Compliance with the IEEE 802.9a IsoEthernet standard.

  ■ Compatibility with future ATM-based networks.

FIG. 6.2
Luxcom isoMAX
Solution.

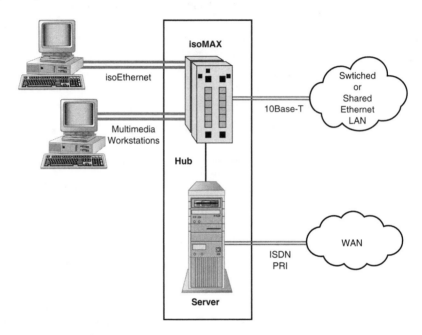

In order to accommodate voice, the server component offers some of the same features of PBX systems for controlling calls between the IsoEthernet workstation and the WAN. Through Q.931 signaling, the system maintains compatibility with any local or long-distance switching service, and narrowband and wideband ISDN.

The server module also supports SQL databases for management, and can be managed from a local console or externally via Telnet or an SNMP manager. The SNMP agent allows it to be controlled either from the isoMAX Manager application, or from OpenView, NetView, or SunNet. The management functions can be used to monitor system status and activity, the server incorporates SQL database technology for all necessary management functions, and can be managed from a local console, or via an external Telnet or SNMP manager. The included SNMP agent can be managed from the isoMAX Manager application, or from OpenView, NetView, or SunNet Manager. The management functions can track the following:

  ■ System status and activity

  ■ Users and user groups with access privileges based on time, bandwidth, and geography

  ■ Hub port and WAN interface configurations

- Telephone directory and dialing information
- SNMP agent, MIB II, and private MIB variables
- Event and alarm logs
- Software download and software configuration
- Loopback and other diagnostic tests

The isoMAX comes ready to run, and establishes a full multimedia network for IsoEthernet stations upon plug-in.

Summary

IsoEthernet integrates ISDN and Ethernet technologies over the same circuit. Using an encoding scheme, IsoEthernet is able to extract an additional 6.144Mbps of bandwidth out of Ethernet's 10Mbps. This additional 6.144Mbps is subdivided into 96 ISDN B channels, which are used for multimedia traffic.

Integrating IsoEthernet into an existing 10Base-T network can be done seamlessly and with very little trouble and expense. An IsoEthernet hub is required, and all workstations must be equipped with an IsoEthernet attachment unit interface (AUI), which is connected to the IsoEthernet hub.

IsoEthernet can operate in one of three modes: multiservice, all-isochronous, and Multiservice. Multi-service accommodates the 10Mbps channel, as well as all of the ISDN channels; the all-isochronous mode makes the full bandwidth available for isochronous data transfer. The 10Base-T mode does not include any provisions for the ISDN channels, and is the equivalent of standard 10BaseT. ●

Ch
6

Switched Multimegabit Data Service (SMDS)

Need to connect a branch office in Tombstone, Arizona with the New York headquarters? Blow away the tumbleweeds and hitch up the wagons to SMDS. Switched Multimegabit Data Service is one of the lesser-known technologies, although it was initially developed by Bellcore in the 1980s, and deployed in 1991 with the formation of the SMDS Interest Group (**http://www. smds-ig.org**), which can be used to internetwork multiple LANs over a wide geographical distance using standard telephone lines. SMDS is often used to connect remote branch offices to headquarters, and it is one of a very few switched broadband services that is capable of carrying network traffic throughout the country or even internationally. SMDS can be an especially valuable alternative for companies currently using costly private or dedicated lines between sites. In the U.S., SMDS has not yet gained widespread acceptance, although the technology is solid and is becoming more widely available. In Europe, however, SMDS has been more widely used, although it is referred to as Connectionless Broadband Data Service (CBDS) on that continent. ■

SMDS is used to internetwork LANs through the public telephone network. Because it is a connectionless technology, carrier switches do not need to establish a call path between two transmission points as they do with frame relay. Instead, the SMDS access devices generate 53-byte cells and pass them to the carrier switch. Each cell's header contains address information. The switch reads this address information and forwards each cell over any available path to the destination.

Even though the cells may travel over different paths, they still arrive in the correct order. Connectionless technology eliminates the need for physical connections between each fixed location, and overcomes the need for precise traffic flow predictions. This model permits the data to travel over the least congested routes, which, in turn, contributes to a faster data transmission rate.

The past few years have seen the development of numerous high-performance LAN and WAN technologies, such as ATM, Gigabit Ethernet, HiPPI, and Fibre Channel. As these and other high-speed technologies take hold, users respond by demanding more access and bigger applications. As a result of the increase in high-speed LANs, there is a corresponding need for a high-performance, wide-area LAN interconnect service. SMDS, a switched, connectionless broadband data service, is designed to meet this interconnect requirement. It can accommodate a transmission rate of 45Mbps in the U.S. and 34Mbps in Europe, and eventually will achieve rates of 155Mbps. It is easy to move from an existing LAN interconnect framework based on leased lines and private switched networks to SMDS, and the service is especially good for traffic that requires a low transit delay.

SMDS's nationwide networking capabilities were demonstrated for the first time in 1994, at a NetWorld+Interop conference, where demonstrations were carried out by the National SMDS Inter-Carrier Interface (ICI) Consortium. These early trials were successful in demonstrating this nationwide capability, as well as the incredibly rich interoperability level of SMDS switches.

Local SMDS clouds across the country can be connected using an SMDS link, running from 56Kbps to 34Mbps. Ultimately, establishing a connection through inter-LATA (Local Access and Transport Area) SMDS will be as simple as placing a long-distance telephone call.

Although wide-area links can be made with ATM or frame-relay services, inter-LATA SMDS does not require users to preconfigure network connections, or to reconfigure the network for every new business condition. A new site can be added easily, and at a low incremental cost. The phone company does most of the work, connecting local SMDS clouds and plugging in the SMDS switch.

Although SMDS has not caught on in the United States to any great extent, it is widely used in Europe, especially in Germany and the U.K. British Telecom and Deutsche Telekom have numerous SMDS access points. The British providers in particular offer the service at a comparatively low cost, making it more cost-effective than frame relay.

Because SMDS is connectionless, users do not have to establish permanent virtual circuits (PVCs), as is required with a frame relay configuration. Having to establish a PVC requires some second-guessing on the part of the user, which may lead to ordering more bandwidth than is actually necessary. Also, whenever the network configuration changes, the PVCs must also be changed, which brings the network administrator quite a lot of work indeed.

Overview of Switched Multimegabit Data Service (SMDS)

SMDS is a connectionless, cell-switching public data transport service. The technology-independent service can operate with frame relay, FDDI, and ATM, as well as dedicated private lines. SMDS, like ATM, is a packet-based service and can be used to establish a high-speed network with up to 45Mbps of throughput. SMDS was originally created by Bellcore and is likely to be widely utilized by telephone companies as the framework of their data networks. It is currently offered by several of the Regional Bell Operating Companies (RBOCs) and MCI.

SMDS has not enjoyed nearly as much press as the more high-profile fast networking technologies, such as ATM or Fast Ethernet. However, for connecting LANs or communicating with business partners, SMDS is worth a second look, and in fact, offers some significant advantages over frame relay and ATM. Network design is much simpler with SMDS, and in many cases, SMDS may be less costly. Although it cannot reach the same ultra-high speeds as ATM, SMDS may be the ideal technology for companies that need to connect several remote branch offices for data exchange, communications, and some limited multimedia.

A frame relay network requires the administrator to assign PVCs between locations, and assign each PVC a committed information rate (CIR). ATM also has complex design requirements. SMDS, on the other hand, establishes any-to-any connectivity with little complexity. Every location that needs to connect with the network has an E.164 address (which is very similar to a standard telephone number). The administrator selects the port connection speed and nothing else—everything else is left to the phone company. After the connection has been established, any node can communicate with any other node on the SMDS network.

Ch

7

However, the sender must know the recipient's E.164 address. The E.164 address is globally valid, and each subscriber network interface (SNI) can be given as many as 16 separate E.164 addresses. All data is sent at the specified port connection speed; individual connections are not configured separately. The technology is highly scalable; adding a site is fairly inexpensive and straightforward. The only extra expense is the extra port connection charge and the usage fees. However, usage fees can be difficult to anticipate, but some providers offer a flat billing service that some users may find to be more convenient.

SMDS is one of a handful of existing cell relay technologies that uses a fixed, 53-byte cell format. Cell relay is a high-bandwidth, low-delay, switching/multiplexing packet technology that is used in B-ISDN-based networks. SMDS includes facilities for simplified error and flow control and uses fixed-length cells to facilitate high-speed switching. ATM is the best-known implementation of cell relay and is defined to work over different physical media at speeds of up to 622Mbps. SMDS, like ATM, is a standards-based cell relay architecture. Transmission speeds range from 1.5 to 45Mbps.

Technically speaking, SMDS is not a true cell-relay service, it is a connectionless packet-switched service. In reality, SMDS provides a datagram service, with packets that contain a 40-octet header and up to 9,188 octets of data. These large packets obviously cannot be transported on top of a connection-oriented ATM service.

However, some users may consider SMDS to be a de facto cell-relay service, because the SMDS Subscriber Network Interface (SNI) uses the IEEE 802.6 Distributed Queue Dual Bus (DQDB) access. DQDB is a type of cell relay. Before SMDS can use DQDB, SMDS must divide its packets into fixed-size, 53-byte cells, with 5-octet headers and 48-octet payloads for transport.

SMDS is very similar to ATM, which also uses 53-byte cells, although many administrators have shown a preference to ATM, largely because of the ability to deploy ATM down to the desktop level. There is, however, a very clear migration path for moving from SMDS to ATM, and a mechanism for ATM and SMDS interworking. The two technologies are highly complementary and ideal for using SMDS to connect branch offices to an ATM-based headquarters operation.

Although SMDS does have many similarities to ATM switching, it provides for a more scaled approach. As users' requirements increase, SMDS provides a good migration path to the higher-bandwidth ATM. SMDS includes facilities for high-speed LAN interconnection.

One major advantage SMDS may bring corporate users is that it can help to reduce transmission costs by replacing multiple dedicated lines with a single packet-switched line.

In California, SMDS is available to almost all of Pacific Bell's customers and is available at bandwidths that align with native LAN speeds of 4Mbps, 10Mbps and 15Mbps.

Some of the advantages of SMDS include:

- High-speed, low-delay, connectionless data transport. Call setup is not required, and packets are sent out as soon as they are received.
- Any-to-any connectivity
- Multicasting
- E.164 addressing (similar to standard telephone numbers)
- Support for major LAN/WAN protocols
- Scalability
- Ability to be managed by SNMP-based systems
- Call blocking, validation, screening, and other security mechanisms

SMDS can be used to seamlessly internetwork Ethernet, Token Ring, FDDI, and ATM LANs over a large geographic area using the regular telephone lines. The basics of connecting a LAN to the SMDS cloud are only a router, SMDS-compatible DSU/CSU, and an SMDS host adapter card.

Smaller companies can also enjoy the benefits of SMDS by purchasing a fractional line in increments of 56Kbps or 64Kbps. Services can be offered at these speeds through the SMDS Data Exchange Interface (DXI).

SMDS, because it is based on E.164 addressing, is easy to interconnect. Just like regular telephone service, if an SMDS address is known, an SMDS user can simply call it up and send data. SMDS can make an efficient alternative to dedicated leased lines, and computers and peripheral devices can be directly attached.

SMDS can coexist with dedicated lines, which means customers can create their own hybrid private/public networks. New sites are easy to add and require little configuration, all that is needed to add a node to the SMDS network is to update the database on the SMDS switch.

Also, because it is technology-independent, several different network technologies can be used in the SMDS internetwork.

Standards Development

The SMDS Interest Group (SIG) shares a common goal with the ATM Forum and Frame Relay Forum in promoting widespread and cost-effective availability of fast-packet and broadband services. Members of all three forums are moving toward consensus on the underlying technology. The three associations have many members in common, but each also has its own unique roster. Because SMDS is complementary to frame relay, the SIG has close ties to the Frame Rely Forum (FRF). Recently, close ties have also been established with the ATM Forum to promote the interworking of both technologies.

SMDS was developed by Bellcore. In Europe, the standard has been adapted to include European transmission speeds by the European SMDS Interest Group (ESIG) and the European Telecommunications Standards Institute (ETSI).

The American SIG was founded in 1990, just months before the creation of the ATM Forum and Frame Relay Forum. The North American organization has international affiliates, with members including users, consultants, providers, and equipment vendors.

SMDS service can be carried on different network platforms, and is not specific to any given network technology. Currently, the primary platform used for SMDS is DQDB, which is defined by the IEEE 802.6 Metropolitan Area Network (MAN) standard.

Implementation and Infrastructure

In order to provide its connectionless data service, SMDS is based on variable-length packets (*datagrams*). Each datagram includes source and destination information, so it can be sent independently over the network. One SMDS packet can be up to 9,188 bytes long. Because the SMDS data unit can contain as many as 9,188 bytes, it can encapsulate a full IEEE 802.3, 802.4, 802.5, or FDDI frame.

Although SMDS is used primarily for data communications, there have been some demonstrations that show SMDS as an effective medium for low-cost videoconferencing. Although an SMDS-based video transmission may experience a little delay and jitter, the versatility and low cost of an SMDS videoconferencing solution may far outweigh these minor inconveniences for many users. Furthermore, SMDS's group addressing scheme can also enhance videoconferencing, by allowing a user to broadcast a videoconference to multiple sites. Also, because of its addressing scheme and its capability to reach far across the country to many remote sites, SMDS is very well-suited to workgroup collaboration. SMDS's group addressing feature can be used to create multiple, virtual private networks (VPNs). These VPNs are easy to create and modify.

Another major advantage that lends itself to workgroup collaboration is SMDS's flexibility and any-to-any connectivity, which makes it simple to add and drop sites as needed.

SMDS is made up of three layers:

- A switching infrastructure, with SMDS switches
- The Subscriber Network Interface (SNI), which is the delivery system made up of nondedicated T-1 and T-3 circuits
- An access control system, used by end users to connect to the switching infrastructure

The SMDS service is not tied to any specific underlying network type and can be carried over different network platforms. As a result, users are free to alter their underlying network technology while still maintaining the SMDS service.

Addressing Scheme

The unique SMDS addresses are in the E.164 format and are the same type used for ISDN numbers. Every SMDS connection has at least one address but can have multiple addresses. An address group can be defined for multicast transmissions, and further screening applications can be implemented to accommodate closed user groups.

The first 4 bits of the address represent the address type, and the remaining 60 represent the address. When the first 4 bits are 1100 (OxC), the address is a unicast address; when the first 4 bits are 1110 (OxE), the address is a multicast address. The remaining 60 bits are in binary-coded decimal (BCD) format, with each 4 bits representing a single digit, which allows for up to 15 digits. It is necessary to specify at least 11 digits, which is the same amount of numbers that must be dialed on a telephone for a long-distance number. For example, a unicast address may be: C14085551212FFFF. A multicast address would be: E14085551212FFFF. The trailing F's are usually not displayed, and it is not necessary to type them in when entering the address. The addresses can be entered with periods (C140.8555.1212), or as a string (C14085551212).

SMDS addresses are assigned by the service provider. The addresses can be applied to either individuals or groups, and are entered into the SMDS configuration software manually. Most SMDS-compliant software packages, including Cisco's Internetwork Operating System (IOS) software, require the addresses to be entered in the 64-bit E.164 format.

Before configuring SMDS, the addresses must have already been obtained. The following address types will be required:

- Group address, for broadcasts
- SMDS hardware address for each router that interfaces with the SMDS network

Ch

7

Besides unicast and multicast addressing, SMDS also offers some other addressing features. A source address is validated by the network to verify that it has been assigned to the originating SNI. This protects against address spoofing, where a sender masquerades as another user.

Source and destination address screening may also be achieved; with source screening looking at addresses as the data units leave the network, and destination screening looking at addresses as the data units enter the network. This screening capability can be used to establish a private virtual network that weeds out all unwanted traffic. Besides adding security to the network, this model also adds more efficiency, because the SMDS-attached devices are handling less traffic.

Tariffs and Access Classes

SMDS providers typically offer a range of tariffs and services to accommodate different performance options and link speeds. The access classes offered by the providers establish limits on the user's sustained data rate and burst size. The provider tracks this by giving each access point its own credit count. This account shows the maximum amount of data that can be sent at any given time. When a packet is received, the SMDS network will refer to the access point's count. If the packet is less than the count shown, the packet length is subtracted from the credit count. If the packet is larger than the count, it is discarded.

The credit count can be as high as 9188 bytes. See Figure 7.1 for an overview of the credit count.

FIG. 7.1
SMDS providers track users' sustained data rate and burst size with credit counts.

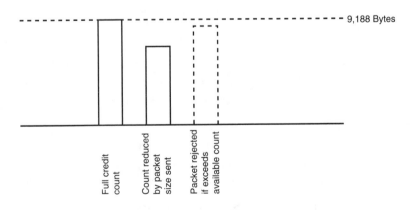

These account restrictions only apply to data moving out of the network; data coming into the network is not subject to credit counts by the receiving network.

SMDS supports several different access classes, each of which determines the maximum sustained information transfer rates and degree of burstiness.

Several access classes are available, starting at a 1.5Mbps class, which is provided through a 2Mbps link. On the 34Mbps link, access classes are available at 4, 10, 16, and 25Mbps. The full amount of bandwidth is unavailable, because of the amount of overhead involved in encapsulating the LAN packets. Because of this overhead, users are limited to approximately 75 percent; that is, the 2Mbps link can deliver only a maximum of 1.5Mbps, and the 34Mbps link can deliver only a maximum of 25Mbps.

Access classes can be changed via software; no new hardware is required so long as the link stays the same. That is, although a new hardware infrastructure would be required to move from the 1.5Mbps class to a higher class, moving between the four classes available on the 34Mbps link can be done completely through software.

Configuration

An SMDS connection requires very little in the way of hardware and software. A typical connection is shown in Figure 7.2.

FIG. 7.2
A typical SMDS connection requires very little hardware.

The following steps enable SMDS:

1. Enable the service on the interface using the SMDS Encapsulation command.
2. Specify the SMDS Address.
3. Establish Address Mapping using the Address Resolution Protocol.
4. Map a Multicast Address to an SMDS Address.
5. Enable ARP (Address Resolution Protocol).
6. Enable Broadcast ARP Messages.
7. Enable Dynamic Address Mapping for IPX over SMDS.

The routing tables used in address mapping are dynamically configured when DECnet, extended AppleTalk, IP, IPX, and ISO CLNS routing is configured. Otherwise, static mapping can be configured if needed.

Ch

7

The SMDS network is similar to an X.25 cloud; with the Customer Premises Equipment (CPE) existing at the edge of the cloud. The service provider facilitates communications across the cloud. The user must configure equipment properly before communications can occur, however, and configuration will be different depending on the protocol being used.

One of the biggest differences in protocols is whether it deploys dynamic or static routing between the edge routers. IP facilitates dynamic routing across the SMDS cloud, and the user need take no action to map higher-level protocol addresses to SMDS addresses.

After SMDS has been enabled, it can be further configured in the following ways, as needed:

- Configure Specific Protocols.
- Enable Transparent Bridging over SMDS.
- Configure SMDS Subinterfaces for Multiple Logical IP Subnetworks.
- Reenable the Data Exchange Interface version 3.2 with Heartbeat Support.
- Configure Pseudobroadcasting.
- Enable Fast Switching.
- Configure Specific Protocols.

Again, those protocols that are dynamically routed require no further action. For other protocols, however, a static entry must be made for every peer router. Different protocols again may have different requirements; some of these are listed here:

- Static maps need to be configured for DECnet.
- Multicasts must be configured for CLNS; no static maps are required.
- Multicast addresses must be configured for IPX. A static map entry is made for each remote peer.
- Multicast addresses must be configured for XNS. A static map entry must also be made for each remote peer.
- For AppleTalk, AppleTalk routers will treat the SMDS cloud as either extended (Phase II AppleTalk) or nonextended (Phase I AppleTalk); these two types cannot be mixed on the same SMDS cloud.
- For Banyan VINES, multicast addresses must be configured. VINES only works with static maps.

A single SMDS interface can be treated as multiple, logical IP subnetworks. If multiple logical IP subnetworks are being used, the router will route between subnetworks using

IP addresses on the SMDS interface. Each subnetwork has its own IP address, unicast and multicast E.164 addresses, which are configured at the SMDS interface.

SMDS provides for the Data Exchange Interface (DXI) 3.2 heartbeat process, which encapsulates SMDS packets in a DXI frame before transmission. This mechanism generates a heartbeat poll frame every 10 seconds, although this default can be changed if desired.

For hosts that do not support multicast E.164 addresses, pseudobroadcasting can be configured. If a multicast address is not available to a particular destination node, pseudobroadcasting will broadcast packets to those destinations with a unicast address.

Enabling Fast Switching will provide for faster packet transfer on serial links with speeds over 56Kbps. Fast Switching should be enabled if using high-speed, packet-switched, datagram-based WAN technologies (such as frame relay).

The Customer Premises Equipment (CPE) can be configured in a single-CPE or multi-CPE configuration. In a single-CPE configuration (see Figure 7.3), the access-oriented DQDB connects the carrier network's switch to a single CPE device.

FIG. 7.3
The DQDB connects the carrier switch to a single CPE device in this single-CPE configuration.

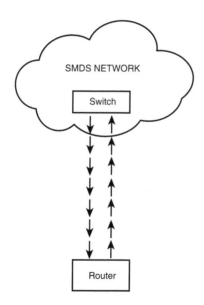

In a multi-CPE configuration (see Figure 7.4), the distributed queue dual bus (DQDB) connects the carrier network's switch to multiple, connected CPE devices.

Ch

7

FIG. 7.4
The DQDB connects to the carrier switch through multiple, interconnected CPE devices in this multi-CPE Configuration.

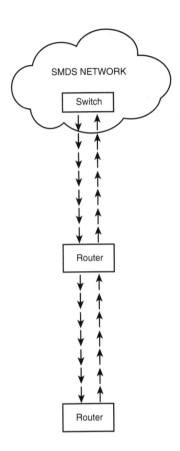

Connectionless Broadband Data Service

The European version of SMDS, Connectionless Broadband Data Service (CBDS), offers access at E1 (2.048Mbps) and E3 (34Mbps) speeds. Essentially, SMDS is a subset of the options available in CBDS. Both use the same addressing structure, although the two use somewhat different terminology, as follows in Table 7.1.

Table 7.1 SMDS and Corresponding CBDS Terminology

SMDS	CBDS
Customer Premises Equipment (CPE)	Customer Network (CN)
Subscriber Network Interface (SNI)	User-MAN Interface (UMI)
Customer	User
L3 PDU (Protocol Data Unit)	IMPDU (Initial MAC Protocol Data Unit)

SMDS	CBDS
L2 PDU	DMPDU (Derived MAC PDU)
Errored L3 PDU Ratio	Undetected Error Ratio
Misdelivered L3 PDU Ratio	Misdelivered SDU Ratio
L3 PDU Not Delivered Ratio	Lost SDU (Service Data Unit) Ratio

SMDS Internetworking

The SMDS Interface Protocol (SIP) defines the connection between the CPE and the SMDS network equipment. It is based on the IEEE protocol for MANs (IEEE 802.6 Distributed Queue Dual Bus standard). This protocol allows the CPE to be attached to the SMDS network for the purpose of internetworking.

Access can be provided over a 1.544Mbps (DS1) or 44.736 (DS3) connection. A typical SMDS internetworking configuration is shown in Figure 7.5.

FIG. 7.5
SMDS internetworking connects LANs to the carrier network.

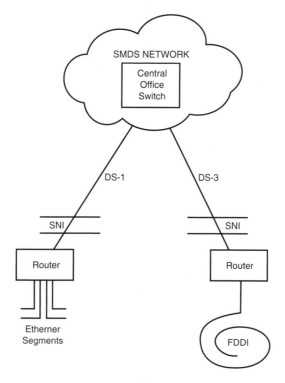

Ch
7

In the previous internetworking diagram, DS1 access can be established over either fiber or copper media; fiber is required for the DS3 connection. The point at which the CPE and the carrier's SMDS network meet is the Subscriber Network Interface (SNI).

The main platform used for SMDS access is the Distributed Queue Dual Bus (DQDB). DQDB is defined in the IEEE 802.6 Metropolitan Area Network (MAN) standard and uses a fixed-length cell of 53 bytes (the same as ATM). Since SMDS uses a larger, variable-length packet, the SMDS packet has to be segmented into 53-byte cells before transport over DQDB.

DQDB access from a customer site to the network switching center is defined by the SMDS Interface Protocol (SIP). In addition, DQDB can be used internally. The Data Exchange Interface (DXI) protocol supports SMDS over serial links.

DQDB defines a MAC-layer protocol that lets multiple systems interconnect through two unidirectional logical buses. DQDB can be used to create private, fiber-based MANs capable of supporting data, voice, and video.

The DQDB has two parts: the protocol syntax, and the distributed queuing algorithm used for shared medium access control.

A LAN is connected to an SMDS network through Optical Line Termination Equipment (OLTE) at both the LAN and network exchange, with both OLTEs connected by optical fiber. Figure 7.6 illustrates a typical connection.

FIG. 7.6

Connecting a LAN to a public SMDS network exchange runs an optical fiber from the customer site to the public network, with each end connected to optical line termination equipment.

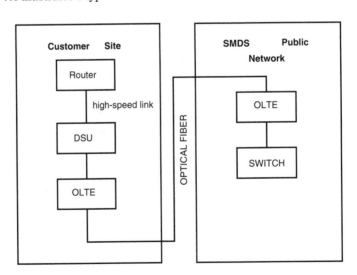

The OLTE establishes an optical/electronic interface. On the customer premises, the OLTE is connected to a Data Service Unit (DSU). The DSU is connected via a high-speed local link to the LAN's router. The DSU converts between DQDB, which is employed by the wide area link, and HDLC, which is employed by the router.

Additional DSUs may be deployed for connecting the router to point-to-point lines and ATM networks. Many routers include SMDS interfaces, and several protocols, including TCP/IP, can be routed over SMDS.

The router-based software processes the packets to and from the SMDS network. The whole process starts when a LAN data packet gets addressed to another LAN on the same SMDS network. That packet will be sent through the router that is connected to the SMDS network. The LAN packet is then inserted into the SMDS packet's payload. Addressing information is added, and the SMDS packet is then sent to the DSU over the high-speed link. When the SMDS packet gets to the DSU, the SMDS packet is divided into cells sized appropriately for putting into the payload of the DQDB cells. The DSU will then send these fixed-size cells to the SMDS switching center. The SMDS network then sends the SMDS packet to the destination LAN, where the payload is extracted and the sending process is reversed. The SMDS network essentially functions as a WAN that interconnects the two LANs involved in the transaction.

The SIP, which defines the interface between the CPE and the SMDS network, can be shown in three levels (see Figure 7.7).

FIG. 7.7
The SMDS Interface Protocol (SIP) is broken down into three levels.

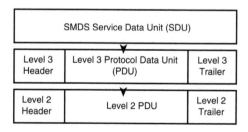

At level 3, the SMD Service data units (SDUs) are encapsulated in a Level 3 header and trailer. These Protocol Data Units (PDUs) are then broken down into Level 2 PDUs as needed to conform to the Level-2 specifications. The Level 3 PDU is shown in Figure 7.8.

Ch

7

FIG. 7.8
The SMDS SDU is broken down into the Level 3 Protocol Data Unit (L3 PDU).

Level 3 Protocol Data Unit
(L3 PDU)

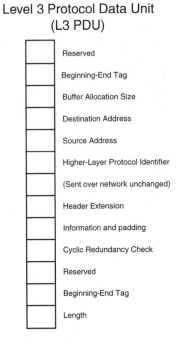

Reserved

Beginning-End Tag

Buffer Allocation Size

Destination Address

Source Address

Higher-Layer Protocol Identifier

(Sent over network unchanged)

Header Extension

Information and padding

Cyclic Redundancy Check

Reserved

Beginning-End Tag

Length

The L3 PDUs are segmented into fixed-size, 53-byte L2 PDUs, or cells. The L2 PDU is shown in Figure 7.9.

FIG. 7.9
The Level 3 Protocol Data Unit is broken down further into the Level 2 Protocol Data Unit.

Level 2 Protocol Data Unit
(L2 PDU)

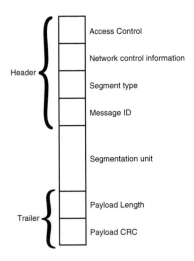

Header {

Access Control

Network control information

Segment type

Message ID

Segmentation unit

Trailer {

Payload Length

Payload CRC

Level 1 provides the physical link protocol, which again operates at DS3 or DS1 and connects the CPE to the SMDS network. Level 1 is divided into the transmission system sublayer and the Physical Layer Convergence Protocol (PLCP). The transmission system sublayer is where the link type (DS3 or DS1) is specified. The PLCP establishes how the L2 PDUs are arranged in the DS3 or DS1 frame.

The 802.6 protocol and SIP were both modeled after ATM, which also uses a fixed-size, 53-byte cell. This fixed-size model is ideal for high speeds, because the smaller cells can be processed and switched via hardware very quickly. Use of fixed cells is ideal for video, voice, or other delay-sensitive applications.

Internet Protocol over SMDS   Figure 7.10 shows a sample of running multiple logical IP subnetworks over SMDS.

FIG. 7.10
Multiple logical IP
subnetworks can exist
in the same SMDS
cloud.

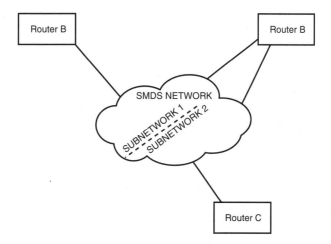

In this example, the three routers are connected to the SMDS cloud through two logical subnetworks (subnet 1 and subnet 2). Router A can recognize both IP subnetworks and can therefore communicate directly with either of the other two routers. Router B can communicate directly with Router A, but only indirectly with Router C by way of router A. Router C, on the other hand, can communicate directly with router A, but only with router B by way of router A. A packet moving from Router B to Router C must therefore make two hops.

SMDS and ATM Interworking   The SMDS Interest Group and ATM Forum established a protocol interface specification for implementing SMDS over ATM public user network interfaces (UNIs). The UNI presents SMDS users with a clear migration path to networks with ATM backbones. The specification will allow SMDS traffic to travel over the ATM switching fabric. ATM is deployed as both a local and wide area solution, and it can be used to simultaneously carry SMDS and other fast packet and broadband traffic.

Ch

7

ATM's Adaptation Layers 3 and 4 were designed to carry connectionless services such as SMDS, making SMDS the only available connectionless ATM service. In fact, SMDS is sometimes referred to as "connectionless ATM."

SMDS lends itself to interconnecting ATM LANs, as well as Ethernet, Token Ring, and FDDI LANs over a wide geographical area. Because the SMDS service layer, which is technology-independent, is separated from the access layer, which is technology-dependent, SMDS can be supported by several different switching technologies and UNIs.

The SMDS Interface Protocol (SIP) has three layers and, like ATM, uses a 53 octet cell. In addition, the SIG has defined a DXI-SNI (Data eXchange Interface), which uses packets instead of cells.

The first SMDS layer is the physical layer; layer two is the 53 octet cell layer; and the third layer includes the E.164 addresses and is similar to the MAC layer in a standard LAN environment.

SMDS internetworking with ATM is straightforward, and has been defined by both the ATM Forum and the SMDS Interest Group. To accomplish this interworking, SMDS packets are mapped into ATM Adaptation Layers (AAL) 3/4 packets at an interworking unit, and then carried from within the AAL 3/4 cells. In SMDS, the IEEE 802.6 access protocol is used to provide the cell-relay facility.

To run SMDS over an ATM UNI, AAL 3/4's Segmentation and Reassembly Layer (SAR) sublayer and the ATM layer must both be provided. However, the SIP layer 2 is connectionless, while the ATM layer is connection-oriented. There are two ways to establish this connection; the first option uses a router that implements SIP_L3, and the SMDS DXI.TA-LAN (a CSU/DSU) will then establish the SAR sublayer of the AAL 3/4 adaptation layer, ATM layer, and physical layer.

In SMDS over AAL 3/4, on the other hand, the ATM layer furnishes the cell-relay facility, and AAL 3/4 provides SMDS's connectionless packet service. The SMDS connectionless service is then emulated by a connectionless server in the ATM network. This ATM-based server receives the SMDS packets, and then forwards them based on the encapsulated SMDS address. There have also been procedures defined for mapping SMDS access classes to ATM Quality of Service parameters.

This SMDS and ATM interworking capability lets users take advantage of SMDS at the present time, and then utilize ATM at a later date when the additional bandwidth is required. The SMDS/ATM UNI specification ensures interoperability and gives users the best of both technologies; that is, the connectionless data services of SMDS, and the bandwidth guarantees and Quality of Service levels found in ATM.

By adding AAL 5 to the specification, terminal equipment that may not support AAL 3/4 will be able to still run SMDS. However, this may present somewhat of an interoperability problem between older SMDS customers running AAL 3/4 equipment and newer ones running AAL5 equipment. However, this limitation can be overcome. Some vendors, including ADC Kentrox, offer equipment that supports interoperability between AAL 3/4 and AAL 5 equipment.

If AAL 5 has not been introduced to the network, interworking between multiple SMDS User-to-Network interfaces with AAL 3/4 only is fairly straightforward. The SMDS PDU (protocol data unit, or packet) is technology-independent, so several different SMDS-to-ATM interface types can interoperate. Different SMDS-to-ATM interfaces are shown in Figure 7.11.

FIG. 7.11

Here are some examples of SMDS-to-ATM interfaces.

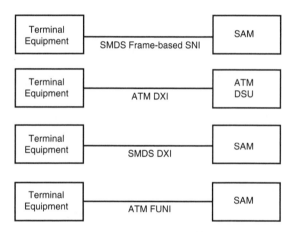

When only AAL 3/4 is deployed, interoperability issues do not arise, because an Interworking Function (IF) is only required between the SMDS cell-based interface and the ATM UNI. In fact, the AAL 3/4 PDU and the SMDS PDU are functionally identical in both payload size and structure. This makes interworking over the UNI very simple, and the SMDS terminal equipment need not perform any specialized processing to establish compatibility with ATM. The SMDS-enabled terminal equipment or router can establish ATM compatibility simply by adding an external device, in the form of the ATM DSU or the Service Access Multiplexer (SAM).

There are two separate ways to route an SMDS packet over an ATM network: one takes a centralized approach and the other a distributed one. In the centralized model (see Figure 7.12), it is not necessary for the terminal equipment or the IF to be able to map between the SMDS-based E.164 address and the ATM Virtual Connection (VCC).

Ch
7

FIG. 7.12

Centralized routing of SMDS over ATM does not require mapping of the SMDS address to the ATM Virtual Connection.

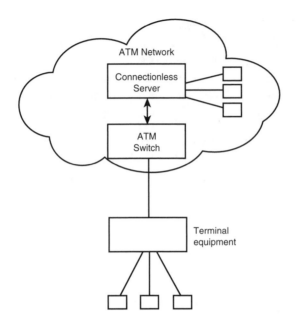

Each user interface is configured with its own Virtual Channel Connection (VCC), connecting it to the closest connectionless server (which is connected to the ATM switch). The connectionless server will receive the SMDS packets and route them to their destinations. This configuration is the least expensive and is dependent on the external connectionless server.

In the distributed model, however, the Interworking Function (IWF) examines each E.164 address and determines the best route. This routing information is then mapped into each VCC, which then ships each SMDS packet through the ATM network directly to the destination site. The IWF takes place in the SAM. This option is less prevalent, and there are less hardware options.

If AAL 5 has been introduced to the ATM UNI, interoperability can be achieved with AAL 3/4 devices. A new specification, proposed by ADC Kentrox and agreed to by the SIG, simplifies interoperability by containing the L3_PDU within the AAL 5 PDU.

An AAL 3/4 to AAL 5 interworking function is needed to facilitate full interoperability; the interworking function is typically implemented in the DCE equipment.

The interworking function reassembles cells received from the source interface using the SAR process. The IWF converts the PDUs to the type required by the destination interface and then segments them as needed for transmission. When the IWF is implemented in the DCE, the DCE must be able to support both AAL 3/4 and AAL 5, and the DCE must be capable of E.164 routing. A DCE that is not capable of E.164 routing will not be able to determine which destination node runs AAL 3/4 and which runs AAL 5, and so it must be limited to only one AAL type.

ATM offers the ability to access SMDS through a physical interface that is common to multiple services. The service interworking function lets SMDS customers accessing the SMDS service through the ATM UNI communicate with other SMDS customers accessing the SMDS service through the SNI. This Service Interworking feature presents a cost-effective way for branch offices to communicate with headquarters; with the branch offices using low-speed SNIs, and headquarters running a high-speed SONET STS-3c (155Mbps) UNI.

SMDS and Frame Relay   Frame Relay is a connection-oriented technology, typically executed at 56Kbps. It requires a specific permanent virtual circuit (PVC) connection to be established between two nodes before they can exchange data. Frame relay users can access SMDS through the SMDS Interface Protocol Relay Service (SIP Relay) standard, which allows SMDS to be encapsulated in Frame Relay.

The SIP transports the SMDS cells on one of the reserved Frame Relay Data Link Connection Identifiers. SIP Relay can be used to add SMDS services to the Frame Relay network at a small cost. This may be especially useful for establishing domestic long-distance or international connections.

SMDS and SONET   SONET is a fiber-optic transmission standard for broadband transmission. Its line rates operate at multiples of 51.840Mbps, and can scale up to multiples of gigabits. Presently, work is underway to allow SMDS to run at speeds of up to 155Mbps on a SONET STS-3c interface.

SMDS and the Internet   Leased lines are not the only way to achieve a high-speed Internet connection. SMDS can be an effective network solution to bring high-speed Internet access to the LAN or WAN.

Vendors

Ch
7

Several companies are active in developing SMDS, and offer a wide variety of products and services. Most of the RBOCs, as well as some long-distance providers, offer SMDS service.

Bay Networks

http://www.baynetworks.com
4401 Great America Parkway
Santa Clara, CA 95052

Bay Networks' line of multiprotocol bridge/routers supports SMDS. Because the products adhere to the DXI 3.2 standard, Bay Network's bridge/routers offer full compatibility with SMDS-compatible DSUs. The Bay Networks products also support routing of several protocols, including IP, IPX, AppleTalk, DECNet, APPN, XNS and VINES, as well as bridging and source route bridging, over SMDS. Furthermore, Bay Networks' product line supports RFC 1209 for IP encapsulation, which offers a greater level of multivendor interoperability over the SMDS network.

Cisco Systems, Inc.

http://www.cisco.com
170 West Tasman Drive
San Jose, CA 95134
Voice: 408-526-4000 or (800) 553-NETS (6387)
Fax: 408-526-4100

Cisco Systems offers several internetworking products that support SMDS interfaces including routers, bridges, communication servers, protocol translators, LAN switches, and ATM switches. Cisco also provides a router with an SMDS over ATM native interface capability with support for SDH/SONET, T3, and E3 interfaces.

MultiAccess Computing Corporation

http://www.multiaccess.com
55 Hollister Ave., Suite C
Santa Barbara, CA 93111
Voice: 800-800-SMDS or 805-964-2332
E-mail: **multiacc@silcom.com**

MultiAccess offers a line of adapter cards for Novell, Novell MultiProtocol Router, Windows, Windows NT, and Apple Macintosh platforms that take advantage of each operating system's built-in routing capabilities. The adapters come equipped with all the drivers required and are easy to install.

QPSX Communications Limited

Private Bag 24
West Perth,
Western Australia 6004
Voice: +61 9 262 2000
Fax: +61 9 324 1642

QPSX's QP2000 family of SMDS WAN adapters supports access rates from 56Kbps to 2Mbps. The adapters are used to interface customer servers and workstations to the public carrier's SMDS access link. The QPSX adapters are integrated with Novell NetWare.

QPSX provides a public network cell switch supporting configuration of hierarchical, resilient looped, and generally meshed network deployment using public transmission standards. Customer service interfaces include on-premises equipment supporting direct interconnection with SMDS, frame relay, LAN, voice, and other customer premises and also exchange interfaces to U.S. and European standards. QPSX also provides public network operator management.

ADC Kentrox

http://www.kentrox.com
14375 N.W. Science Park Dr.
Portland, OR 97229
Voice: 800-ADC-KTRX or 1-503-643-1681
E-mail: info@kentrox.com

ADC Kentrox offers a wide range of access products at all available standard connection rates. Access Concentrators and DataSMART SMDSUs feature in-band SNMP/TELNET for connection to cell-based SMDS services. The D-SERV and DataSMART product families support economical access to frame-based SMDS DXI services. The CellSMART, AAC-1 and AAC-3 ATM Access Concentrators are ideal for hybrid SMDS/FR/ATM applications.

Ch
7

Digital Link Corporation

http://www.dl.com
217 Humboldt Court
Sunnyvale, CA 94089
Voice: 408-745-4146
Fax: 408-745-0492
E-mail: **info@dl.com**

Digital Link's DL200 Encore SMDS Converter gives users access to T1/E1 SMDS network services. The DL200 Encore supports DXI 3.2, DXI 2.1, and Cisco DX1- compatible internetworking devices and HDLC-based channel extenders. An embedded SNMP agent is included for easy management. The DL3200 Digital Service Interface provides users access to T3/E3 SMDS networks at speeds up to 44.2Mbps. An embedded SNMP agent is provided with the unit. The DL3202 Digital Cell Multiplexer provides multiple users access to T3/E3 SMDS. The DL3202 has downloadable code and an embedded SNMP agent. Digital Link Corporation supports SMDS at T1, T3, E1, and E3 transport speeds.

Alcatel Network Systems

1225 North Alma Road
MS 407-421
Richardson, TX 75081
Voice: 972-996-5986
Fax: 972-996-6943

Alcatel's 1000 AX is an ATM VP/VC switch capable of carrying SMDS and frame relay services in an ATM environment. It supports DS0, DS1, DS3, E1, E3, OC-3c, and OC-12c.

AT&T Network Systems

http://www.att.com
Liberty Corner Road
Warren, NJ 07059

AT&T's BNS-2000 family of SMDS switches uses the SMDS standard for high-speed, connectionless public-network switching. The product line can be used to effectively extend LAN performance far beyond the customer site. The BNS-2000 architecture provides SMDS for telecommunications carriers and large private enterprises via access interfaces that connect to industry-standard SMDS routers and terminal adapters in customer equipment.

Cascade Communications Corp.

http://www.casc.com
5 Carlisle Road
Westford, MA 01886
Voice: 508-692-2600 or 800-647-6926
Fax: 508-692-5052
E-mail: mktg@casc.com

Cascade provides an SMDS access server for the STDX 3000/6000-Frame Relay Switch and the B-STDX 8000/9000 Multiservice Switches, providing TR-TSV-001239 low-speed SMDS capability. DS0, T1/E1, T3/E3, and access class service are supported.

Brooktree Corporation

http://www.brooktree.com/brooktree/index.html
9868 Scranton Road
San Diego, CA 92121
Voice: 800-228-2777

The Bt8210 SCARF (SMDS Control and Reassembly Formatter) performs SMDS interface protocol functions in an IC including PDU formatting, SAR, PLCP, and head-of-bus functions. The Bt8209 is a lower-cost pin and software-compatible version of the Bt8210 for T1/E1 only applications. Access to all levels of the protocol is available along with additional features for test equipment. Both terminal and switch functions are provided for DS1, DS3, E1, and E3. The Bt8330 combines a DS3 and an E3 framer as a companion chip to SCARF. The chip also operates as an HDLC formatter running up to 52Mbps for the SMDS DXI interface for HSSI. The Bt8360 is a T1 framer that directly connects to SCARF. The Bt8510 is an E1 framer that directly connects to SCARF. The Bt8210 Evaluation Module is a complete SMDS DSU reference design using the Bt8210 for T1/E1 and DS3/E3 rates.

Brooktree Corporation's Strategic Business Unit (SBU) manufactures a family of integrated circuits for high-speed digital communications applications. Brooktree has a fully integrated SMDS network interface device, which consolidates multi-ASIC solutions into a single chip. The company's SMDS Control and Reassembly Formatter (SCARF) is the only commercially available silicon for SMDS, and implements the full Subscriber Network Interface (SNI) for both CPE and central office applications. It is also the only device that offers full support for the SMDS protocol at T1/E1 and T3/E3 rates.

Ch
7

UUNET Technologies

http://www.uunet.com
3060 Williams Drive
Fairfax, VA 22031
Voice: 703-206-5600 or 800-488-6383

UUNET Technologies, the first commercial Internet service, offers a variety of services for companies needing high throughput for Internet access. Besides a tiered T-3 service, UUNET's AlertNet SMDS service gives companies a platform for high-volume Web sites and intranets. SMDS gives subscribers access speeds of up to 34Mbps through a public SMDS cloud. By using the public data network used by several companies, SMDS gives users an inexpensive alternative to point-to-point connections. The SMDS service lets users change their throughput configuration as needed, and add new bandwidth capacity as required—without having to install new CPE devices.

The AlertNet service is distance-insensitive and is available in several major U.S. cities.

Summary

SMDS is a technology originally developed by Bellcore, which can be used to interconnect LANs over a wide geographic distance. It is often used to connect remote branch offices to headquarters.

SMDS moves LAN traffic through the public telephone network. As a connectionless technology, the carrier switches do not need to establish a call path between the two transmission points. Instead, the access device generates fixed, 53-byte cells, which are then sent on to the carrier switch. The switch will then read each cell's address information, and send it on over any available path.

SMDS can coexist with dedicated lines, which means customers can create their own hybrid private/public networks. New sites are easy to add and require little configuration, all that is needed to add a node to the SMDS network is to update the database on the SMDS switch. SMDS is technology-independent, so several different network technologies can be used in the SMDS internetwork. ●

CHAPTER 8

Synchronous Optical Network (SONET)

In the chapter on SMDS, we saw how SMDS technology can carry data over the public telephone system for great distances. SONET uses fiber-optic rings to accomplish the same thing over greater distances, and to provide a much higher rate of transfer with some unusual availability guarantees.

Synchronous Optical Network (SONET) was created by Bellcore in 1985 to provide a cost-effective platform for multivendor interworking. SONET has several advantages over asynchronous methods, including the ability to offer back-to-back multiplexing, compatibility with other standards, and ultra-high performance. Because it is a transmission technology, SONET can be used to carry a wide variety of traffic, including ATM cells. ■

N O T E   SONET's basic building blocks are 125 microsecond frames, which come in two sizes;
             the STS-1 and STS-3c frame. STS-1's bit rate is 51.84Mbps; STS-3c's is three times
that of STS-1, or 155.52Mbps. Older multiplexing formats connect frame structure and bit-
oriented multiplexing to the constituent signal. SONET, on the other hand, completely separates
the overhead and payload fields. All SONET signals, with one exception, are developed by
interleaving one of the two base formats (STS-1 and STS-3c). The exception is STS-12c
(622Mbps), which is used for exceptionally large payloads. Because no overhead is added
from multiplexing, the resulting bit rates are exact multiples of the STS-1 base rate. ■

SONET technology has since evolved into a set of ANSI standards and is widely deployed
by telecommunications carriers. Synchronous Digital Hierarchy (SDH) is the European
equivalent of SONET, as defined by the ITU.

Overview of SONET

Services like SONET and SDH differ from frame relay and SMDS. SONET serves as both
carrier infrastructure and customer-premises based services. SONET exists at Layer 1
(Physical layer) of the OSI stack, providing the mechanism for transmission of high-speed
services like ATM. Frame relay and SMDS, on the other hand, ride on top of ATM. However, SONET can function as the underlying transport mechanism for ATM, which in
turn, supports other services such as frame relay and SMDS.

Another major difference is that while ATM is a switching technology, SONET is a transmission technology. Switching is concerned with how data is routed across the network;
while transmission covers how data is encoded and transported across the network.

While SONET is not applied directly to switch devices, it is used to specify the interface
between the switches that are linked by optical fibers. As such, standard ATM or LAN
switches are equipped with a SONET interface in order to comply with the SONET
specification.

A SONET/SDH transmission starts at 51.84Mbps (OC-1). However, this rate is close to
the 45Mbps rate offered by a common T3 line, and so most vendors do not offer OC-1
SONET rates. SONET comes into its own at OC-3 speeds of 155Mbps and above. SONET
is also available at OC-12 (622Mbps) and OC-48 (2.488 Gbps). A SONET backbone is often
deployed at OC-48 to ensure adequate capacity.

N O T E   SONET building block signals are referred to as STS-1, STS-3, STS-9, STS-12, STS-18,
             STS-24, STS-36, and STS-48. STS stands for Synchronous Transport Signal. When an
STS is converted to an optical format for transmission, the signal is then referred to as optical
carrier (OC), but still has the same bit rate as STS. ■

Typical SONET-based applications include:

- LAN-to-LAN interconnection
- Host-to-host interconnection
- Videoconferencing
- Team engineering
- Distributed processing
- Advanced scientific research

SONET and Synchronous Digital Hierarchy (SDH)

SONET and SDH are remarkably similar, but not truly interoperable. SONET is based on an STS-1 (Synchronous Transport Signal Level 1), which operates at 51.84Mbps; while SDH is based on the STM-1 (synchronous transport module), which operates at 155.52Mbps. Consequently, payload mapping differs somewhat; although three STS-1s fit exactly into a single STM-1.

Here's a comparison chart between STS and STM.

Table 8.1 North American STS and European STM

U.S.	Europe	Bit Rate
STS-1	n/a	51.84Mbps
STS-3	STM-1	155.52Mbps
STS-12	STM-4	622.08Mbps
STS-24	STM-8	1244.16Mbps
STS-48	STM-16	2488.32Mbps
STS-192	STM-64	9953.28Mbps

There are a few other minor differences. However, most SONET-compliant physical interface chips include an STM operation mode, which in reality, makes the two almost interchangeable.

SONET and SDH are basically the same; SDH was specified after SONET and incorporates SONET in full. There are a few minor differences, such as payload size and framing, but both are interoperable. European SONET networks, however, do not enjoy as high an availability rate as those in the United States, although their availability is still generally more than 99 percent.

Advantages of SONET

Optical fiber technologies such as SONET carry with them numerous advantages over coaxial or twisted-pair cabling, including:

- Higher bandwidth
- The capability to be carried over a longer distance without repeaters
- Immunity to interference
- Greater security, because it is difficult to tap
- Less expensive to maintain

As with any technology, there is the inevitable downside, however. Only users in major metropolitan areas are likely to be able to utilize SONET services; some RBOCs and other carriers are not yet SONET-capable.

Implementation and Infrastructure

SONET is a CCITT standard for optical signals with a synchronous frame structure for multiplexing digital traffic onto the fiber-optic line. SONET has a hierarchical signaling architecture, which allows a higher-rate signal to be built out of multiple lower-rate signals.

Several of the Regional Bell Operating Companies have upgraded their telecommunications facilities with fiber-optic networks. SONET plays a part in this upgrade, and also adds additional value by delivering more reliability, stability, and enhanced compatibility between LANs and WANs.

Super-high-speed technologies like SONET are already in use on carrier backbones, and a few network managers are also starting to put it to use in larger corporate networks. Several carriers are also starting to offer public ATM services based on a high-speed SONET transport. These public networks offer near-perfect uptime and extremely high speeds measured in the tens of gigabits.

A Step Beyond Synchronous Transfer Mode

SONET is the next step from STM (synchronous transfer mode), the technology that underlies the country's digital telephone network. STM relies on time-division multiplexing to send asynchronous traffic, such as the traffic on T1 and T3 circuits. Speed and reliability are two of the biggest advantages of SONET.

Self-Healing Mechanism

SONET has the remarkable capability to heal itself and to provide a high service guarantee. SONET can protect communications with a self-healing ring, which provides 100 percent connectivity between business sites and the Bell wiring centers.

Actually, by referring to itself as "self-healing" the folks who designed SONET are being a little misleading. The SONET ring does not actually heal itself; if the cable is cut, human technicians must actually go out and put it back together. However, to the end user, SONET's Bidirectional Line-Switched Ring (BLSR) technology has the effect of creating self-healing. In reality, BLSR is not a technique for self-healing, but a technique used to achieve a high level of survivability. The SONET rings also provide for automatic network backup and 100 percent redundancy; so even if there is a point of failure on the SONET ring, the service will continue.

This remarkable self-healing feature makes a SONET ring quite different from a traditional telecom network. SONET/SDH networks are point-to-point synchronous networks using TDM multiplexing over a ring or mesh topology. These rings lay the Physical Layer framework for FDDI, SMDS, or ATM implementation. Most of the RBOCs have upgraded their infrastructures with fiber optics. SONET's survivability options deliver an incredibly high rate of reliability and flexibility, enough to keep a mission-critical network moving on a 24 by 7 basis. The self-healing nature of SONET rings establishes a method of automatic network backup with complete redundancy, so in the event of ring failure, the service continues uninterrupted. Some of the advantages of SONET include:

1. Service is fully survivable around failed fiber facilities or electronics
2. On-demand provisioning of new services
3. Nearly error-free data transmission with the lowest bit-error rate available
4. Service guarantees
5. Real-time network alarming and performance monitoring
6. Prompt initiation of service restoration

SONET's superior fault tolerance is based on its unusual self-healing mechanism. This rerouting works in this way: Each ring has dual circuits; if one circuit suffers a cut, the traffic reverses and flows in the opposite direction on the same ring to avoid the cut. If the ring is broken in two places, however, the traffic will be automatically rerouted onto the second circuit. This rerouting happens almost instantaneously.

Another type of protection called path-protection switching (1+1 protection switching) sends traffic over both the working and protection fiber pairs. Each packet is compared at the receiving end and the best copy is used.

Traffic running on SONET/SDH circuits is automatically rerouted within a matter of milliseconds in the event of a cut cable or other type of outage. Every SONET/SDH frame carries instructions that tell each frame where to go if its original destination is unreachable. The software that runs on the add-and-drop muxes will detect these rerouted frames, and will then communicate to the switch to send the rest of the traffic directed at the outage to go onto the alternative path. Because the traffic travels so quickly, end users on the SONET services usually are not even aware of the outage.

The older STM technology, on the other hand, deals with outages manually. Although an alarm will be generated, technical staff had to find an alternative path manually. SONET enjoys 99.99 percent and higher uptime levels. Several providers go so far as to back up their guarantees with promises to refund the service charge if the SONET circuit is down for any significant amount of time. All major worldwide carriers deploy SONET or SDH on their backbones, and some also offer these services to corporate users.

If this level of reliability is unnecessary, however, point-to-point service may be the better option. A local point-to-point service merely furnishes a circuit that links a site to the nearest switch. A long-distance point-to-point SONET service is very similar to a leased line; a company purchases a connection between two points, but the traffic is actually sent over several SONET rings within the public network. Therefore, the buyer is not literally purchasing a specific SONET ring but still gets the reliability benefits that come from using them.

Carriers

Carriers deploy SONET in their backbones differently; some use a dual ring pair configuration for redundancy. Others use a meshed network model, where several redundant circuits are provided for each switch in the network.

Although all of the major long distance carriers have SONET rings, Sprint was the first to deploy the technology and has the biggest SONET infrastructure to date. The company expects its network to be 100 percent SONET by 1998. The first international SONET ring was completed by Sprint. The company created a 1,174 mile connection between the U.S. and Canada, using the four-fiber, bidirectional, ring-switched, ring topology.

Although SONET is widely used by major carriers, corporate users are still few and far between. The service is costly, and none of the long-distance carriers have a formal pricing structure for the service. Some carriers recommend that corporate users with six to eight T1 lines connected to two or three locations consider a SONET ring; in this case, an OC-3 ring connecting the sites will be less costly than the expense of the T1 lines.

Some carriers are creating new services that divide a high-capacity SONET OC-12 trunk into multiple T1 or T3 circuits, which can then be sold to individual users. This option gives customers the reliability of SONET, without having to pay the full price.

As the carriers move toward replacing their existing infrastructure with SONET, more day-to-day traffic will be carried over the SONET infrastructure, which means that everyone will benefit with more reliable service at a lower cost. Sometimes, it is possible to request that your dedicated service be run over the carrier's SONET backbone.

Options For corporate use, managers can choose between point-to-point dedicated SONET/SDH lines or a dual-fiber SONET/SDH ring. The ring configuration consists of a fiber ring connected by a high-speed synchronous transport. This option offers the best speed and reliability, although the point-to-point option also offers high speed. The fiber ring option has the advantage of guaranteeing automatic rerouting around an outage.

Although long-distance carriers have been promoting their SONET services, the Regional Bell Operating Companies (RBOCs) also have less well-known SONET services. Most local carriers offer SONET services that can bring the SONET ring directly into your building or office, and establish either a shared or dedicated circuit back to the RBOC's central office or to the long-distance carrier's point of presence. SONET services from local carriers will not be for everyone. It is not likely to even be available now except for larger, metropolitan and surrounding areas.

A SONET ring can be used to connect several buildings on a campus, or to connect a city to redundant carrier switches.

Bandwidth SONET services range from 51.84Mbps (OC-1) to 13.22 Gbps (OC-255). The technology is very flexible and can be used to transport a wide variety of digital signals. The optical standard promotes interworking of multiple vendors' transmission devices; it consists of a physical interface, Optical Carrier (OC) signals, a frame format, and the OAM&P (Operations, Administration, Maintenance, and Provisioning) protocol.

The First SONET Ring

Sprint's 1,174 mile ring connects the U.S. and Canada through points that include Montreal, Toronto, Buffalo, and Springfield, MA. The Sprint ring uses the same four-fiber, bidirectional, line-switched ring topology used in Sprint's domestic network. Sprint's SONET deployment began in 1993; full deployment is expected in 1997. In the event of a network failure, Sprint's SONET ring can reroute traffic in under 60 milliseconds. Interestingly, shortly after the international ring was installed, a storm severed the fiber-optic cable. However, Sprint customers suffered no disruption in service, and the ring performed as anticipated.

The rerouting offered by the BLSR methodology works like this: Visualize the SONET ring as the face of a clock. The user is at 6:00, and wants to send a message to someone at 2:00. The message gets transmitted simultaneously clockwise and counterclockwise. Of course, the counterclockwise path gets there first; but if, for example, there is a cut in the ring at 4:00, the clockwise path will still get to the destination.

Elements of SONET

Let's have a look at the different elements of a SONET internetwork:

- *Path Terminating Equipment (PTE)*. This device is a network element that multiplexes/demultiplexes the STS payload. The PTE can originate, access, modify, or terminate the path overhead.

- *Line Terminating Equipment (LTE)*. This device is the network element used to originate or terminate the line signal. It can originate, access, modify, or terminate line overhead.

- *Section Terminating Equipment (STE)*. A section consists of any two adjacent SONET network elements. The STE can take the form of a terminating network element or regenerator. It can originate, access, modify, or terminate section overhead.

Because the various SONET network elements are synchronous, there is no need for sending preambles for clock synchronization. Framing bits are used to indicate the beginning of a frame. The STS-N frame is sent every 125 microseconds, regardless of the presence or absence of data. The SONET functions map approximately into the physical layer of the OSI stack.

The synchronicity of SONET also may be an advantage over asynchronous modes of transmission. Asynchronous systems are typically point-to-point mechanisms; whereas SONET supports a multi-point, or hub-based configuration.

SONET's frame length is 125 microseconds, with a frame rate of 8,000 frames per second. STS-1 (synchronous transport signal Level 1) is the basic signal rate; each frame can be viewed in a 9-row by 90-column format, which totals 810 bytes.

SONET's line rate is designed with a synchronous hierarchy that can accommodate signals of varying capacities. The OC-1 line rate (51.84Mbps) can accommodate 28 DS1 signals and one DS3 signal. Higher level signals are obtained merely by synchronous multiplexing of the lower-level signals.

The STS-N signal, on the other hand, is formed by byte-interleaving a number of STS-1 signals.

As the rate increases, so does the percentage of overhead. Additional overhead is used for control bits, alarms, signaling, parity bits, and stuffing. Therefore, as the rate increases, the percentage of useable capacity decreases.

Each level in the SONET hierarchy is called a digital stream (DS); the lower level DSs are multiplexed to make higher level digital streams. The lowest level, DS0, carries a single voice channel and has a bit rate of 64Kbps. A DS1 stream is made up of 24 DS0 streams, for a combined bit rate of 1.544Mbps. A DS3 stream is made up of 28 DS1s, for a total bit rate of 44.736Mbps.

The digital multiplexing system is actually asynchronous at DS3 and lower levels. Bit-stuffing is required when DS0 signals are multiplexed into a DS1 stream. This process places additional bits to account for variations in individual streams. SONET does perform synchronous multiplexing at all levels, through a system of pointers used for synchronizing frames. Lower-level streams can be extracted from a higher-level stream synchronously.

Synchronous, as used in the term Synchronous Optical Network, refers to the multiplexing method used to combine channels. This is done by guaranteeing that all the input channels into the multiplexer have synchronized clocks. An OC-3 channel can be achieved simply by combining three OC-1 channels.

SONET is compatible with existing networks; the most notable SONET-compatible network is the public telephone network.

Some existing network architectures require lower speed channels to be fully demultiplexed or multiplexed before they are allowed to combine or decombine into a higher-speed line. This can be costly however, especially if there are a lot of low-speed channels. SONET bypasses this problem with the use of Add/Drop Multiplexers (ADMs). These permit low-speed signals to be added or dropped without having to demultiplex the entire signal. A SONET frame can be sent across different network types; to do so, it is essential that clocks in both networks be synchronized. SONET uses a clock hierarchy to maintain synchronization.

Signaling   SONET's synchronous nature allows for the adding or dropping of signals with a single multiplexing process. It further integrates OAM&P into the network to minimize transmission costs. The SONET standard defines, in addition to rates and formats, the physical layer, network element, architectural features, and network operational criteria.

A major problem of traditional internetworking is that each local network has a different signal hierarchy, encoding technique, and multiplexing strategy. For example, a DS1 signal includes one framing bit per frame and has 24 voice channels. It has a rate of 1.544Mbps, or 64Kbps per channel. However, because it utilizes the Alternate Mark Inversion (AMI) encoding scheme, it takes one bit from each byte for signaling and so has a rate of 56Kbps per channel.

But if B8ZS encoding is utilized, all bits are used for transmission, so it would enjoy a rate of 64Kbps. In addition, sending a signal between LANs requires multiplexing/demultiplexing to convert signals between schemes.

B8ZS Encoding Scheme

The B8ZS (Bipolar with 8 Zero Substitution) signal encoding scheme represents a one alternately as a positive or negative voltage. Zero is represented uniformly as zero voltage. Under B8ZS, at least one bit of every eight bits must be a one. Therefore, eight consecutive zeroes cannot possibly occur. This minimum number of one values is necessary, because the values are used for timing. Too many zero values will cause the sender and receiver to lose their synchronized state. By adding a one value in at least every eight bits, it is not possible for the transmission to get too far out of synchronization.

SONET overcomes the translation problem by standardizing rates and formats. The Synchronous Transport Signal (STS) makes up the SONET interface, at a 51.84Mbps rate. STS is made up of a payload and overhead; the payload carries data, and the overhead carries signaling and protocol information. Signals are converted to STS before traveling through the SONET network; terminating equipment on the receiving end will then convert the STS into the format employed by the user. An example of the flow in a SONET network is shown in Figure 8.1.

FIG. 8.1
Note how the SONET data flows through the network.

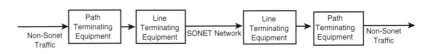

The path terminating equipment (PTE) multiplexes and demultiplexes the STS payload. The line terminating equipment (LTE) originates and terminates the line signal. The section terminating equipment (STE) consists of two adjacent SONET network elements. The STE may be a terminating network element or regenerator.

An STS-N frame (where N equals a variable multiplier of OC-1) is sent every 125 microseconds (8,000 frames per second), regardless of whether or not data needs to be sent. Because data arrives in an asynchronous manner, data may start at any location on the SPE.

The STS-1 (synchronous transport signal Level 1) is SONET's basic signal rate, with a frame resembling a 9-row, 90-column structure with a total actually of 810 bytes. The first three columns make up the transport overhead as follows: nine bytes for section overhead, 18 for line overhead. The STS-1 or OC-1 rate is 51.84Mbps and can accommodate 28 DS1 signals and one DS3 signal. Higher signals are simply created by multiplexing lower-level signals.

The STS-N signal is created by byte-interleaving N STS-1 signals. Transport overhead channels of each STS-1 signal must be frame-aligned before interleaving takes place. Every STS-1 signal has a unique payload pointer to show the location of each SPE; therefore, each associated STS SPE does not have to be aligned.

STS-1 rates can be concatenated to create a higher, STS-Nc signal that can be multiplexed, switched, and transported over the network as a signal entity.

As the rate of the signal increases, the percentage of overhead also increases. Additional overhead is required for control bits, alarm and signaling, parity bits, and bit stuffing. The percentage of overhead relative to the frame is 2.7 percent for DS2; but 6.6 percent for DS4.

The first three rows of the transport overhead is the section overhead. Framing bytes are allocated to each STS-1 line to indicate the beginning of each STS-1 frame.

The last six rows of the transport overhead is the line overhead. The line overhead consists of pointers, which are used to align the STS-1 SPE in the STS-N signal.

Path overhead is contained within the payload and created by the path terminating equipment as part of the SPE. Path overload is extracted when the terminating path equipment demultiplexes the payload.

There are two types of SONET frames, both of which are sent every 125 microseconds. STS-1 can be represented by a 9 row by 90 column byte matrix, with three columns of transport overhead and 87 columns of payload. This amounts to a bit rate of 51.84Mbps.

The STS-3c format is nine rows by 270 columns, with nine columns of overhead and 261 of payload. The bit rate is equal to three times that of STS-1, or 155.52Mbps. Other SONET signals are created by byte-interleaved multiplexing of these two formats.

Multiplexing does not require any additional overhead, so when multiplexing the STS signals, the new bit rate is a multiple of the base rate. Once STS is converted to an optical format, the signal is referred to as an optical carrier (OC), but it still has the same bit rate. Because SONET's overhead and payload fields are separate, it can easily be used for many different types of traffic.

Layers of SONET   SONET has four optical interface layers (see Figure 8.2): the Path Layer, Line Layer, Section Layer, and Photonic Layer.

FIG. 8.2
Optical Interface
Layers.

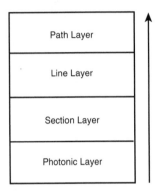

Each of the four layers build on the services of the lower layers; each layer communicates to equipment in the same layer and passes information to the next highest layer.

These layers do not correspond with the OSI model; SONET as a whole corresponds to the OSI Physical Layer only. The layers are as follows:

- *Photonic Layer.* Accommodates the transport of bits over the physical medium and converts STS signals to OC signals.

- *Section Layer.* Sends STS frames and Section Overhead (SOH) over the transport medium. Framing, scrambling, and error monitoring all occur in the Section Layer.

- *Line Layer.* Responsible for the transport of user data in the form of Synchronous Payload Envelopes (SPE) and Line Overhead (LOH) over the medium. Synchronization and multiplexing occur on this layer. The main functions include synchronization, multiplexing, error monitoring, line maintenance, and protection switching.

- *Path Layer.* Responsible for the transport of services between Path Terminal Equipment (PTE). Services and Path Overhead data is mapped into the PTE. Signals are mapped into the appropriate format, as required by the Line Layer. The Path Layer also reads and interprets the path overhead for the purpose of performance monitoring.

Interleaving

The optical cable can transmit at an extremely high rate. This makes multiplexing several STS-1 signals practical. An interleaving process is used to allow multiple STS-1 signals to appear as a single STS-1 signal.

Interleaving interlaces a signal's individual bytes, so that each signal can be seen within the combined signal. Interleaving involves aligning the STS-1 signals by frame and then byte-interleaving the frames to form an STS-N signal.

The interleaving of multiple STS-1 signals can be done in a one-stage or two-stage process. The two-stage process is necessary to accommodate the European rates; first byte interleaves the STM-1 signals into STS-3 signals, and the STS-3 signals are then interleaved to a higher, STS-N signal. The single-stage process is more direct and interleaves N STS-1 signals to create a larger, STS-N signal without the intermediate step of first creating STS-3 signals.

However, if the rate is less than or equal to an STS-3c, the concatenated signal needs to be fully contained within an STS-3 block. If the rate is more than that of an STS-3c, all of the combined signals need to be fully contained within blocks that are multiples of STS-3.

Clock timing is derived from the incoming OC-N signal. A preamble for clock synchronization is not needed. Framing bits are necessary to indicate the beginning of the frame. Synchronization characters and message framing for clock synchronization are unnecessary in SONET. SONET uses a synchronization network that instead transports timing references between multiple locations. As such, the clock's accuracy is particularly important.

SONET's digital signals, you will notice, do not fit perfectly into the SPE; this requires signal mapping. The difference is made up through bit-stuffing.

Ring Architecture

The two main ring architectures in SONET are the bidirectional line-switched ring (BLSR) and the unidirectional path switched ring (UPSR). BLSRs can be made up of either two or four fibers, although the four-fiber model is more survivable. The UPSR, on the other hand, achieves survivability while sending traffic in one direction on one fiber. The traffic is duplicated and sent over the protection fiber in the opposite direction.

SONET/SDH takes full advantage of the extremely high bandwidth inherent in the fiber-optic medium, as well as its reliability. SONET/SDH uses point-to-point connections, making the technology well-suited for WAN backbones.

Mapping can be done to conventional telecommunications signals, such as DS1 and DS3, as well as other formats. Individual SONET lines can be configured in 1.544Mbps (DS1 channel) increments or 45Mbps (DS3 channel) increments. Unfortunately, the full amount of bandwidth is unavailable when mapping to these signals, because of a hold-over from DS1 mapping developed several years ago. Two of the payload columns are designated as "fixed stuff," and cannot be used to carry traffic. Although these columns are now completely unnecessary, the folks who make the standards have not eliminated them.

The number of stations that can be connected is nearly without limit, and is restricted only by the capacity of the multiplexers. The SONET rates are as follows:

OC-1	52Mbps
OC-3	155Mbps
OC-9	466Mbps
OC-12	622Mbps
OC-18	933Mbps
OC-24	1.2 Gbps
OC-36	1.9 Gbps
OC-48	2.5 Gbps

Some typical SONET applications are:

- LAN-to-LAN and host-to-host interconnection
- Videoconferencing
- Team engineering and design
- Distributed processing
- Advanced scientific research

A fiber network offers a number of advantages. It does not suffer from signal transmission latency, or the atmospheric interference sometimes suffered by satellite configurations.

Sending a signal to a different network requires a complex multiplexing and demultiplexing encoding process to convert the signals between schemes. SONET addresses this problem with a series of standardized formats. The Synchronous Transport Signal (STS) forms the basis of SONET optical interfaces and has a rate of 51.84Mbps. STS is made up of the STS payload and STS overhead. The payload holds the information, while the overhead portion holds signaling and protocol information. Because the STS holds signaling information, intelligent nodes can communicate and the network can be controlled from a central location.

Signals are converted to STS and then travel through SONET networks until termination. Terminating equipment will then convert the STS back to the end user format.

Virtual Tributary

Virtual tributaries are used to allow SONET to multiplex lower-capacity (sub STS-1) channels, down to 64Kbps (DS0). A sub STS-1 channel is called a virtual tributary. An STS-1 signal can hold up to 28 DS1 signals. SONET can also accommodate signals lower than the STS-1 rate (sub-STS-1). A sub-STS-1 signal is known as a Virtual Tributary (VT).

There are four sizes of VTs, each one meant to accommodate a different-sized digital signal. The signals are shown in Table 8.2.

Table 8.2   Sub-STS-1 Rates

Virtual Tributaries		Digital Signals	
VT 1.5	1.728Mbps	DS1	1.544Mbps
VT 2	2.304Mbps	CEPT-1	2.048Mbps
VT 3	3.456Mbps	DSIC	3.152Mbps
VT 6	6.912Mbps	DS2	6.312Mbps

A VT Group (VTG) is a structure that permits a mixture of different VTs to be carried in an STS-1 SPE, created by interleave multiplexing one VT-6, two VT-3s, three VT-2s, and four VT 1.5s. Seven VTGs can be mapped into one STS-1 SPE. A VT can operate in either locked or floating mode.

The locked mode is used mainly to promote efficiency of network elements performing the DS0 switching; floating mode is used primarily to minimize delay for distributed VT switching. In locked mode, a fixed mapping establishes a direct line between the tributaries and their locations. Floating mode lets the payload float within the VT payload capacity. In floating mode, four consecutive 125 microsecond frames of STS-1 SPE make up a single 500 microsecond superframe.

The superframe includes a VT payload pointer, VT synchronous payload envelope, and VT path overhead.

Jitter and Wander

No, this isn't the biggest dance craze since the Macarena. Jitters come from multiplexing and regenerator equipment. Differences in temperature in different portions of the cable may be the cause of wander. *Jitter* is the phase variation that is buffered and filtered by a phase locked loop. *Wander* is the phase variation tracked and passed on by a phase locked loop.

When a signal travels over a long distance, temperature changes over the length of the cable may result in some propagation delay, which over time, can shift pulse position. Wander can also be caused by a drift in regenerator laser wavelength over time. This problem can be addressed by sending each bit stream to a phase locked loop (PLL) or surface acoustic wave filter, to separate the timing from the bit stream.

Jitter can be caused by multiplexing; wander can be caused by temperature differences throughout the length of the cable.

Standards

In 1991, several companies, including AT&T Microelectronics, BT&D Technologies, Hitachi, and Fujitsu, agreed to establish internationally compatible sources of fiber-optic transmitter and receiver modules in support of the SONET/SDH standards. The agreement allows manufacturers to construct their equipment from compatible, board-level modules.

The SONET standards define the rates and formats for optical networks as specified in ANSI T1.105, ANSI T1.106, and ANSI T1.117. The European SDH standard has been established in Europe by the UTI-T. Both are technically consistent.

The synchronous nature of SONET permits the adding and dropping of signals to take place with single multiplexing. The cost of transmission is further minimized by the inclusion of the OAM&P protocol.

SONET was originally established by ANSI after being initiated by Bellcore for the RBOCs. The goal of SONET was to provide a cost-effective framework for multivendor internetworking. The advantages of SONET over asynchronous transmission include the availability of back-to-back multiplexing, an easy migration path to broadband transport, and compatibility with existing operations standards. The SONET equipment interleaves the STSs to establish the synchronous, high-speed signal. This approach eliminates the necessity for demultiplexing to access lower-speed signals.

SONET Internetworking

Because SONET's format separates the overhead and payload fields, it lends itself to carrying virtually any type of digital traffic. SONET promotes compatibility between local and wide area networks.

High Performance Parallel Interface over SONET

A HiPPI/SONET gateway can be used to send HIPPI traffic over long distances. This has been demonstrated by the Los Alamos National Laboratory (LANL). LANL has developed a HiPPI/SONET Gateway as part of its CASA Gigabit Testbed and ACTS satellite system. The gateway sends HiPPI traffic over a distance of 2000 km for the CASA project and over 70,000 km for the satellite link.

The gateway maps HiPPI frames into SONET payload for transport over the WAN link. In order to maintain the full HiPPI speed, the laboratory stripes data over six OC-3c channels of 155Mbps each.

In the outbound direction, the gateway takes HiPPI frames, packages them into a SONET payload, and uses the appropriate number of OC-3c stripes. In the inbound direction, the operation is reversed; HiPPI data is extracted from the SONET payload and recombined into an HiPPI frame.

The SONET standard has been widely adopted by the RBOCs and other telecom carriers as the primary means of communicating over optical fiber.

Many companies have adopted HiPPI as a way of establishing high-speed I/O in their computing products. The high-performance LANs used in the LANL test were made using off-the-shelf HiPPI crossbar switches and interfaces.

The OC-3 SONET rate is the most widely available service provided to end users. LANL rejected the OC-12 rate because of costs and limited availability; and the OC-24 rate suffers from a lack of terminal equipment. The OC-48 rate is the backbone rate most carriers use for cross-country traffic. The carriers' terminal equipment divides the OC-48 rate into 16 OC-3 stripes. The CASA project used an aggregate of eight OC-3 stripes, for a total of 1.2Gbps.

The CASA researchers reported sustained data transmission over TCP/IP of 550Mbps over the 2000 km link between LANL and the San Diego Supercomputer Center. The bandwidth was the maximum that could be sustained by the supercomputers involved in the transmission; the wide-area link itself did not limit the bandwidth. The project constructed a total of 13 HIPPI-SONET gateways.

ATM over SONET

SONET goes with ATM like coffee with donuts. SONET/SDH is defined as a transmission medium for B-ISDN, on which ATM is based. ATM serves as the Layer 2 protocol on the OSI stack. The combination of SONET and ATM makes for an incredibly fast and stable switched public network capable of carrying almost any type of traffic. Most of the long-distance carriers offer ATM, frame relay, or SMDS services over a SONET backbone.

A major advantage of ATM is that it can be used for both local and wide area networking. The ATM Forum recommends, among other physical layer structures, SONET for transmitting high-speed traffic over optical fiber in a public network. Because the SONET format can carry almost any size payload over the network for thousands of miles, it is an ideal technology for an ATM-based internetwork.

There are SONET specifications for the User-to-Network Interface (UNI), and for use in the LAN between a workstation and an ATM LAN switch, or between two local ATM switches. Figure 8.3 illustrates some of the potential uses for SONET on ATM.

FIG. 8.3
ATM on SONET.

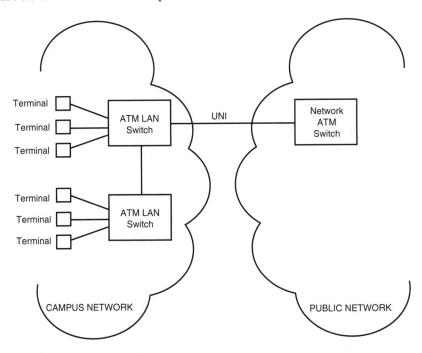

One of the biggest advantages of SONET is its flexibility, and its capability to accommodate several LAN and WAN configurations.

Better internetworking between LANs on a WAN will lead to fewer bottlenecks. Ultimately, the LAN and the WAN should use the same technology, or as close to the same technology as is practically possible. SONET can be used as the physical layer for both the LAN and WAN. With SONET as the LAN protocol, traffic will flow more seamlessly from the PC to the LAN, and across the WAN. There will be no need for rate conversion or buffering, and processing would be faster.

ATM is rate-independent and scalable. SONET, too, is highly scalable because the higher rates are simple multiples of lower rates. Originally, the ATM selected STS-3c as the SONET format for use with ATM, although some manufacturers prefer the STS-1 rate that can be used over twisted-pair.

STS-3c can transport cells at a highly efficient rate, with the STS-3c rate of 155.52Mbps transporting cells at 149.76Mbps.

In terms of the ATM LAN protocol stack, SONET exists at the physical layer, to support the ATM LAN; and also at the ATM Adaptation Layer (AAL), where the ATM cells are created and eventually turned into SONET frames.

The SONET physical layer consists of two sublayers: the Transmission Convergence sublayer (TC) and Physical Medium Dependent sublayer (PMD). The TC sublayer performs the following tasks:

- Header Error Check generation
- Scrambling
- SONET STS-3c frame structure generation
- Cell delineation
- Header error checking
- Performance monitoring

Basically, the TC sublayer exists to take cells from the ATM layer and place them inside of SONET frames for transmission over the SONET internetwork. At the receiving end, the TC sublayer retrieves the ATM cells out of the SONET frame and passes them onto the ATM layer. The PMD sublayer, on the other hand, adds the additional line coding necessary for using SONET over twisted pair.

The ATM Forum has formally defined only STS-3c/OC-3 for use as the SONET physical layer standard for the ATM LAN and UNI. However, Bellcore has defined a method to map ATM cells into an STS-1 frame.

The process of running ATM over SONET starts with accepting ATM cells from the Layer 2 (ATM Layer) process. The ATM layer makes cells out of higher-level data and management information; the SONET physical layer's TC sublayer generates the Header Error Check (HEC) byte for use in the ATM cell's header.

HEC is a single-byte error correcting code and ensures that cells are not delivered incorrectly due to header errors. The TC sublayer then scrambles the 48-byte payload of each ATM cell to decrease the possibility of the user data generating a false framing indication. The cell can then be encapsulated within the SONET frame. The ATM layer delivers a constant stream of cells to the TC process. The ATM layer is required to generate empty cells with null addresses if no data is available for transmission, in order to maintain a steady flow to the TC sublayer. The TC sublayer then hands the frames off to the PMD sublayer. Here, transport overhead of all frames is aligned to allow for faster framing. At the receiving end, after demultiplexing, the ATM frames are taken from the SONET frame.

The PMD sublayer accepts the SONET frame created at the TC sublayer and sends it out over a physical medium (optical fiber).

The ATM Forum has established three interfaces for ATM equipment:

- ■ *I1*. Interfaces between a terminal and local ATM LAN switch.
- ■ *I2*. Defines the interface between local ATM switches.
- ■ *I3*. Defines the interface between a local switch or terminal device, and the public network (UNI).

All three of these interfaces can use SONET. I1 and I2 can use single or multimode fiber or twisted pair; the I3 interface must use single mode fiber.

There are three possibilities for interfacing the ATM LAN with the public network: leased fiber, leased STS-1 or STS-3c, or a public ATM service.

The first option, leased fiber, is straightforward and simple, most local service providers will lease dark fiber between two locations with little restriction. Leased fiber is typically single-mode and can be used for either the I1 or I2 interfaces. This can accommodate a distance of up to about seven miles. Although technically, this is a public interface, there are few restrictions on its use. Dark fiber is merely fiber through which no light (signal) is transmitted by the carrier. In this option, the carrier does not lease SONET capacity, but merely the fiber over which the company can transmit.

The second option, leasing SONET capacity from public carriers in the form of an STS-1 or STS-3c line, provides for more flexibility, because the leased line is carried over the carrier network. Quality-of-service information is sent back across the UNI to the customer, but most of the links are transparent to the user because the carrier is responsible for maintenance. This option provides for almost unlimited range between interconnected equipment, since the leased facility is sent over one or more carrier networks.

Ch
8

The third option, a public ATM service, resembles the leased option, with a minor difference. Path overhead is terminated instead of transported end-to-end. The path is terminated by the first ATM entity encountered by the signal, usually an ATM switch. This option lacks the end-to-end visibility of the second option.

At first glance, the combination of SONET (*synchronous* optical network) and ATM (*asynchronous* transfer mode) sounds like it would mix about as well as peanut butter and pickles. However, terminal equipment is typically loop-timed by the ATM LAN switch, so the link between the two will be inherently synchronous. If the ATM LAN switch and the SONET network have somewhat different clocks, the output buffers contained in the switch will mitigate the difference.

If the switch is slower, an empty cell can be sent to make up the difference. However, for time-sensitive applications, some synchronization between the LAN and the SONET network will be necessary. These time-sensitive applications will require timing information to be carried with the signal (an isochronous signal). Because the signal is sent as an ATM cell, no timing information is exchanged between source and destination ATM LAN switches. However, both switches can be synchronized to the network itself.

Vendors

Some carriers offering SONET services include:

Ameritech Corp. (155Mbps, 622Mbps, 2.4Gbps)

AT&T (T.155)

Bellsouth Corp. (155Mbps, 622Mbps)

British Telecommunications PLC (BT)

Colt Telecommunications Ltd.

Energis Communications Ltd. (2Mbps, 34Mbps, 140Mbps)

LDDS Worldcom (155Mbps, 622Mbps)

MFS Datanet Inc. (155Mbps)

Nippon Telephone and Telegraph Corp. (NTT) (51Mbps, 155Mbps)

Nynex Corp. (155Mbps, 622Mbps, 2.4Gbps)

Pacific Bell (1.544Mbps through 2.488Gbps)

Sprint Corp. (155Mbps, 622Mbps, 2.4Gbps)

Teleport Communications Group (155Mbps, 622Mbps, 2.4Gbps)

US West Advanced Communications Services (1.544Mbps, 45Mbps, 155Mbps, 622Mbps, 1.2Gbps, 2.4Gbps)

Hitachi

http://www.hitachi.com

Voice: 770-446-8820

Fax: 770-242-1414

Hitachi's AMN series of SONET network elements furnish third generation SONET technology for rates from OC-1 to OC-192. Hitachi's AMN 5000 product line focuses on advanced bandwidth management. The first generation of SONET network elements had basic time-slot assignment (TSA) capabilities, which allowed STS-1 traffic to be added, dropped, or passed through at any SONET network element.

Hitachi's AMN 5003 Advanced Multiservices Node (an OC-3 network element) consists of a tributary interface section and a common equipment section. The interface section encompasses the DS1 interface, DS3 interface, STS-1 interface, OC-1 interface, and Protection Switch cards. The AMN 5003 shelf can support as many as 84 DS1, 3 DS3, 3 STS-1, and 6 OC-1 tributaries.

SONET terminals are connected by two pairs of optical fibers: a working fiber pair and a protection fiber pair. The dual pair design allows for network survivability through diverse routing.

At the high end is the AMN 5192 Advanced Multiservices Node (an OC-192 product).

MetaSolv Software

http://www.metasolv.com

14900 Landmark

Suite 530

Dallas, TX 75240

Voice: 972-239-0623

Fax: 972-239-0653

MetaSolv's ASAP software is one of only a handful of packages available that can be used to design and manage SONET networks. A Windows-based package, ASAP offers a set of graphical tools for both designing and tracking the SONET network.

Northern Telecom

http://www.nortel.com

2221 Lakeside Blvd.

Richardson, TX 75082

Voice: 800-4-NORTEL or 214-684-5930

Nortel's DSS II places at the network manager's disposal a set of network management capabilities for operating synchronous networks such as SONET. This technology allows the SONET network to be completely controllable via software.

Nortel's software architecture complies with the ITU TMN (Telecommunications Management Network) model, particularly in relation to the recommended interfaces to the Service and Business Management Layers and the Element Management Layer. The software gives users the ability to configure end-to-end paths, and provides for bandwidth on demand and disaster recovery. It can monitor and respond to faults, and can gather and analyze performance metrics.

The DSS II subsystems include the following:

Operator Workstation (OWS). Manages the user environment and controls end user access to all the various subsystems. Also establishes security management, giving the administrator the ability to configure user accounts and subsystem accessibility.

Event Logging System (ELS). Logs and displays unsolicited messages reported by network elements. Through an SQL database, ELS will display and report on current events in real time. Includes alarm functions and event monitoring.

Service Inventory Management (SIM). Manages network inventory of both physical and logical objects.

Application Management (APM). Manages configuration of other subsystems.

Services Management (SMS) (optional). Lets network operators create DS1 and DS3 paths by specifying end points on a graphical display. Can be used to predefine alternate paths in the event of network failure.

Alarm Status (ALS) (optional). Correlates messages gathered by Event Logging subsystem. Graphically tracks status of network equipment and facilities.

Nortel engineers recommend distributing the DSS II functions over multiple computers on the LAN.

Ameritech

http://www.ameritech.com
30 South Wacker
Floor 34
Chicago, IL 60606

Ameritech's SONET services provide dedicated, point-to-point or multipoint transmission of voice, data, and video at very high speeds. SONET is provided in bandwidths of 155Mbps and 622Mbps; and individual SONET lines can be configured in increments of 1.544Mbps (DS-1 channels) or increments of 45Mbps (DS-3 channels), or a combination of the two.

Ameritech's performance objective is 99.9975 percent error-free seconds; one of the major advantages of the service is the capability to integrate voice, data, and video over a single facility.

Optivision

http://www.optivision.com
3450 Hillview Drive
Palo Alto, CA 94304
Voice: 415-855-0200

Optivision's HIPPI-SONET Single Channel Gateway is used to interconnect two HIPPI networks through SONET fiber. The gateway can be attached to an HIPPI host or a port of an HIPPI network switch. HIPPI data and control lines from the HIPPI network or host are packed into SONET frames, and sent over a single SONET OC-3c link at 132Mbps to another HIPPI host. The receiving host then reconstructs the data stream. Transporting HIPPI data through SONET is transparent to the HIPPI hosts.

Bell Atlantic

http://www.bellatlantic.com

Bell Atlantic includes the following SONET services:

> IntelliLight SONET Transport Service: This basic service provides high-capacity access services in a shared SONET ring with local loop protection.

IntelliLight Dual Wire Center: This service eliminates the risk of disruption to faults in the local loop, wiring center, or interoffice facilities.

IntelliLight Custom SONET Ring: This service provides a dedicated SONET ring, also with automatic rerouting at point-of-failure.

Ch 8

Summary

SONET uses fiber-optic rings to offer extremely high transmission rates over long distances. SONET offers an unusual availability technology that automatically and transparently reroutes traffic in the event of a severed cable.

SONET is available in multiples of STS-1 rates (51.84Mbps), sub-STS-1 rates as low as 56Kbps, and multiples of STS-3 rates (622Mbps). Because the payload and overhead are kept separate, SONET can be used to transmit almost any type of traffic, including ATM and HIPPI. ●

CHAPTER 9

HiPPI

Back in the '60s, a small group of Beatniks migrated from North Beach to the Haight-Ashbury district, grew their hair long, and rebelled against the system. Perhaps one of them eventually wandered southeast of San Francisco to Silicon Valley. Maybe then this person went on to become an engineer, laying down the groundwork for the *High-Performance Parallel Interface (HiPPI)*.

HiPPI was initially developed to connect heterogeneous supercomputers with IBM mainframes. It is a connection-oriented, circuit-switched mechanism that offers a data rate of up to 1.6Gbps. Besides connecting big iron, it can be used to address areas that need tremendous amounts of bandwidth, such as scientific visualization, cinematic special effects, or structural analysis.

The first 800Mbps HiPPI specification was established at New Mexico's Los Alamos National Laboratory as a high-speed data pipe for connecting Cray supercomputers to visualization displays. Since that time, HiPPI has found its way into everything from PC network adapters to backbone switches. Furthermore, the price per switch port has decreased significantly, as has the cost of fiber—making the technology even more attractive. ∎

Overview of HiPPI

Created in the late 1980s, the original application of HiPPI was as a supercomputer technology but the latest version can be applied to internetworks and workstation clusters. It is limited to 50 m in point-to-point copper wire connections, but can span 300 m over multimode fiber, and 10 km over single-mode fiber. Furthermore, the latest proposed standards extend the 50 m copper limitation by allowing cascading multiple switches, which allows an effective length of 200 m.

Some of the advantages of HiPPI include:

■ Simplicity

■ Efficient physical-level flow control

■ HiPPI networks use crossbar switches, which have multiple inputs and outputs, and a separate connection path between each input and output, allowing for simultaneous connections.

■ An efficient tester is available that allows vendors to test implementations in-house, effectively making the interconnection with other vendors' equipment a straightforward process.

■ Several products with HiPPI interfaces are on the market, including switches, chassis, and adapter cards.

■ Crossbar switches are available from several vendors.

■ Longer distances can be accommodated with HiPPI-to-SONET adapters, giving HiPPI the ability to operate over the same Metropolitan Area Network (MAN) as any SONET ring.

Although HiPPI provides an incredible amount of bandwidth when compared with other technologies, there are still a few limitations:

■ A few applications require the enormous bandwidth of HiPPI, so it is not a mass-market item and, as a result, has higher prices.

■ It does not support speeds of less than 800Mbps.

■ It does not support multiplexing.

■ It does not support isochronous or time-critical data.

■ It provides little support for network administration tools.

HiPPI conforms to ANSI X3T9.3, and operates in 32-bit parallel mode at 800Mbps. Operating in parallel gives it an effective rate of 1.6Gbps. Actually a simplex channel, HiPPI transmits data in only one direction, but because it is configured in pairs, the end result is full duplex, 1.6Gbps operation. Through driver software, users can operate the HiPPI channel directly or indirectly via TCP or UDP sockets. HiPPI is a general-purpose channel, and is well-suited to several different types of high-performance applications. These include:

- *Distributed applications.* HiPPI's speed makes applications such as data acquisition and analysis more suited for distributed processing.
- *Raster graphics.* Real-time animated graphics offering motion picture quality are possible when HiPPI is used with a high-speed frame buffer. This capability has pressed HiPPI into service in Hollywood, adding fabulous special effects to movies.
- *High-speed file transfer.* HiPPI can be used to transfer files quickly between high-end systems much faster than with any other type of channel architecture. Software for file transfers includes FTP and RCP which use TCP sockets.
- *Shared mass storage.* With NFS, a remote system's files can be accessed as if they were local. Using NFS over HiPPI between high-end systems gives the effect of shared mass storage.

As a point-to-point connection technology, HiPPI was originally designed to connect two devices—such as a supercomputer and a peripheral device—at rates of 800Mbps or 1.6Gbps over a 25 m cable. However, HiPPI has evolved significantly to become an important method for high-speed data communications and gigabit services.

The Evolution of HiPPI

In the 1980s, researchers at the Los Alamos National Laboratory reviewed their connections between supercomputers, storage devices, and other peripherals. Seeing potential for bottlenecks, the lab started to look for a higher-speed connection. The network had an existing transmission rate of 50Mbps—more than adequate for most networks, but not quite enough for this high-powered national lab. Data simulation, for example, called for showing 30 frames per second on a 24-bit color monitor. This required a transmission rate of nearly 750Mbps—quite impossible on its existing system.

In 1987, the proprietary Cray HSX interface ran at 850Mbps. However, Los Alamos wanted an interoperable, multivendor solution.

During that same year, researchers at Los Alamos presented their own design for a Gbps channel, now called HiPPI, to the ANSI working group on high-speed data transmission. The standard was soon underway, and the first HiPPI product appeared in 1988 in the form of an IBM 3090 HiPPI port. That year, Los Alamos also built a prototype HiPPI switch, and in 1989, the first commercial HiPPI switches hit the market. In 1991, HiPPI was officially ratified by ANSI, becoming the very first national standard for gigabit per second data transmission.

Ch
9

Beyond Supercomputers

Engineers have been working to extend HiPPI below the supercomputer level and create HiPPI applications for an Ethernet internetwork. HiPPI can work with most LAN and WAN technologies, including Ethernet, FDDI, ATM, Fibre Channel, and TCP/IP. It can link workstations and a variety of hosts, storage systems, and more at extremely high speeds.

HiPPI may eventually combine with ATM to benefit managers with ATM's wide-area capabilities, as well as HiPPI's speed over the local area.

HiPPI-ATM Interface

A HiPPI-ATM interface, which is under development by the HiPPI Networking Forum and ANSI, would encapsulate HiPPI data for transport over the ATM network, then reconstruct the HiPPI data at the receiving end. Such an interface would give users the best of both technologies: HiPPI's extremely high throughput in the local area, and ATM's wide-area connectivity. A HiPPI-ATM interface could potentially end multimedia data from HiPPI servers to ATM desktops.

Unfortunately, there are tremendous obstacles to creating a HiPPI-ATM gateway. Although both are connection-oriented, HiPPI is circuit-switched, and ATM is cell-switched. Once established, the gateway would divide HiPPI frames into ATM cells, tunnel it through the ATM network, and reassemble it at the other end.

As a switch-based LAN/WAN technology, HiPPI presents a simple, connection-oriented scheme to allow two devices to communicate. It is also possible to establish a permanent connection between two point-to-point links.

N O T E   At the present time, multiple connections cannot be multiplexed over the same line. ▨

Implementation and Infrastructure

The physical elements of a HiPPI network include ports for the devices connected to the network, cables for network links, and a switch used to connect devices.

As a machine-room networking technology, the HiPPI standard first specified copper cables with a maximum length of 25 m. Some vendors now supply fiber-optic cables that can extend the HiPPI links to 10 km. This extension is part of an implementors agreement, however, and not part of the official HiPPI standard.

HiPPI has become the technology of choice for short-distance, gigabit-per-second needs. Simplicity was a major part of its design, and the interface is easy to understand and implement. Numerous interfaces have come to connect HiPPI with SONET, ATM, and Fibre Channel, establishing long-distance interconnections.

Under HiPPI, there are two ways to establish a connection: Two hardware components can be connected directly with a HiPPI link, or a switch can be used. A HiPPI switch can accommodate four input components and four output destinations.

HiPPI signaling sequences are very simple, and consist of three messages:

- *Request.* This message is used by the source to request a connection.
- *Connect.* This message is used by the destination to indicate that the connection has been established.
- *Ready.* This message is used by the destination machine to indicate it is ready to accept packet streams.

HiPPI offers protocol independence. The HiPPI channels can accommodate raw HiPPI data, which is data formatted in compliance with the HiPPI framing protocol and without any upper-layer protocols. HiPPI can also accommodate TCP/IP datagrams and IPI-3 (Intelligent Peripheral Interface) framed data. IPI-3 is used to connect RAID devices to computers. HiPPI can also be used for internetworking and high-speed data storage. Physical-layer flow control is enabled by a simple mechanism, whereby the source tracks the Ready signals and sends data only when the destination is prepared to handle them.

A HiPPI packet is sent as a sequence of bursts, each one containing up to 256 words. At 800Mbps, each word is 32 bits; at 1.6Gbps, each word is 64 bits wide. Only the first burst in a packet can be less than 256 words; other bursts must be exactly 256 words. HiPPI uses variable-length packets; a packet can be as little as 2 bytes or as large as 4G. Also, all HiPPI packets contain a higher layer protocol identifier and 1,016 bytes of control information.

HiPPI Protocols

Under the ISO Reference Model, HiPPI functions in the Physical and Data Link layers. At higher levels, HiPPI supports IPI-3 for storage connectivity, and TCP/IP for networking. As such, it is compatible with Ethernet, FDDI, Token Ring, and other wide-area protocols. HiPPI also offers support for Address Resolution Protocol (ARP), allowing a HiPPI network to self-configure.

Ch

9

In addition, HiPPI technology makes provisions for physical-layer flow control, effectively eliminating errors or data loss that would be caused by congestion. Both data transfer and flow are executed in small bursty increments, with each burst containing 1,024 or 2,048 bytes. Error reporting is also provided from the physical layer.

CAUTION

HiPPI provides error detection but not error correction. Error correction will be included in the new HiPPI 6400 implementation once it becomes available.

The various protocols outlined in the HiPPI 6400 standard include:

■ *HiPPI 6400 PH (Physical layer).* This specifies the physical layer, point-to-point, full duplex link for transmitting user data at 6.4Gbps per direction over parallel copper cable or parallel fiber-optic cable. The specification calls for small, fixed-size micropackets, which establish a low-latency, efficient structure for sending messages of any size. In addition, services are provided here for sending data associated with other protocols.

■ *HiPPI 6400 SC (Switch Control).* This protocol establishes procedures for controlling the physical layer switches based on HiPPI 6400 PH.

Physical Layer   HiPPI uses a parallel data path with copper cable. 800Mbps HiPPI requires a 32-bit data bus; 1600Mbps HiPPI requires a 64-bit data bus. HiPPI is a simplex channel that can transfer data in only one direction, but two HiPPI channels can be used in combination to create a full duplex channel. As a point-to-point technology, HiPPI does not support multi-drop operations. Although this may be somewhat limiting, HiPPI's point-to-point nature greatly simplifies its specification. Some of the limitations may be mitigated through use of crossbar switches.

Once a connection has been made, packets can be sent from the source to the destination. Each packet contains one or more bursts, or it may be a null packet with no bursts. A burst contains up to 256 words, each of which is made up of 32 or 64 bits. One word is sent for each contiguous clock period. Wait time between packets is dependent on the data flow between the physical layer and the upper layer protocols.

For distances of up to 25 m, 50-pair, shielded twisted-pair (STP) cables can be used. One cable is required to achieve 800Mbps, two for 1600Mbps.

A HiPPI connection is very similar to that of a telephone conversation. The source inputs a numeric field through the data bus and issues a REQUEST signal. The destination must then issue a CONNECT signal in order to accept the call. If the destination does not wish to accept the call, it can either not react to the REQUEST signal, or it can issue a CONNECTION REJECT signal, which allows the source to disconnect the line immediately.

Once a connection is established, single or multiple packets may be transferred from the source to the destination. Packets, which are made up of multiple bursts, are delimited with a TRUE packet signal. Bursts, on the other hand, are delimited by a TRUE burst signal. Packets are delimited by the PACKET signal being true.

The destination node controls the data flow by issuing a READY signal every time it is ready to accept a burst from the source node. When the READY signal arrives back at the source before the source is ready to send out the next burst, there is no time lag between bursts. This method means that if the cable length time is shorter than the amount of time required to send a burst, flow control is distance-independent. This independence can be maintained by adding one burst buffer for each kilometer of cable.

Framing Protocol   The HiPPI framing protocol (FP) defines how packets are framed for transmission over the HiPPI connection. The FP divides packets into three individual pieces: the Header Area, D1 Area, and D2 Area. Each of the three areas starts and ends on a 64-bit boundary. The sizes and offsets of D1 and D2 are defined in the Header Area. D1 is used to hold control information, and D2 is used to hold data pertaining to the control information.

The interface to the FP layer is defined through a set of three standards: Link Encapsulation, an IPI-3 document, and HiPPI MI. Link Encapsulation (HiPPI LE) encapsulates IEEE 802.2 Logical Link PDUs (Protocol Data Units) inside of HiPPI packets, which allow IP traffic to travel on HiPPI connections. The IPI-3 document addresses mapping between the IPI-3 command sets and HiPPI-FP packets. HiPPI MI (Memory Interface) is a generic memory interface protocol, used for remote memory reads and writes over the HiPPI interface.

Switch Control   HiPPI SW (switch control) implements an innovative switch control standard. The switch control protocol is used to control switches connected to the HiPPI cable. The protocol describes the Carrier-to-Carrier Interface (CCI), or I-field, and defines how switches interpret them in order to route connection requests. The current document also contains references to the possibility of doing a broadcast operation, although this function may not remain part of the official standard.

In addition, the ANSI X3T9.3 committee has a draft proposal for encapsulating IP on HiPPI. This proposal would use ANSI standard HiPPI hardware and protocols over the Internet, and includes using HiPPI switches as LANs, and interoperating with other networks. This draft proposal is intended to become an Internet standard.

Ch
9

HiPPI 6400

The next-generation HiPPI interface is currently under development by the ANSI X3T11 HiPPI subcommittee. HiPPI 6400 will furnish a data rate of 6400Mbps (6.4Gbps), while still maintaining the low latency and distance advantages of standard HiPPI. The objectives of the proposal, which were initially made by Silicon Graphics and Cray Research, include:

- Ultra-high bandwidth and throughput
- Latency of less than one microsecond
- Predictability
- Distance of over 1 km at full speed
- Use of copper wire for lower costs at shorter distances
- Multiplexing capability
- Compatibility with older HiPPI standards
- Flow control
- Error detection and recovery
- More network management features including auto-configuration

HiPPI 6400 uses coaxial cable at distances up to 25 m, or multi-mode optical fiber for distances up to 1 km. Single-mode optical fiber can extend the distances to up to 10 km. HiPPI 6400 is a full-duplex technology that runs at 3.2Gbps in each direction for a total of 6.4Gbps. A HiPPI 6400 network offers several advantages over older HiPPI networks. Some of these advantages include:

- The capability to build a HiPPI 6400 network using switches.
- HiPPI 6400 switches can still accommodate older HiPPI 800 connections through adapter boxes.
- HiPPI 6400 can use copper cable and parallel fiber cable.

The ANSI X3T11 HiPPI 6400 working group started work on the HiPPI 6400 specification in 1996. The group hopes to establish a new version of HiPPI capable of running reliably at 6.4Gbps. Besides an upgrade path for 800Mbps HiPPI, HiPPI 6400 includes several new innovations. It inserts high-latency protocol functions directly into the Physical Layer, and includes error detection, retransmission, flow control, and logical level message-size based multiplexing. This new design significantly minimizes latency and cuts down on software overhead. The previous HiPPI specification implemented these features through software.

N O T E HiPPI 6400 will be able to accommodate a much larger marketplace through its added reliability and its unique, message-size dependent, Physical Layer multiplexing capability. Control operations and small messages will only compete with each other on one of the four virtual channels (VC). HiPPI-6400 recognizes the Ethernet and IP LAN protocols, and the HiPPI-6400 MAC header closely resembles the Ethernet MAC header for easy translation. In addition, IP support is included for simple integration into current IP networks. ■

HiPPI 6400's Link layer runs 32-byte micropackets for low latency multiplexing and easy retransmission.

In addition, a scheduled transfer interface (HiPPI ST) establishes a predetermined data transfer feature, which lets two hosts set up and reserve everything needed for data transfer.

HiPPI 6400 goes far beyond the capabilities of the first HiPPI by adding reliability, multiplexing, and other features. Furthermore, the HiPPI 6400 Media Access Control (MAC) Header recognizes Ethernet and IP, making translation and IP support straightforward. HiPPI 6400 will also support SNMP and ARP, making it easy to incorporate a HiPPI connection into an existing network.

HiPPI Goes to the Movies

HiPPI, although it was originally meant as a mechanism for connecting supercomputers, has found its way into the motion picture industry. Digital technology has become more prevalent in motion pictures over the past few years as a means of producing dramatic special effects. Digital films, however, require a huge volume of information to be sent back and forth. A single frame may consume 40M of information. At 24 frames per second, that's 960M—almost a whole gigabyte—per second. Fast Ethernet and FDDI, at 100Mbps, is obviously inadequate for sending digital video across the wires. Even ATM, running at its maximum at 622Mbps, would still be slow.

Fibre Channel may offer more appropriate speeds, but HiPPI is the more established technology. Serial HiPPI provides signaling of 1.2Gbps over distances as great as 10 km; a full line of devices and software is widely available and cost-effective. HiPPI technology has been widely used in Hollywood, in films such as Clint Eastwood's *In the Line of Fire*, to provide special effects for some of the biggest hits on the big screen.

Integration with Other Technologies

The simplest implementation of HiPPI is a connection between two computers with a HiPPI channel consisting of two 50-pair copper cables. However, HiPPI-Serial can establish a fiber connection to as long as 10 km, allowing multiple switches to be connected to a

HiPPI backbone. HiPPI has also come to be used as a mechanism for interconnecting LANs. HiPPI has also long been used as a high-speed channel for connecting disk and tape controllers, various storage devices, and more.

Ultimately, HiPPI can present a simple way to build a gigabit-rate switched TCP/IP network. It can be used to link workstations and hosts, connect workstations with storage systems, and attach display peripherals to promote real-time visualization. In the workstation cluster, HiPPI lends itself to applications such as animation or scientific visualization.

HiPPI and ATM The ATM market, on the other hand, does not generally achieve the rates offered by HiPPI. The two, however, can work together effectively. A gateway running from a HiPPI cluster to ATM would give end users HiPPI's throughput at the LAN level, along with the wide-area connectivity of ATM.

A HiPPI-ATM connection would work by encapsulating the HiPPI data for transport over the ATM network, and then reassembling it at the other end. This would be accomplished through ATM's AAL5 (adaptation layer 5). The proposed HiPPI-ATM gateway specification is still a draft standard, but some companies, including NetStar, have HiPPI-ATM interface devices based on the draft standard.

HiPPI and Fibre Channel   HiPPI also complements Fibre Channel technology. Both technologies are the product of the same ANSI X3T11 committee, although Fibre Channel is much more complex. An ANSI standard has been defined for sending upper-layer Fibre Channel protocols over lower-layer HiPPI media. A complementary standard for sending HiPPI upper-layer protocol over Fibre Channel lower-layer media is also under development.

An ANSI standard has been defined to specify how to transmit upper-layer Fibre Channel protocols over lower-layer HiPPI media. A complementary ANSI standard, which defines how to transmit HiPPI upper-layer protocols over Fibre Channel lower-layer media, is still underway. The standard for sending HiPPI upper-layer protocol over Fibre Channel will describe a point-to-point, physical layer of the high-performance serial link. It will support the higher protocols from HiPPI, Intelligent Peripheral Interface (IPI), and SCSI. This standard will specify a signaling rate of at least 132.8M baud, and no more than 1.0625G baud. The standard will establish a method of transport for the upper layers of HiPPI, IPI, and SCSI, and will be capable of replacing their existing physical interfaces. IPI commands, SCSI commands, and HiPPI data link operations will be able to be combined on the Fibre Channel.

HiPPI and SONET Over long distances, HiPPI can take advantage of SONET technology. Under a HiPPI/SONET network, the HiPPI network extends to a HiPPI/SONET gateway, which frames the HiPPI data for transport over SONET. HiPPI maps directly to a single SONET OC-12c circuit (622-Mbit/sec) circuit or multiple SONET OC-3 circuits.

Los Alamos National Laboratories developed the HiPPI/SONET gateway for use in its CASA Gigabit Testbed and ACTS satellite system. This gateway is used to send HiPPI traffic over long distances, of up to 2,000 km in the case of CASA, and a whopping 70,000 km for the satellite link. CASA presents HiPPI LANs connected by a wide-area SONET fiber-optic circuit. The HiPPI-SONET gateway maps HiPPI frames into SONET payloads for transmission over the wide-area links. Six SONET OC-3c channels of 155Mbps each are required to realize the full HiPPI bandwidth potential of 800Mbps, although the gateway can support eight OC-3c channels.

Standards Development

The ANSI standards that specify HiPPI are as follows:

- Physical Layer: X3.183-1991
- Switch Control: X3.222-1993
- Link Encapsulation: X3.218-1993
- Framing Protocol: X3.210-1992

ANSI/ISO specifications are:

- Disk Connections: 9318-3
- Tape Connections: 9318-4

Further standards work is being done to map HiPPI to ATM.

HiPPI MIB

The HiPPI Networking Forum and ANSI X3T11 Technical Committee are both working to make HiPPI even easier to manage. A proposal for a HiPPI MIB (management information base) is underway, and some developers are working to integrate HiPPI with management platforms such as IBM's NetView and HP's OpenView.

A HiPPI MIB is being developed for SNMP, which includes features for self-discovery of switch addresses, and address resolution between MAC addresses and HiPPI addresses.

Serial HiPPI

Serial HiPPI is not a formal ANSI standard, but rather an agreement between manufacturers. It establishes an extended standard that is used for sending data serially between

HiPPI PH nodes. Serial HiPPI outlines both optical and electrical interfaces. This Implementers Agreement (IA) defines a method for running HiPPI over single-mode fiber for distances of up to 10 km.

Product Overview

Several vendors offer HiPPI paraphernalia, along with other high-speed, fiber-optic products.

Essential Communications

http://www.esscom.com/
4374 Alexander Blvd. NE, Suite T
Albuquerque, NM 87107
505-344-0080
800-278-7897
Fax: 505-344-0408
E-mail: **info@esscom.com**

Essential Communications is very active in gigabit networking. The company provides hardware and software for building and managing everything from small, high-performance workgroups to high-speed, enterprise-wide backbones. Essential was the first company to introduce a full line of HiPPI and Serial HiPPI products, providing signaling rates up to 1,200 Mbit/sec (in each direction simultaneously). While Serial HiPPI is the fastest networking technology available today, Essential is positioning itself to be at the forefront of all gigabit networking technologies, including ATM, Fibre Channel, Gigabit Ethernet, and HiPPI-6400. Essential offers a full range of HiPPI products, including switches, base chassis, and adapter cards. In addition, the company's management software facilitates switch management, traffic routing, alternative path routing, and other administrative functions.

Applied Micro Circuits Corporation

http://www.amcc.com
6195 Lusk Blvd.
San Diego, CA 92121
619-450-9333

AMCC offers a selection of HiPPI interface circuits for 800Mbps connections.

GigaLabs

http://www.gigalabs.com

290 Santa Ana Court

Sunnyvale, CA 95086

408-481-3030 or 800-LAN-8120

Fax: 408-481-3045

E-mail: **info@gigalabs.com**

GigaLabs offers a selection of HiPPI switches, test equipment, frame buffers, and adapter boards.

Broadband Communications Products (BCP)

305 East Drive

Melbourne, FL 32904

407-984-3671

Fax: 407-728-0487

E-mail: **fiberlink@bcpinc.com**

BCP, Inc. specializes in the development and manufacture of high-speed fiber-optic communications and test equipment. BCP offers a large selection of HiPPI and other gigabit technology.

Cray Research (A Silicon Graphics Company)

655 Lone Oak Drive

Eagan, MN 55121

612-452-6650

Fax: 612-683-7199

Cray, a leader in supercomputer technology, has an impressive selection of HiPPI equipment, including computer adapter boards.

Hewlett-Packard

http://www.hp.com/

Workgroup Networks Division and Direct Connect Operation

8000 Foothills Blvd.

Roseville, CA 95747-5551

Hewlett-Packard, an active participant in the Serial HiPPI Implementors Agreement, offers a selection of Serial HiPPI chips.

IBM Corp.

http://www.rs6000.ibm.com/hardware/index.html#adapters
800-IBM-4YOU (Canada)
800-IBM-3333 (U.S.)
E-mail: **askibm@info.ibm.com**

IBM supports HiPPI on its RS/6000 platform, delivering some of the highest throughput in the industry. IBM uses HiPPI to enhance the performance of its file transfer and clustering capabilities. IBM's offerings open up HiPPI networks to the RS/6000 platform, bringing supercomputer technology to the RS/6000.

Optivision

415-855-0200
3450 Hillview Dr.
Palo Alto, CA 94304

Optivision offers equipment for establishing a HiPPI-SONET gateway, HiPPI repeaters, and other equipment.

Silicon Graphics

800-800-7441
2011 N. Shoreline Blvd.
Mountain View, CA 94043

Silicon Graphics has been a driving force in bringing HiPPI to the motion picture and high-end graphics industry. Silicon Graphics' offerings include a selection of both HiPPI and Serial HiPPI adapter boards.

Silicon Graphics is active in the development of the HiPPI 6400 specification. The company is designing an Application-specific Integrated Circuit (ASIC) capable of implementing HiPPI 6400 for use in contracts and on Silicon Graphics' own computer line.

Summary

HiPPI was first created in the late 1980s as a technology to interconnect supercomputers, although the latest implementation can be applied to internetworks and workstation clusters. Although it was not originally created as a MAN or WAN technology, longer distances have been achieved through a HiPPI-to-SONET gateway. In addition, new developments and evolving standards may significantly add to HiPPI's potential networking distance.

HiPPI operates in 32-bit parallel mode at 800Mbps, giving it an effective rate of 1.6Gbps. Although it is a simplex channel technology that transmits data in only one direction, because it is configured in pairs, the end result is a de facto full duplex, 1.6Gbps operation.

The next step in the development of HiPPI is the proposed HiPPI 6400 standard, which will operate at an incredible 6.4Gbps. ●

Ch

9

CHAPTER 10

Fibre Channel

There are two kinds of protocols for device connection: channels and networks. A *channel* is a link between a master host computer and a slave peripheral device. It is used to send very large quantities of data at high speeds, usually over small distances. There is little software overhead once data transmission begins. A *network*, on the other hand, interfaces multiple users over both short and long distances, and supports many smaller transactions. A network can endure much higher overhead than a channel link.

Channels are closed environments, where all devices that can communicate with the host are known in advance. These slave peripherals are connected directly to the host system. In a channel, a direct or switched point-to-point connection is established. Channels are typically a hardware-intensive environment with very little software overhead.

Networks, on the other hand, are open and less structured. In a network, any host or device can communicate with any other host or device. Although in some environments, such as NetWare, the nodes cannot directly communicate with each other, there is at least node-to-host communications in any event. The network consists usually of several distributed nodes, which can interact with each other either directly or indirectly, and with centralized servers. Networks are much more software-intensive than a channel system, and usually slower.

Fibre Channel combines the best of channel and network systems into a new I/O interface. ■

Overview

Fibre Channel is not a true channel, nor is it a true network topology. It establishes an intelligent interconnection mechanism called a *fabric* for connecting devices. The high-performance serial link can support not only its own protocol, but several other higher-level protocols as well. The switch(es) connecting the devices are collectively known as the *fabric*. The link is established by two unidirectional fibers moving in opposite directions. Each fiber has a transmitter at one end and a receiver at the other end.

There are three possible applications for Fibre Channel:

- *Clustering*, or connecting processors in a point-to-point link for the purpose of parallel processing
- Linking processors to storage arrays
- LAN backbone technology

Although the latter usage is still controversial, there is some interest in using Fibre Channel for this purpose. There are advantages to using Fibre Channel as a high-speed LAN backbone. It is designed to be friendly, and is able to map into existing computer methodologies. On the other hand, Fibre Channel is less scalable and more expensive than technologies such as Asynchronous Transfer Mode (ATM).

Fibre Channel is well-suited for connectivity with high-speed storage access and server clustering, gigabit enterprise backbones, and gigabit LANs.

Initially, Fibre Channel was used in enterprise networking and point-to-point RAID and large storage subsystems. It has since expanded to accommodate On-Line Transaction Processing (OLTP) servers, video and graphics, video editing, and imaging systems.

Why Is It Called "Fibre Channel?"

The standards bodies are not trying to be pretentious by using the European spelling of *fiber*. Rather, the French spelling, *Fibre*, is used for a very specific reason. The older fiber channel standard could run on fiber media only. Later, when the standards bodies advanced the standard to allow it to run over any serial media, including copper coaxial or twisted pair, the term *fiber* no longer applied. However, they still wanted to retain the term because it had come to be widely recognized. So, they decided to replace *fiber* with *fibre* to reflect the new specification, while still keeping some level of name recognition.

Furthermore, use of the term *channel* does not indicate that Fibre Channel is strictly a channel protocol. Indeed, it can be applied to either channels or networks. Fibre Channel can support a variety of transmission methods, including ATM, IEEE 802, Internet Protocol (IP), and High Performance Parallel Interface (HiPPI). The two types of interfaces (channels and networks) can share the same physical medium. That is, information can be transmitted to the network via Fibre Channel, and Fibre Channel can also be used to allow a machine to communicate with its directly-attached peripherals.

Ch 10

Standards Development

Development on the Fibre Channel standard started in 1988, as an outgrowth of work being done on the *Intelligent Peripheral Interface (IPI)* Enhanced Physical standard. Although it is not practical to deploy Fibre Channel on low-end PCs, it is widely used in systems ranging from workstations to mainframes.

The *Fibre Channel Association (FCA)* consists of more than 120 member companies dedicated to promoting Fibre Channel technology. The organization hopes to develop an interconnected technology to promote full interoperability between products, ultimately resulting in a plug-and-play environment.

The development of Fibre Channel is primarily the responsibility of the ANSI X3T11 committee. There has been a lot of work on extending Fibre Channel, particularly in faster link speeds and new classes of service. The official Fibre Channel standard documents include the following:

- *FC-PH*. Fibre Channel Physical Interface.
- *FC-PH-2*. Fibre Channel Enhanced Physical Interface.
- *FC-PH-3*. Fibre Channel Physical and Signaling Interface.
- *FC-IG*. Fibre Channel Implementation Guide.

- *FC-FP*. Fibre Channel Mapping to HiPPI-FP Framing Protocol.

- *FC-LE*. Fibre Channel, Link Encapsulation.

- *FC-SB*. Single Byte Command Code Sets.

- *GPP*. SCSI-3 Generic Packetized Protocol.

- *FCP SCSI-3*. Fibre Channel Protocol.

- *FC-FG*. Fibre Channel Fabric Generic Requirements.

- *FC-SW*. Fibre Channel Switched Fabric Requirements.

- *FC-AL*. Fibre Channel Arbitrated Loop.

- *FC-AL-2*. X3T11/Project 1133.

- *FC-FLA*. FC Loop Attachment.

- *FC-PLDA*. FC Private Loop Attachment.

- *FC-ATM*. Fibre Channel mapping to ATM.

- *FC-GS*. Fibre Channel Generic Services.

- *FC-FLA*. FC Loop Attachment.

- *FC-PLDA*. FC Private Loop Attachment.

- *IP (Internet Protocol)* and *ARP (Address Resolution Protocol)* on *FC*.

- *10-Bit Interface Specification (8b/10b encoding)*.

IBM, Sun Microsystems, and Hewlett-Packard did the early development of Fibre Channel, having founded the *Fibre Channel Systems Initiative (FCSI)*. The FCSI later disbanded and was succeeded by the FCA, which includes some of the founders of the FCSI.

Implementation and Infrastructure

Fibre Channel was developed to offer a practical and inexpensive way to transfer data quickly between workstations, mainframes, supercomputers, and peripherals.

Many existing protocols suffer from high system overhead or low data transmission speeds. Fibre Channel achieves very high performance while still providing a system with low overhead. The technology is extremely fast, serial, scalable, asynchronous, and switched. It is independent of the type of data being transferred, and can therefore carry multiple higher-level protocols such as SCSI and HiPPI on channels, or TCP/IP and ATM for networks.

The same protocols that suffer from high overhead often suffer from a progressively degrading efficiency level in heavier traffic. Protocols that use asynchronous transfer, on the other hand, maintain high throughput under heavy loading. Fibre Channel uses a switched topology as opposed to a shared media or shared bandwidth concept. A *switched fabric* is used to connect all participating nodes, making it possible to achieve multiple, concurrent connections.

Fibre Channel nodes can be connected directly in a point-to-point topology, or cabled through a switch or hub. Because each node functions as a repeater for every other node on a Fibre Channel loop, a single disconnected or failed node can bring down the entire loop. A *concentrator* can automatically bypass a downed node, and is essential to providing continuous availability on the network.

Using a concentrator offers some advantages, including fault tolerance and easier trouble-shooting. However, the concentrator itself can be a single point of failure. Redundant cabling and concentrators offer additional fault tolerance if needed. One way to provide redundancy in a Fibre Channel system is to establish two independent, redundant loops. This scheme furnishes two independent data paths with redundant hardware. This is, however, a costly solution, and for all but the most sensitive networks, the concentrator will be adequate.

With Fibre Channel, you can cascade up to 126 nodes per concentrator. Ethernet can be bridged to Fibre Channel with a Fibre Channel-to-Ethernet router. Fibre Channel can be managed through the Simple Network Management Protocol (SNMP) interface, and a draft for an SNMP Management Information Base (MIB) is under consideration by the Internet Engineering Task Force (IETF).

Any number of Fibre Channel nodes can be connected, although only 127 nodes can be active at any one given time because of addressing concerns.

Types of Optics Used in Fibre Channel

There are two types of optics used: *Optical Fibre control (OFC)* and *non-OFC lasers*. OFC is employed when using a high-powered transmitter and short-wave laser. The OFC system uses a handshake procedure to protect against possible eye damage. If the receiver detects a loss of light, which may indicate a disconnected or broken cable, it will automatically shut down the transmitter. OFC must be used on all medium power and high power short-wave 870 nanometer (nm) lasers, and on high powered short-wave 850 nm lasers. The OFC must be installed on both ends of the Fibre Channel link.

Non-OFC optics uses a lower-powered laser that is safe to the eye; the protective measures needed in medium and high-power short-wave are not required.

Ch
10

Fibre Channel Frame Format

Every Fibre Channel port has two fibers: one for transmitting and one for receiving. The information is sent out and received over these fibers in the form of *frames*. Fibre Channel frames are grouped into *sequences*, which are in turn grouped into exchanges. The *exchange* is the largest unit, and consists of the entire file or message that needs to be transferred. The exchange is divided into multiple sequences; each sequence is further divided into frames before transfer can occur.

A frame is made up of several *Transmission Words (TWs)*, each one of which is 4 bytes long. A frame (see Figure 10.1) can be as long as 2,148 bytes, with a 2,112-byte payload and 64-byte headers. The *header* includes control information in which the sender and destination is identified, protocol, and type of information.

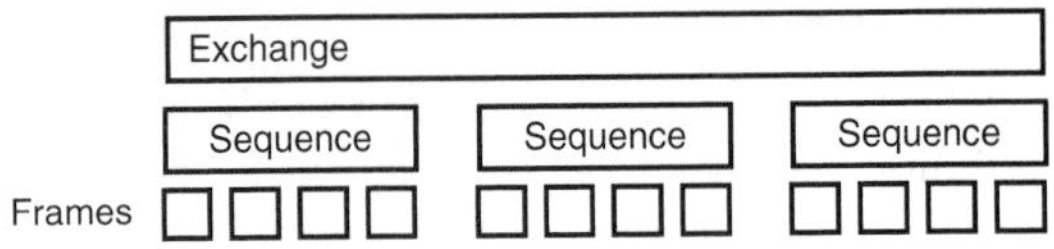

FIG. 10.1
Fibre Channel frames are grouped into sequences, which are in turn grouped into a single exchange.

The Fibre Channel frame uses a 4-byte marker at the beginning and end, with the starting marker followed by a 24-byte frame header with addressing information. After the frame header is the *data field*, which can hold up to 2,112 bytes, including a 2,048-byte payload and a 64-byte header. Then comes a 4-byte field used for cyclical redundancy, then the 4-byte end of frame marker. Despite the overhead, a 266Mbps Fibre Channel link can still transmit 200Mbps of user data. Because it is hardware-intensive, the overhead is very low and primarily emanates from the 8B/10B encoding mechanism.

Encoding

Encoding is the process of transmitting digital signals over the network, typically by representing binary values as a current level or a voltage differential. Fibre Channel uses a *8B/10B signal encoding scheme*, where 8-bit components are encoded as 10-bit symbols. 8B/10B encoding is related to 4B/5B encoding, and is used in IBM's SNA networks. The 8B/10B scheme is more efficient than Manchester encoding schemes common to most local area networking technologies such as Ethernet. Manchester is a simple biphase encoding mechanism, whereas 8B/10B includes the extra preprocessing step to achieve greater efficiency. Encoding takes place in the FC-1 layer of the Fibre Channel standard, along with error detection and order-of-word transmission.

Protocol Stack

Fibre Channel architecture consists of five layers, FC-0 through FC-4, as follows:

- *FC-0.* The physical layer, which includes the Open Fibre Control system. If a connection is broken, Open Fibre Control permits the receiving device to change over to a lower-level laser pulse for safety purposes.
- *FC-1.* The transmission protocol layer.
- *FC-2.* The signaling protocol layer. FC-2 defines four service classes: Class 1 is a dedicated connection, Class 2 provides for shared bandwidth, and Class 3 is the same as 2 except that it does not confirm frame delivery. A fourth service class that uses virtual connections is under development by the ANSI X3T11 subcommittee (document FC-PH-2).
- *FC-3.* Defines common services such as striping, multicast, and hunt groups.
- *FC-4.* Includes the Upper Layer Protocols (network and channel protocols).

FC-0 Layer   FC-0 defines the physical layer, including the Fibre, connectors, and optical and electrical parameters. Coax and twisted-pair versions are defined. FC-0 defines the electrical and mechanical specifications for the four supported transmission speeds (133Mbps, 266Mbps, 531Mbps, and 1.06Gbps). FC-0 also specifies the OFC safety system (see the "Types of Optics Used in Fibre Channel" section previously for a more detailed discussion of OFC).

FC-1 Layer   FC-1 defines the transmission protocol, including serial encoding and decoding, and error control. It also defines timing recovery and serial line balance. This layer uses the 8B/10B transmission coding scheme (licensed from IBM). Under this mechanism, 8 bits are transmitted as a 10-bit group, with the other 2 bits used for error detection and correction. This mechanism is known as *disparity control.*

FC-2 Layer   FC-2 defines the signaling protocol which includes the frame structure and byte sequences. This is where data framing, class of service, and congestion control are defined. FC-2 performs signaling and framing, and defines the transport mechanism for data from upper layers of the stack for transmission via the FC-0 layer. It can also accept transmission from the FC-0 layer, and reframe and resequence them for use by the upper layers.

Because the amount of overhead needed to send a frame is constant, regardless of frame size, Fibre Channel is quite efficient for high-volume data transfers. Layer FC-2 also offers traffic management functions, including flow control, link management, buffer memory management, error detection, and correction. FC-2 is also where the four classes of service are defined.

Ch
10

Voice and video traffic requires precise delivery. If a frame of a video, for example, arrives out of order, the picture quality would be affected. In voice, too, packets not arriving in sequence can cause garbled audio. Fibre Channel accommodates different classes of service, in order to provide for the special needs of voice and video traffic. While some of the classes support a lossless service, suitable for data, others support a lossy scheme, which suppresses any frames that arrive out of order. The FC-2 (signal protocol) layer defines four classes of service.

Class 1   Class 1, a dedicated connection, delivers frames in the same order in which they are transmitted, and the receiving device sends an acknowledgment for each frame it receives. This class is best for applications, such as imaging or full-motion video. The Class 1 definition also includes a service called *Intermix*, under which all classes of services can be multiplexed, while enjoying the bandwidth guarantees of the Class 1 connection.

Class 1 service establishes a dedicated connection and is guaranteed by the fabric. Maximum bandwidth between two *N*-Ports is guaranteed, making Class 1 the best service for sustained, high-throughput transactions. Under Class 1, frames are delivered to the destination port in the same order in which they are sent.

Class 2   Class 2 services permits shared bandwidth. In this class, multiple frames are multiplexed over a connection. The connection can be made up of multiple channels. There is no guarantee of delivery, and frames are not necessarily received in the same order in which they are transmitted.

Class 2 is a connectionless service that lets bandwidth be shared by multiplexing frames from several sources onto the same channel. The fabric does not guarantee order of delivery, and some frames may be delivered out of sequence. Both Class 1 and 2 send acknowledgment frames to confirm delivery.

Class 2 is more interactive, because it is not necessary to establish the dedicated connections. Consequently, a stream of frames can be sent to multiple destinations quickly.

Class 3   Class 3 service has the same characteristics as Class 2, except that Class 3 does not send acknowledgment frames to confirm delivery.

Class 3 is identical to Class 2, except that delivery is not confirmed. This type of transfer is the fastest available, and is ideal for real-time broadcasts.

Class 4   Class 4 is a connection-oriented mode, but uses virtual connections instead of dedicated connections, and distributes a port's bandwidth between several destinations. Additional classes of service are currently being defined, including an *isochronous* (accepts data at guaranteed intervals, sometimes called *constant bit rate*) service for voice and video, and a buffered class of service.

Fibre Channel offers extremely low latency levels in all service classes. Packetized video can be carried by any of the four classes of service, although Class 4's isochronous service may be best suited for packetized video in order to achieve minimum jitter without buffering.

FC-3 Layer   FC-3 defines common services that exist over multiple ports of a node. The FC-3 Layer provides common services such as:

- *Striping*. Used to multiply bandwidth with multiple *N*-Ports in parallel, thereby transmitting a single information unit over multiple links. An *N*-Port is any port in a point-to-point connection.

- *Hunt groups*. Using more than a single port to respond to the same alias address. This technique enhances efficiency by making it less likely that a busy *N*-Port will be reached.

- *Multicast*. Delivers a single transmission to multiple destination ports.

FC-4 Layer   FC-4 defines mapping between the lower levels of the Fibre Channel and the Intelligent Peripheral Interface (IPI) and SCSI command sets, HiPPI data framing, IP, and other upper level protocols. This layer of the five-layer Fibre Channel protocol stack includes an application interface, which is used to transparently convert TCP/IP to Fibre Channel sequences. Fibre Channel data is made up of frames, which can be much larger than ATM cells.

These network and channel protocols are all specified or proposed for FC-4:

- Small Computer System Interface (SCSI)
- Intelligent Peripheral Interface (IPI)
- High Performance Parallel Interface (HiPPI) Framing Protocol
- Internet Protocol (IP)
- ATM Adaptation Layer for computer data (AAL5)
- Link Encapsulation (FC-LE)
- Single Byte Command Code Set Mapping (SBCCS)
- IEEE 802.2

Ch
10

Topology

Three topologies are supported: *point-to-point*, *arbitrated loop*, and *fabric switching*. The topology is transparent to attached devices, and all three topologies are interoperable.

Ports in a point-to-point connection are called *N-Ports*; ports in a loop are referred to as *NL-Ports*. Ports in a fabric are known as the F-Ports. Data can flow between two ports in both directions at the same time. The mechanism of exchanging information in this manner is simply called the *Exchange*. The port that starts the Exchange is the *Originator*, and the port on the other end is the *Responder*.

Arbitrated Loop   The arbitrated loop topology is a low-cost way to attach multiple devices without a hub or switch (see Figure 10.2). The arbitrated loop topology may contain up to 127 ports, and all ports are connected in a loop. Each NL-Port will request permission to use the loop when necessary. If the loop is available, the requesting port will establish a bi-directional connection with the destination port. The connection can then be used to deliver any class of service between the two ports.

FIG. 10.2
Fibre Channel
Arbitrated Loop
Topology.

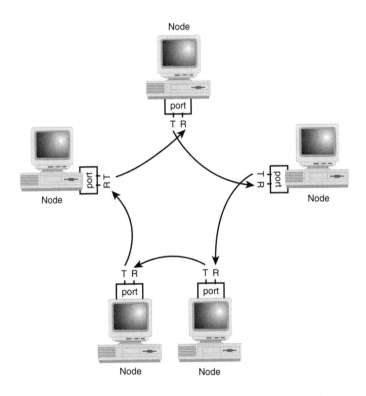

T = Transmitter
R = Receiver

Only a single pair of loop ports can communicate at any given time. When the two ports are finished, another connection between two other ports can be established. The loop can be attached to a switch fabric port (*FL Port*), or directly to a single host system.

All ports must be compatible. The arbitrated loop is simpler and less costly than the fabric model. However, this is a shared-bandwidth topology. Only two ports are active at any given time, with the intervening ports acting as repeaters.

The arbitrated loop is somewhat similar to Token Ring, in that all messages are passed from port to port through a token protocol.

Fabric   A fabric topology offers the greatest connection possibilities and largest aggregate throughput. In this topology, every device is connected to a switch (fabric), and paths are then established to all other connections on the switch (see Figure 10.3). Multiple switches are connected together. Often, switches are connected with multiple paths in order to provide redundancy.

FIG. 10.3
A Fibre Channel Fabric Topology.

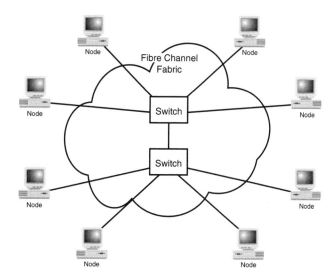

The fabric topology facilitates dynamic interconnections between nodes, through ports connected to a central fabric. This represents an any-to-any type of connection.

The fabric is akin to a switch. Every port is attached to the fabric through a specific link. The ports in the fabric are used as an intermediate level, allowing any node to communicate with any other node through the fabric. The fabric itself performs routing, as opposed to the ports themselves.

Ch
10

In a fabric topology, several connections may take place simultaneously. The link is established through the *address identifier*, which determines the fabric domain and the specific destination port.

The fabric may make use of other networks, such as ATM or SONET (Synchronous Optical Network), between the different fabric elements that may be distributed through a large geographic area. The individual fabric elements themselves can be linked through expansion ports (E Ports). There is no limit to the number of ports that can exist in a fabric.

FIG. 10.4

A Fibre Channel Point-to-Point Topology.

Node

Node

T = Transmitter
R = Receiver

Point-to-Point Topology   The simple point-to-point topology connects two ports through a single link (see Figure 10.4).

Both ports must run the same protocols and at the same speed. The transmitter of each port is connected to the receiver of the opposite port. Point-to-point connections may be used to link two computers, or one computer to a disk. This topology uses a single, full-duplex cable between the two devices. This simple topology provides the greatest possible bandwidth, because no other devices are present to cause any type of delay.

Mixed Topology   Some implementations will combine these three topologies: the arbitrated loop, fabric, and point-to-point (see Figure 10.5). An arbitrated loop could serve a workgroup; one of the ports in the loop would then be connected to the fabric, which allows the workgroup to communicate with the broader enterprise.

Cabling

Serial media allows for easy and inexpensive cables. There is no need for the thick, rigid cables or multi-pin connectors used in other technologies.

Fibre Channel runs on fiber optic or electronic cable, with bandwidth dependent on the grade of cable. The standard supports a variety of cable grades, including single mode and multimode fiber. Fiber Channel can function with a laser or a light-emitting diode (LED) as light source; light source wavelength can vary from 780 to 1,300 nm.

Optical and electrical (copper) cable can be combined in a single system, if a media converter or fabric topology is used. Distances are dependent on the type of media being used.

FIG. 10.5
Fibre Channel Mixed Topology.

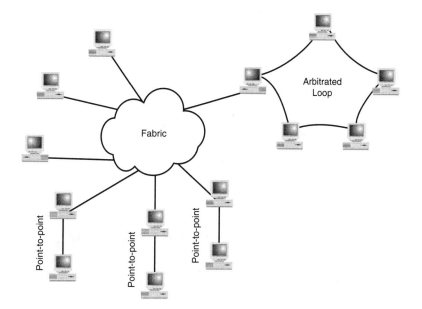

N O T E Fibre Channel does not support unshielded twisted pair (UTP) cabling.

Fibre Channel supports the following distances, as shown in Tables 10.1 and 10.2.

Table 10.1 Optical Fiber Network Distances

Fiber Type	Mbps	Distance (in Kilometers)
Single mode (short wave)	100	10
Single mode (long wave)	25	10
50 Micron Multimode (shortwave)	100	0.5
50 Micron Multimode (shortwave)	25	2
50 Micron Multimode (longwave)	25	2
62.5 Micron Multimode (shortwave)	100	0.175
62.5 Micron Multimode (shortwave)	25	0.7
62.5 Micron multimode (longwave)	25	1.5

Table 10.2   Electrical Cable

Type	Mbps	Distance (in Meters)
Video coax fiber	100	25
Video coax fiber	25	75
Miniature coax fiber	100	10
Miniature coax fiber	25	25
Shielded twisted pair	25	50

Although either can be used, there are a number of reasons for deploying fiber-optic cable over copper. Fiber will generate less signal attenuation, and can accommodate a longer distance. Copper is more susceptible to noise and interference that could potentially cause damage to equipment.

Fibre Channel and Other Network Technologies

Fibre Channel functions as a transport mechanism for upper-level protocols, including IPI and SCSI command sets, HiPPI data framing, IP, IEEE 802.2, and other protocols. It is also considered a viable backbone technology.

The FC-4 layer defines mapping between Fibre Channel and the command sets that run over Fibre Channel, such as SCSI, HiPPI, IEEE 802, and ATM. As part of this mapping, the connecting technologies retain their own command sets and functions on a higher level, but replace their lower levels with Fibre Channel.

Fibre Channel is superior for use in clustering, as well as LAN and MAN applications, but is not meant as a WAN technology by itself because of its distance limitations. It is, however, complementary to other WAN technologies such as ATM, because of its ability to support the transmission of ATM and other types of network traffic. Fibre Channel can support 16 million switched port connections, making its switched topology very much like that of ATM. Fibre Channel's many point-to-point links are configured into a fabric topology. Fibre Channel does support the ATM protocol, so ATM can be mapped over Fibre Channel's physical layer.

Fibre Channel is able to map multiple networking protocols. It does this by defining a MAC layer protocol, over which any Level 2 layer protocol can run. Data packets or datagrams map directly into the Fibre Channel sequence, which is segmented into frames, transmitted through the Fibre Channel fabric, and then reassembled for delivery to the remote level 2 protocol.

Although Fibre Channel does not have a command set of its own, it does allow other protocols to be superimposed over itself. This is done by using Fibre Channel as a carrier of other protocols' command sets, allowing multiple command sets to be used simultaneously, with a single physical medium defined for all of the supported command sets. That is, Fibre Channel is merely used to provide the connection, and the protocols that run on top of Fibre Channel actually carry out the packets and commands.

The ANSI Fibre Channel standard offers higher available bandwidth than ATM, and more products supporting Fibre Channel are available in the marketplace than for ATM. Sun and Hewlett-Packard both have workstations that support Fibre Channel networks.

ATM was designed as a cell-based, high-speed network architecture for data and voice traffic; Fibre Channel, on the other hand, is a high-speed architecture for connecting network devices, such as PCs and workstations, and high-speed hardware, such as hard drives, that are usually connected directly to a system bus.

Ch
10

The Fibre Channel bus (channel) offers the combination of high transmission speed with low overhead. The standard supports four speeds: 133Mbps, 266Mbps, 530Mbps, and 1.06Gbps. Fibre Channel network interface cards (NICs) supporting these speeds are currently available. ANSI has approved 2.134Gbps and 4.25Gbps Fiber Channel specifications, although the technology for these rates have not yet been made commercially available.

Commercially available ATM products, on the other hand, usually support only the middle of the ATM transmission rate range.

Fibre Channel is meant to be the successor to HiPPI, which was developed to connect heterogeneous supercomputers with IBM mainframes. Like HiPPI, the primary application for Fibre Channel has been clustering. Also like HiPPI, Fibre Channel can be used to link the processor to a storage array.

The advantage of Fibre Channel over HiPPI is that processors can be located several kilometers apart, whereas HiPPI had a much shorter maximum distance (at least during its earlier incarnation, the newer HiPPI 6400 standard offers greater distance flexibility). Fibre Channel is not currently used as a LAN backbone technology, although it is being proposed for that purpose.

Like HiPPI, Fibre Channel was originally meant to connect high-speed devices, although the technology is starting to compete with FDDI, Fast Ethernet, and ATM for a position in the LAN backbone.

Vendors

Fiber Channel NICs and switches are available from several vendors to support 266Mbps or 1.06Gbps.

Four Fibre Channel developers—Gadzoox Microsystems, Inc.; Interphase Corp.; Seagate Technology, Inc.; and W.L. Gore & Associates—announced in March 1997 a plan to bundle their gigabit-speed Fibre Channel products in the first integrated Fibre Channel "Starter Kit." The "best-of-breed" solution offers a turnkey solution for deploying Fibre Channel in *Storage Area Network (SAN)* environments.

The SAN represents the next generation of storage architectures, made necessary by newer, data-intensive applications such as data warehousing. The SAN is a server-storage connectivity architecture, with a high-performance storage infrastructure designed for the enterprise. The SAN architecture, built on Fibre Channel arbitrated loop (FC-AL) technology, is complementary to ATM, Fast Ethernet, and Gigabit Ethernet, and is designed to relieve server-storage bottlenecks. A Fibre Channel SAN is cost-effective, and facilitates long-term scalability and migration to server-clustering applications.

The starter kit itself includes all of the equipment needed to configure a dual-host SAN topology. It includes two Interphase 5526 PCI adapter cards with Windows NT drivers, a Gadzoox 9-port active hub, a Seagate Barracuda 9G Fibre Channel drive in a single disk enclosure, W.L. Gore's Fibre Channel cables, and documentation. The kit is distributed by Bell Microproducts.

Emulex Corporation

http://www.emulex.com
714-662-5600 or 800-854-7112
14711 NE 29th
Bellevue, WA 98007

Emulex offers a growing family of Fibre Channel products, including hubs and adapter cards, as well as a five-port mini-hub that simplifies loop management and extends node-to-node distances. The five-port hub is the smallest solution available for Fibre Channel. It supports automatic bypassing of unused or unpowered ports, bringing a degree of flexibility to the network and simplifying the process of adding and removing users. The mini-hubs can be connected to make a larger configuration, but by themselves are an ideal solution for smaller workgroups.

Adaptec

http://www.adaptec.com
691 South Milpitas Boulevard
Milpitas, CA 95035
Voice: 408-945-8600
Fax: 408-262-2533

Adaptec is a strong supporter of the standardization of Fibre Channel. The company has plans for releasing Fibre Channel chips, boards, and controller silicon for original equipment manufacturers (OEMs). Further, it plans to build host-based Fibre Channel connections into its RAID controller family, which can support 30 connections of 25 meters each. Adaptec's Fibre Channel family includes both 32-bit and 64-bit PCI solutions.

Ancot Corporation

http://www.ancot.com
115 Constitution Drive
Menlo Park, CA 94025
Voice: 415-322-5322
Fax: 415-322-0455

Ancot is a leading vendor of Fibre Channel networking and test equipment. Ancot is also strong in the area of SCSI, and offers a Fibre Channel-to-SCSI bridge device. Ancot also offers a set of tools for development, integration, and repair of Fibre Channel systems.

Ancot's Fibre Channel Analyzer, the FCA-5000, is used to develop, integrate, and repair Fibre Channel systems. A self-contained unit, the *FCA-5000* is a two-channel analyzer with data displayed in plain English. Transfer rates are 266Mbps, 531Mbps, and 1Gbps for fiber or copper media supporting fabric, arbitrated loop, and point-to-point topologies. The instrument will attach to both in and out fibers to monitor and record all activity.

The company's Fibre Channel To SCSI Bridge/Extender, the *SB-8001/8010*, is used to connect parallel SCSI devices to Fibre Channel networks. The unit offers automatic operation and support for point-to-point, switched or arbitrated loop topologies, as well as both optical fiber and copper media.

Two of the devices can be connected back-to-back to form an SCSI bus extender, which extends the SCSI bus distances to more than 2 km. The bridge operates bi-directionally, and can function as a Fibre Channel originator or responder, or as an SCSI initiator or target. It is especially useful for extending the SCSI bus over a very long distance. When using it as an SCSI bus extender, the extender is transparent to the host and connected devices.

Digital Equipment Corporation

http://www.dec.com
Voice: 800-344-4825
Fax: 800-676-7517

Digital's 64-bit Alpha processor, one of the fastest computers available, can be matched with Fibre Channel through Digital's *High Performance Interconnect (HPI)* program.

Fujikura America

743 Pastoria Avenue
Sunnyvale, CA 94086
Voice: 408-245-8810
Fax: 408-245-5165

Fujikura has a newly developed optical gigabit transceiver for high-speed data communications applications, including Fibre Channel. The devices support hot pluggability and short wavelength operation at 1,062Gbps.

Gadzoox Microsystems

http://www.gadzoox.com
6840 Via Del Oro, Suite 290
San Jose, CA 95119
Voice: 408-360-4950 or 888-423-3222
Fax: 408-360-4951
e-mail: **info@gadzoox.com**

Gadzoox released the first gigabit Fibre Channel hub in 1996, and now offers a starter kit as part of a cooperative effort between itself and Interphase, W.L. Gore, and Seagate. The company is also planning to release a complete line of Fibre Channel Arbitrated Loop hubs, bridges, and switches to connect disk drives, disk arrays, and servers.

Hitachi Data Systems

http://www.htshq.com
750 Central Expressway
P.O. Box 54996
Santa Clara, CA 95056
Voice: 408-970-1000
Fax: 408-727-8036

Hitachi plans to incorporate Emulex's Fibre Channel chipset into its own next generation RAID systems. Emulex's Firefly chipset offers conformance to industry standards, and high performance and scalability.

LSI Logic

http://www.lsilogic.com
1551 McCarthy Boulevard
Milpitas, CA 95035
Voice: 408-433-8000
Fax: 408-433-8989

LSI has a strong commitment to Fibre Channel. In 1996, it released the world's first Complementary Metal Oxide Semiconductor (CMOS) gigabit-per-second transceiver for Fibre Channel, and a full-featured dual-loop Fibre Channel controller. Both products are part of LSI's CoreWare library of ASIC building blocks.

Raidtec Corporation

http://www.raidtec.com
105-C Hembree Park Drive
Roswell, GA 30076
Voice: 770-664-6066
Fax: 770-664-6166
e-mail: **raidtec@raidtec.com**

At the 1996 Comdex, Raidtec demonstrated an incredible 1 terabyte FC-AL array, consisting of 16 FibreArrays and 112 Seagate 9G drives connected through a FibreRAID controller to a Windows NT server. The FibreARray FC-AL drive subsystem features hot replaceable drive bays, power supplies, and a Fibre Channel RAID controller with up to 128M of cache.

Seagate Technology

http://www.seagate.com
920 Disc Drive
Scotts Valley, CA 95066

Seagate has long supported Fibre Channel, and introduced the first FC-AL disk drive to the market last year.

Sun Microsystems

http://www.sun.com
2550 Garcia Avenue
Mountain View, CA 94043

Sun is strong in FC-AL storage solutions, and has recently achieved an installed base of more than 1.5 petabytes of Fibre Channel attached storage, which is more than all other Fibre Channel storage vendors combined.

W.L. Gore & Associates

133 S. Van Gordon, Ste. 200
Lakewood, CO 80288
Voice: 303-989-7752
Fax: 303-985-2278

Gore has a full line of physical layer Fibre Channel devices, copper interconnects, and other products to facilitate a seamless migration from copper to optics.

Summary

A channel is a link between a master host computer and a slave peripheral. It is used to send large quantities of data at high speeds, usually across small distances. A network, on the other hand, interfaces multiple users over both short and long distances. Fibre Channel is an attempt to combine the best features of both models.

Fibre Channel is well-suited for connectivity with high-speed storage access and server clustering, gigabit enterprise backbones, and gigabit LANs.

Fibre Channel achieves very high performance while still providing a system with low overhead. The technology is extremely fast, serial, scalable, asynchronous, and switched. It is independent of the type of data being transferred, and can therefore carry multiple higher-level protocols such as SCSI and HiPPI on channels, or TCP/IP and ATM for networks.

Fibre Channel nodes can be connected directly in a point-to-point topology, or cabled through a switch or hub. Because each node functions as a repeater for every other node on a Fibre Channel loop, a single disconnected or failed node can bring down the entire loop. A *concentrator* can automatically bypass a downed node, and is essential to providing continuous availability on the network.

The Fibre Channel architecture consists of five layers, FC-0 through FC-4, as follows: FC-0 (physical layer), FC-1 (transmission protocol layer), FC-2 (signaling protocol layer/service classes), FC-3 (common services), and FC-4 (upper layer protocols). ●

Ch
10

CHAPTER 11

IEEE 1394 (Fire Wire)

This book has covered a number of different approaches to transporting large amounts of data over a long distance. But how about sending data at high speeds from your PC to a printer or other peripheral device?

IEEE 1394 originated in 1986 by Apple Computer as a method of alleviating the *spaghetti syndrome* where dozens of cables protrude from the back of the computer to connect printers, modems, and other peripherals. Apple's design was accepted as an industry standard in 1995.

The IEEE 1394 standard, sometimes referred to as *Fire Wire,* may well revolutionize the transport of digital data for computers and other consumer electronics. IEEE 1394 establishes a *universal I/O connection*, an inexpensive and open high-speed way to interconnect multiple digital devices. Because it is scalable and uses a flexible peer-to-peer topology, IEEE 1394 can be used to connect a wide range of devices, including printers, hard drives, digital audio, and video hardware, all on the same bus. ■

Overview of IEEE 1394

1394 was originally designed to replace parallel SCSI in computer applications, and provides an innovative new way to send and receive digital data over a low-cost and lightweight cable.

1394 is an incredibly versatile technology. Peripheral devices with different transport rates can be interconnected, and because the IEEE 1394 serial bus functions as a digital interface, there is no need to convert digital data to analog. Because it is physically small, it is easy to use; there is no need for complex setup or terminators. Devices can be added or removed while the bus is active, so there is no need to turn off the system to add or remove a device. And because it is inexpensive, it has quickly become an ideal technology for consumer products. The scalable architecture can mix 100Mbps, 200Mbps, and 400Mbps devices onto a single bus.

1394 has come to be especially useful for video editing and other multimedia applications. It offers half-duplex transmission at 100, 200, and 400Mbps. At 200Mbps, uncompressed 640×480 video can be transmitted at 30 frames per second (fps).

An innovative feature of 1394 is its peer-to-peer transfer of data. Each node can transmit or receive data from any other node on an equal basis. A 1394 network typically contains a host PC, but the host is not required to intervene in bus arbitration. Nodes can be interchanged, even when turned on. Each node receives and retransmits data to its neighbor as a repeater. If the topology changes, the system will automatically reconfigure itself, so dip switches are unnecessary.

Implementation and Infrastructure

The 1394 Serial Bus Standard describes a peripheral bus for the cable medium, and a backplane bus as backup to the parallel backplane. The cable medium allows 16 cable hops of 4.5 m each, for a maximum of 72 m between the two farthest nodes. 100, 200, and 400Mbps devices can run on the same bus, and up to 63 devices can connect to a single bus segment. Bus segments can be bridged, so up to 63,000 devices can be interconnected.

Although 1394 is a bus with nodes arbitrating for access, it resembles a network, and is divided into three protocol layers:

- *Transaction Layer*. This layer implements the request-response protocol. The Transaction Layer is implemented in firmware.

- *Link Layer.* This layer generates an acknowledgment datagram to the transaction layer. All packet transmission and reception is handled at this layer. The Link Layer is hardware-based.

- *Physical Layer.* This layer furnishes initialization and arbitration services, which guarantee that only one node at a time sends data. The Physical Layer is also hardware-based.

1394 is a transaction-based packet technology. The serial bus organization can address 1,023 networks of 63 nodes each, each with as much as 281 terabytes of memory. Each bus entity is a *node*, which can be individually addressed, reset, and identified. 1394 offers live connect/disconnect, also known as *hot-plugging*, and the ability to dynamically address nodes as they are added to the serial chain.

1394 can directly link 63 devices without additional hardware such as hubs. Connection may be to a PC, or to one another. Sony was actually the first to commercialize the formal IEEE standard, with its Digital Video Handycam product line in 1995. Sony continues to use the technology in an ever-increasing line of digital cameras, digital video camcorders, and other multimedia peripherals.

1394 supports both asynchronous and isochronous data transfer; the *asynchronous format* sends data and Transaction Layer information to an explicit address. Under the *isochronous format*, data is broadcast based on channel numbers. A unique feature of 1394 is that transactions of different speeds can occur on a single device medium.

IEEE 1394 may be deployed as a network technology in some limited situations, although it is not meant for full-scale network operation.

The standard specifies three signaling rates: 98.304, 196.608, and 393.216Mbps. These figures are usually rounded up to 100, 200, and 400. Most consumer electronics equipment uses the 100Mbps speed, although most of the PC adapter cards are capable of supporting up to 200Mbps. The bus's signaling rate is dependent on the slowest active node, although if the bus controller deploys a Topology Map and Speed Map for specific node pairs, the bus can support more than one signaling speed between the pair.

A bus management scheme is specified in the standard to allow a variety of devices to interconnect. Bus management is offered in the form of three services:

- *Cycle master.* The cycle master broadcasts cycle start packets, which are required for isochronous operation. An isochronous resource manager, for DV and DA applications, is also included for those nodes that support isochronous operation. Also included is an optional bus master.

- *Isochronous Data Transport.* This transport provides the bandwidth guarantees necessary for high-speed data transfer over multiple channels. The isochronous resource manager's Bandwidth Available register shows the remaining bandwidth available to all isochronous nodes. Whenever the bus is reset, or when an isochronous node is added to the bus, the node will request a bandwidth allocation.

- *The isochronous resource manager.* This manager will give each node requesting isochronous bandwidth a channel number between 0 and 63. The isochronous packets are then identified by that channel number. When nodes no longer need isochronous resources, it releases its bandwidth and its channel number.

Industry Support

Several developers, including IBM, Compaq, Dell, Digital Equipment, Microsoft, and Apple support the 1394 specification.

Microsoft   Microsoft's *Simply Interactive PC (SIPC)* initiative adds new support to the 1394 standard. Microsoft has also entered into an agreement with Sony Electronics to create open device driver interfaces, application programming interfaces (APIs), and an open host controller interface for 1394. Microsoft has also agreed to work with Compaq to facilitate the adoption of 1394 as a standard in the PC industry.

The standard, along with support from Microsoft and other companies, will make it easier to connect PCs with high-speed peripherals. Microsoft's support will have the result of integrating PCs with multimedia consumer electronics, and could eventually be used as a high-speed method of connecting to the Internet and other communications systems.

Apple Computer   Apple Computer plans to introduce FireWire to its entire product line, and will build it into the motherboards of all its desktops and notebooks by 1998.

Sun Microsystems   Sun Microsystems also announced support for the standard. Sun plans to work with other industry supporters to create an open, industry-wide extension of 1394 to offer multi-gigabit rates.

Universal Serial Bus

1394 does not truly compete against the Universal Serial Bus (USB) design, but rather is complementary to it. The 1394 specification allows for a transfer rate of up to 400Mbps. Intel's USB design, on the other hand, allows for a transfer rate of only up to 12Mbps. USB is more applicable for peripherals that do not require a high-speed interface. USB technology can connect multiple low- to medium-speed peripherals, such as keyboards, mice, telephones, CD-ROM drives, and printers. USB makes a 1.5 Mbps subchannel available for lower-data-rate devices, such as mice or keyboards.

The USB, like 1394, was also designed to minimize the tangle of cables that protrude from the back of the PC. It connects peripherals in a tiered-star topology, and uses a four-wire connector with one twisted pair for signaling, a 5-volt power connector, and a ground conductor. However, its transfer rate is only 12Mbps. Still, USB is enough to accommodate MPEG-1, Digital Video Disks (DVDs), and MPEG-2 compressed video. The advantage of 1394 over USB, besides greater speeds, is that 1394 devices can be used without having to go through a PC or other microprocessor-based controller.

Physical Infrastructure

Up to 63 devices can be connected to a single bus segment, with each device up to 4.5 m apart. Greater distances can be achieved via repeaters. More than 1,000 bus segments can be connected to bridges, and the standards bodies are currently working on extending the 4.5-meter limitation to 25 meters.

Bus Categories   There are two defined bus categories: backplane and cable. A *backplane bus* supplements parallel bus structures by providing a serial path between devices plugged into the backplane. The *cable bus*, on the other hand, is used to make up a network of peripherals.

The backplane version of the standard runs at 12.5, 25, or 50Mbps; the cable version runs at 100, 200, and 400Mbps. Both are compatible at the link layer and above.

The application of the cable version is primarily connectivity at the back panel of the PC using a low-cost, high-speed serial interface. 1394 was developed to accommodate the growing need for high-speed, high-volume data transfer. A standard LAN or WAN cannot furnish inexpensive connectivity capabilities. Furthermore, SCSI (a parallel high-speed communication mechanism) cannot support long distances or live connect/disconnect, which means that configuration can be time-consuming.

Cabling   Because the cable transports both data and power, the 1394 cable is the only cable required to connect a device to its peripheral.

Electrical contact is made inside of the structure, and cable terminators are not required. There is also no addressing ID that needs to be set.

The physical 1394 cable is made up of six copper wires. Two of them carry power, and the other four are grouped into two twisted-wire pairs. Each twisted pair is shielded, and the entire cable is shielded on top of that.

100, 200, and 400Mbps nodes can all be supported in the same technology. However, a different chip set is required for each speed. 1394 uses a six-wire STP cable. The type of internal bus on the PC is irrelevant; the PCI bus can take full advantage of 1394. PCs with

Ch
11

built-in 1394 connectivity are not expected until the end of 1997, although several firms do offer general-purpose 1394-to-PCI adapters, including Adaptec, Texas Instruments, and Skipstone.

Digital Video and Multimedia

The speed and isochronous features of 1394 are well-suited to digital video, and the first applications to take advantage of the technology have been video editing, digital imaging, and videoconferencing. The music industry has elected to use IEEE 1394 through its MIDI standard as the next interface for electronic musical instruments and music editing systems.

In addition to MIDI, VCR manufacturers have selected 1394 as the video interface for the next generation of VCRs. Furthermore, the Video Electronics Industry Standards Association (VESA) has agreed to adopt IEEE 1394 for its home distribution network, which will use it in set-top boxes, HDTV, and household local networks.

The 1394 standard provides a way to interconnect a wide variety of consumer electronics, such as digital audio devices, digital VCRs, and digital video cameras to multimedia PCs. The standard provides for simultaneous real-time data transfers and non-time dependent data transfers, which allows devices with real-time requirements, such as live digital video being sent from a camcorder, to share the same bus as a non-real time device. Most PCs use an asynchronous (time-independent) bus; using an isochronous (real-time) bus such as 1394 ensures that data is delivered at a constant rate, and eliminates the need for memory buffers.

Advantages

Because it is not proprietary, 1394 establishes an easy and affordable interconnect for all digital devices.

Advantages of Fire Wire are as follows:

- Widely supported and currently available.
- Cross-platform, and can transport any type of digital data.
- Low cost.
- Easy to use; any device can be attached or removed at any time without turning off the system.
- Fast—speeds of up to 400Mbps, with 1,000Mbps under development.
- Ability to operate under an asynchronous mode to accommodate connectivity to legacy devices.

In some limited situations, 1394 can be used as a network technology, although it is not optimized for a full network operation. Rather, it is more ideal for connecting multiple peripherals.

A *bus bridge* can be used to connect multiple buses of the same or different types. For example, a bus bridge can connect a 1394 to a PCI interface, or can also be used to connect a 1394 cable and a 1394 backplane bus. Up to 16 nodes can be daisy-chained through connectors with cables up to 4.5 m, making a total cable length of 72 m. Additional devices can be connected in a leaf configuration.

The standard allows up to 27 connectors to be present on a device, although all existing 1394 devices currently have only one connector.

1394 and Asynchronous Transfer Mode

Asynchronous Transfer Mode (ATM) is an excellent way to send large amounts of information over a WAN. However, it can be a costly method to attach to every device in the office. IEEE 1394 can be very complementary to ATM. It has a similar packet structure and can be used as the local connection mechanism for ATM networks.

Standards Development

The *1394 Trade Association* was established in 1994 to promote the development of computer and consumer electronics, which can be connected to each other through a single serial multimedia link. Members include Sun Microsystems, Texas Instruments, Philips Semiconductor, Apple Computer, IBM, Microsoft, Adaptec, Molex, Sony, Mitsubishi, AMD, and Skipstone. The trade association operates as a confederation of volunteers with the following three goals:

- Driving technical efforts to promote the IEEE 1394 market.
- Promoting 1394 as the multimedia interface of choice.
- Providing a focal point for the 1394 community to establish industry agreements.

ON THE WEB

The 1394 Trade Association can be found at **http://www.firewire.org/**

The standard actually started to unfold in 1986 when the IEEE's Microcomputer Standards Committee wanted to unify multiple serial bus implementations—specifically the VME (Versa Module Europa), Multibus II, and Future Bus standards.

N O T E The VMEBus is standardized as IEEE 1014. It is a popular backplane interconnection
bus system, originally developed by a consortium of vendors led by Motorola. The
VMEBus is flexible, and can support several compute-intensive tasks.

In 1995, the IEEE released the 1394 specification based on Apple Computer's original
FireWire bus. Apple's original design was created to replace or supplement the SCSI bus
used on Mac and PowerMac machines.

Updates and Improvements

The 1394 Trade Association is already working on an initiative to improve the 1394
specification.

1394a is a minor fix with small changes; these products are backward-compatible with
1394 products. A 1394b fix is expected to raise the speed factor to 800Mbps.

1394.1 is a subsequent fix to accommodate a four-wire connector used by Sony
camcorders, and to establish a standard for 1394 bridges.

1394.2 is incompatible with 1394, and is used to interconnect a cluster of workstations
at speeds of up to 1Gbps. This specification requires a loop architecture (which is not
allowed in standard 1394). The 1394.2 proposal is somewhat controversial because it
is so much different from the original standard. 1394.2 is designed on supercomputer
technology, and is meant primarily as a way to interconnect computers instead of
peripherals.

Operating System Support

1394 support will be built into the Mac operating system and Windows 97. There will be
no support for 1394 in Windows 3.1, Amiga computers, and UNIX systems.

The digital revolution has brought about digital audio and video, and greater quality than
was previously available with analog devices. However, although video cameras have been
moving to a digital format, it was still necessary to convert the digital video signal to analog for output to a cable; the device at the receiving end (the computer) then had to convert the analog signal back to digital. The conversion process leads to some degradation
of the image quality. Fire Wire presents a way to retain the digital format as the signals
are sent over the cable.

Vendors

Within two years, gigabyte IEEE 1394 devices will be on the market. PCs with on-board 1394 connectors are expected to be announced this year. 1394-compliant PC peripherals, such as disk drives, are not expected to be released until the market has been saturated with 1394-compliant PCs to hold them.

Because it represents a new technology for interconnecting computer and consumer multimedia equipment, the availability of 1394 may well trigger a new wave of multimedia applications, such as video mail, videoconferencing, and other high-end video applications.

3A International

http://www.3a.com
4014 E. Broadway Road #402
Phoenix, AZ 85040
Voice: 602-437-1751
Fax: 602-437-5313

3A's 1394 Data Analyzer uses passive bus snooping technology, which lets the administrator listen in to all bus activity without affecting regular bus traffic. This allows all events, whether asynchronous or isochronous, to be logged into an online buffer for subsequent offline analysis.

Ch
11

Adaptec

http://www.adaptec.com/serialio/
691 South Milpitas Boulevard
Milpitas, CA 95035
Voice: (408) 945-8600
Fax: (408) 262-2533

Adaptec has been very active in the development of the 1394 standard, and in providing products that support it. The company's 1394 host adapter allows both PCs and Macintoshes to connect to 1394 peripherals, including DV camcorders, digital VCRs, color printers, scanners, digital still cameras, and DVD players. Adaptec also has a 1394 Fire Wire Developer's Kit for Windows NT and 95, for use by developers creating products that comply to the 1394 standard.

Kenwood

http://www.kenwoodtmi.co.jp/e/news/ieee1394fe.html
1-16-2 Hakusan, Midori-ku,
Yokohama 226 JAPAN
Tel:+81-45-939-7030
Marketing Dept.: +81-45-939-7053

Kenwood, in cooperation with Firefly, Inc., has also developed a rich set of 1394 products. Firefly was founded by the inventors of the 1394 technology, and they offer a set of software libraries. The two companies jointly released a 1394 bus analyzer.

Matsushita

2-15, Matsuba-cho
Kadoma Osaka 571
Japan
Voice: +81-75-956-9517
Fax: +81-75-957-3677

Matsushita offers the world's slimmest and lightest LCD digital video movie camera, with a 4-inch LCD monitor and 1394 bus.

Sony

http://www.sony.com
3300 Zanker Rd
San Jose, CA 95134
Voice: 408-955-5024
Fax: 408-955-5704

Sony's digital camera complies with the 1394 standard. Sony was the first to offer commercial 1394 products with its Digital Video Handycam product line. Microsoft, along with Sony, Adaptec, and others, announced its intention to support 1394 in subsequent versions of Windows.

Skipstone

Skipstone is the leading OEM supplier of 1394 products and services, including computer adapters, drivers, prototype design, turnkey solutions, chip development, and embedded applications. Skipstone has recently agreed to be purchased by Adaptec.

Texas Instruments

http://www.ti.com/sc.1394
Mixed Signal Products
Texas Instruments MS 8710
P.O. Box 660199, 8505 Forest Lane
Dallas, TX 75243
Voice: 972-480-3404

TI's peripheral link layer controller device was designed for 1394 peripheral applications. It performs bidirectional asynchronous/isochronous (ISO) data transfers to and from an IEEE-1394 serial bus physical layer device (PHY).

Toshiba

http://www.toshiba.com
Toshiba America Electronic Components
1060 Rincon Circle
San Jose, CA 95131
Voice: 408-526-2620
Fax: 408-456-9002

Toshiba offers a 1394-compliant CD-ROM drive.

Philips Semiconductors

http://www.semiconductors.philips.com
M/S 55
9201 Pan American Freeway NE
Albuquerque, NM 87113
Voice: 505-858-2893
Fax: 505-822-7802

Philips offers a 1394-compliant audio/video link layer controller with an embedded A/V layer interface. The hot-pluggable device lets peripherals be used in Plug and Play mode, so devices such as camcorders can be connected without having to first turn off the computer system.

Ch
11

Summary

IEEE 1394 establishes a universal method to interconnect multiple digital devices. It is highly scalable, and can be used to connect printers, hard drives, digital audio, video hardware, and more, all on the same bus.

1394 allows peripheral devices with different transfer rates to be interconnected. In addition, because the 1394 serial bus operates as a digital interface, there is no need to convert digital to analog.

The 1394 Serial Bus Standard describes a peripheral bus for the cable medium, and a backplane bus as backup to the parallel backplane. The cable medium allows 16 cable hops of 4.5 m each, for a maximum of 72 m between the two farthest nodes. 100, 200, and 400Mbps devices can run on the same bus, and up to 63 devices can connect to a single bus segment. Bus segments can be bridged, so up to 63,000 devices can be interconnected.

1394 is a transaction-based packet technology. The serial bus organization can address 1,023 networks of 63 nodes each, each with as much as 281 terabytes of memory. Each bus entity is a *node*, which can be individually addressed, reset, and identified. 1394 offers live connect/disconnect, also known as *hot-plugging*; and the capability to dynamically address nodes as they are added to the serial chain.

The 1394 standard is often used to interconnect a wide variety of consumer electronics, such as digital audio devices, digital VCRs, and digital video cameras to multimedia PCs. The standard provides for simultaneous real-time data transfers and non-time dependent data transfers, which allows devices with real-time requirements, such as live digital video being sent from a camcorder, to share the same bus as a non-real-time device. ●

CHAPTER 12

High-Speed Telephony and Internet Access

If Harry S. Truman were president today, he may well have changed his famous line, "A chicken in every pot, a car in every garage" to "A computer in every home, and fast Internet over every POTS."

We have seen several ways to establish high-speed corporate networks capable of sending tremendous volumes of data throughout the enterprise at unbelievable speeds. But for most telecommuters, home business owners, and freelance writers, our only link to the outside world is a 28.8 analog modem and a standard telephone line. While corporate users enjoy the ability to download multi-megabit files from the corporate server in seconds, we must still wait endless minutes for the same files.

Fortunately, there are several options now for faster access to intranets and the Internet, including ISDN, advances in high-speed telephony, Asynchronous Digital Subscriber Lines, and more. ∎

ISDN

ISDN is one of the more mature technologies that delivers fast access to intranets or the Internet. Most major metropolitan areas offer ISDN services, and the biggest online information services also offer ISDN service. ISDN means fast file downloads over the Internet, far beyond anything that can be achieved with a 28.8Kbps modem. Unlike analog modem communications, ISDN transfers are not affected by line noise, because it is a digital technology.

Several vendors offer ISDN hardware devices. ISDN modems have come down in price significantly since they were first introduced, and are available for a few hundred dollars. ISDN has advanced in popularity very rapidly. Although ISDN was first published as one of the 1984 CITT/ITU-TSB Red Book recommendations, the 1988 Blue Book recommendations added many of the features that are currently enjoyed. In 1995, Motorola introduced the first commercial ISDN modem: the BITSURFER TA210 digital modem.

ISDN is made up of three channels: two "B" channels for data, and a narrow "D" channel for instructions. This configuration is the *Basic Rate Interface (BRI)*. Each B channel accommodates up to 64Kbps of data, for a total of 128Kbps of bandwidth. ISDN uses plain copper telephone wires, and can combine voice with data. Most individual users will need a BRI configuration.

The other configuration is a *Primary Rate Interface (PRI)*, which consists of 23 "B" channels and one "D" channel, for a total of 1,536Kbps. The vast majority of small office/home office (SOHO) users will be more than satisfied with the BRI connection.

ISDN pricing structures vary tremendously, depending on the individual phone company, although service may be found for as little as $29 a month in certain areas.

High-Speed Telephony: xDSL

Digital Subscriber Line (DSL) technology builds on ISDN to offer an even faster access rate. xDSL (the x stands for the various flavors of DSL) technology includes high bit rate DSL (HDSL), symmetric DSL (SDSL), asymmetric DSL (ADSL), and very high bit rate DSL (VDSL). The most mature and widely available of these is ADSL, created as an alternative to T1 service. These DSL technologies offer a new level of capabilities over standard copper telephone wire. DSL models the distortion inherent in copper lines and dynamically adjusts their transmission characteristics to match.

N O T E Like ISDN, xDSL technologies also require a specialized modem. ADSL modems are the most common and are currently available from several companies, including PairGain Technologies, Motorola, and AT&T Microelectronics. ▓

ISDN marked the beginning of digital telephony. DSL has significantly expanded its capability starting at HDSL, running at 1.5 and 2Mbps. However, HDSL requires four wires or two twisted pairs, but ADSL only requires one twisted pair, an early standard found in even the most rural of areas.

The Coming of VDSL

Beyond ADSL, the next standard under development is VDSL (very high speed digital subscriber line). VDSL will be targeted at phone companies that install fiber to neighborhoods, and then provide up to 51Mbps data rate over a copper pair to homes within 3,000 feet of the fiber.

Asynchronous Digital Subscriber Line (ADSL)

There has been a tremendous interest in ADSL, as Internet service providers struggle to differentiate themselves and offer customers faster access to the Internet. At 6.144Mbps, ADSL can offer over 200 times the speed of a 28.8 modem, and can also provide simultaneous POTS, real-time video, and Internet access.

ADSL runs on standard copper pair telephone lines, providing interactive telephony and digital services directly to the home or office. This transport technology significantly increases the capacity of the existing telephone wire.

With ADSL, those lengthy file transfers—during which you visit the coffee room, restroom, take a walk around the block, and catch up on your phone calls—may now execute in seconds at speeds of up to 6Mbps—many times that of your old 28.8Kbps modem.

Troubled by the single-line dilemma? Standard dial-up systems do not allow users to talk on the phone while using the Internet. ADSL, on the other hand, preserves the POTS connection while adding fast access to the Internet.

Another advantage ADSL has over other services, such as ISDN, is that no new telephone equipment is necessary.

ADSL lets multiple users, or a single user, use the phone service for several tasks at once. This happens in the phone company switching office, where the phone company connects phone lines to the Internet, video switches, and the regular audio phone matrix through their ADSL access multiplexer. End users connect to this access mux through their ADSL

Ch
12

modems. No additional fiber or coax is required to the customer site; everything takes place, incredibly, over the existing copper phone infrastructure. A standard modem takes the computer's digital data, converts it to analog for transmission over the phone lines, and then converts it back to digital on the other end. ADSL modems work in much the same way. ADSL modems format digital data into analog signals that are carried on the standard phone line, in a discrete multitone (DMT) modulation technique. The remote ADSL modem then converts the DMT signals back into digital bits and routes the different signals to each appropriate application.

With ADSL, the customer enjoys a data rate of up to 6Mbps inbound (from the phone company's central office to the user's site) and as high as 1Mbps outbound. The actual rate varies depending on the length of the telephone line. A shorter phone line of under 1.5 miles, which will suffer from lower attenuation, will enjoy a faster rate than a longer phone line. Other factors, such as crosstalk and other types of signal noise, may also affect the actual rate. ADSL is, however, immune to impulse noise. Electronic noise caused by nearby electronics—such as refrigerators, hair dryers, or vacuum cleaners—may impact a regular modem connection. However, ADSL's selected discrete multitone (DMT) mechanism takes impulse noise and spreads it equally between all tones in order to dilute it as much as possible and minimize its effect. The modem calculates the information about the phone line, and then reports the highest possible data rate to the network maintenance center. Downstream rates for up to 1.5 miles is 8Mbps; 2.5 miles is 6Mbps, 3.5 miles is 4Mbps, and 3.5 to 5 miles is 1.5 to 2Mbps. At the highest rate, users enjoy tremendously fast Internet access, with simultaneous access to other applications such as broadcast digital television, video-on-demand movies, or other futuristic applications.

N O T E   Most of the major telephone companies are already experimenting with ADSL; some of the European phone companies have already advanced to experimenting with video-on-demand movies. Additionally, several hardware vendors are planning to offer standards-compliant ADSL modems.

DMT line coding divides the signal into 256 tones, each 4kHz wide. Each tone carries a data rate of up to 60Kbps each. The amount of data each tone carries is dependent on the DMT loading algorithm.

DMT enjoys strong immunity to *impulse noise*, or interference caused by nearby electronics, simply by dividing any interfering impulse noise equally among the 256 tones in order to dilute it.

While other digital technologies, such as ISDN, do not accommodate the lifeline telephone requirements that phone service continues in the event of a power failure, ADSL does leave phone service intact if a power failure occurs. Users can enjoy simultaneous access to multiple services, including video channels, video conferencing, Internet access, and normal telephone service.

Ultimately, phone companies will replace all of their copper with fiber, although this may take years. ADSL takes advantage of existing copper wire. The design here is to run optical cable to neighborhoods (optical network units), and to use existing copper to connect to individual homes. This is a much more cost-effective measure than placing fiber to each home. Under this design, fiber runs to the neighborhood switch center, and personal lines run ADSL over existing copper to connect to the switch center.

The customer deploys an ADSL modem, and the phone company deploys an ADSL circuit switch in the switching center. Three channels are then created to connect the user to the switch: a unidirectional data channel, a medium-speed duplex channel, and a POTS connection. The unidirectional channel runs at speeds of up to 6.1Mbps inbound; the duplex channel offers 640Kbps outbound data rates. Forward error correction (FEC) is used by ADSL to minimize data errors caused by line noise. To run over existing copper, ADSL uses digital signal processing and compression algorithms. But because signals moving over copper suffer from attenuation and crosstalk, there is a distance limitation of five miles between the central switching office and the ADSL modem.

ADSL Applications   ADSL may not only lend itself to entertainment but also to many practical applications. An ideal technology for home-based workers and telecommuters, ADSL can be used to establish a low-cost connection to a WAN switching center or corporate headquarters. It supports all protocols and requires no additional wiring; and the only extra equipment required is the device in the phone company central office and the ADSL modem at the user end.

Also, because it can be used for two-way communications, it could also potentially be used for interactive cable television. Because it is new, ADSL modems are still fairly expensive—nearly $1,000. However, as support for the technology becomes pervasive, costs will go down.

ADSL may be just the ticket for SOHO workers desiring faster access and interactivity. If all you need is access to the Internet, ISDN's 64Kbps or 128Kbps rate may be more than adequate. ADSL promises much more than a fast way to download Web pages, however. Ultimately, it could be used to give couch potatoes access to downloadable videos and music on demand, interactive cable television, and many more entertainment goodies.

For corporate users, ADSL could provide shared CD-ROM access, fast access to huge databases over the Internet, speedy data transfer, and tremendous efficiency. Entertainment and business features like this could have a potentially dramatic effect on the Internet, and could provide a new way for telephone companies and others to profit by providing these services over the Internet.

Ch
12

ADSL Service Classes and Capacity   ADSL's downstream capacity ranges from 2.048Mbps to 6.144Mbps, with longer distances possible at lower speeds. There are three transport classes in ADSL: 2M-1, 2M-2, and 2M-3. Maximum capacity is shown in Table 12.1.

Table 12.1   ADSL Capacity

Service Class	2M-1	2M-2	2M-3
Downstream	6.144Mbps	4.096Mbps	2.048Mbps
Upstream	640Kbps	448Kbps	160Kbps

HDSL

HDSL is very similar to ADSL, but it provides fast throughput in a symmetric and full-duplex manner—in other words, the full 6.1Mbps is available in both directions, instead of just inbound. Although it was designed for running over two pairs of twisted copper wire, it has been demonstrated running successfully over a single copper wire. However, ADSL is further along in development than HDSL, and is significantly cheaper to operate. HDSL may instead be limited to specialty areas, such as cities with several high-rise buildings or advanced cellular systems.

VDSL

VDSL still runs over twisted-pair copper, but uses ATM technology to provide up to 55Mbps throughput through the local telephone loop. VDSL is even younger than HDSL, but offers a tremendous amount of potential. The architecture of VDSL is again similar to that of ADSL. It is made up of several channels, with inbound rates of up to 55Mbps and outbound at about 13Mbps.

Standards

ANSI's T1E1.4 working group has approved standards for ADSL devices with a throughput of up to 6.1Mbps. Furthermore, the ATM Forum has embraced ADSL as a physical layer transmission protocol for running over UTP media. The new ADSL Forum, established in 1994, promotes the technology and has more than 60 members from the telecommunications industry. The ADSL Forum is working on enhancing the standard. Enhancements include a new bit interface for connecting ADSL to Ethernet and ATM networks.

DSL and ATM

Several communications equipment vendors have licensed Advanced Telecommunications Modules Ltd.'s "ATM-on-a-chip" technology for the next generation of Internet access equipment for Digital Subscriber Line (DSL) networks. By incorporating ATM into these end-point devices, carriers will be able to use these products to provide a low-cost ATM/DSL network, and value-added services such as transparent LAN services and high-speed Internet connections. The incorporation of ATM into DSL technology will also eventually result in the development of more applications, such as electronic commerce, remote management, and distance learning. Combining ATM with DSL gives carriers the ability to offer full-service networking of data, voice, and video.

Advanced Telecommunications Modules' integrated ATM ASIC and software solution will lay the groundwork for a high-bandwidth, end-to-end ATM solution for DSL networks using existing copper telephone wire. The product, called the ATOM Accelerator, will give a boost to equipment manufacturers by decreasing costs and time to market for the development and manufacture of DSL modems, Digital Subscriber Loop Access Multiplexers (DSLAMs), and network interface cards (NICs).

The ATOM ASICs are the first CPU-embedded ASICs with ATM capability and a fully integrated software environment. The ATOM Accelerator features ATM Ltd's ATOM ASIC chips which are optimized for xDSL products.

The ATOM ASICs include two universal end-point chips: the Hydrogen and Helium, both which are used for building NICs, modems, and DSLAM line cards. The Hydrogen chip has an ATM25 interface and ATM SAR functions. The Hydrogen chip includes traffic management features to manage flow control. Through adaptive rate-pacing, Hydrogen can be used for all xDSL applications and speeds.

Ch
12

Next-Generation Network Technology

At the time of this writing, six communications equipment vendors have licensed Advanced Telecommunications Modules' ATM-on-a-chip technology as the next step in developing next-generation Internet access equipment for xDSL networks. By incorporating ATM technology into xDSL end-point devices, carriers will be able to offer low-cost ATM/DSL networks as well as several value-added services, including transparent LAN services and high-speed Internet access.

Advanced Telecom's ATOM Accelerator is an integrated, ATM application-specific integrated circuit (ASIC) and an accompanying software development kit.

Vendors

Telephone companies have already started to offer xDSL services, both to consumers and businesses. To meet the demand, however, the telephone companies must provision their customers with the appropriate type of modems for xDSL, and offer assistance with configuration.

U.S. Robotics is likely to play a leading role in the xDSL market by taking advantage of its technical, marketing, and distribution expertise. The company has made a number of alliances for its new xDSL product line. U.S. Robotics' xDSL modems are equipped with GlobeSpan Technologies' RADSL (Rate Adaptive Digital Subscriber Line) chipset. RADSL technology offers a rate-adaptive transmission speed, which is based on the length and signal quality of the existing telephone line. RADSL-based products can select the highest practical operating speed either automatically, or as specified by the telecommunications service provider. In addition, the French telecom integration company CS Telecom has chosen U.S. Robotics to provide xDSL products. Several other companies around the globe, including Spain's Telefonica public telephone and telegraph company, are also working with U.S. Robotics to provide xDSL services.

Paradyne's HotWire DSL systems have been incorporated into Ingram Micro's Telecom Integration Division's family of CTI Total Solutions. Under the reseller agreement, Ingram will distribute Paradyne's HotWare DSL and other related products to VARs in the U.S. and Canada. Paradyne is one of the early pioneers in the DSL Industry, and offers a large product line. HotWire suite includes multiservices DSL Access Multiplexer (DSLAM) platforms, endpoint products, and management utilities.

U.S. Robotics DSL remote access solution provides small businesses and consumers with high-speed remote access to both corporate LANs and the Internet over standard telephone lines. Telecommunications service providers are already starting to offer DSL services to small businesses, consumers, and branch offices.

Multilink Channel Aggregation

Wouldn't it be nice if you could put together those two 28.8Kbps modems and get a single 57.6 connection to the Internet? Microsoft's Windows NT operating system gives you a way to do it. Two phone lines and two analog modems can be combined and connected to the same PC to create a greater aggregate bandwidth. Windows NT's Remote Access

Service (RAS) feature offers something called *Multilink Channel Aggregation*. With Multilink, multiple communications lines, whether analog or digital, can be combined into a single link. For example, if you have two 28.8Kbps modems, you can combine it to form a single 57.6Kbps link. Multilink can be used to combine analog modems, multiple B-ISDN channels, or a combination of the two.

The process is remarkably straightforward, and starts simply by hooking up a multiport adapter to the PC. The multiport adapter can be used to connect two or more analog modems to the PC.

Multilink can be used in several different ways. It can be used to allow a Windows NT workstation to establish a direct connection with a Windows NT Server machine, or it can be used to establish a high-speed connection to the Internet. As a simple, high-speed technology, multilink adapters can be especially useful for the small office/home office (SOHO) market.

In addition to multilink, RAS also offers users access to the Point-to-Point Tunneling Protocol (PPTP), which can be used to create a virtual private network over the Internet. Microsoft's Steelhead beta release enhances RAS with more sophisticated PPTP and other features.

Microsoft Steelhead Beta

In its present state, RAS establishes a client-to-server connection only. Microsoft's new Steelhead beta promises to build on RAS' already sophisticated features, including multilink, and to go beyond the point-to-point nature of RAS.

The existing RAS features are used for making high-speed and efficient point-to-point connections—for example, allowing a telecommuter to link to headquarters. Steelhead goes a step further by allowing server-to-server connections, thereby facilitating the linkage of entire branch offices to headquarters.

Under Steelhead's Point-to-Point Tunneling (PPT) facility, it is possible to use the Internet as a Virtual Private Network (VPN). Although RAS does already support the PPTP, Steelhead adds to its functionality by allowing server-to-server connections. With Steelhead, not only can you link a remote client to the corporate server, but you can now also link a branch office's server to headquarter's server, thereby allowing everyone in the branch office to enjoy the connection. Using a VPN, a remote user, or even a server at a remote branch could communicate with a distant headquarters office for the price of a local call. This is done by dialing up an ISP and then establishing a secure, encrypted tunnel over the Internet, back to the RAS server.

Ch
12

Intranets

The Internet has given way to another technology revolution known as an *intranet*, a technology that uses the Internet and World Wide Web's architecture as a way to disseminate information internally on a LAN. Intranets have evolved as a handy way to allow remote workers, customers, and others to access corporate data through a standard Internet connection and a Web browser interface from their LAN. They are inexpensive, cross-platform, and enormously convenient.

But again, in order for an intranet to be most effective, it must be able to support mission-critical data in large quantities. Intranet services can be integrated with existing LAN infrastructures, and in particular, Asynchronous Transfer Mode (ATM) technology can be used to implement a highly efficient and fast intranet.

Although a text-only intranet can present some significant opportunities for efficiency, data with video, graphics, executable code, and more—as well as very large files necessary for applications such as data warehousing and multi-dimensional analysis—cry out for more. Over the past few years, the nature of data that moves over the network has changed significantly. PCs and workstations have evolved to the point where they can easily handle many types of rich data; it is now necessary to move these large quantities of data over the network at high speeds.

Several elements are necessary before a mission-critical intranet can be deployed. First, the intranet must have adequate bandwidth to host business applications and to deliver large amounts of data. Furthermore, the network must be highly available and robust. Scalability is also critical, so the intranet can send information not only to the desktop, but also across a backbone and through a WAN. Of course, it must also be secure, affordable, and easily manageable.

There are three basic types of intranets: the data center intranet, campus intranet, and wide-area intranet. All three can make use of ATM technology to realize the high speeds necessary to operate in a modern environment.

The speed at which data is served through an intranet will greatly affect its popularity and efficiency. Some of the technologies described previously, such as ISDN and xDSL, give the end users a high-speed pipe to the ISP. Multilink channel aggregation can be used to forge a direct, high-speed link either to the ISP or directly to the data center.

But, even if the end users can connect with a fast pipe, the servers themselves can slow the system down if they are not part of a high-speed network. The servers that hold the data must be able to access the back-end data the users want, and quickly, in order to send it out through those fast pipes. Placing the Web servers in a core ATM network, which also holds the corporate data servers, will facilitate faster access.

Data Center Intranet

Occasionally, for security and cost reasons, corporate servers may be centralized. In the Figure 12.1, the Web server or intranet server is connected directly to the core ATM network and indirectly to the surrounding Ethernet or Token-Ring networks.

FIG. 12.1

A data center intranet.

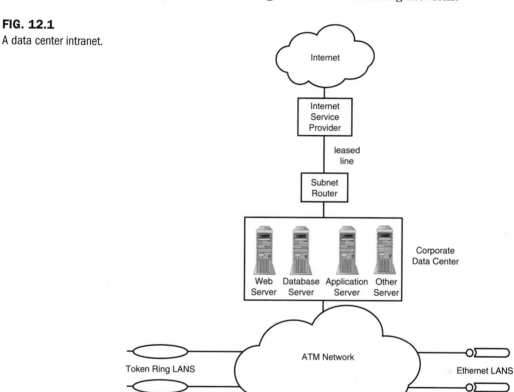

This configuration allows data to flow easily between the servers in the data center, and the legacy Token Ring and Ethernet LANs; and also between the LANs themselves. Translation between the legacy networks to the ATM environment takes place in an edge router, or a device that contains LAN Emulation (LANE) software. The edge router allows the legacy networks to maintain their own identities and operate with the ATM network unchanged.

Ch

12

Campus Intranet

A campus intranet (see Figure 12.2) adds a new layer of complexity to accommodate a larger area.

FIG. 12.2

A campus intranet.

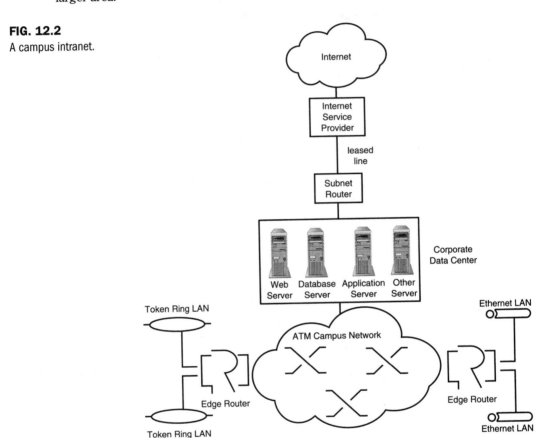

Wide Area Intranet

This model encompasses operations with several remote branch offices and allows them to exchange information between themselves and with headquarters. A wide area intranet may require all of ATM's features, including bandwidth reservation and Quality of Service, to make the most efficient use of the WAN.

FIG. 12.3
A wide area intranet.

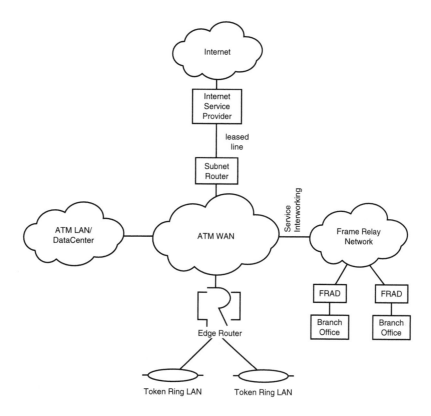

Cable Access

Cable TV companies know a good thing when they see it, and want to use their existing cable infrastructure to send the Internet into your homes. This strategy fits in quite well with the latest innovation of Internet appliances that connect to the television.

There are only a handful of cable modems on the market at the present time, but this new model holds a great deal of potential. Through cable modems, you could access the Internet at rates of more than 500 times that of a standard 28.8Kbps analog modem. Some of the vendors offering cable modems include Hewlett-Packard, Motorola, Nortel, and Zenith.

Theoretically, a cable modem could offer downstream speeds of up to 36Mbps, although most will be limited to 2Mbps–10Mbps. Like xDSL, cable modems will have an asynchronous type of operation, with a higher downstream speed than upstream speed. Nonetheless, the high rate of speed available through cable could lead to applications such as video-on-demand and other interactive services.

This concept of the cable modems is still quite young, and there are no standards bodies governing the technology. Furthermore, there is significant doubt in the industry as to whether it will ever become successful. This is largely because even if the end user has a 10Mbps connection to the Internet, providers still can only send the data out at substantially lower ISDN rates. Cable modems would then be of little use except for in point-to-point connections.

Satellite

We have discussed several options for logging on to the Internet through telephone lines. One option is to bypass the phone company altogether and use satellite technology. DirecPC services pipe Internet data directly to your computer via a satellite dish at about 400Kbps.

Summary

Significant advances have been made in modem technology. While most home users still rely on a 28.8 or even a 14.4 modem over POTS, more powerful options are starting to emerge.

ISDN is one of the more mature technologies for fast access. Most of the bigger cities have ISDN services. With ISDN, users enjoy fast file downloads and a tremendous increase over standard 28.8 modem technology. In addition, ISDN transfers are not affected by line noise; because they have been around longer than the other technologies discussed in this chapter, ISDN modems are coming down in price and are currently available for a few hundred dollars.

Digital Subscriber Line (DSL) technology builds on ISDN to offer an even faster access rate. xDSL technology includes high bit rate DSL (HDSL), symmetric DSL (SDSL), asymmetric DSL (ADSL), and very high bit rate DSL (VDSL). The most mature and widely available of these is ADSL, created as an alternative to T1 service. These DSL technologies offer a new level of capabilities over standard copper telephone wire. DSL models the distortion inherent in copper lines and dynamically adjust their transmission characteristics to match. ●

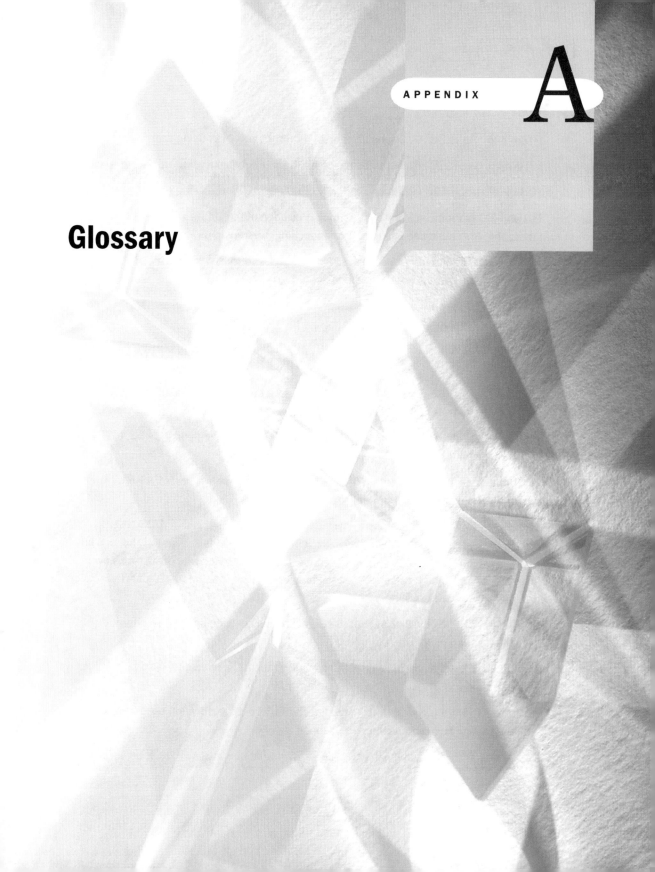

Glossary

Numbers

10Base-2   An IEEE 802.3 specification for Ethernet networks using thin coaxial cable.

10Base-5   An IEEE 802.3 specification for Ethernet networks using thick coaxial cable.

10Base-F   An IEEE 802.3 specification for Ethernet networks using fiber-optic cable.

10Base-FB (Fiber Backbone)   A sub-specification of the 100BaseF Fiber Optic Ethernet specification used for making connections between buildings.

10Base-FL (Fiber Link)   A sub-specification of the 100BaseF Fiber Optic Ethernet specification used for intermediate hubs or workgroups.

10Base-FP (Fiber Passive)   A sub-specification of the 100BaseF Fiber Optic Ethernet specification used for desktop connections.

100Base-FX   A Fast Ethernet (100BaseT) specification that supports two-strand fiber optic cable.

10Base-T   An IEEE 802.3 specification for Ethernet networks. 10BaseT uses UTP copper wire, and provides up to 10Mbps of bandwidth.

100Base-T4   A Fast Ethernet (100BaseT) specification that supports CAT-3, CAT-4, or CAT-5 cabling and requires four pairs of wires.

100Base-TX   A Fast Ethernet (100BaseT) specification that supports CAT-5 UTP and STP cabling and requires two pairs of wires.

100Base-VG/Any LAN   A proprietary extension of the IEEE LAN/MAN (IEEE 802.12) standard, developed by Hewlett-Packard. 100Base VG is similar to Ethernet, but does not use the CSMA/CD protocol. It supports a transmission rate of 100Mbps over four pairs of CAT-3 UTP cable, and uses a demand priority scheme to assign priority to data packets.

1000Base-CX   A physical layer of the Gigabit Ethernet specification used for interconnection of equipment clusters.

1000Base-LX   A physical layer of the Gigabit Ethernet specification used for horizontal building cabling.

1000Base-SX   A physical layer of the Gigabit Ethernet specification used for backbone building cabling and campus interconnections.

1000Base-T   The Gigabit Ethernet specification that operates at 1000Mbps.

4B/5B Encoding   A data translation scheme in which a group of four bits is represented as a five-bit symbol, which is then associated with a bit pattern.

5B/6B Encoding   A data translation scheme in which each group of five bits is represented as a six-bit symbol, which is then associated with a bit pattern.

56K line   A digital leased line capable of carrying a throughput of 56Kbps of data.

64K line   A digital leased line capable of carrying a throughput of 64Kbps of data. Physically, a 64Kbps line is the same as a 56Kbps line.

8B/10B Encoding   A data translation scheme based on 4B/5B Encoding, in which each group of eight bits is represented as a ten-bit symbol, which is then associated with a bit pattern.

802.1   An IEEE standard for LAN architecture, internetworking, and network management.

802.10   An IEEE working group in charge of LAN security issues, including data encryption and network management.

802.11   An IEEE working group charged with establishing standards for wireless networks.

802.12   An IEEE working group covering LAN/MAN standards, including 100Base-VG's Demand Priority mechanism.

802.2   An IEEE standard that outlines the Logical Link Control (LLC) layer for a CSMA/CD bus network. The LLC layer is used to interface between media access methods and the network layer.

802.3   An IEEE standard that specifies the parameters for the Media Access Control (MAC) layer for a CSMA/CD bus network.

802.4   An IEEE standard that specifies the Media Access Control (MAC) layer for a token-passing bus network.

802.5   An IEEE standard that specifies the Media Access Control (MAC) layer for a token-passing ring network.

802.6   An IEEE standard that specifies a Metropolitan Area Network (MAN) with a 30-mile fiber-optic ring.

802.9   An IEEE standard for integrating voice and data.

802.x   The full suite of IEEE 802 standards.

A

AAL Connection (ATM Adaptation Layer Connection)   An association established by the AAL between multiple higher-layer entities.

AAL-1 (ATM Adaptation Layer Type 1)   The set of AAL methods used to support constant bit rate traffic.

AAL-2 (ATM Adaptation Layer Type 2)   The set of AAL methods used to support variable bit rate video transmission.

AAL-3/4 (ATM Adaptation Layer Type 3 / 4)   The set of AAL methods used to support variable bit rate traffic that is more delay-tolerant than video transmissions, but requires error detection.

AAL-5 (ATM Adaptation Layer Type 5   The set of AAL methods used to support variable bit rate traffic that is more delay-tolerant than video transmission, and requires little or no error detection.

Access Line   A communications line used to connect a frame relay device (DTE) with a frame relay switch (DCE).

Access Rate (AR)   The user access channel's data rate in a Frame Relay network.

ADM (Add/Drop Multiplexer)   A device used to allow low-speed signals to be added or dropped dynamically, without having to demultiplex the entire signal. This device, commonly used in SONET networks, overcomes the restriction found in some other network architectures that require lower speed channels to be completely demultiplexed before they can be recombined into a higher-speed signal.

Address Resolution   A procedure used by a network client to associate a LAN destination with the ATM address of another client or the Broadcast and Unknown Server (BUS).

Address Resolution Protocol (ARP)   Part of the Internet Protocol (IP) suite. ARP is used to determine a destination node's physical address so data transmission can take place. ARP maps between IP addresses and hardware-based data-link addresses associated with a particular machine.

ADSL (Asymmetric Digital Subscriber Line)   A modem technology designed to offer 6.144Mbps of downstream and 640Kbps upstream bandwidth over standard telephone copper wire. The technology is limited to about five miles.

Alternate Routing   A mechanism used to establish a new data path, if a previously established path fails.

American National Standards Institute (ANSI)   A standards body responsible for data communications and terminal standards.

American Standard Code for Information Interchange (ASCII)   A seven-bit code used to exchange data between communications devices.

AMI (Alternate Mark Inversion)   A bipolar encoding scheme used in FDDI and ISDN. Under this method, there are three possible values: positive voltage, zero voltage, and negative voltage. *Zero* bits are encoded as zero voltage, *one* bits are alternately encoded as positive and negative. An external clock is necessary for timing.

Application layer (OSI Model)   The seventh layer in the OSI Reference Model. The application layer grants end users access to the network, and connects with the transport layer on the source machine.

APPN (Advanced Peer-to-Peer Networking)   Part of IBM's Systems Application Architecture (SAA) environment. APPN allows two network computers (PU 2.1 devices) to communicate directly, without having to go through an intermediate SNA device.

Arbitrated Loop   A Fibre Channel topology that interconnects several ports. Traffic is managed with a token-acquisition protocol, and only one connection can be maintained within the loop at a time.

arbitration   A set of rules used to mitigate conflicts that arise when two systems request access to the same computer resource.

asynchronous   A way of transmitting data, in which each characters or blocks may start at any time. Each individual character or block, however, must be equal in length. Stop and start bits are placed at the beginning and end of each block to indicate the beginning and end of each character, as opposed to a constant timing mechanism.

Asynchronous Time Division Multiplexing (ATDM)   A type of multiplexing that organizes the data into unassigned time slots, which are then assigned to cells based on current need.

Asynchronous Transfer Mode (ATM)   A high-speed, cell-based method of communication where units of information are organized into fixed-size cells of 53 bytes each. ATM is a connection-oriented and packet-switched architecture, based on B-ISDN technology. It is capable of offering very high bandwidth rates of up to 622Mbps. It includes a Quality of Service (QoS) specification, which makes it possible to transmit many different types of data over an ATM network.

ATM Adaptation Layer (AAL)   A method used to adapt higher-layer protocols for transport over an ATM network.

ATM Inverse Multiplexing (AIMUX)   A device used to combine multiple T1 or E1 links into a single broadband facility, over which ATM cells can then be transmitted.

ATM Peer-to-Peer Connection   A virtual channel connection (VCC) or virtual path connection (VPC).

ATM Traffic Descriptor   A list of traffic parameters used to identify the characteristics of a particular ATM connection.

ATM User-User Connection   An ATM Layer association used to support communication between multiple ATM users on an ATM network. Communications over the ATM Layer can be bidirectional or unidirectional.

ATS (Abstract Test Suite)   A test suite that is independent of any specific implementation.

AUI (Attachment Unit Interface)   The interface between a network device and a medium attachment unit (MAU). The AUI can be a cable that attaches a computer to a network hub.

Attenuation   A type of distortion that occurs as a signal passes through physical media. Attenuation becomes greater with distance.

Auto-Negotiation   A handshaking process whereby two intelligent devices, such as modems or hubs, determine the highest common denominator between the two, thereby determining the best available parameters for communication.

Asymmetric Digital Subscriber Line (ADSL)   A communications technology that significantly increases the capacity of existing copper telephone connections, and allows concurrent data and voice to be transmitted and received.

Available Bit Rate (ABR)   A type of ATM traffic that does not require a specific amount of bandwidth.

B

B Channel   The bearer channel in an ISDN circuit. The B channel can transmit voice or data bidirectionally at the rate of 64Kbps. Multiple B channels can be multiplexed into a higher-rate H channel.

backbone   An internetworking structure used to establish a central connection path. Network segments, subnetworks, or individual devices can be attached directly to the backbone.

bandwidth The signaling rate possible for a connection, expressed in bits per second (bps). Bandwidth determines the rate at which data can travel over the physical medium.

bandwidth-on-demand A virtual circuit's ability to exceed its committed information rate (CIR).

Baseband A system that transmits signals without first converting them to another frequency. Baseband systems, such as Ethernet, support only one frequency of signals.

Basic Rate Interface (BRI) An ISDN interface between the user and the ISDN switch. The BRI is made up of two 64-Kbps B channels and one 16-Kbps D channel. The two B channels are used for voice and data, and the D channel holds addressing and other information.

baud rate A serial communications rate that indicates the speed at which a signal changes. The baud rate is the same as the bit rate if each signal represents a single bit; but if each signal represents several bits, the bit rate is a multiple of the baud rate.

binary synchronous communications (BISYNC) A type of communication used in IBM mainframe environments, in which a SYN character is used to determine a data block's synchronization. The recipient acknowledges the receipt of each block with ACK characters.

bit stuffing A technique that inserts additional bits in order to guarantee that a specific bit pattern does not appear as part of data in a transmission. The additional bits are removed after the transmission is processed.

bridge A hardware device used to connect two or more networks or network segments. The frames are forwarded between the two networks based on information held in the data-link header. The bridge filters out all packets not meant for the destination network. Because it is protocol-independent, it can handle packets from multiple higher-level protocols; but the bridge itself operates at the Data Link Layer.

broadband A transmission technology that multiplexes several different types of signals over a single cable, allowing several networks to exist on the same cable. Every network's conversations occur on a different frequency so there is no interference.

Broadband ISDN Inter-Carrier Interface (B-ICI) An ATM Forum standard used to establish inter-switch communications in public networks.

broadband network A network that uses broadband technology to send several data streams over the same cable. Each of several channels are divided by a guard channel, which is a small band of unused frequency that sits between each transmission channel.

Backward Explicit Congestion Notification (BECN)   A type of control cell generated either by the destination node or the Frame Relay network itself. This cell indicates that the network is in a congested state for traffic that is flowing in the direction opposite of the BECN cell, and that the sending device should initiate congestion avoidance procedures.

bidirectional line-switched ring (BLSR)   A survivability technology employed in SONET networks. A BLSR configuration implements dual circuits. If one circuit suffers a cut, the traffic reverses and flows in the opposite direction on the same ring to avoid the cut. If the ring is broken in two places, however, the traffic will be automatically rerouted onto the second circuit. This rerouting happens almost instantaneously.

binary logarithmic access method (BLAM)   A proposed alternative to the IEEE 802.3 backoff algorithm.

Bit Error Rate (BER)   A metric used to indicate transmission quality by showing a ratio of erroneous bits to the total number of bits.

Broadcast and Unknown Server (BUS)   A server in an ATM network. The BUS is used to broadcast traffic to multiple destinations, and to send packets to their destinations when the destination address is not known.

buffered repeater   A device used to boost signals before re-transmitting them. A buffered repeater can hold data temporarily, for example, if a transmission is already occurring on the network. Use of a buffered repeater is proposed as a means of enhancing performance of Gigabit Ethernet. This mechanism alters the CSMA/CD access mechanism, and proposes placing collision detection on the repeater. Consequently, end stations do not have to retransmit after a collision. This mechanism allows end stations to transmit over a full-duplex link, reduces the possibility of packet collision, and permits a larger network diameter.

Burst excess (Be)   A parameter used to control Permanent Virtual Circuits (PVCs) in a frame relay network. Be is defined as the highest number of uncommitted data bits the network will attempt to deliver over a specified period of time.

Burstiness   A quality of data that uses bandwidth inconsistently. A bursty transmission has pauses during which no traffic is flowing. Most LAN traffic is bursty by nature.

Building Integrated Timing Supply (BITS)   A SONET clock synchronization scheme for transporting a timing reference between locations. SONET's model of synchronization uses a single clock, which is designated as the Building Integrated Timing Supply (BITS). All other clocks receive their timing references from the BITS.

C

carrier extension   A proposal for modifying the CSMA/CD access mechanism for Gigabit Ethernet. Under carrier extension, when a device on the network transmits, the signal stays active for a longer time before another device can attempt to transmit. This lets an Ethernet frame travel a longer distance, and thereby increases the potential network diameter.

carrier-to-carrier interface (CCI)   A protocol contained in the HiPPI SW (switch control) standard. HiPPI SW is used to control switches connected to the HiPPI cable. The CCI, also known as the I-field, is described in the standard. The HiPPI switch interprets the CCI in order to route connection requests.

Carrier Sense Multiple Access/Collision Detection (CSMA/CD)   A media access protocol designed to mitigate the results of packet collision. CSMA/CD is used in Ethernet/802.3 networks, and functions on the MAC sublayer of the OSI Reference Model. A node implementing CSMA/CD will first determine whether there is traffic on the network. If traffic is detected, the node waits before attempting to transmit. If two nodes transmit at the same time, a collision occurs. In this case, the packets will be discarded, and each node will retransmit after a random period of time.

Categories 1-5   A set of cabling standards established by the Electronics Industry Association/Telecommunications Industry Association (EIA/TIA). Often abbreviated CAT 1-5. The categories are as follows:

- **Category 1**. Unshielded twisted pair (UTP) telephone cable.
- **Category 2**. UTP cable for use at speeds of up to 4Mbps.
- **Category 3**. UTP cable for use at speeds of up to 10Mbps.
- **Category 4**. UTP cable for use at speeds of up to 16Mbps in a Token Ring network.
- **Category 5**. UTP cable for use at speeds of up to 100Mbps.

cell   The unit of data used for transmitting information in an Asynchronous Transfer Mode network. An ATM cell contains 53 bytes, 48 of which are used for data and five for the header.

Cell Loss Priority   A bit in an Asynchronous Transfer Mode header, used to indicate a cell's priority level. A cell set with a CLP bit to zero has higher priority than a cell with the CLP bit set to one. In the case of congestion, cells with a CLP bit set to one may be discarded.

Cell Loss Ratio   A negotiated Quality of Service parameter in an Asynchronous Transfer Mode network. This parameter indicates a ratio of lost cells to total transmitted cells.

Cell-Relay   A type of network, such as Asynchronous Transfer Mode, where data is divided into small, fixed-size packets that can be switched throughout the network very quickly.

Channel   A direct connection between two devices, typically designed for high-speed data transfer.

Channel Capture   A condition that occurs when the Ethernet MAC layer temporarily becomes biased toward one workstation on a loaded network, thereby making that one station the contention winner more times than would randomly occur.

Channel Service Unit (CSU)   A device used in a Frame Relay network used to interface the Data Terminal Equipment (DTE) to the frame relay switch.

Circuit emulation switching (CES)   Part of the ATM Forum's proposed Service Aspects and Applications (SAA) standard.

client/server model   A network that distributes processing between the server and the individual workstations.

coaxial cable   A cable with a central solid wire, surrounded by insulation. A braided-wire conductor sheath covers the insulation, and a plastic jacket surrounds the sheath.

collision   A state that occurs when two network devices transmit data at the same time.

collision domain   The part of an Ethernet network that includes all end stations and repeaters that are interconnected without a bridge, switch, or router.

Committed Burst (Bc)   The amount of data (expressed in bps) that a Frame Relay network transfers under normal conditions during a set time interval.

Committed Information Rate (CIR)   The rate of information transfer (expressed in bps) offered by a Frame Relay service provider under normal conditions.

Common management information protocol (CMIP)   A network management protocol used in the OSI Reference Model, and similar to (but less frequently used than) the Simple Network Management Protocol (SNMP). CMIP defines how management information is transmitted between stations.

computer telephony integration (CTI)   Intelligent telephony features that are implemented through a computer, such as automatic dialing, caller ID, and other customer service functions.

concentrator   A hardware device with one bus and many connections. A concentrator can be used to send many input channels out to fewer output channels, or to connect multiple network elements with different cabling schemes. A concentrator can be used as a hub.

connection-oriented network   A type of network where communication occurs only after first setting out a predetermined path between sender and recipient.

connectionless network   A type of datagram delivery in the Internet Protocol, where communication occurs without having to first establish a direct connection between sender and recipient.

Constant Bit Rate (CBR)   An Asynchronous Transfer Mode connection under the Class A Quality of Service level. CBR is used for voice and video, and other data that is loss-intolerant.

Convergence Sublayer   A sublayer of the ATM Adaptation Layer, used to convert data between ATM and non-ATM formats.

crosstalk   Interference that can occur when two wires are in close proximity.

Customer Premises Equipment (CPE)   Hardware that is leased or owned by the customer, and used at the customer's location.

cut-through   A type of switching common to token ring, in which data is forwarded as soon as the first 20 or 30 bytes of a frame have been received, as opposed to waiting for the whole frame to be received.

cycle master   Part of the bus management scheme used in the IEEE 1394 connection technology. The cycle master broadcasts cycle start packets, which are required for isochronous operation. An isochronous resource manager, for DV and DA applications, is also included for those nodes that support isochronous operation. Also included is an optional bus master.

Cyclic Redundancy Check (CRC)   A calculation meant to ensure the accuracy of frames sent between devices. The CRC calculates a value before transmission, where the value is dependent on the frame's payload. The value is recalculated at the destination; if it is the same, it is assumed that no errors occurred during transmission.

D

daisy chain   A series of serially-linked components. Also known as cascading.

dark fiber   An unused fiber optic cable through which no light (signal) is being transmitted. A carrier occasionally sells dark fiber only, without transmission service, if the customer prefers to install their own equipment.

Data Communications Equipment (DCE)   Switching equipment in a Frame Relay network.

data exchange interface (DXI)   An ATM Forum specification. The DXI is a frame-based interface that exists between a packet-based router and an ATM-based data service unit (DSU).

Data Link Layer (OSI Model)   The second layer in the seven-layer OSI Reference Model. The Data Link layer packages and addresses data, and controls transmission flow over communication lines.

Data Service Unit   Equipment used to connect a customer's computing equipment to a public network.

Data Terminal Equipment   External network interface equipment.

data warehousing   A type of relational database technology that stores large quantities of corporate transactional data, often in different formats, in a central location for subsequent analysis.

datagram   A packet containing information and address information that is routed through a packet-switching network.

dedicated line   A leased or private communications line that is always available.

dedicated router   A device that operates solely as a router.

Defense Advanced Research Projects Agency (DARPA)   A U.S. Department of Defense agency, formerly known as ARPA, that was instrumental in the development of TCP/IP. ARPA's ARPANET network formed the basis of the modern Internet.

Demand Priority   The mechanism used in 100VG networks to replace CSMA/CD. Demand priority replaces the contention-oriented CSMA/CD mechanism with a priority-based scheme that eliminates collisions.

demodulator   A device, often combined with a modulator, that removes the modulating signal from the carrier signal on which it travels.

demultiplexer   A hardware device that is used to separate multiplexed material sent from a single input, and then disseminate the material out to their various destinations.

Derived MAC PDU (DMPDU)   A Connectionless Broadband Data Service (CBDS) term that corresponds to the L2 PDU in Switched Multimegabit Data Service (SMDS). CBDS is the European equivalent of SMDS.

Digital Service Unit (DSU)   A device that sits between a user's Data Terminal Equipment (DTE) and a common carrier's digital circuits.

Digital Signal Level 0 (DS-0)   The 64Kbps transmission rate common to ISDN and other digital transmission technologies.

Digital Signal Level 1 (DS-1)   A 1.544Mbps transmission rate. DS-1 can support 24 simultaneous DS-0 signals, and is the equivalent of a T-1 link..

Digital Signal Level 2 (DS-2)   A 6.312Mbps transmission rate. Ds-2 can support 96 simultaneous calls, and is the equivalent of a T-2 link.

Digital Signal Level 3 (DS-3)   A 44.736 transmission rate. DS-3 can support 28 DS-1 connections, and is the equivalent of a T-3 link.

Digital stream (DS)   A level in the SONET hierarchy. Lower-level DSs are multiplexed into higher-level digital streams. DS0, the lowest level, carries a single voice channel, and runs at 64Kbps. A DS1 stream consists of 24 DS0 streams (1.544Mbps), and a DS3 stream consists of 28 DS1 streams (44.736Mbps).

digital subscriber line (DSL)   A digital line that links a customer's equipment to the phone company's central switching office over ordinary copper telephone wire. A DSL can carry both voice and data simultaneously in both directions.

Discard Eligibility (DE)   A bit set by the user in a Frame Relay network, to indicate that a frame may be discarded in the event of congestion.

discrete multitone (DMT)   A modulation technique employed by ADSL modems. The modem formats digital data into analog signals, which are then carried over a standard telephone line using DMT. The remote modem will then convert the DMT signals back into digital bits.

disparity control   A function of the 8B/10B transmission encoding scheme, in which the two remaining bits are used for error detection and correction. 8B/10B transmits 8 bits as a 10-bit group, thereby leaving two additional bits for disparity control.

distributed queue dual bus (DQDB)   A function of the IEEE 802.6 standard. DQDB provides a cell-relay, fast packet MAN technology, which can transparently connect multiple LANs to a public carrier service. DQDB is capable of facilitating the delivery of connectionless datagrams, virtual circuits, and isochronous data service. Each site involved must have Optical Line Terminating Equipment (OLTE) as a bridge between the private and public networks.

E

E1   A communications line with a transmission rate of 2.048Mbps.

E.164   A public network addressing standard similar to the public telephone number scheme that can use up to 15 digits.

Edge Device A physical device, such as a router, that can forward packets between legacy networks and a core ATM network.

Edge Router A hardware device used to integrate legacy Token Ring or Ethernet LANs with a core ATM network. Conversion between ATM cells and Ethernet or Token Ring packets take place in the edge router.

ELAN (Emulated LAN) An Ethernet or token ring LAN that is connected to an ATM network using LAN Emulation (LANE).

Encapsulation The process of placing one end device's protocol-specific frames within a different type of frame for transmission.

end node The computer or other hardware unit that exists at the origin and destination of network traffic. The end node does not relay traffic to other nodes.

End-of-Frame Delimiter A character or symbol used to denote the end of a frame.

enterprise network An internetwork that connects multiple sites and runs mission-critical applications.

Ethernet A type of shared-media, packet-switching, contention-oriented LAN. Ethernet uses the CSMA/CD media access method, and can operate over several different media. The original standard specified a transmission rate of 10Mbps, although it has since been extended to accommodate 100Mbps and 1000Mbps.

Ethernet packet A variable-length packet that contains header information and a payload, and is transmitted over an Ethernet network.

Excess Burst(Be) The maximum amount of uncommitted data over the Bc rate that a Frame Relay network can attempt to deliver during a given time period.

F

fabric An interconnection mechanism used in Fibre Channel networks. The fabric connects all participating nodes, making it possible to achieve multiple concurrent connections.

Fast Ethernet An extension of the Ethernet standard, defined as 100Base-T that allows for a transport rate of 100Mbps. Fast Ethernet is compatible with 10Base-T Ethernet, but cannot accommodate as wide a network diameter as can 10Base-T.

F Port A port in a Fibre Channel fabric to which an N Port is attached.

Fiber Distributed Data Interface (FDDI)   A type of LAN that uses fiber optic cable as the physical medium. FDDI is based on a ring topology, and operates at 100Mbps using a token-passing transport mechanism.

Fiber Optic Cable   A cable used for high-speed data transmissions, typically over long distances. The fiber itself is made from a thin strand of glass, and is surrounded by a protective cladding. Light pulses travel through the strand to transmit data.

Fibre Channel   A high-speed architecture for connecting network devices and other hardware.

Fire Wire   A term created by Apple Computer to refer to IEEE 1394 cabling. Fire Wire connects peripheral devices to a host computer over a high-speed interface cable. The technology is often applied to video equipment.

FL Port   A port in a Fibre Channel fabric to which an NL Port is attached.

floating mode   In SONET networks, a mode of operation for a Virtual Tributary (VT) group. Floating mode is used to minimize delay for distributed VT switching.

Forward Error Correction (FEC)   A technique for detecting and correcting errors in a digital data stream.

Forward Explicit Congestion Notification (FECN)   A bit that is set in a Frame Relay network to notify Data Terminal Equipment that the network is in a congested state, and that the receiving device should implement congestion avoidance techniques.

Frame   A packet data format used in serial communications. A frame includes start bits, data bits, a parity bit, and stop bits.

Frame Check Sequence (FCS)   The 16-bit cyclic redundancy check used in High-Level Data Link Control (HDLC) and Frame Relay frames.

Frame Header   A series of bytes in a data frame that holds information, such as addresses and control data.

Frame Relay   A packet-based networking mechanism that allocates dedicated resources between end points in order to provide bandwidth-on-demand.

Frame Relay Access Device (FRAD)   A hardware device used in a Frame Relay network to connect a workstation to the Frame Relay cloud. Also known as Frame Relay Assembler/Disassembler.

Frame Relay Frame   A variable-length unit of data that is sent through the Frame Relay network.

Frame User Network Interface (FUNI)   An ATM service that converts between Frame Relay and ATM networks.

Full Duplex   A type of communications where transmission occurs in both directions simultaneously.

G

Gateway   A link that exists between two dissimilar networks.

generic cell rate algorithm   An ATM function that is carried out at the user-to-network interface (UNI) level. It guarantees that traffic matches the negotiated connection that has been established between the user and the network.

Gigabit Ethernet   An extension of the Ethernet standard that operates at 1000Mbps. Also known as 1000Base-T. Gigabit Ethernet is backward-compatible with 100Base-T and 10Base-T, but cannot accommodate as wide a network diameter.

Gigabit Medium Independent Interface (GMII)   The GMII replaces the Medium Independent Interface (MII) used in Fast Ethernet to connect the Media Access Control (MAC) layer to the physical layers. The GMII allows Gigabit Ethernet to remain compatible with Fast Ethernet.

H

Half Duplex   A type of communications where transmission occurs only in one direction.

Hamming code   A forward error correction mechanism for detecting and correcting single-bit transmission errors.

Header   Information contained at the beginning of a packet that includes control information and addressing data.

header error check (HEC)   A single-byte error correcting code, contained in the header of an ATM cell. The HEC is used to ensure that cells are not delivered incorrectly due to header errors.

heartbeat support   A function that generates a frame periodically, even if no data is being sent, for network management purposes.

High Bit Rate Digital Subscriber Line (HDSL)   A high-speed technology similar to ADSL. HDSL provides fast throughput of up to 6.1Mbps over one pair of twisted copper wire, in both downstream and upstream directions.

High Level Data Link control (HDLC)   A link-level communications protocol used to manage synchronous, serial data transfers over a connection.

High Performance Parallel Interface (HiPPI)   An ANSI standard for high-speed data transfer over short distances.

high performance routing (HPR)   A method used in IBM networks to give SNA/APPN networks native access to an ATM network.

High Speed Serial Interface (HSSI)   Serial connections that transmit at over 20Kbps.

Hop   A single circuit between two switches in a network, with no intervening hubs or other hardware.

Hop count   The number of routers or other devices a packet must pass through between its source and destination.

Hot pluggable   The ability to remove and replace a device while the computer is still operating.

Hub   A device used to expand the network with additional workstations. A hub concentrates wiring that goes out to multiple end nodes, and may modify transmission signals.

Hybrid multiplexing (HMUX)   A multiplexing technique that multiplexes both network data from the MAC layer, and isochronous data such as voice or video.

I

Initial MAC Protocol Data Unit (IMPDU)   A Connectionless Broadband Data Service (CBDS) term that corresponds to the L3 PDU in Switched Multimegabit Data Service (SMDS). CBDS is the European equivalent of SMDS.

Institute of Electrical and Electronic Engineers   A standards body that establishes networking standards for cabling, electrical topology, physical topology, and access schemes.

Integrated Services Digital Network (ISDN)   A digital communications mechanism for carrying voice and data communications. ISDN is provided to end users by the public telecommunications carriers.

Integrated frame relay assembler/disassembler (IFRAD)   A device that can accommodate voice, data, and fax over a public or private frame relay network. These devices will negotiate delay and jitter that would otherwise occur in voice traffic through a series of bandwidth management techniques. A standard FRAD accommodates data only.

Integrated Private Network-to-Network Interface (IPNNI)   A method used to send IP traffic over an ATM network. IPNNI is an alternative to more traditional routing protocols, such as the Routing Information Protocol (RIP) and Open Shortest Path First (OSPF), and takes into account ATM parameters such as QoS and delay constraints.

Inter-Carrier Interface (ICI)   An interface that exists between different carriers' networks.

Inter frame gap (IFG)   A period between transmission of Ethernet frames during which no transmissions occur. The IFG gives stations an opportunity to detect when no transmissions are occurring.

Interim Interswitch Signal Protocol   A call routing scheme used in ATM networks. Formerly known as PNNI Phase 0. IISP is an interim technology meant to be used pending completion of PNNI Phase 1. IISP uses static routing tables established by the network administrator to route connections around link failures.

Internet Engineering Task Force (IETF)   A committee of the Internet Activities Board that helps establish Internet standards.

Internet Protocol (IP)   An industry standard, session-layer protocol suite. Network nodes in a heterogeneous environment are able to communicate using IP.

Intelligent Peripheral Interface (IPI)   A hard disk interface that supports transfer rates of up to 25Mbps. IPI also accommodates a multi-gigabyte storage capacity.

Internetwork   Two or more networks that are connected by a router, bridge, or gateway.

intranet   A private network that is based on the same technology as the Internet, but is inaccessible by the general public.

IsoEthernet   An IEEE standard that uses compression to realize 16Mbps out of a standard 10BaseT connection; and then separate out the additional 6Mbps for use in transporting real-time multimedia over the network.

isochronous   A type of transmission that is time-sensitive. An isochronous transmission includes a constant time interval between both synchronous and asynchronous transmissions, thereby allowing asynchronous data to be sent over a synchronous link.

J

Jitter   A timing variation that can cause a video transmission to appear jumpy and irregular.

K

Kbps   Kilobits per second. A metric used to reflect the speed of data transfer in thousands of bits per second.

L

L Port   A Fibre Channel port in an arbitrated loop topology.

LAN Emulation (LANE)   An ATM technology that allows applications designed for Ethernet to operate over an ATM network.

LAN Emulation Client (LEC)   An entity in an ATM network that performs data forwarding, address resolution, and control functions.

LAN Emulation Configuration Server (LECS)   A server in an ATM network responsible for configuration of LAN Emulation clients, and providing details about virtual LANs.

LAN Emulation Server (LES)   A server in an ATM network used to resolve MAC-to-ATM addresses. The LES learns the MAC address of a remote LAN Emulation client, thereby allowing an end node on the ATM network to communicate with an end node on an emulated LAN.

LAN Emulation User-Network Interface (LUNI)   The interface between a LAN Emulation client, and one of the three LAN Emulation servers (LAN Emulation Configuration Server, Broadcast and Unknown Server, or LAN Emulation Server).

Leaky Bucket   A buffering technique used in ATM networks, which applies a sustained cell flow rate to bursty traffic.

link consolidation   The ability of a single frame relay access link to support multiple virtual circuits.

link encapsulation (LE)   A function of the HiPPI Framing Protocol (FP) layer. LE encapsulates IEEE 802.2 Logical Link PDUs (Protocol Data Units) inside of HiPPI packets, thereby allowing IP traffic to travel over a HiPPI connection.

locked mode   In SONET networks, a mode of operation for a Virtual Tributary (VT) group. A VT group can function in either locked or floating mode. While floating mode minimizes delays in distributed VT switching, locked mode is used to enhance the efficiency of the network devices performing the switching.

line overhead (LOH)   One of three types of overhead in a SONET frame. The other two are path overhead and section overhead. The line overhead consists of pointers, which are used to align the STS-1 SPE in the STS-N signal.

Line Terminating Equipment (LTE)   A device in a SONET network used to originate or terminate the line signal. The LTE can also originate, access, modify, or terminate the line overhead.

long wavelength   A wavelength that exceeds one micrometer.

M

Management Information Base (MIB)   A database used for network management. The MIB contains definitions of management objects that are accessed by a management agent.

maximum transmission unit (MTU)   The biggest datagram that a given network interface is able to accommodate.

Media Access Control (MAC)   The sublayer specified in the OSI reference model that sits between the physical and Data Link layers, and controls access to transmission media.

Media Independent Interface (MII)   A part of the Fast Ethernet specification. The MII replaces 10Base-T Ethernet's Attachment Unit Interface (AUI), and is used to connect the MAC layer to the physical layer. The MII establishes a single interface for the three 100Base-T media specifications (100Base-TX, 100Base-T4, and 100Base-FX).

Memory interface (MI)   A function of the HiPPI Framing Protocol (FP) layer. The MI is a generic memory interface protocol, and is used for remote memory reads and writes over the HiPPI interface.

Metropolitan Area Network (MAN)   A network designed to carry data over an area of intermediate size, such as a city or metropolitan region.

modulator   A device, often combined with a demodulator, that generates a modulating signal that is overlaid on the carrier signal on which it travels.

Multicasting   A type of transmission where a single station transmits a single message to multiple destinations

Multimode Fiber   A type of fiber over which multiple beams of light can be transmitted.

Multiplexer   A device used to combine multiple, lower-speed transmissions into a single, higher-speed channel.

Multiplexing   A function by which information from multiple connections are interleaved into a single connection.

Multiprotocol over ATM (MPOA)   An ATM protocol used to run multiple network layer protocols over ATM by mapping external network layer addresses to ATM.

N

N Port   A Fibre Channel port used in point-to-point or fabric topology.

Network control protocol   ARPA's original standard for communication. NCP was later replaced by the TCP/IP protocol suite.

Network Interface Card (NIC)   A PC expansion card that plugs into the PC or server and is connected to the network media, and allows it to connect with the network.

Network Layer   The third layer in the seven-layer OSI reference model. The network layer facilitates the arrival of information at its intended destination.

network service access point   In the OSI Reference Model, the point at which a network service is made available to a transport entity. The NSAP is identified by a globally unique OSI Network Address.

NL Port   Any Fibre Channel port attached to a node.

Non-return to Zero Inverted (NRZI)   A signal encoding mechanism used to promote high read/write speeds. NRZI is a variation of the Non-Return to Zero (NRZ) encoding mechanism. In NRZ, ones and zeroes are represented by alternating high and low voltages, with no return to a reference zero voltage between encoded bits. NRZI, on the other hand, inverts the signal for a *one* bit value, and leaves it unchanged for a *zero* bit value.

O

Online Transaction Processing (OLTP)   A type of application processing that divides the many interactions between a user and application, and allows them to be processed in small parts, or transactions, as they are received by the system. TP environments have rigorous routing requirements, and require multithreading. In an OLTP, the master files are updated every time an entry is entered at the terminal; as opposed to batch processing, which updates the master files only periodically.

Open Fibre Control (OFC)   A Fibre Channel safety mechanism used to control the optical power of an open optical fiber cable.

Open Shortest Path First (OSPF)   A routing protocol used in TCP/IP networks. The protocol analyzes network loading and available bandwidth when routing data over the network, in order to derive the best optimal routing path.

Optical Carrier (OC)   When the SONET Synchronous Transport Signal (STS) is converted to an optical format for transmission, the signal is then referred to as an optical carrier (OC), but still has the same bit rate.

optical fibre control (OFC)   One of two types of optical technology used in fibre channel. OFC is used with high-powered transmitters and shortwave lasers. OFC uses a handshake procedure to protect against the possibility of eye damage. If the receiving node detects a loss of light (which may be indicative of a broken cable), it will automatically power down the transmitter. OFC is not used with lower-powered lasers, because protective measures are not required.

optical line termination equipment (OLTE)   A connection device that exists both at the customer premises and the public network, at the point where the optical fiber terminates. At the customer site, this is before the DSU; in the public network, the OLTE is placed before the switch.

Organizationally Unique Identifier (OUI)   A unique 48-bit identifier used to identify the manufacturers of Ethernet network interface cards. The OUI is divided into two 24-bit sections; the first denotes a manufacturer, and the second is used by the manufacturer to denote a unique address for each Ethernet interface.

OSI Reference Model   A networking reference model that divides communications into seven connected layers, each of which builds on the functions of the one below it.

- Layer 7: Application Layer
- Layer 6: Presentation Layer
- Layer 5: Session Layer
- Layer 4: Transport Layer
- Layer 3: Network Layer
- Layer 2: Data Link Layer
- Layer 1: Physical Layer

P

Packet   A group of binary digits that include a payload and control data. A packet is transmitted over a packet-switching network, but the packets that make up an entire message may not travel consecutively. They are, however, assembled in proper order at the receiving end.

Packet burst   A packet burst protocol transmits multiple packets before requiring the acknowledgment of previously transmitted packets. Packet bursts are more efficient, because requiring acknowledgment immediately for every packet upon receipt causes greater network delays.

Packet-Switching Network   A communications network based on packet-switching technology, where an individual connection is occupied only for the duration of the packet transmission.

path layer   One of four optical interface layers in a SONET network. The other three are the photonic layer, section layer, and line layer. The path layer is responsible for the transport of services between Path Terminal Equipment (PTE). Services and Path Overhead data is mapped into the PTE. Signals are mapped into the appropriate format, as required by the line layer. This layer also reads and interprets the path overhead for the purpose of performance monitoring.

path terminating equipment (PTE)   A device used in SONET networks. The PTE multiplexes/demultiplexes the Synchronous Transport Signal (STS) payload. The PTE can originate, access, modify, or terminate the path overhead.

Payload   The data contained in a frame besides headers and footers.

Permanent Virtual Circuit (PVC)   A logical communications path between two stations in a Frame Relay network that has been established in advance, and is always available.

Physical Layer   The first layer in the seven-layer OSI reference model. This layer details the network topology, including transmission media and signaling.

Physical Layer Convergence Protocol   A Level 1 SMDS physical link protocol. Level 1 is divided into the transmission system sublayer and the Physical Layer Convergence Protocol (PLCP). The transmission system sublayer is where the link type (DS3 or DS1) is specified. The PLCP establishes how the L2 PDUs are arranged in the DS3 or DS1 frame.

Physical signaling   A sublayer of the OSI Physical Layer. This sublayer interfaces with the MAC sublayer, and performs bit symbol encoding, transmission, reception, and decoding.

Plain Old Telephone Service (POTS)   Basic access to the public switched telephone service from single-line telephones.

Point-to-Point   A direct communications link.

Point-to-Point Tunneling Protocol   A protocol that can be used to create a virtual private network over the public Internet.

Primary Rate Interface (PRI)   An ISDN standard that specifies a 1.544Mbps (DS-1) ISDN line. PRI supports 23 B channels of 64Kbps each, and a single D channel.

Private Branch Exchange (PBX)   A device used to provide private local voice switching and other related services within a private network.

Private Network   A type of network that connects branch offices or remote sites together, using switching equipment that is owned and operated by the user instead of the telephone service carrier.

Private Network-to-Node Interface (PNNI)   A routing information protocol used in ATM networks. PNNI allows multivendor ATM switches to be used in the same network.

Protocol Data Unit (PDU)   A message made up of protocol-specific control information and a payload. A PDU is transmitted over the protocol interfaces that sit between the layers of protocols.

Public switched telephone network   The worldwide telephone network.

Pulse code modulation (PCM)   A method used by North American telephone systems to digitize voice transmissions.

Q

Quality of Service (QoS)   An ATM standard that defines specific characteristics of a connection, and what type of traffic can run over the connection. Service is determined based on Cell Loss Ratio, Cell Transfer Delay, and Cell Delay Variation.

R

Remote Monitoring (RMON)   A type of network management that uses agents or probes to gather statistics and monitor network activity.

Repeater   A hardware device that is defined in the physical layer of the OSI Reference Model. A repeater merely sends any signal from one node to another connecting node without change. The primary purpose is to extend the length of the transmission medium beyond normal cable length limits.

Residential broadband (RBB)   A proposed ATM Forum standard. RBB would establish an end-to-end, residential ATM system that could ultimately be used to connect common household devices and appliances, including set-top boxes and PCs.

Resource Reservation Protocol (RSVP)   An IETF protocol used to reserve bandwidth on an Ethernet connection.

Router   An intelligent device used to transmit data packets to the correct destination and control traffic flow throughout the network. A router can support LAN-to-LAN communications, relying on network layer addresses to filter out packets that are not destined for one particular network.

Routing Information Protocol (RIP)   A protocol in the TCP/IP protocol suite. RIP is used to allow routers to communicate with each other in order to determine optimal routes.

route server   ATM-based routing can take on a centralized model or distributed model. A centralized ATM implementation uses a route server that stores topology and resource information in a central server. The central route server must be constantly connected to the network; and has the disadvantage of having a single point of failure.

S

Secure Data Exchange (SDE)   Part of the IEEE 802.10 Standard for Interoperable LAN/MAN Security (SILS), designated as 802.10b.

Section Layer   One of four optical interface layers in a SONET network. The other three are the line layer, photonic layer, and path layer. The section layer sends synchronous transport signal (STS) frames and Section Overhead (SOH) over the transport medium. Framing, scrambling, and error monitoring all occur in the Section Layer.

Section Terminating Equipment (STE)   A device used in a SONET network. The STE consists of two adjacent SONET network elements, and may be a terminating network element or regenerator. It can originate, access, modify, or terminate section overhead.

Segment   A LAN or section of a LAN that has no additional routers or bridges.

Segmentation and Reassembly (SAR)   A sublayer of the ATM Adaptation Layer, used to break up higher-layer packets into 48-byte data segments for transport via ATM cells. SAR then reassembles the ATM cells into the larger data units on the receiving end.

Self-healing   A quality of SONET networks. A SONET ring achieves a high degree of survivability, because it can automatically reroute traffic in the other direction, or in the event of two breaks on the ring, onto a second, redundant ring.

Serial   Tasks that are carried out consecutively; or in communications, when each byte is transferred a bit at a time.

Service Aspects and Applications (SAA)   An ATM Forum standard. SAA includes application programming interfaces (APIs), interworking with Frame Relay, SMDS, and Circuit Emulation Services. The Frame UNI specification is complete; the Circuit Emulation Switching (CES) Interoperability Specification is still underway. The ATM Forum's SAA should not be confused with IBM's Systems Application Architecture, which is a standard used across IBM operating environments.

Service Access Multiplexer (SAM)   A device that allows interworking between ATM and other networks, such as SMDS.

Service Data Unit (SDU)   A packet, as described in the OSI Reference Model, which is passed from one layer to the layer below it.

Service interworking   A carrier service that renders protocol conversion software unnecessary when running both ATM and frame relay. Service interworking is used to transparently link ATM and frame relay sites. Protocol translation is done by the carrier, and requires no special software on the customer premises.

Shielded Twisted Pair Cable (STP Cable)   Cable with a foil shield and copper braid over a pair of twisted copper wires.

Short-wave laser   A device that generates short-wave radiation of between 780 nm and 850 nm.

Single Byte Command Code Set (SBCCS)   An IBM protocol used in the FC-4 layer of Fibre Channel networks.

Signal Computing System Architecture (SCSA)   A bus architecture developed by Dialogic for sending signals, including voice channels, to a PC. SCSA specifies a real-time bus, and a scalable switching mechanism that promotes equal access between all connected clients.

Single-Mode Fiber   A type of fiber over which only one ray of light can be transmitted.

Small Computer Systems Interface (SCSI)   An ANSI standard used to attach peripheral devices to host computers.

Star Topology   A way of connecting nodes in a network, where a central wiring hub or concentrator is placed at the center, and each node is connected directly to the hub in a star-like formation.

Start-of-Frame Delimiter   A character or symbol used to denote the beginning of a frame.

Statistical Multiplexing   A function that interleaves data from multiple devices onto a single channel for transmission over a Frame Relay network.

Store-and-Forward   A routing or messaging mechanism that stores messages, or data packets, temporarily, for later transmission to their destinations.

Subscriber network interface   The point at which the customer's network connects with the public carrier's line.

Switch   A network hardware device used to group data by destination, and route it out on the basis of predetermined rules. A switch is an intelligent device that can check packets for errors, direct them to the appropriate network, and translate packets into a different format.

Switched Frame Transfer Mode   A frame relay networking technology that gives permanent virtual circuits (PVCs) some of the same benefits offered by switched virtual circuits (SVCs). Switched Frame Transfer Mode lets users switch voice and data over a public or private frame relay network. SFTM overcomes the traditional methodology of using PVCs, which calls for a point-to-point connection between each location for each application.

Switched Multi-Megabit Data Services (SMDS)   A connectionless service used to allow LANs, MANs, and WANs to exchange data. SMDS is based on the IEEE 802.6 Metropolitan Area Network (MAN) standard.

SMDS Interface Protocol (SIP)   The SIP defines the connection between the customer premises equipment and the SMDS network equipment. It is based on the IEEE protocol for MANs (IEEE 802.6 Distributed Queue Dual Bus standard), which allows the CPE to be attached to the SMDS network for the purpose of internetworking.

Switched Virtual Circuit (SVC)   A virtual circuit that is established and cleared dynamically as needed.

Symmetric Digital Subscriber Line (SDSL)   A digital subscriber line technology that offers 384Kbps both upstream and downstream. SDSL can be used for videoconferencing.

Synchronous   A way of transmitting data, which uses timing to control the transmission. In a synchronous transmission, a synchronization sequence is followed by a predefined number of bits which are sent at a constant rate.

Synchronous communications   A type of data transfer where information is transmitted in blocks that are separated by equal time intervals.

Synchronous Data Link Control (SDLC)   A bit-oriented protocol developed by IBM for use in SNA networks.

Synchronous Digital Hierarchy   The European equivalent of SONET, as defined by the ITU. SONET and SDH are remarkably similar, but not truly interoperable. SONET is based on an STS-1 (synchronous transport signal), which operates at 51.84Mbps; while SDH is based on the STM-1, which operates at 155.52Mbps. Consequently, payload mapping differs somewhat; although three STS-1s fit exactly into a single STM-1.

Synchronous Optical Network (SONET)   An ANSI standard for transmitting information long distances over optical fiber at extremely high rates of speed.

Synchronous Payload Envelopes   A SONET optical interface line layer function, responsible for the transport of user data.

Synchronous Time Division Multiplexing   A type of multiplexing which relies on a hardware clock, as opposed to software, to control the multiplexer and channel source.

Synchronous transport signal (STS)   The basic building block of SONET networks. An STS signal operates at 51.84Mbps. All other signals are multiples of that base figure.

T

T1   A long-distance, point-to-point circuit. A T1 link has 24 channels, each with 64Kbps of bandwidth, for a total of 1.544Mbps.

T2   A communications channel with 6.312Mbps of bandwidth. A T2 circuit is the equivalent of four T1 circuits.

T3   A communications channel with a 44.736Mbps bandwidth. A T3 circuit is the equivalent of 28 T1 circuits.

Telephony Applications Programming Interface (TAPI)   A call control protocol developed by Microsoft. TAPI allows telephone equipment to be controlled by a PC.

Time Division Multiplexing (TDM)   A data transmission mechanism that allocates a fixed amount of bandwidth to all connected devices, whether they are active or not.

Token Ring   A network topology where nodes are connected in a consecutive pattern. A token, or specific bit pattern, is passed between all the nodes on the network, the node that holds the token is allowed to transmit while all the others wait.

Traffic policing   An ATM function that guarantees that the traffic running over each connection is within the parameters that have been established for each individual connection. Policing is done through a switch-level buffering technique.

Traffic shaping   An ATM function that guarantees that the traffic matches the negotiated connection that has been established between the user and network. Traffic shaping is accomplished through the Generic Cell Rate Algorithm (GCRA), which has been defined as part of the UNI 3.0 standard by the ATM Forum. Traffic shaping can be implemented by the ATM network adapter, hub, bridge, or router.

Transmission Control Protocol   A connection-oriented, transport layer protocol and part of the TCP/IP protocol suite. TCP provides for the sequenced delivery packets to the network layer.

transmission convergence   A sublayer of the SONET physical layer. This layer performs Header Error Check generation, scrambling, SONET STS-3c frame structure generation, cell delineation, header error checking, and performance monitoring. It takes cells from the ATM layer and places them inside of SONET frames for transmission over the SONET internetwork. At the receiving end, the TC sublayer retrieves the ATM cells out of the SONET frame and passes them onto the ATM layer.

Transport Layer   The fourth layer in the seven-layer OSI Reference Model. This layer specifies the end-to-end delivery of data and detects transmission errors.

U

Unidirectional path switched ring (UPSR)   One of two main SONET ring architectures. UPSR achieves survivability while sending traffic in one direction on one fiber. The traffic is duplicated and sent over the protection fiber in the opposite direction.

Universal serial bus (USB)   A bus architecture designed by Intel. USB offers a transfer rate of up to 12Mbps, divided into multiple 1.5 subchannels, and was designed to alleviate the tangle of multiple cables that often occurs in the backs of PCs. It connects peripherals to the host CPU in a tiered star topology, and can be used to connect multiple low- to medium-speed peripherals.

Unshielded Twisted Pair (UTP)   Cable with two or more pairs of twisted copper wire, with an outer jacket but no additional shielding layer.

Unspecified Bit Rate (UBR)   An ATM Quality of Service parameter that does not specify a service guarantee.

User Datagram Protocol   A method used to allow two programs in a TCP/IP network to communicate directly.

User-Network Interface (UNI)   The interface between end users and an ATM switch, or between the ATM switch and a public carrier ATM network.

V

Variable Bit Rate (VBR)   An ATM service category which supports variable bit rate data traffic with average and peak traffic parameters.

Variable Bit Rate-Non Real Time (VBR-NRT)   One of the four Quality of Service parameters in an ATM network. VBR-NRT is designated as Class C, and is useful in applications where a slight delay may be more acceptable, such as in video playback, or transaction processing.

Variable Bit Rate-Real Time(VBR-RT)   One of the four Quality of Service parameters in an ATM network. VBR-RT is designated as Class B. It is a "reserved bandwidth" service, in which the network allocates the necessary resources to establish a connection with an end station to match the parameters requested by that end station. This quality level is appropriate for voice or video applications.

Very High Bit Rate Digital Subscriber Line (VDSL)   A proposed digital subscriber line technology that would use ATM to provide up to 55Mbps of bandwidth over the local telephone loop.

Virtual Channel Connection (VCC)   The basic switching unit in broadband ISDN. A concatenation of virtual channel links between two endpoints. Multiple VCCs can be bundled into one Virtual Path Connection (VPC).

virtual circuit   A network connection that appears to the end user as if it were a dedicated, point-to-point circuit. However, a virtual circuit is actually implemented via software, and the data is sent via the most appropriate route over the network.

Virtual Local Area Network (VLAN)   Workstations that are connected to an intelligent device that defines LAN membership via software.

virtual path connection (VPC)   A concatenation of virtual path links between two points. Multiple VCCs can be bundled into a single VPC.

Virtual Private Network   A network that uses the public Internet as the means of transport, but behaves as if it were a private network. A virtual private network can be established using tunneling protocols such as Point-to-Point Tunneling Protocol (PPTP).

Virtual Tributary (VT)   In SONET, a sub STS-1 rate. A VT can operate at four speeds: 1.728Mbps, 2.304Mbps, 3.456Mbps, or 6.912Mbps.

VLAN Trunk Protocol (VTP)   A mapping protocol developed by Cisco Systems. VTP can be applied to automatically configure an ATM VLAN across a campus network, regardless of backbone type. The protocol is used for both switch-to-switch and switch-to-router communications, and propagates all VLAN configuration data throughout the network.

W

wavelength division multiplexing   A multiplexing mechanism similar to frequency division multiplexing, except that different signals are transmitted at different wavelengths along the same physical circuit.

Wide Area Network (WAN)   A network made up of multiple LANs, that may span a large geographic distance.

X

X.25   A CCITT standard that outlines the connection between a terminal and a public packet-switched network. ●

A Brief History of Networking

The earliest concept of networking was introduced with the invention of the telegraph in 1844 by Samuel Morse. It later grew to encompass the telephone, but didn't go far beyond that until much later. Computers and networking were not put together until the 1960s, and then it was limited to connecting dumb terminals to a host, either via modem or serial link connections. The first computer, ENIAC (Electronic Numerical Integrator and Computer), designed in 1945, was as big as a house, didn't have a monitor, and was filled with vacuum tubes. The mere idea of networking these early behemoths would have been preposterous. In fact, Thomas Watson, chairman of IBM in 1943, once uttered these now famous words: "I think there is a world market for maybe five computers."

After the telegraph, the next major networking milestone was the invention of the telephone. The first telephones sent analog signals over copper wire, with one circuit being required for each conversation. ∎

The Dividing Line

Telephone network technology changed very little until the 1960s. The phone worked by multiplexing an analog voice signal unchanged through the network. Conversion to digital transmission marked a new level of quality, and improvements in utilization of the network. The first algorithm for 64Kbps digital transmission, Pulse Code Modulation (PCM), was followed by Adaptive Differential Pulse Code Modulation (ADPCM), which doubled the amount of traffic that could be transmitted.

The first, primitive move towards bandwidth optimization came in the form of frequency-division multiplexing, which allowed multiple calls to be carried over a single wire. In the 1960s, Bell Laboratories introduced Time Division Multiplexing (TDM), a technique that digitized and multiplexed 24 voice conversations onto a single, four-wire copper trunk. TDM, however, divides the conversation into packets, regardless of periods of silence—effectively generating a series of empty packets. Later, packet switching was introduced as a way to enhance the efficiency of TDM. IBM's Systems Network Architecture (SNA), introduced in 1974, is an example of a packet technology.

Integrated Services Digital Network (ISDN) was soon introduced as another form of switched TDM, although the first implementation of ISDN still suffered from the same limitations as TDM, that is, empty packets that resulted from periods of silence during a voice conversation. The second version of ISDN, or Broadband ISDN (B-ISDN), addressed the empty packets inefficiency, and by design, allowed video, data, and voice traffic to be transmitted over the same line. B-ISDN is based on a cell relay technique that was first described in 1968 by Bell Laboratories as Asynchronous Time Division Multiplexing (ATDM). It was not until 1986 that this technique saw the light of day and became the centerpiece of B-ISDN. The creation of B-ISDN then gave birth to Asynchronous Transfer Mode (ATM) in 1988.

New regulations allowed customers to attach their own equipment to telephone company lines in the late 1970s. As a result, network managers in larger companies could create their own private networks to transmit both voice and data throughout the company using existing telephone lines. Private networks became more popular, and manufacturers started to create voice digitization algorithms to minimize bandwidth usage. These algorithms, however, typically resulted in low quality audio.

One of the first packet technologies was X.25, a method that allowed several users to multiplex onto a single physical line. Later, fast packet technologies, such as Frame Relay and ATM, were created to offer greater speed and a higher level of reliability. These fast packet technologies were more efficient and could generate higher throughput, largely due to reduced protocol overhead. While X.25 often resulted in long delays, Frame Relay provided the benefit of a low overhead-to-payload ratio due to its variable packet size methodology. Frame Relay initially used only permanent virtual circuits (PVCs), much like X.25. Only recently have Frame Relay implementers moved to Switched Virtual Circuits (SVCs), a technology that makes better use of existing facilities, and is easier to set up and manage.

Early Network

One of the first known computer networks was the radio-based Aloha network, developed at the University of Hawaii in the 1960s. AlohaNet furnished a simple way for multiple nodes to communicate over the same frequency channel. This system, invented by Norman Abramson, formed the basis of modern packet broadcast systems, including Ethernet. Under this simple model, any user on the network could transmit at any time. However, because anyone could transmit at any time, data collisions were inevitable. If the transmission was successful, an acknowledgment was received. If not, the user would attempt to retransmit again. AlohaNet offered no guarantees, but it represented a valuable first step in the world of computer networking.

Inspired by Abramson's earlier Aloha network, Bob Metcalfe created Ethernet in 1974 while he was working at Xerox's Palo Alto Research Center (PARC). Metcalfe saw that AlohaNet could use only a small percentage of its total capacity, because of its lack of guarantees and tendency toward packet collision. Metcalfe hoped to improve on Abramson's model with a mathematical queuing algorithm that would, in the case of a data collision, automatically retransmit after a random period of time. This simple addition significantly improved the efficiency of the AlohaNet model, and paved the way for widespread networking.

Like AlohaNet, Ethernet is a simple design that has withstood the test of time. Newer Ethernet paradigms, including switched Ethernet and Fast Ethernet, promise to extend this technology's long life; although ultimately it may be replaced by ultra high-speed technologies such as ATM which are capable not only of delivering data at incredibly high rates of speed, but are also capable of delivering multiple types of data, and unifying a large WAN.

Between the late 1970s and early 1980s, the Ethernet standard 802.3, based on Metcalfe's design, was created by the Institute of Electrical and Electronic Engineers (IEEE). The first Ethernet standard, 10Base-5, was known as Thick Wire Ethernet, and was limited to a length of 500 meters per segment. The network trunk can have up to five segments, two of which can be link segments (with no end nodes attached), and three of which can be trunk segments (with end nodes attached). Each trunk segment can have up to 100 nodes attached, for a total of up to 300 nodes in all. Later, the Thin Wire standard, 10Base-2, presented a less costly and more manageable solution. However, Thin Wire is limited to 185 meters per segment and up to five segments. Still later, in 1990, the 10Base-T standard came into being, which allowed Ethernet to run over a twisted-pair telephone wire.

Standardization of Ethernet quickly led to commercialization of the technology. Xerox introduced the first Ethernet LAN with the Star Ethernet Series in 1981, a system that connected workstations, servers and printers, and other peripherals, giving end users the ability to share files and printing services for the first time.

Also in 1981, Novell introduced its Sharenet program, which later turned into the popular NetWare network operating system. Sharenet introduced the concept of using one of the network nodes as a central repository, or server.

In 1982, Metcalfe formed a new company called 3Com, and released the very first Ethernet adapter card for the PC. The EtherLink product was accompanied by 3Com's own network operating system.

Token Ring was introduced in 1985 as an alternative to Ethernet. This new technique presented a token, which was passed from device to device. When a device held the token, it could transmit data. Ethernet was a contention-based mechanism, whereas Token Ring was deterministic and avoided the possibility of collision.

Later, Ethernet switching isolated collision domains and extended the viable life of Ethernet. A switched Ethernet environment minimizes some of the advantages of Token Ring, because it significantly reduces the possibility of collision. The switching model also gave each end node more available bandwidth. Under a traditional routed Ethernet environment, all end nodes on the network share that 10Mbps; under a switched network, each segment shares the 10Mbps.

Switching did give Ethernet networks the advantage of full-duplex communications. Previously, an Ethernet node could only transmit or receive at any given time; Ethernet switching brought the capability of simultaneous transmission and reception. Even with switching, however, the 10Mbps limit was still in place, even though it could be divided between fewer users. This was acceptable for most smaller file-and-print networks, but limited for growing networks full of multimedia applications and huge files.

In recent years, computer networking has followed the general trend of giving the end user greater access to corporate data, as well as access to larger files such as multimedia.

Eventually, network companies and standards bodies recognized the need for more speed and bigger pipes. The Internet, intranets, multimedia, and just a bigger demand for corporate data in general started to put pressure on standard LAN technology. One of the first viable high-speed network technologies was Fast Ethernet, which was developed primarily by Grand Junction Networks in 1992. Fast Ethernet increased the speed of standard Ethernet tenfold, going in one leap from 10Mbps to 100Mbps. Fast Ethernet eventually became an IEEE standard (802.3u) in 1995.

The Internet and More Standardization

No history of networking would be complete without a look at the Internet. This important development has come to be integrated with internal company networks, and has presented companies with new ways to communicate, share information, and access data. In fact, the intranet has been a major driving force behind the growth of high-speed networking.

App
B

The Internet itself first saw the light of day in 1969, when the Advanced Research Projects Agency (ARPA), currently known as the Defense Advanced Research Projects Agency (DARPA), linked together computers at UCLA, Stanford Research Institute, University of California at Santa Barbara, and University of Utah. At first, it was quite complicated, and typically used only by scientists and engineers running what was, at the time, high-powered workstations. TCP/IP, the protocol that currently forms the framework of the Internet, was developed in the late 1970s specifically for use on ARPA's Arpanet network by Vinton Cerf at Stanford University.

The Internet became the commercial phenomenon it is today after the European Laboratory for Particle Physics (CERN), led by Tim Berners-Lee, developed the World Wide Web in 1989. Marc Andreeson then commercialized it after he developed the graphical browser called Mosaic while at the National Center for Supercomputing Applications (NCSA), and marketed it through what was to become Netscape Communications Corp.

At first, ARPANET was built on a packet-switching technology and used a small set of tools for terminal access, file transfer, and mail. TCP/IP was adopted as the standard protocol of the Internet years later. Because the government did eventually adopt TCP/IP as a standard, every computer vendor wanting to do business with the government had to support TCP/IP, thus giving it a wide base of acceptance. Since those early years, most UNIX networks ran TCP/IP; in the 1990s when the Internet started to grow in popularity, most other computer manufacturers and software vendors began to support TCP/IP also.

During the early evolution of the Internet, IBM introduced its revolutionary Systems Network Architecture (SNA) in 1974. Most major mainframe-based networks are still based on SNA. This technology served to bring mainframe data out into the open, and to connect more end users to the data center.

Digital Equipment Corp.'s DECnet, originally introduced in 1976 as part of the Digital Network Architecture (DNA), came soon after IBM's introduction of SNA. DECnet was used to connect a variety of terminals, workstations, VAXes, and other computers.

Multi-User Operating Systems Advance Networking

One of the most popular network operating systems is UNIX, developed by Bell Laboratories in 1969 for the DEC PDP-7. The project grew out of the Multics (Multiplexed Information and Computing Service) project, an attempt to design an operating system for up to a thousand simultaneous users. The creation and evolution of UNIX was a major milestone in networked computing for the masses. This project, which rumor has it was originally designed by engineers to play computer games, gave the end user, for the first time, enormous control over their computing environments, although they had to suffer through learning the arcane commands that UNIX users still face to this day.

By 1971, Bell had decided to devote significant resources to its development by creating the UNIX Systems Laboratory. However, until about 1976, UNIX was used mostly on an internal basis at AT&T; the first public version was not available until that time. Because UNIX had been used at a variety of educational institutions, several variants of the operating system evolved over time, until it was fractured beyond all recognition and several incompatible versions existed. When AT&T released the seventh version of UNIX in 1978, development on the operating system also began at the University of California, Berkeley. The work done at Berkeley was crucial in the further development of UNIX and was later funded by DARPA with the intention of producing a standardized UNIX implementation for use by military contractors. Many of Berkeley's innovations found their way into subsequent versions of UNIX Systems Laboratory's implementations, including use of virtual memory. A standardization effort has been underway for the past few years, and title to UNIX has changed hands from AT&T, to Novell, and then to SCO. Trademark rights to UNIX are currently owned by the X/Open standards body, which created Spec 1170, also known as the UNIX Standard Specification; a mostly successful attempt at bringing the state of UNIX back into a unified mode.

While UNIX was bringing a new networking paradigm to workstation users, PCs were still largely single-user, stand-alone devices. The early Sinclairs, Osbornes, TRS-80s, and Lisas were interesting, but limited. Until the 1980s, when PCs became more popular and less of a novelty item, mainframe data had to be accessed through dumb 3270 terminals. Although for the most part, in those early days PCs were stand-alone, the first, primitive steps toward assimilating PCs into a meaningful corporate role took place when the IRMA board was introduced in 1982. This terminal emulation board allowed the PC to function as a mainframe terminal, thereby giving the PC user access to the mainframe without having to have both a PC and a terminal on the same desk.

The Wave of the Future

In the future, networking will take on an even broader role. Novell's marketing model of "pervasive computing" sums it up; not only will everything be computerized, but it will be networked as well. There have been many steps toward achieving this goal, some successful, some not. Microsoft's failed "At Work" strategy was an innovative attempt at networking common office equipment, although perhaps a little ahead of its time. The concept of the "information appliance," introduced by Oracle's Larry Ellison, may well herald the trend of commodity networking. These devices, meant to cost less than $500, will be attached to a television in much the same way as a VCR—allowing ordinary couch potatoes to surf the Net. Advances in hardware, integrated circuit (IC) technology and embedded operating systems will further the cause of the networked household. The day may yet come, where you water your lawn, control your thermostat, and operate your toaster all from a console in the wall. ●

OUI Listing

The following table lists the 48-bit Ethernet addresses used in Ethernet network interface cards, or the Organizationally Unique Identifier (OUI), for each manufacturer. This address is divided into two 24-bit sections; the first denotes a manufacturer, and the second is used by the manufacturer to denote a unique address for each Ethernet interface. ■

Table C.1   48-bit Ethernet Addresses

Company	OUI (Hex)	Company ID (Base 16)
FUJITSU, LTD.	00-00-0E	00000E
NOVELL, INC.	00-00-lb	0000lb
ABB AUTOMATION AB	00-00-23	000023
QPSX COMMUNICATIONS PTY, LTD.	00-00-31	000031
OXFORD METRICS, LTD.	00-00-37	000037
AUSPEX SYSTEMS, INC.	00-00-3C	00003C
SYNTREX, INC.	00-00-3F	00003F
OLIVETTI NORTH AMERICA	00-00-46	000046
APRICOT COMPUTERS, LTD.	00-00-49	000049
NEC CORP.	00-00-4C	00004C
RADISYS CORP.	00-00-50	000050
HOB ELECTRONIC GMBH & CO. KG	00-00-51	000051
OPTICAL DATA SYSTEMS	00-00-52	000052
RACORE COMPUTER PRODUCTS, INC.	00-00-58	000058
USC INFORMATION SCIENCES INSTITUTE	00-00-5E	00005E
SUMITOMO ELECTRIC IND., LTD.	00-00-5F	00005F
GATEWAY COMMUNICATIONS	00-00-61	000061
YOKOGAWA DIGITAL COMPUTER CORP.	00-00-64	000064
NETWORK GENERAL CORP.	00-00-65	000065
ROSEMOUNT CONTROLS	00-00-68	000068
CRAY COMMUNICATIONS, LTD.	00-00-6D	00006D
ARTISOFT, INC.	00-00-6E	00006E
MADGE NETWORKS, LTD.	00-00-6F	00006F
RICOH COMPANY, LTD.	00-00-74	000074
NETWORTH, INC.	00-00-79	000079
CRAY RESEARCH SUPERSERVERS, INC.	00-00-7D	00007D
LINOTYPE-HELL AG	00-00-7F	00007F
CRAY COMMUNICATIONS A/S	00-00-80	000080

Company	OUI (Hex)	Company ID (Base 16)
DATAHOUSE INFORMATION SYSTEMS	00-00-8A	00008A
ASANTE TECHNOLOGIES	00-00-94	000094
CROSSCOMM CORP.	00-00-98	000098
MEMOREX TELEX CORP.	00-00-99	000099
NETWORK APPLICATION TECHNOLOGY	00-00-A3	0000A3
ACORN COMPUTERS, LTD.	00-00-A4	0000A4
COMPATIBLE SYSTEMS CORP.	00-00-A5	0000A5
NETWORK COMPUTING DEVICES, INC.	00-00-A7	0000A7
STRATUS COMPUTER, INC.	00-00-A8	0000A8
NETWORK SYSTEMS CORP.	00-00-A9	0000A9
XEROX CORP.	00-00-AA	0000AA
DASSAULT AUTOMATISMES ET TELECOMMUNICATIONS	00-00-AE	0000AE
ALPHA MICROSYSTEMS, INC.	00-00-B1	0000B1
MICRO-MATIC RESEARCH	00-00-B6	0000B6
DOVE COMPUTER CORP.	00-00-B7	0000B7
ALLEN-BRADLEY CO., INC.	00-00-BC	0000BC
OLICOM A/S	00-00-C1	0000C1
DENSAN CO., LTD.	00-00-CC	0000CC
INDUSTRIAL RESEARCH, LTD.	00-00-CD	0000CD
DEVELCON ELECTRONICS, LTD.	00-00-D0	0000D0
SBE, INC.	00-00-D2	0000D2
INTEGRATED MICRO PRODUCTS, LTD.	00-00-E3	0000E3
APTOR PRODUITS DE COMM INDUST.	00-00-E6	0000E6
STAR GATE TECHNOLOGIES	00-00-E7	0000E7
ACCTON TECHNOLOGY CORP.	00-00-E8	0000E8
ISICAD, INC.	00-00-E9	0000E9
APRIL	00-00-ED	0000ED
SPIDER COMMUNICATIONS	00-00-F2	0000F2

App
C

continues

Table C.1   Continued

Company	OUI (Hex)	Company ID (Base 16)
ALLIED TELESIS, INC.	00-00-F4	0000F4
DIGITAL EQUIPMENT CORP.	00-00-F8	0000F8
RECHNER ZUR KOMMUNIKATION	00-00-FB	0000FB
NODE RUNNER, INC.	00-02-67	000267
RACAL-DATACOM	00-07-01	000701
LEXMARK INTERNATIONAL, INC.	00-20-00	002000
SERITECH ENTERPRISE CO., LTD.	00-20-02	002002
PIXEL POWER, LTD.	00-20-03	002003
YAMATAKE-HONEYWELL CO., LTD.	00-20-04	002004
SIMPLE TECHNOLOGY	00-20-05	002005
GARRETT COMMUNICATIONS, INC.	00-20-06	002006
SFA, INC.	00-20-07	002007
CABLE & COMPUTER TECHNOLOGY	00-20-08	002008
PACKARD BELL ELEC., INC.	00-20-09	002009
SOURCE-COMM CORP.	00-20-0A	00200A
OCTAGON SYSTEMS CORP.	00-20-0B	00200B
ADASTRA SYSTEMS CORP.	00-20-0C	00200C
CARL ZEISS	00-20-0D	00200D
SATELLITE TECHNOLOGY MGMT, INC.	00-20-0E	00200E
TANBAC CO., LTD.	00-20-0F	00200F
JEOL SYSTEM TECHNOLOGY CO., LTD.	00-20-10	002010
CANOPUS CO., LTD.	00-20-11	002011
CAMTRONICS MEDICAL SYSTEMS	00-20-12	002012
DIVERSIFIED TECHNOLOGY, INC.	00-20-13	002013
GLOBAL VIEW CO., LTD.	00-20-14	002014
ACTIS COMPUTER SA	00-20-15	002015
SHOWA ELECTRIC WIRE & CABLE CO.	00-20-16	002016
ORBOTECH	00-20-17	002017

Company	OUI (Hex)	Company ID (Base 16)
CIS TECHNOLOGY, INC.	00-20-18	002018
OHLER GMBH	00-20-19	002019
N-BASE SWITCH COMMUNICATIONS	00-20-1A	00201A
NORTHERN TELECOM/NETWORK SYSTEMS CORP.	00-20-lb	0020lb
EXCEL, INC.	00-20-1C	00201C
KATANA PRODUCTS	00-20-1D	00201D
NETQUEST CORP.	00-20-1E	00201E
BEST POWER TECHNOLOGY, INC.	00-20-1F	00201F
MEGATRON COMPUTER INDUSTRIES PTY., LTD.	00-20-20	002020
ALGORITHMS SOFTWARE PVT., LTD.	00-20-21	002021
TEKNIQUE, INC.	00-20-22	002022
T.C. TECHNOLOGIES PTY., LTD.	00-20-23	002023
PACIFIC COMMUNICATION SCIENCES	00-20-24	002024
CONTROL TECHNOLOGY, INC.	00-20-25	002025
AMKLY SYSTEMS, INC.	00-20-26	002026
MING FORTUNE INDUSTRY CO., LTD.	00-20-27	002027
WEST EGG SYSTEMS, INC.	00-20-28	002028
TELEPROCESSING PRODUCTS, INC.	00-20-29	002029
ADVANCED TELECOMMUNICATIONS MODULES, LTD.	00-20-2B	00202B
WELLTRONIX CO., LTD.	00-20-2C	00202C
TAIYO CORP.	00-20-2D	00202D
DAYSTAR DIGITAL	00-20-2E	00202E
ZETA COMMUNICATIONS, LTD.	00-20-2F	00202F
ANALOG & DIGITAL SYSTEMS	00-20-30	002030
ERTEC GMBH	00-20-31	002031
ALCATEL TAISEL	00-20-32	002032

App

C

continues

Table C.1   Continued

Company	OUI (Hex)	Company ID (Base 16)
SYNAPSE TECHNOLOGIES, INC.	00-20-33	002033
ROTEC INDUSTRIEAUTOMATION GMBH	00-20-34	002034
CPN ARCHITECTURES/IBM CORP.	00-20-35	002035
BMC SOFTWARE	00-20-36	002036
SEAGATE TECHNOLOGY	00-20-37	002037
VME MICROSYSTEMS INTERNATIONAL CORP.	00-20-38	002038
SCINETS	00-20-39	002039
DIGITAL BIOMETRICS, INC.	00-20-3A	00203A
WISDM, LTD.	00-20-3B	00203B
EUROTIME AB	00-20-3C	00203C
NOVAR ELECTRONICS CORP.	00-20-3D	00203D
LOGICAN TECHNOLOGIES, INC.	00-20-3E	00203E
JUKI CORP.	00-20-3F	00203F
DATAMETRICS CORP.	00-20-42	002042
NEURON COMPANY, LTD.	00-20-43	002043
GENITECH PTY., LTD.	00-20-44	002044
SOLCOM SYSTEMS, LTD.	00-20-45	002045
CIPRICO, INC.	00-20-46	002046
FORE SYSTEMS, INC.	00-20-48	002048
COMTRON, INC.	00-20-49	002049
PRONET GMBH	00-20-4A	00204A
AUTOCOMPUTER CO., LTD.	00-20-4B	00204B
MITRON COMPUTER PTE, LTD.	00-20-4C	00204C
INOVIS GMBH	00-20-4D	00204D
NETWORK SECURITY SYSTEMS, INC.	00-20-4E	00204E
DEUTSCHE AEROSPACE AG	00-20-4F	00204F
KOREA COMPUTER, INC.	00-20-50	002050

Company	OUI (Hex)	Company ID (Base 16)
PHOENIX DATA COMMUNUNICATIONS CORP.	00-20-51	002051
RAGULA SYSTEMS	00-20-52	002052
HUNTSVILLE MICROSYSTEMS, INC.	00-20-53	002053
EASTERN RESEARCH, INC.	00-20-54	002054
ALTECH CO., LTD.	00-20-55	002055
NEOPRODUCTS	00-20-56	002056
TITZE DATENTECHNIK GMBH	00-20-57	002057
ALLIED SIGNAL, INC.	00-20-58	002058
MIRO COMPUTER PRODUCTS AG	00-20-59	002059
COMPUTER IDENTICS	00-20-5A	00205A
SKYLINE TECHNOLOGY	00-20-5B	00205B
INTERNET SYSTEMS/FLORIDA, INC.	00-20-5C	00205C
NANOMATIC OY	00-20-5D	00205D
CASTLE ROCK, INC.	00-20-5E	00205E
GAMMADATA COMPUTER GMBH	00-20-5F	00205F
ALCATEL ITALIA S.P.A.	00-20-60	002060
DYNATECH COMMUNICATIONS, INC.	00-20-61	002061
SCORPION LOGIC, LTD.	00-20-62	002062
WIPRO INFOTECH, LTD.	00-20-63	002063
PROTEC MICROSYSTEMS, INC.	00-20-64	002064
SUPERNET NETWORKING, INC.	00-20-65	002065
GENERAL MAGIC, INC.	00-20-66	002066
ISDYNE	00-20-68	002068
ISDN SYSTEMS CORP.	00-20-69	002069
OSAKA COMPUTER CORP.	00-20-6A	00206A
MINOLTA CO., LTD.	00-20-6B	00206B
EVERGREEN TECHNOLOGY CORP.	00-20-6C	00206C
DATA RACE, INC.	00-20-6D	00206D
XACT, INC.	00-20-6E	00206E

App
C

continues

Table C.1   Continued

Company	OUI (Hex)	Company ID (Base 16)
FLOWPOINT CORP.	00-20-6F	00206F
HYNET, LTD.	00-20-70	002070
IBR GMBH	00-20-71	002071
WORKLINK INNOVATIONS	00-20-72	002072
FUSION SYSTEMS CORP.	00-20-73	002073
SUNGWOON SYSTEMS	00-20-74	002074
MOTOROLA COMMUNICATION ISRAEL	00-20-75	002075
REUDO CORP.	00-20-76	002076
KARDIOS SYSTEMS, CORP.	00-20-77	002077
RUNTOP, INC.	00-20-78	002078
MIKRON GMBH	00-20-79	002079
WISE COMMUNICATIONS, INC.	00-20-7A	00207A
LEVEL ONE COMMUNICATIONS	00-20-7B	00207B
AUTEC GMBH	00-20-7C	00207C
ADVANCED COMPUTER APPLICATIONS	00-20-7D	00207D
FINECOM CO., LTD.	00-20-7E	00207E
KYOEI SANGYO CO., LTD.	00-20-7F	00207F
SYNERGY (UK), LTD.	00-20-80	002080
TITAN ELECTRONICS	00-20-81	002081
ONEAC CORP.	00-20-82	002082
PRESTICOM, INC.	00-20-83	002083
OCE GRAPHICS USA, INC.	00-20-84	002084
EXIDE ELECTRONICS	00-20-85	002085
MICROTECH ELECTRONICS, LTD.	00-20-86	002086
MEMOTEC COMMUNICATIONS CORP.	00-20-87	002087
GLOBAL VILLAGE COMMUNICATIONS	00-20-88	002088
T3PLUS NETWORKING, INC.	00-20-89	002089
SONIX COMMUNICATIONS, LTD.	00-20-8A	00208A

Company	OUI (Hex)	Company ID (Base 16)
LAPIS TECHNOLOGIES, INC.	00-20-8B	00208B
GALAXY NETWORKS, INC.	00-20-8C	00208C
CMD TECHNOLOGY	00-20-8D	00208D
CHEVIN SOFTWARE ENG., LTD.	00-20-8E	00208E
ECI TELECOM, LTD.	00-20-8F	00208F
ADVANCED COMPRESSION TECHNOLOGY, INC.	00-20-90	002090
J125, NATIONAL SECURITY AGENCY	00-20-91	002091
CHESS ENGINEERING B.V.	00-20-92	002092
CUBIX CORP.	00-20-94	002094
RIVA ELECTRONICS	00-20-95	002095
SIEBE ENVIRONMENTAL CONTROLS	00-20-96	002096
HECTRONIC AB	00-20-98	002098
BON ELECTRIC CO., LTD.	00-20-99	002099
THE 3DO COMPANY	00-20-9A	00209A
ERSAT ELECTRONIC GMBH	00-20-9B	00209B
PRIMARY ACCESS CORP.	00-20-9C	00209C
LIPPERT AUTOMATIONSTECHNIK	00-20-9D	00209D
BROWN'S OPERATING SYSTEM SERVICES, LTD.	00-20-9E	00209E
MERCURY COMPUTER SYSTEMS, INC.	00-20-9F	00209F
OA LABORATORY CO., LTD.	00-20-A0	0020A0
DOVATRON PRODUCTS DIVISION	00-20-A1	0020A1
GALCOM NETWORKING, LTD.	00-20-A2	0020A2
DIVICOM, INC.	00-20-A3	0020A3
MULTIPOINT NETWORKS	00-20-A4	0020A4
API ENGINEERING	00-20-A5	0020A5
PROXIM, INC.	00-20-A6	0020A6
PAIRGAIN TECHNOLOGIES, INC.	00-20-A7	0020A7

App
C

continues

Table C.1   Continued

Company	OUI (Hex)	Company ID (Base 16)
WHITE HORSE INDUSTRIAL	00-20-A9	0020A9
NTL	00-20-AA	0020AA
MICRO INDUSTRIES CORP.	00-20-AB	0020AB
INTERFLEX DATENSYSTEME GMBH	00-20-AC	0020AC
LINQ SYSTEMS	00-20-AD	0020AD
ORNET DATA COMMUNICATION TECH.	00-20-AE	0020AE
3COM CORP.	00-20-AF	0020AF
GATEWAY DEVICES, INC.	00-20-B0	0020B0
COMTECH RESEARCH, INC.	00-20-B1	0020B1
GKD GESELLSCHAFT FUR KOMMUNIKATION UND DATENTECHNIK	00-20-B2	0020B2
SCLTEC COMMUNICATIONS SYSTEMS	00-20-B3	0020B3
TERMA ELEKTRONIK AS	00-20-B4	0020B4
YASKAWA ELECTRIC CORP.	00-20-B5	0020B5
AGILE NETWORKS, INC.	00-20-B6	0020B6
NAMAQUA COMPUTERWARE	00-20-B7	0020B7
PRIME OPTION, INC.	00-20-B8	0020B8
METRICOM, INC.	00-20-B9	0020B9
CENTER FOR HIGH PERFORMANCE COMPUTING OF WPI	00-20-BA	0020BA
ZAX CORP.	00-20-BB	0020BB
JTEC PTY., LTD.	00-20-BC	0020BC
NIOBRARA R & D CORP.	00-20-BD	0020BD
LAN ACCESS CORP.	00-20-BE	0020BE
AEHR TEST SYSTEMS	00-20-BF	0020BF
PULSE ELECTRONICS, INC.	00-20-C0	0020C0
TAIKO ELECTRIC WORKS, LTD.	00-20-C1	0020C1
TEXAS MEMORY SYSTEMS, INC.	00-20-C2	0020C2

Company	OUI (Hex)	Company ID (Base 16)
COUNTER SOLUTIONS, LTD.	00-20-C3	0020C3
EAGLE TECHNOLOGY	00-20-C5	0020C5
NECTEC	00-20-C6	0020C6
AKAI ELECTRIC CO., LTD.	00-20-C7	0020C7
LARSCOM, INC.	00-20-C8	0020C8
VICTRON BV	00-20-C9	0020C9
DIGITAL OCEAN	00-20-CA	0020CA
PRETEC ELECTRONICS CORP.	00-20-CB	0020CB
DIGITAL SERVICES, LTD.	00-20-CC	0020CC
HYBRID NETWORKS, INC.	00-20-CD	0020CD
LOGICAL DESIGN GROUP, INC.	00-20-CE	0020CE
TEST & MEASUREMENT SYSTEMS, INC.	00-20-CF	0020CF
VERSALYNX CORP.	00-20-D0	0020D0
MICROCOMPUTER SYSTEMS (M) SDN.	00-20-D1	0020D1
RAD DATA COMMUNICATIONS, LTD.	00-20-D2	0020D2
OST (OUEST STANDARD TELEMATIQU)	00-20-D3	0020D3
ZEITNET, INC.	00-20-D4	0020D4
VIPA GMBH	00-20-D5	0020D5
LANNAIR, LTD.	00-20-D6	0020D6
JAPAN MINICOMPUTER SYSTEMS CO.	00-20-D7	0020D7
PANASONIC TECHNOLOGIES, INC./ MIECO-US	00-20-D9	0020D9
XYLAN CORP.	00-20-DA	0020DA
XNET TECHNOLOGY, INC.	00-20-DB	0020DB
DENSITRON TAIWAN, LTD.	00-20-DC	0020DC
AWA, LTD.	00-20-DD	0020DD
JAPAN DIGITAL LABORAT'Y CO., LTD.	00-20-DE	0020DE
KYOSAN ELECTRIC MFG. CO., LTD.	00-20-DF	0020DF
PREMAX ELECTRONICS, INC.	00-20-E0	0020E0

App
C

continues

Table C.1 Continued

Company	OUI (Hex)	Company ID (Base 16)
ALAMAR ELECTRONICS	00-20-E1	0020E1
INFORMATION RESOURCE ENGINEERING	00-20-E2	0020E2
MCD KENCOM CORP.	00-20-E3	0020E3
LIDKOPING MACHINE TOOLS AB	00-20-E6	0020E6
B&W NUCLEAR SERVICE COMPANY	00-20-E7	0020E7
DATATREK CORP.	00-20-E8	0020E8
DANTEL	00-20-E9	0020E9
EFFICIENT NETWORKS, INC.	00-20-EA	0020EA
CINCINNATI MICROWAVE, INC.	00-20-EB	0020EB
TECHWARE SYSTEMS CORP.	00-20-EC	0020EC
GIGA-BYTE TECHNOLOGY CO., LTD.	00-20-ED	0020ED
GTECH CORP.	00-20-EE	0020EE
U.S.C. CORP.	00-20-EF	0020EF
ALTOS INDIA, LTD.	00-20-F1	0020F1
MAXIMUM STRATEGY, INC.	00-20-F2	0020F2
RAYNET CORP.	00-20-F3	0020F3
SPECTRIX CORP.	00-20-F4	0020F4
PAN DACOM TELECOM'CATIONS GMBH	00-20-F5	0020F5
NET TEK AND KARLNET, INC.	00-20-F6	0020F6
CYBERDATA	00-20-F7	0020F7
CARRERA COMPUTERS, INC.	00-20-F8	0020F8
PARALINK NETWORKS, INC.	00-20-F9	0020F9
GDE SYSTEMS, INC.	00-20-FA	0020FA
OCTEL COMMUNICATIONS CORP.	00-20-FB	0020FB
MATROX	00-20-FC	0020FC
ITV TECHNOLOGIES, INC.	00-20-FD	0020FD
TOPWARE, INC. /GRAND COMPUTER CORP.	00-20-FE	0020FE

Company	OUI (Hex)	Company ID (Base 16)
SYMMETRICAL TECHNOLOGIES	00-20-FF	0020FF
ZERO ONE TECHNOLOGY CO., LTD.	00-40-01	004001
TACHIBANA TECTRON CO., LTD.	00-40-09	004009
GENERAL MICRO SYSTEMS, INC.	00-40-0C	00400C
LANNET DATA COMMUNICATIONS, LTD.	00-40-0D	00400D
SONIC SYSTEMS	00-40-10	004010
NTT DATA COMM. SYSTEMS CORP.	00-40-13	004013
COMSOFT GMBH	00-40-14	004014
ASCOM INFRASYS AG	00-40-15	004015
COLORGRAPH, LTD.	00-40-1F	00401F
PINACL COMMUNICATION SYSTEMS, LTD.	00-40-20	004020
LOGIC CORP.	00-40-23	004023
MOLECULAR DYNAMICS	00-40-25	004025
MELCO, INC.	00-40-26	004026
SMC MASSACHUSETTS, INC.	00-40-27	004027
CANOGA-PERKINS	00-40-2A	00402A
XLNT DESIGNS, INC.	00-40-2F	00402F
GK COMPUTER	00-40-30	004030
DIGITAL COMMUNICATIONS ASSOCIATES, INC.	00-40-32	004032
ADDTRON TECHNOLOGY CO., LTD.	00-40-33	004033
OPTEC DAIICHI DENKO CO., LTD.	00-40-39	004039
FORKS, INC.	00-40-3C	00403C
SSANGYONG COMPUTER SYSTEMS CORP.	00-40-3F	00403F
FUJIKURA, LTD.	00-40-41	004041
NOKIA DATA COMMUNICATIONS	00-40-43	004043
SMD INFORMATICA S.A.	00-40-48	004048
HYPERTEC PTY., LTD.	00-40-4C	00404C

App
C

continues

Table C.1   Continued

Company	OUI (Hex)	Company ID (Base 16)
TELECOMMUNICATIONS TECHNIQUES	00-40-4D	00404D
SPACE & NAVAL WARFARE SYSTEMS	00-40-4F	00404F
IRONICS, INC.	00-40-50	004050
STAR TECHNOLOGIES, INC.	00-40-52	004052
THINKING MACHINES CORP.	00-40-54	004054
LOCKHEED - SANDERS	00-40-57	004057
YOSHIDA KOGYO K. K.	00-40-59	004059
FUNASSET, LTD.	00-40-5B	00405B
STAR-TEK, INC.	00-40-5D	00405D
HITACHI CABLE, LTD.	00-40-66	004066
OMNIBYTE CORP.	00-40-67	004067
EXTENDED SYSTEMS	00-40-68	004068
LEMCOM SYSTEMS, INC.	00-40-69	004069
KENTEK INFORMATION SYSTEMS, INC.	00-40-6A	00406A
COROLLARY, INC.	00-40-6E	00406E
SYNC RESEARCH, INC.	00-40-6F	00406F
CABLE AND WIRELESS COMMUNICATIONS, INC.	00-40-74	004074
AMP, INC.	00-40-76	004076
WEARNES AUTOMATION PTE, LTD.	00-40-78	004078
AGEMA INFRARED SYSTEMS AB	00-40-7F	00407F
LABORATORY EQUIPMENT CORP.	00-40-82	004082
SAAB INSTRUMENTS AB	00-40-85	004085
MICHELS & KLEBERHOFF COMPUTER	00-40-86	004086
UBITREX CORP.	00-40-87	004087
TPS TELEPROCESSING SYS. GMBH	00-40-8A	00408A
AXIS COMMUNICATIONS AB	00-40-8C	00408C
DIGILOG, INC.	00-40-8E	00408E

Company	OUI (Hex)	Company ID (Base 16)
WM-DATA MINFO AB	00-40-8F	00408F
PROCOMP INDUSTRIA ELETRONICA	00-40-91	004091
ASP COMPUTER PRODUCTS, INC.	00-40-92	004092
SHOGRAPHICS, INC.	00-40-94	004094
R.P.T. INTERGROUPS INT'L, LTD.	00-40-95	004095
TELESYSTEMS SLW, INC.	00-40-96	004096
DRESSLER GMBH & CO.	00-40-98	004098
NETWORK EXPRESS, INC.	00-40-9A	00409A
TRANSWARE	00-40-9C	00409C
DIGIBOARD, INC.	00-40-9D	00409D
CONCURRENT TECHNOLOGIES, LTD.	00-40-9E	00409E
LANCAST/CASAT TECHNOLOGY, INC.	00-40-9F	00409F
ROSE ELECTRONICS	00-40-A4	0040A4
CRAY RESEARCH, INC.	00-40-A6	0040A6
VALMET AUTOMATION, INC.	00-40-AA	0040AA
SMA REGELSYSTEME GMBH	00-40-AD	0040AD
DELTA CONTROLS, INC.	00-40-AE	0040AE
3COM K.K.	00-40-B4	0040B4
VIDEO TECHNOLOGY COMPUTERS, LTD.	00-40-B5	0040B5
COMPUTERM CORP.	00-40-B6	0040B6
MACQ ELECTRONIQUE SA	00-40-B9	0040B9
STARLIGHT NETWORKS, INC.	00-40-BD	0040BD
VISTA CONTROLS CORP.	00-40-C0	0040C0
BIZERBA-WERKE WILHEIM KRAUT GMBH & CO. KG	00-40-C1	0040C1
APPLIED COMPUTING DEVICES	00-40-C2	0040C2
FISCHER AND PORTER CO.	00-40-C3	0040C3
FIBERNET RESEARCH, INC.	00-40-C6	0040C6
MILAN TECHNOLOGY CORP.	00-40-C8	0040C8

App
C

continues

Table C.1   Continued

Company	OUI (Hex)	Company ID (Base 16)
SILCOM MANUF'G TECHNOLOGY, INC.	00-40-CC	0040CC
STRAWBERRY TREE, INC.	00-40-CF	0040CF
PAGINE CORP.	00-40-D2	0040D2
GAGE TALKER CORP.	00-40-D4	0040D4
STUDIO GEN, INC.	00-40-D7	0040D7
OCEAN OFFICE AUTOMATION, LTD.	00-40-D8	0040D8
TRITEC ELECTRONIC GMBH	00-40-DC	0040DC
DIGALOG SYSTEMS, INC.	00-40-DF	0040DF
MARNER INTERNATIONAL, INC.	00-40-E1	0040E1
MESA RIDGE TECHNOLOGIES, INC.	00-40-E2	0040E2
QUIN SYSTEMS, LTD.	00-40-E3	0040E3
E-M TECHNOLOGY, INC.	00-40-E4	0040E4
SYBUS CORP.	00-40-E5	0040E5
ARNOS INSTRUMENTS & COMPUTER SYSTEMS (GROUP) CO., LTD.	00-40-E7	0040E7
ACCORD SYSTEMS, INC.	00-40-E9	0040E9
PLAIN TREE SYSTEMS, INC.	00-40-EA	0040EA
NETWORK CONTROLS INT'L, INC.	00-40-ED	0040ED
MICRO SYSTEMS, INC.	00-40-F0	0040F0
CHUO ELECTRONICS CO., LTD.	00-40-F1	0040F1
CAMEO COMMUNICATIONS, INC.	00-40-F4	0040F4
OEM ENGINES	00-40-F5	0040F5
KATRON COMPUTERS, INC.	00-40-F6	0040F6
COMBINET	00-40-F9	0040F9
MICROBOARDS, INC.	00-40-FA	0040FA
LXE	00-40-FD	0040FD
TELEBIT CORP.	00-40-FF	0040FF
3COM CORP.	00-60-8C	00608C

Company	OUI (Hex)	Company ID (Base 16)
MULTITECH SYSTEMS, INC.	00-80-00	008000
ANTLOW COMPUTERS, LTD.	00-80-04	008004
CACTUS COMPUTER, INC.	00-80-05	008005
COMPUADD CORP.	00-80-06	008006
DLOG NC-SYSTEME	00-80-07	008007
JUPITER SYSTEMS	00-80-09	008009
VOSSWINKEL F.U.	00-80-0D	00800D
SEIKO SYSTEMS, INC.	00-80-15	008015
WANDEL AND GOLTERMANN	00-80-16	008016
KOBE STEEL, LTD.	00-80-18	008018
DAYNA COMMUNICATIONS, INC.	00-80-19	008019
BELL ATLANTIC	00-80-1A	00801A
NEWBRIDGE RESEARCH CORP.	00-80-21	008021
INTEGRATED BUSINESS NETWORKS	00-80-23	008023
KALPANA, INC.	00-80-24	008024
NETWORK PRODUCTS CORP.	00-80-26	008026
TEST SYSTEMS & SIMULATIONS, INC.	00-80-2A	00802A
THE SAGE GROUP PLC	00-80-2C	00802C
XYLOGICS, INC.	00-80-2D	00802D
TELEFON AB LM ERICSSON CORP.	00-80-37	008037
DATA RESEARCH & APPLICATIONS	00-80-38	008038
APT COMMUNICATIONS, INC.	00-80-3B	00803B
SURIGIKEN CO., LTD.	00-80-3D	00803D
SYNERNETICS	00-80-3E	00803E
FORCE COMPUTERS	00-80-42	008042
NETWORLD, INC.	00-80-43	008043
SYSTECH COMPUTER CORP.	00-80-44	008044
MATSUSHITA ELECTRIC IND. CO	00-80-45	008045
UNIVERSITY OF TORONTO	00-80-46	008046

continues

Table C.1   Continued

Company	OUI (Hex)	Company ID (Base 16)
NISSIN ELECTRIC CO., LTD.	00-80-49	008049
CONTEC CO., LTD.	00-80-4C	00804C
CYCLONE MICROSYSTEMS, INC.	00-80-4D	00804D
FIBERMUX	00-80-51	008051
ADSOFT, LTD.	00-80-57	008057
TULIP COMPUTERS INT'L B.V.	00-80-5A	00805A
CONDOR SYSTEMS, INC.	00-80-5B	00805B
INTERFACE CO.	00-80-62	008062
RICHARD HIRSCHMANN GMBH & CO.	00-80-63	008063
SQUARE D COMPANY	00-80-67	008067
COMPUTONE SYSTEMS	00-80-69	008069
ERI (EMPAC RESEARCH, INC.)	00-80-6A	00806A
SCHMID TELECOMMUNICATION	00-80-6B	00806B
CEGELEC PROJECTS, LTD.	00-80-6C	00806C
CENTURY SYSTEMS CORP.	00-80-6D	00806D
NIPPON STEEL CORP.	00-80-6E	00806E
ONELAN, LTD.	00-80-6F	00806F
SAI TECHNOLOGY	00-80-71	008071
MICROPLEX SYSTEMS, LTD.	00-80-72	008072
FISHER CONTROLS	00-80-74	008074
MICROBUS DESIGNS, LTD.	00-80-79	008079
ARTEL COMMUNICATIONS CORP.	00-80-7B	00807B
SOUTHERN PACIFIC, LTD.	00-80-7E	00807E
PEP MODULAR COMPUTERS GMBH	00-80-82	008082
COMPUTER GENERATION, INC.	00-80-86	008086
VICTOR COMPANY OF JAPAN, LTD.	00-80-88	008088
TECNETICS (PTY), LTD.	00-80-89	008089
SUMMIT MICROSYSTEMS CORP.	00-80-8A	00808A

Company	OUI (Hex)	Company ID (Base 16)
DACOLL, LTD.	00-80-8B	00808B
WESTCOAST TECHNOLOGY B.V.	00-80-8D	00808D
RADSTONE TECHNOLOGY	00-80-8E	00808E
MICROTEK INTERNATIONAL, INC.	00-80-90	008090
JAPAN COMPUTER INDUSTRY, INC.	00-80-92	008092
XYRON CORP.	00-80-93	008093
SATTCONTROL AB	00-80-94	008094
HUMAN DESIGNED SYSTEMS, INC.	00-80-96	008096
TDK CORP.	00-80-98	008098
NOVUS NETWORKS, LTD.	00-80-9A	00809A
JUSTSYSTEM CORP.	00-80-9B	00809B
DATACRAFT MANUFACTUR'G PTY., LTD.	00-80-9D	00809D
ALCATEL BUSINESS SYSTEMS	00-80-9F	00809F
MICROTEST, INC.	00-80-A1	0080A1
LANTRONIX	00-80-A3	0080A3
REPUBLIC TECHNOLOGY, INC.	00-80-A6	0080A6
MEASUREX CORP.	00-80-A7	0080A7
IMLOGIX, DIVISION OF GENESYS	00-80-AC	0080AC
CNET TECHNOLOGY, INC.	00-80-AD	0080AD
HUGHES NETWORK SYSTEMS	00-80-AE	0080AE
ALLUMER CO., LTD.	00-80-AF	0080AF
SOFTCOM A/S	00-80-B1	0080B1
BUG, INC.	00-80-B8	0080B8
SPECIALIX (ASIA) PTE, LTD.	00-80-BA	0080BA
HUGHES LAN SYSTEMS	00-80-BB	0080BB
IEEE 802 COMMITTEE	00-80-C2	0080C2
ALBERTA MICROELECTRONIC CENTRE	00-80-C9	0080C9
MICRONICS COMPUTER, INC.	00-80-CD	0080CD
BROADCAST TELEVISION SYSTEMS	00-80-CE	0080CE

App
C

continues

Table C.1   Continued

Company	OUI (Hex)	Company ID (Base 16)
FANTUM ENGINEERING, INC.	00-80-D7	0080D7
BRUEL & KJAER	00-80-DA	0080DA
GMX, INC/GIMIX	00-80-DD	0080DD
XTP SYSTEMS, INC.	00-80-E0	0080E0
LYNWOOD SCIENTIFIC DEV., LTD.	00-80-E7	0080E7
THE FIBER COMPANY	00-80-EA	0080EA
KYUSHU MATSUSHITA ELECTRIC CO.	00-80-F0	0080F0
SUN ELECTRONICS CORP.	00-80-F3	0080F3
TELEMECANIQUE ELECTRIQUE	00-80-F4	0080F4
QUANTEL, LTD.	00-80-F5	0080F5
HEURIKON CORP.	00-80-F9	0080F9
BVM, LTD.	00-80-FB	0080FB
AZURE TECHNOLOGIES, INC.	00-80-FE	0080FE
CENTILLION NETWORKS, INC.	00-A0-00	00A000
WATKINS-JOHNSON COMPANY	00-A0-01	00A001
LEEDS & NORTHRUP AUSTRALIA PTY., LTD.	00-A0-02	00A002
STAEFA CONTROL SYSTEM	00-A0-03	00A003
NETPOWER, INC.	00-A0-04	00A004
APEXX TECHNOLOGY, INC.	00-A0-07	00A007
NETCORP	00-A0-08	00A008
WHITETREE NETWORK TECHNOLOGIES, INC.	00-A0-09	00A009
R.D.C. COMMUNICATION	00-A0-0A	00A00A
KINGMAX TECHNOLOGY, INC.	00-A0-0C	00A00C
THE PANDA PROJECT	00-A0-0D	00A00D
VISUAL NETWORKS, INC.	00-A0-0E	00A00E
BROADBAND TECHNOLOGIES	00-A0-0F	00A00F
MUTOH INDUSTRIES, LTD.	00-A0-11	00A011

Company	OUI (Hex)	Company ID (Base 16)
CSIR	00-A0-14	00A014
WYLE	00-A0-15	00A015
J.B.M. CORP.	00-A0-17	00A017
CREATIVE CONTROLLERS, INC.	00-A0-18	00A018
BINAR ELEKTRONIK AB	00-A0-1A	00A01A
PREMISYS COMMUNICATIONS, INC.	00-A0-lb	00A0lb
EST CORP.	00-A0-1E	00A01E
TRICORD SYSTEMS, INC.	00-A0-1F	00A01F
GTE GOVERNMENT SYSTEMS CORP.	00-A0-21	00A021
CENTRE FOR DEVELOPMENT OF ADVANCED COMPUTING	00-A0-22	00A022
APPLIED CREATIVE TECHNOLOGY, INC.	00-A0-23	00A023
3COM CORP.	00-A0-24	00A024
REDCOM LABS, INC.	00-A0-25	00A025
TELDAT, S.A.	00-A0-26	00A026
FIREPOWER SYSTEMS, INC.	00-A0-27	00A027
CONNER PERIPHERALS	00-A0-28	00A028
COULTER CORP.	00-A0-29	00A029
TRANSITIONS RESEARCH CORP.	00-A0-2B	00A02B
1394 TRADE ASSOCIATION	00-A0-2D	00A02D
CAPTOR NV/SA	00-A0-30	00A030
GES SINGAPORE PTE., LTD.	00-A0-32	00A032
AXEL	00-A0-34	00A034
CYLINK CORP.	00-A0-35	00A035
APPLIED NETWORK TECHNOLOGY	00-A0-36	00A036
DATASCOPE CORP.	00-A0-37	00A037
KUBOTEK CORP.	00-A0-3A	00A03A
TOSHIN ELECTRIC CO., LTD.	00-A0-3B	00A03B
OPTO - 22	00-A0-3D	00A03D

App
C

continues

Table C.1   Continued

Company	OUI (Hex)	Company ID (Base 16)
ATM FORUM	00-A0-3E	00A03E
COMPUTER SOCIETY MICROPROCES'R & MICROPRO'R STDS COMMITTEE	00-A0-3F	00A03F
APPLE COMPUTER	00-A0-40	00A040
LEYBOLD-INFICON	00-A0-41	00A041
SPUR PRODUCTS CORP.	00-A0-42	00A042
AMERICAN TECHNOLOGY LABS, INC.	00-A0-43	00A043
PHOENIX CONTACT GMBH & CO.	00-A0-45	00A045
SCITEX CORP., LTD.	00-A0-46	00A046
INTEGRATED FITNESS CORP.	00-A0-47	00A047
DIGITECH INDUSTRIES, INC.	00-A0-49	00A049
NISSHIN ELECTRIC CO., LTD.	00-A0-4A	00A04A
TFL LAN, INC.	00-A0-4B	00A04B
INNOVATIVE SYSTEMS & TECH., INC.	00-A0-4C	00A04C
EDA INSTRUMENTS, INC.	00-A0-4D	00A04D
AMERITEC CORP.	00-A0-4F	00A04F
CYPRESS SEMICONDUCTOR	00-A0-50	00A050
LINKTECH, INC.	00-A0-55	00A055
MARQUIP, INC.	00-A0-5B	00A05B
INVENTORY CONVERSION, INC./ NEKOTECH DIVISION	00-A0-5C	00A05C
AES PRODATA	00-A0-62	00A062
KVB/ANALECT	00-A0-64	00A064
NEXLAND, INC.	00-A0-65	00A065
ISA CO., LTD.	00-A0-66	00A066
NETWORK SERVICES GROUP	00-A0-67	00A067
VERILINK CORP.	00-A0-6A	00A06A
DMS DORSCH MIKROSYSTEM GMBH	00-A0-6B	00A06B
AUSTRON, INC.	00-A0-6E	00A06E

Company	OUI (Hex)	Company ID (Base 16)
THE APPCON GROUP, INC.	00-A0-6F	00A06F
COASTCOM	00-A0-70	00A070
OVATION SYSTEMS, LTD.	00-A0-72	00A072
COM21, INC.	00-A0-73	00A073
PERCEPTION TECHNOLOGY	00-A0-74	00A074
ZEOS INTERNATIONAL, LTD.	00-A0-75	00A075
CARDWARE LAB, INC.	00-A0-76	00A076
ALPS ELECTRIC (USA), INC.	00-A0-79	00A079
DAWN COMPUTER, INC.	00-A0-7B	00A07B
TONYANG NYLON CO., LTD.	00-A0-7C	00A07C
SEEQ TECHNOLOGY, INC.	00-A0-7D	00A07D
AVID TECHNOLOGY, INC.	00-A0-7E	00A07E
GSM-SYNTEL, LTD.	00-A0-7F	00A07F
ANTARES MICROSYSTEMS	00-A0-80	00A080
ALCATEL DATA NETWORKS	00-A0-81	00A081
NKT ELEKTRONIK A/S	00-A0-82	00A082
DATAPLEX PTY., LTD.	00-A0-84	00A084
GEC PLESSEY SEMICONDUCTORS	00-A0-87	00A087
ESSENTIAL COMMUNICATIONS	00-A0-88	00A088
XPOINT TECHNOLOGIES, INC.	00-A0-89	00A089
BROOKTROUT TECHNOLOGY, INC.	00-A0-8A	00A08A
MULTIMEDIA LANS, INC.	00-A0-8C	00A08C
JACOMO CORP.	00-A0-8D	00A08D
IPSILON NETWORKS, INC.	00-A0-8E	00A08E
APPLICOM INTERNATIONAL	00-A0-91	00A091
H. BOLLMANN MANUFACTURERS, LTD.	00-A0-92	00A092
JC INFORMATION SYSTEMS	00-A0-97	00A097
NETWORK APPLIANCE CORP.	00-A0-98	00A098
K-NET, LTD.	00-A0-99	00A099

App C

continues

Table C.1   Continued

Company	OUI (Hex)	Company ID (Base 16)
QPSX COMMUNICATIONS, LTD.	00-A0-9B	00A09B
JOHNATHON FREEMAN TECHNOLOGIES	00-A0-9D	00A09D
ICTV	00-A0-9E	00A09E
COMMVISION CORP.	00-A0-9F	00A09F
COMPACT DATA, LTD.	00-A0-A0	00A0A0
EPIC DATA, INC.	00-A0-A1	00A0A1
DIGICOM S.P.A.	00-A0-A2	00A0A2
RELIABLE POWER METERS	00-A0-A3	00A0A3
MICROS SYSTEMS, INC.	00-A0-A4	00A0A4
TEKNOR MICROSYSTEME, INC.	00-A0-A5	00A0A5
VORAX CORP.	00-A0-A7	00A0A7
RENEX CORP.	00-A0-A8	00A0A8
SPACELABS MEDICAL	00-A0-AA	00A0AA
NETCS INFORMATIONSTECHNIK GMBH	00-A0-AB	00A0AB
NUCOM SYSTEMS, INC.	00-A0-AE	00A0AE
FIRST VIRTUAL CORP.	00-A0-B1	00A0B1
SHIMA SEIKI	00-A0-B2	00A0B2
ZYKRONIX	00-A0-B3	00A0B3
TEXAS MICROSYSTEMS, INC.	00-A0-B4	00A0B4
3H TECHNOLOGY	00-A0-B5	00A0B5
SANRITZ AUTOMATION CO., LTD.	00-A0-B6	00A0B6
PATTON ELECTRONICS CO.	00-A0-BA	00A0BA
VIASAT, INC.	00-A0-BC	00A0BC
INTEGRATED CIRCUIT SYSTEMS, INC.	00-A0-BE	00A0BE
DIGITAL LINK CORP.	00-A0-C0	00A0C0
ORTIVUS MEDICAL AB	00-A0-C1	00A0C1
R.A. SYSTEMS CO., LTD.	00-A0-C2	00A0C2
UNICOMPUTER GMBH	00-A0-C3	00A0C3

Company	OUI (Hex)	Company ID (Base 16)
QUALCOMM, INC.	00-A0-C6	00A0C6
TADIRAN TELECOMMUNICATIONS	00-A0-C8	00A0C8
FUJITSU DENSO, LTD.	00-A0-CA	00A0CA
ARK TELECOMMUNICATIONS, INC.	00-A0-CB	00A0CB
SWL, INC.	00-A0-CF	00A0CF
TEN X TECHNOLOGY, INC.	00-A0-D0	00A0D0
INVENTEC CORP.	00-A0-D1	00A0D1
ALLIED TELESIS, INC.	00-A0-D2	00A0D2
INSTEM COMPUTER SYSTEMS, LTD.	00-A0-D3	00A0D3
RADIOLAN, INC.	00-A0-D4	00A0D4
SIERRA WIRELESS, INC.	00-A0-D5	00A0D5
KASTEN CHASE APPLIED RESEARCH	00-A0-D7	00A0D7
SPECTRA - TEK	00-A0-D8	00A0D8
CONVEX COMPUTER CORP.	00-A0-D9	00A0D9
FISHER & PAYKEL PRODUCTION	00-A0-DB	00A0DB
AZONIX CORP.	00-A0-DD	00A0DD
YAMAHA CORP.	00-A0-DE	00A0DE
TENNYSON TECHNOLOGIES PTY., LTD.	00-A0-E0	00A0E0
XKL SYSTEMS CORP.	00-A0-E3	00A0E3
OPTIQUEST	00-A0-E4	00A0E4
NHC COMMUNICATIONS	00-A0-E5	00A0E5
DIALOGIC CORP.	00-A0-E6	00A0E6
CENTRAL DATA CORP.	00-A0-E7	00A0E7
REUTERS HOLDINGS PLC	00-A0-E8	00A0E8
ELECTRONIC RETAILING SYSTEMS INTERNATIONAL	00-A0-E9	00A0E9
FASTCOMM COMMUNICATIONS CORP.	00-A0-EB	00A0EB
TRANSMITTON, LTD.	00-A0-EC	00A0EC
NASHOBA NETWORKS	00-A0-EE	00A0EE

App
C

continues

Table C.1   Continued

Company	OUI (Hex)	Company ID (Base 16)
MTI	00-A0-F1	00A0F1
STAUBLI	00-A0-F3	00A0F3
GE MEDICAL SYSTEMS	00-A0-F4	00A0F4
RADGUARD, LTD.	00-A0-F5	00A0F5
SYMBOL TECHNOLOGIES, INC.	00-A0-F8	00A0F8
BINTEC COMPUTOR SYSTEME GMBH	00-A0-F9	00A0F9
ANT NACHRICHTENTECHNIK GMBH	00-A0-FA	00A0FA
TORAY ENGINEERING CO., LTD.	00-A0-FB	00A0FB
SCITEX DIGITAL PRINTING, INC.	00-A0-FD	00A0FD
BOSTON TECHNOLOGY, INC.	00-A0-FE	00A0FE
TELLABS OPERATIONS, INC.	00-A0-FF	00A0FF
LANOPTICS, LTD.	00-C0-00	00C000
DIATEK PATIENT MANAGEMENT SYSTEMS, INC.	00-C0-01	00C001
SERCOMM CORP.	00-C0-02	00C002
GLOBALNET COMMUNICATIONS	00-C0-03	00C003
JAPAN BUSINESS COMPUTER CO., LTD.	00-C0-04	00C004
LIVINGSTON ENTERPRISES, INC.	00-C0-05	00C005
NIPPON AVIONICS CO., LTD.	00-C0-06	00C006
PINNACLE DATA SYSTEMS, INC.	00-C0-07	00C007
SECO SRL	00-C0-08	00C008
KT TECHNOLOGY (S) PTE., LTD.	00-C0-09	00C009
MICRO CRAFT	00-C0-0A	00C00A
NORCONTROL A.S.	00-C0-0B	00C00B
ADVANCED LOGIC RESEARCH, INC.	00-C0-0D	00C00D
PSITECH, INC.	00-C0-0E	00C00E
QUANTUM SOFTWARE SYSTEMS, LTD.	00-C0-0F	00C00F
INTERACTIVE COMPUTING DEVICES	00-C0-11	00C011

Company	OUI (Hex)	Company ID (Base 16)
NETSPAN CORP.	00-C0-12	00C012
NETRIX	00-C0-13	00C013
TELEMATICS CALABASAS INT'L, INC.	00-C0-14	00C014
NEW MEDIA CORP.	00-C0-15	00C015
ELECTRONIC THEATRE CONTROLS	00-C0-16	00C016
LANART CORP.	00-C0-18	00C018
LEAP TECHNOLOGY, INC.	00-C0-19	00C019
COROMETRICS MEDICAL SYSTEMS	00-C0-1A	00C01A
SOCKET COMMUNICATIONS, INC.	00-C0-lb	00C0lb
INTERLINK COMMUNICATIONS, LTD.	00-C0-1C	00C01C
GRAND JUNCTION NETWORKS, INC.	00-C0-1D	00C01D
S.E.R.C.E.L.	00-C0-1F	00C01F
ARCO ELECTRONIC, CONTROL, LTD.	00-C0-20	00C020
NETEXPRESS	00-C0-21	00C021
TUTANKHAMON ELECTRONICS	00-C0-23	00C023
EDEN SISTEMAS DE COMPUTACAO SA	00-C0-24	00C024
DATAPRODUCTS CORP.	00-C0-25	00C025
CIPHER SYSTEMS, INC.	00-C0-27	00C027
JASCO CORP.	00-C0-28	00C028
KABEL RHEYDT AG	00-C0-29	00C029
OHKURA ELECTRIC CO., LTD.	00-C0-2A	00C02A
GERLOFF GESELLSCHAFT FUR	00-C0-2B	00C02B
CENTRUM COMMUNICATIONS, INC.	00-C0-2C	00C02C
FUJI PHOTO FILM CO., LTD.	00-C0-2D	00C02D
NETWIZ	00-C0-2E	00C02E
OKUMA CORP.	00-C0-2F	00C02F
INTEGRATED ENGINEERING B.V.	00-C0-30	00C030
DESIGN RESEARCH SYSTEMS, INC.	00-C0-31	00C031
I-CUBED, LTD.	00-C0-32	00C032

App
C

continues

Table C.1   Continued

Company	OUI (Hex)	Company ID (Base 16)
TELEBIT COMMUNICATIONS APS	00-C0-33	00C033
DALE COMPUTER CORP.	00-C0-34	00C034
QUINTAR COMPANY	00-C0-35	00C035
RAYTECH ELECTRONIC CORP.	00-C0-36	00C036
SILICON SYSTEMS	00-C0-39	00C039
MULTIACCESS COMPUTING CORP.	00-C0-3B	00C03B
TOWER TECH S.R.L.	00-C0-3C	00C03C
WIESEMANN & THEIS GMBH	00-C0-3D	00C03D
FA. GEBR. HELLER GMBH	00-C0-3E	00C03E
STORES AUTOMATED SYSTEMS, INC.	00-C0-3F	00C03F
ECCI	00-C0-40	00C040
DIGITAL TRANSMISSION SYSTEMS	00-C0-41	00C041
DATALUX CORP.	00-C0-42	00C042
STRATACOM	00-C0-43	00C043
EMCOM CORP.	00-C0-44	00C044
ISOLATION SYSTEMS, LTD.	00-C0-45	00C045
KEMITRON, LTD.	00-C0-46	00C046
UNIMICRO SYSTEMS, INC.	00-C0-47	00C047
BAY TECHNICAL ASSOCIATES	00-C0-48	00C048
CREATIVE MICROSYSTEMS	00-C0-4B	00C04B
MITEC, INC.	00-C0-4D	00C04D
COMTROL CORP.	00-C0-4E	00C04E
TOYO DENKI SEIZO K.K.	00-C0-50	00C050
ADVANCED INTEGRATION RESEARCH	00-C0-51	00C051
MODULAR COMPUTING TECHNOLOGIES	00-C0-55	00C055
SOMELEC	00-C0-56	00C056
MYCO ELECTRONICS	00-C0-57	00C057
DATAEXPERT CORP.	00-C0-58	00C058

Company	OUI (Hex)	Company ID (Base 16)
NIPPONDENSO CO., LTD.	00-C0-59	00C059
NETWORKS NORTHWEST, INC.	00-C0-5B	00C05B
ELONEX PLC	00-C0-5C	00C05C
L&N TECHNOLOGIES	00-C0-5D	00C05D
VARI-LITE, INC.	00-C0-5E	00C05E
ID SCANDINAVIA AS	00-C0-60	00C060
SOLECTEK CORP.	00-C0-61	00C061
MORNING STAR TECHNOLOGIES, INC.	00-C0-63	00C063
GENERAL DATACOMM IND., INC.	00-C0-64	00C064
SCOPE COMMUNICATIONS, INC.	00-C0-65	00C065
DOCUPOINT, INC.	00-C0-66	00C066
UNITED BARCODE INDUSTRIES	00-C0-67	00C067
PHILIP DRAKE ELECTRONICS, LTD.	00-C0-68	00C068
CALIFORNIA MICROWAVE, INC.	00-C0-69	00C069
ZAHNER-ELEKTRIK GMBH & CO. KG	00-C0-6A	00C06A
OSI PLUS CORP.	00-C0-6B	00C06B
SVEC COMPUTER CORP.	00-C0-6C	00C06C
BOCA RESEARCH, INC.	00-C0-6D	00C06D
KOMATSU, LTD.	00-C0-6F	00C06F
SECTRA SECURE-TRANSMISSION AB	00-C0-70	00C070
AREANEX COMMUNICATIONS, INC.	00-C0-71	00C071
KNX, LTD.	00-C0-72	00C072
XEDIA CORP.	00-C0-73	00C073
TOYODA AUTOMATIC LOOM WORKS, LTD.	00-C0-74	00C074
XANTE CORP.	00-C0-75	00C075
I-DATA INTERNATIONAL A-S	00-C0-76	00C076
DAEWOO TELECOM, LTD.	00-C0-77	00C077
COMPUTER SYSTEMS ENGINEERING	00-C0-78	00C078

App
C

continues

Table C.1 Continued

Company	OUI (Hex)	Company ID (Base 16)
FONSYS CO., LTD.	00-C0-79	00C079
PRIVA B.V.	00-C0-7A	00C07A
RISC DEVELOPMENTS, LTD.	00-C0-7D	00C07D
NUPON COMPUTING CORP.	00-C0-7F	00C07F
NETSTAR, INC.	00-C0-80	00C080
METRODATA, LTD.	00-C0-81	00C081
MOORE PRODUCTS CO.	00-C0-82	00C082
DATA LINK CORP., LTD.	00-C0-84	00C084
THE LYNK CORP.	00-C0-86	00C086
UUNET TECHNOLOGIES, INC.	00-C0-87	00C087
TELINDUS DISTRIBUTION	00-C0-89	00C089
LAUTERBACH DATENTECHNIK GMBH	00-C0-8A	00C08A
RISQ MODULAR SYSTEMS, INC.	00-C0-8B	0C08B
PERFORMANCE TECHNOLOGIES, INC.	00-C0-8C	00C08C
TRONIX PRODUCT DEVELOPMENT	00-C0-8D	00C08D
NETWORK INFORMATION TECHNOLOGY	00-C0-8E	00C08E
MATSUSHITA ELECTRIC WORKS, LTD.	00-C0-8F	00C08F
PRAIM S.R.L.	00-C0-90	00C090
JABIL CIRCUIT, INC.	00-C0-91	00C091
MENNEN MEDICAL, INC.	00-C0-92	00C092
ALTA RESEARCH CORP.	00-C0-93	00C093
TAMURA CORP.	00-C0-96	00C096
ARCHIPEL SA	00-C0-97	00C097
CHUNTEX ELECTRONIC CO., LTD.	00-C0-98	00C098
YOSHIKI INDUSTRIAL CO., LTD.	00-C0-99	00C099
RELIANCE COMM/TEC, R-TEC SYSTEMS, INC.	00-C0-9B	00C09B
TOA ELECTRONIC, LTD.	00-C0-9C	00C09C

Company	OUI (Hex)	Company ID (Base 16)
DISTRIBUTED SYSTEMS INT'L, INC.	00-C0-9D	00C09D
QUANTA COMPUTER, INC.	00-C0-9F	00C09F
ADVANCE MICRO RESEARCH, INC.	00-C0-A0	00C0A0
TOKYO DENSHI SEKEI CO.	00-C0-A1	00C0A1
INTERMEDIUM A/S	00-C0-A2	00C0A2
DUAL ENTERPRISES CORP.	00-C0-A3	00C0A3
UNIGRAF OY	00-C0-A4	00C0A4
SEEL, LTD.	00-C0-A7	00C0A7
GVC CORP.	00-C0-A8	00C0A8
BARRON MCCANN, LTD.	00-C0-A9	00C0A9
SILICON VALLEY COMPUTER	00-C0-AA	00C0AA
JUPITER TECHNOLOGY, INC.	00-C0-AB	00C0AB
GAMBIT COMPUTER COMMUNICATIONS	00-C0-AC	00C0AC
MARBEN COMMUNICATION SYSTEMS	00-C0-AD	00C0AD
TOWERCOM CO., INC., DBA PC HOUSE	00-C0-AE	00C0AE
TEKLOGIX, INC.	00-C0-AF	00C0AF
GCC TECHNOLOGIES, INC.	00-C0-B0	00C0B0
NORAND CORP.	00-C0-B2	00C0B2
COMSTAT DATACOMM CORP.	00-C0-B3	00C0B3
MYSON TECHNOLOGY, INC.	00-C0-B4	00C0B4
CORPORATE NETWORK SYSTEMS, INC.	00-C0-B5	00C0B5
MERIDIAN DATA, INC.	00-C0-B6	00C0B6
AMERICAN POWER CONVERSION CORP.	00-C0-B7	00C0B7
FRASER'S HILL, LTD.	00-C0-B8	00C0B8
FUNK SOFTWARE, INC.	00-C0-B9	00C0B9
NETVANTAGE	00-C0-BA	00C0BA
FORVAL CREATIVE, INC.	00-C0-BB	00C0BB
INEX TECHNOLOGIES, INC.	00-C0-BD	00C0BD
ALCATEL - SEL	00-C0-BE	00C0BE

App
C

continues

Table C.1   Continued

Company	OUI (Hex)	Company ID (Base 16)
TECHNOLOGY CONCEPTS, LTD.	00-C0-BF	00C0BF
SHORE MICROSYSTEMS, INC.	00-C0-C0	00C0C0
QUAD/GRAPHICS, INC.	00-C0-C1	00C0C1
INFINITE NETWORKS, LTD.	00-C0-C2	00C0C2
ACUSON COMPUTED SONOGRAPHY	00-C0-C3	00C0C3
COMPUTER OPERATIONAL REQUIREMENT ANALYSTS, LTD.	00-C0-C4	00C0C4
SID INFORMATICA	00-C0-C5	00C0C5
PERSONAL MEDIA CORP.	00-C0-C6	00C0C6
MICRO BYTE PTY., LTD.	00-C0-C8	00C0C8
BAILEY CONTROLS CO.	00-C0-C9	00C0C9
ALFA, INC.	00-C0-CA	00C0CA
CONTROL TECHNOLOGY CORP.	00-C0-CB	00C0CB
COMELTA, S.A.	00-C0-CD	00C0CD
RATOC SYSTEM, INC.	00-C0-D0	00C0D0
COMTREE TECHNOLOGY CORP.	00-C0-D1	00C0D1
SYNTELLECT, INC.	00-C0-D2	00C0D2
AXON NETWORKS, INC.	00-C0-D4	00C0D4
QUANCOM ELECTRONIC GMBH	00-C0-D5	00C0D5
J1 SYSTEMS, INC.	00-C0-D6	00C0D6
QUINTE NETWORK CONFIDENTIALITY EQUIPMENT, INC.	00-C0-D9	00C0D9
IPC CORP. (PTE), LTD.	00-C0-DB	00C0DB
EOS TECHNOLOGIES, INC.	00-C0-DC	00C0DC
ZCOMM, INC.	00-C0-DE	00C0DE
KYE SYSTEMS CORP.	00-C0-DF	00C0DF
SONIC SOLUTIONS	00-C0-E1	00C0E1
CALCOMP, INC.	00-C0-E2	00C0E2
OSITECH COMMUNICATIONS, INC.	00-C0-E3	00C0E3

Company	OUI (Hex)	Company ID (Base 16)
LANDIS & GYR POWERS, INC.	00-C0-E4	00C0E4
GESPAC, S.A.	00-C0-E5	00C0E5
TXPORT	00-C0-E6	00C0E6
FIBERDATA AB	00-C0-E7	00C0E7
PLEXCOM, INC.	00-C0-E8	00C0E8
OAK SOLUTIONS, LTD.	00-C0-E9	00C0E9
ARRAY TECHNOLOGY, LTD.	00-C0-EA	00C0EA
SEH COMPUTERTECHNIK GMBH	00-C0-EB	00C0EB
DAUPHIN TECHNOLOGY	00-C0-EC	00C0EC
U.S. ARMY ELECTRONIC	00-C0-ED	00C0ED
KYOCERA CORP.	00-C0-EE	00C0EE
ABIT CORP.	00-C0-EF	00C0EF
KINGSTON TECHNOLOGY CORP.	00-C0-F0	00C0F0
SHINKO ELECTRIC CO., LTD.	00-C0-F1	00C0F1
TRANSITION ENGINEERING, INC.	00-C0-F2	00C0F2
NETWORK COMMUNICATIONS CORP.	00-C0-F3	00C0F3
INTERLINK SYSTEM CO., LTD.	00-C0-F4	00C0F4
METACOMP, INC.	00-C0-F5	00C0F5
CELAN TECHNOLOGY, INC.	00-C0-F6	00C0F6
ENGAGE COMMUNICATION, INC.	00-C0-F7	00C0F7
ABOUT COMPUTING, INC.	00-C0-F8	00C0F8
HARRIS AND JEFFRIES, INC.	00-C0-F9	00C0F9
CANARY COMMUNICATIONS, INC.	00-C0-FA	00C0FA
ADVANCED TECHNOLOGY LABS	00-C0-FB	00C0FB
ELASTIC REALITY, INC.	00-C0-FC	00C0FC
PROSUM	00-C0-FD	00C0FD
BOX HILL SYSTEMS CORP.	00-C0-FF	00C0FF
RACAL-DATACOM	02-07-01	020701
APPLE COMPUTER, INC.	08-00-07	080007

App
C

continues

Table C.1   Continued

Company	OUI (Hex)	Company ID (Base 16)
HEWLETT PACKARD	08-00-09	080009
UNISYS CORP.	08-00-0B	08000B
INTERNATIONAL COMPUTERS, LTD.	08-00-0D	08000D
SHARP CORP.	08-00-1F	08001F
TEXAS INSTRUMENTS	08-00-28	080028
DIGITAL EQUIPMENT CORP.	08-00-2B	08002B
CERN	08-00-30	080030
SPIDER SYSTEMS, LTD.	08-00-39	080039
EUROTHERM GAUGING SYSTEMS	08-00-48	080048
EXPERDATA	08-00-51	080051
INT'L BUSINESS MACHINES CORP.	08-00-5A	08005A
SILICON GRAPHICS, INC.	08-00-69	080069
CASIO COMPUTER CO., LTD.	08-00-74	080074
CHIPCOM CORP.	08-00-8F	08008F
IBM CORP.	10-00-5A	10005A
DIGITAL EQUIPMENT CORP.	AA-00-00	AA0000
DIGITAL EQUIPMENT CORP.	AA-00-03	AA0003
DIGITAL EQUIPMENT CORP.	AA-00-04	AA0004

Index

A

video applications
Apple QuickTime
(IsoEthernet), 147-148
ATM standards
development, 17

Video Electronics Industry Standard (VESA), VCR video interface standards, 254

videoconferencing (SMDS), 164-165

Virtual Channel Connection (VCC), 304

virtual circuits, 304

virtual collisions
channel capture, 117-118
configuring, 117
Gigabit Ethernet, 116-118
multimedia capabilities, 116-118
network diameters, 118

Virtual LANs (VLANs)
administration, 35
advantages, 94-95
ATM overview, 35
disadvantages, 94-95
dynamic management
capabilities, 109-110
Fast Ethernet
implementation, 94-95
features, 109-110
frame tagging, 109-110
IEEE 802.1Q specification, 108
interoperability, IEEE
802.10 standard, 35-36
packet tagging, 94-95
policy-based management
scheme, 35
security mechanisms, 35
switching versus routing, 109-110
traffic routing, 36
filtering tables, 36
packet tagging, 36

Virtual Network Navigator (VNN),Cascade Communications, 47-48

virtual path connection (VPC), 305

virtual private networks versus frame relays, 64-65

virtual tributaries (VTs)
data rates, 199
floating mode, 199
locked mode, 199
sizes, 199

voice calls
compression, packetized
voice transmission, 65-66
frame relays
intracompany communications, 68-69
quality concerns, 67
"jitters", 65
packet prioritization, 67
plain ordinary telephone
service (POTS), 64
Pulse Code Modulation
(PCM), 64
sending frame relays, 64-65
standards development
(Frame Relay Forum), 68-69

Voice over Frame Relay (VoFR), Frame Relay Forum, 57

W

W.L. Gore & Associates, Fibre Channel, vendor products, 246

wanders from multiplexing, 199-200

WANs (wide area networks), corporate frame relay connections, 52

Watson, Thomas, founder of IBM (International Business Machines), 307

wavelength division multiplexing, 305

Web sites
1394 Trade Association, 255-256
3A International, 257
3Com, 101-102
ACT Networks, 73
Adaptec, 243, 257
ADC Kentrox, 181
Alcatel Network Systems, 182
Alteon Networks, 133-134
Ameritech, 208
Ancot Corporation, 243-244
Applied Micro Circuits
Corporation, 222
Asanté, 101
Ascom Nexion, 153
ATM Forum, 43
Bay Networks, 180
Bell Atlantic, 208-209
Broadband Communications Products, 223
Brooktree Corporation, 183
Cascade Communications, 32, 47
Cisco Systems, 75
Cnet, 102
Cogent Data Technologies, 101
Comsat Corporation, 29
CrossComm, 45
Digital Link Corporation, 182
Emulex Corporation, 242
End2End, 49
Essential Communications, 222
Farallon Computer, 100
Fore Systems, 28
Fujikura America, 244
Gadzoox Microsystems, 244
Gigabit Ethernet
Alliance, 110
GigaLabs, 133, 223
Hewlett-Packard, 223
Hitachi Data Systems, 206, 245
IBM Corporation, 224
IEEE Computer
Society, 109

Complete and Return this Card
for a *FREE* Computer Book Catalog

Thank you for purchasing this book! You have purchased a superior computer book written expressly for your needs. To continue to provide the kind of up-to-date, pertinent coverage you've come to expect from us, we need to hear from you. Please take a minute to complete and return this self-addressed, postage-paid form. In return, we'll send you a free catalog of all our computer books on topics ranging from word processing to programming and the internet.

Mr. ☐   Mrs. ☐   Ms. ☐   Dr. ☐

Name (first) ☐☐☐☐☐☐☐☐☐☐☐☐☐☐   (M.I.) ☐   (last) ☐☐☐☐☐☐☐☐☐☐☐☐☐☐☐☐☐☐

Address ☐☐☐☐☐☐☐☐☐☐☐☐☐☐☐☐☐☐☐☐☐☐☐☐☐☐☐☐☐☐☐☐☐☐☐☐☐☐

City ☐☐☐☐☐☐☐☐☐☐☐☐☐☐☐☐☐☐   State ☐☐   Zip ☐☐☐☐☐ ☐☐☐☐

Phone ☐☐☐ ☐☐☐ ☐☐☐☐   Fax ☐☐☐ ☐☐☐ ☐☐☐☐

Company Name ☐☐☐☐☐☐☐☐☐☐☐☐☐☐☐☐☐☐☐☐☐☐☐☐☐☐

E-mail address ☐☐☐☐☐☐☐☐☐☐☐☐☐☐☐☐☐☐☐☐☐☐☐☐☐☐☐☐☐☐

1. Please check at least (3) influencing factors for purchasing this book.

Front or back cover information on book ☐
Special approach to the content ☐
Completeness of content ☐
Author's reputation ☐
Publisher's reputation ☐
Book cover design or layout ☐
Index or table of contents of book ☐
Price of book ☐
Special effects, graphics, illustrations ☐
Other (Please specify): _____ ☐

2. How did you first learn about this book?

Saw in Macmillan Computer Publishing catalog ☐
Recommended by store personnel ☐
Saw the book on bookshelf at store ☐
Recommended by a friend ☐
Received advertisement in the mail ☐
Saw an advertisement in: _____ ☐
Read book review in: _____ ☐
Other (Please specify): _____ ☐

3. How many computer books have you purchased in the last six months?

This book only ☐   3 to 5 books ☐
books ☐   More than 5 ☐

4. Where did you purchase this book?

Bookstore ☐
Computer Store ☐
Consumer Electronics Store ☐
Department Store ☐
Office Club ☐
Warehouse Club ☐
Mail Order ☐
Direct from Publisher ☐
Internet site ☐
Other (Please specify): _____ ☐

5. How long have you been using a computer?

☐ Less than 6 months   ☐ 6 months to a year
☐ 1 to 3 years   ☐ More than 3 years

6. What is your level of experience with personal computers and with the subject of this book?

	With PCs	With subject of book
New	☐	☐
Casual	☐	☐
Accomplished	☐	☐
Expert	☐	☐

Source Code ISBN: 0-7897-1294-6

7. Which of the following best describes your job title?

Administrative Assistant .... ☐
Coordinator .... ☐
Manager/Supervisor .... ☐
Director .... ☐
Vice President .... ☐
President/CEO/COO .... ☐
Lawyer/Doctor/Medical Professional .... ☐
Teacher/Educator/Trainer .... ☐
Engineer/Technician .... ☐
Consultant .... ☐
Not employed/Student/Retired .... ☐
Other (Please specify): _____ ☐

8. Which of the following best describes the area of the company your job title falls under?

Accounting .... ☐
Engineering .... ☐
Manufacturing .... ☐
Operations .... ☐
Marketing .... ☐
Sales .... ☐
Other (Please specify): _____ ☐

9. What is your age?

Under 20 .... ☐
21-29 .... ☐
30-39 .... ☐
40-49 .... ☐
50-59 .... ☐
60-over .... ☐

10. Are you:

Male .... ☐
Female .... ☐

11. Which computer publications do you read regularly? (Please list)

_____
_____
_____
_____
_____
_____
_____
_____
_____
_____

Comments: _____
_____
_____

Fold here and scotch-tape to mail

Check out Que® Books on the World Wide Web
http://www.quecorp.com

As the biggest software release in computer history, Windows 95 continues to redefine the computer industry. Click here for the latest info on our Windows 95 books

Make computing quick and easy with these products designed exclusively for new and casual users

Examine the latest releases in word processing, spreadsheets, operating systems, and suites

The Internet, The World Wide Web, CompuServe®, America Online®, Prodigy®—it's a world of ever-changing information. Don't get left behind!

Find out about new additions to our site, new bestsellers and hot topics

In-depth information on high-end topics: find the best reference books for databases, programming, networking, and client/server technologies

A recent addition to Que, Ziff-Davis Press publishes the highly-successful *How It Works* and *How to Use* series of books, as well as *PC Learning Labs Teaches* and *PC Magazine* series of book/disc packages

Stay on the cutting edge of Macintosh® technologies and visual communications

Find out which titles are making headlines

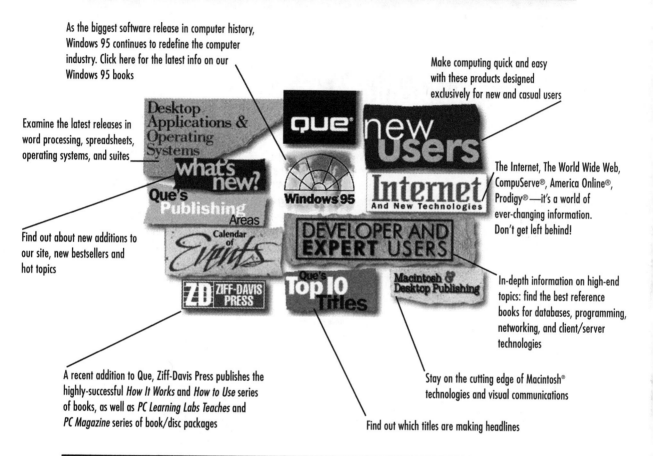

With 6 separate publishing groups, Que develops products for many specific market segments and areas of computer technology. Explore our Web Site and you'll find information on best-selling titles, newly published titles, upcoming products, authors, and much more.

- Stay informed on the latest industry trends and products available
- Visit our online bookstore for the latest information and editions
- Download software from Que's library of the best shareware and freeware

MACMILLAN COMPUTER PUBLISHING USA
A VIACOM COMPANY

Technical Support:

If you need assistance with the information in this book or with a CD/Disk accompanying the book, please access the Knowledge Base on our Web site at **http://www.superlibrary.com/general/support**. Our most Frequently Asked Questions are answered there. If you do not find the answer to your questions on our Web site, you may contact Macmillan Technical Support **(317) 581-3833** or e-mail us at **support@mcp.com**.